From Irving to Olivier

*A Social History of the
Acting Profession in England
1880–1983*

From Irving to Olivier

A Social History of the
Acting Profession in England
1880–1983

MICHAEL SANDERSON

Foreword by Athene Seyler CBE

LIBRARY

THE ATHLONE PRESS · LONDON
ST MARTIN'S PRESS · NEW YORK

First published 1984 by The Athlone Press Ltd
44 Bedford Row, London WC1R 4LY

First published in the United States of America in 1984
by St Martin's Press, Inc., 175 Fifth Avenue, New York, NY 10010

British Library Cataloguing in Publication Data

Sanderson, Michael
    From Irving to Olivier.
    1. Theatre – England – History – 19th century
    2. Theatre – England – History – 20th century
    3. Acting – History – 19th century
    4. Acting – History 20th century
    I. Title
    792'.028'0942   PN2581

    ISBN 0-485-11252-3

Library of Congress Cataloging in Publication Data
Sanderson, Michael.
    From Irving to Olivier.
    Bibliography: p.
    Includes index.
    1. Actors – England. 2. Acting – History – 20th century.
    3. Theater – England – History – 20th century. 4. Theater
    and Society – England. I. Title.
    PN2595. S25   1984   792'.028'0942   84-40050

    ISBN 0-312-30768-3

Printed in Great Britain at
the University Press, Cambridge

PN
2595
.S25
.S25
1984

Contents

For my wife
Anne Hilary Sanderson

Foreword by Athene Seyler CBE

I am glad to be associated by this foreword to this most entertaining and instructive book on the theatre. Its span is almost exactly my working life on the stage and says, I think, everything that should be remembered. I have only one observation to add, and that is that I feel acting as a whole is of a higher standard now in many ways than in my early years – the twenties and thirties – the great names in the theatre then were known for the personalities of the performers, and plays were chosen and written solely to exploit these. One cannot imagine Gerald du Maurier, for instance, appearing successfully in a great tragedy, and Charles Hawtrey turned down my suggestion of his playing a Shakespearian part with unbelieving laughter. Audiences went to see the admired personality of an actor in a play designed to show it off to the best advantage. Nowadays, our leading actors are famed and admired for their interpretation of many different kinds of parts and a great reputation is hardly achieved without appearing in the classics. The young ones seem to me much more adventurous in their work. So on this congratulatory note I introduce you to a splendid picture of the theatre as it was in the days of great actors – noting that what survives is our devotion to my beloved profession.

Acknowledgements

This book could not have been written without the kind co-operation of many people in various walks of theatrical and academic life, and it is a great pleasure to be able to thank them.

I am grateful to the Social Science Research Council for a research grant for travel and work away from Norwich. The University of East Anglia also provided travel funds, research leave and secretarial assistance essential to the book's completion. In London I am indebted to the British Theatre Museum where the curator, Miss Jennifer Aylmer MBE, helped both with advice and the provision of documents. I am very much obliged to Mr Peter Plouviez, the General Secretary of British Actors' Equity Association, and Mrs R. B. Haseler, the Research Officer, for permission to use their early records. Other trade-union material was made available at the Library of the TUC at Congress House.

The Royal Academy of Dramatic Art generously allowed me to use their early letterbooks and other material and to work there at various times. I thank the Registrar, Mr Richard O'Donoghue, for his help and interest. Likewise at the Central School of Speech and Drama Mrs Joanna Jeffrey made available their collections to me. A major collection of documents concerning drama education was that of the London University Diploma in Drama. Mr J. H. Burrows drew my attention to these and Mr Peter Burtt-Jones gave permission for me to use them.

Major N. E. Thackeray, RM, the Secretary of the Garrick Club, permitted me to use their records and Dr Geoffrey Ashton was most helpful on my visits to their library. Dr Robert Hutchison entertained me at the Arts Council and suggested which of their early CEMA materials would prove useful. The Rev. Michael Hurst-Bannister, the Senior Chaplain of the Actors' Church Union, gave

viii

me permission to use their records and I am indebted to him and Miss Phyllis Brown, the Secretary of the ACU, for discussion of their work. The Rev. Henry Dodd and the Committee of the Catholic Stage Guild likewise allowed me to use their records, which the Secretary, Mrs Marjorie Hogan, made available. Mrs Gwendoline Rye, the widow of the former Secretary Mr Alan Rye, wrote to me about the early days of the revival of the Guild and made available some additional documentation concerning it. The Matron of Denville Hall, Mrs Kay Kirby, allowed me to visit the Hall and generously gave of her time to show me round and discuss its work. Miss A. G. Marks of the Actors' Benevolent Fund provided me with some information about the present activities of the Fund. In Bristol Miss Ann Brooke Barnett, Keeper of the University of Bristol Theatre Collection, allowed me to use the papers of Sir Herbert Beerbohm Tree and I am grateful for the helpful interest of both her and Dr George Rowell during my time there. Finally, I am indebted to the staffs of the Colindale and the Westminster Libraries, which hold runs of specialist theatrical journals and newspapers.

I have benefited greatly from the kindness of a number of actors and actresses and other people of the Theatre who allowed me to interview them. They were Miss Fabia Drake, Miss Kathleen Harrison, Mr Esmond Knight, the late Mr John Laurie and Mrs Laurie, the late Miss Marie Ney, Miss Athene Seyler CBE, Miss Nora Swinburne, the late Mr Austin Trevor, Mr Timothy West. Miss Gwynneth Thurburn OBE, the former Principal of the Central School of Speech and Drama, gave me her valuable reminiscences of drama training developments since the 1920s. From them I not only learnt much about the history of the acting profession but also experienced something of its generosity and outgoing interest, which I greatly appreciated. I have also had interviews and conversations with less well-known ladies and gentlemen with off-stage connections with the theatre. Mrs Elizabeth Anderson told me of theatre-going before 1914 and working in Tree's theatre; Mr Jack Berkeley, in whose office at Equity I worked, helped me with reminiscent explanatory conversation; Miss Edna Farrand told me about the Actors' Association and Actors' Church Union in the interwar years and Mrs Nessa Hughes Smith was illuminating on the Guildhall School and theatre-going in the same period.

ACKNOWLEDGEMENTS

I have also benefited from contact with other scholars in contiguous fields. I have had interesting talk from time to time with Brian Crozier and Lois Rutherford, both of Cambridge; the former made available his typescript on theatre audiences before 1914 and the latter some of her early findings on the variety comedian. Dr Derek R. Layder of the University of Leicester kindly lent me his important doctoral thesis on the present-day state of the profession. Most of the typing has been done by Miss Judith Sparks and Mrs Christine Jope, and I am grateful for their careful skill.

I am especially grateful to Miss Athene Seyler CBE for most graciously agreeing to write the Foreword to this book. Finally, especial thanks are due to my wife and two anonymous readers for their careful reading of the text, which has been improved by their suggestions. My wife has been a constant encouragement and support during the research and writing of the book, which has been a labour of love and which is dedicated to her.

List of Illustrations

Equity). The meeting of actors and unions called for greater
government support for the film industry.

Introduction

In 1914 an observer noted: 'it is safe to say that the theatrical industry receives less attention from social students than any other industry of the same size'. This has been partly because the actor has been thought of as a 'romantic accessory' rather than as a serious professional worker in an important trade.[1] The traditional approach to theatre history has been that of the literary history of drama or of aspects of staging, but in recent years more interest has been directed to the socio-economic aspects of the theatre and its actors.

The purpose of this present work is to examine the social history of the modern acting profession in England roughly from Sir Henry Irving's knighthood in 1895 to the 1980s and Lord Olivier's admission to the Order of Merit in 1981. Both were important 'firsts' in the development of the profession of actor and its public recognition. Our concern is with the legitimate stage, that is to say, the straight spoken drama. This distinction of legitimate and other forms of entertainment had grown up in the eighteenth and early nineteenth centuries, since before 1843 only patented theatres were permitted to perform straight plays without musical interludes, songs or dances. After the Theatres Act of 1843 this distinction has of course ceased to have legal effect, but the rough division remains and sets a necessary boundary to our present theme. Accordingly we are not concerned with the variety artist, the musical theatre and still less with opera and ballet. This is not contradicted by the fact that Chapter 6 deals with the actor in the music hall. This focuses not on the music hall for its own sake, nor on the variety artist proper, but on the problem of legitimate stage actors in their dealing with this important borderland to their own art. On the other hand, the work of the legitimate actor has not been confined to the stage and the twentieth-century media of film, radio and television have opened

1

fruitful areas for the dramatic actor's art, with inevitable reactions back on the traditional stage. Geographically our concern is with England. The focus of theatrical life was London, and this centripetal tendency increased with the problems of the provincial theatre in the 1930s and 1950s. Accordingly leading Scottish and Welsh playwrights and actors, from J. M. Barrie onwards, have developed their careers in a London and English context rather than by staying exclusively in their homelands. Reference is made from time to time to Scotland and Wales and inevitably many of the developments experienced in England were common to those countries also, but our focus is the theatrical heartland of London and the English provinces. This is not a general history of all aspects of the theatre, nor of the literary history of plays. It is essentially a study of actors and the development of their profession in its changing context over the last hundred years.

In the 1890s actors were jocularly known as 'the Profession' while still being regarded by many as little better than the 'rogues and vagabonds' they had been in Elizabethan times. Yet since the 1890s acting has acquired many of the characteristics of a genuine profession in the many social changes that have shaped it in the last hundred years.

It is the mark of a profession that it is based on a certain level of education and training. In Victorian times there was virtually no formal training for the actor. But since the 1900s, with the creation of RADA in 1904 and the Central School in 1906, drama education has grown apace. Moreover this has established links with the universities, the traditional founts of professional training. This was evident with the interesting experiment of the London University Diploma from the 1920s whereby the University co-operated with the major drama schools in higher academic education for the stage. Since the last war the creation of university drama departments has further strengthened the links between higher education and the training of the actor. It has also contributed to the increasing tendency for actors and actresses to be graduates. Accordingly many actors have been to university before going on to drama school. This has further raised the status of drama schools, putting them in a position analogous to the post-graduate training found in the medical, legal and teaching professions. This concern with academic education has

2

been given meaning by the development of a coherent body of learned knowledge which should be part of the actor's stock in trade. This in turn has developed from the acceptance of English and foreign literature and drama as respectable subjects of study. The adding of intellectual content to the vocational and mechanical voice and physical training of the actor has increased its professional quality. The balance between the academic and the practical is a recurrent dilemma in drama education.

It tends to be a characteristic of professions that attract the respect of the public that their entrants and practitioners come from a fairly homogeneous and elevated social class and carry over its manners and lifestyle into their professional conduct. In scarcely any other area has there been such a change as in the acting profession. In the mid-nineteenth century actors usually came from theatrical families, and for a respectable middle-class son to go on the stage was regarded as a shameful retrograde step. From around the 1890s it became much more usual and acceptable for actors to come from backgrounds in the traditional professions and business. Few came from the working class and fewer than before from theatrical families. This situation lasted from the 1890s to the last war. This new type of gentlemanly actor brought into the profession many features of a new lifestyle appropriate to their social status. These ranged from such characteristics as the fashionable social life of the London restaurants and clubs, notably the Garrick, playing golf, forming military corps and religious organizations, mixing with royalty and the beau-monde. In these ways actors of acceptable social origins could associate with high-prestige groups who would never have encountered actors in the mid-nineteenth century. It all enhanced the actors' pretensions to be regarded as members of a profession on a parity with others. Since the 1950s something of this homogeneity has been lost with entrants coming from a wider social sphere, with fewer public schoolboys and a change away from the kind of fashionable lifestyle which characterized the 1890–1945 generations.

Professions have their own professional organizations which serve to set standards of conduct, discipline members and control entry. When Equity was created in 1929 it took on this role, making it clear that it was not merely a trade union concerned to defend its members at all costs. On the contrary it would punish actors who brought the

3

profession into disrepute through unprofessional conduct. This it did to striking effect in a number of cases. Equity has also paid great attention to the problem of the restriction of entry into the profession. An occupation continually flooded by casual outsiders without qualifications finds it difficult to be taken seriously as a profession or as any kind of career at all. So it was with acting prior to the 1930s. An important part of the move towards professionalization was the exclusion of the amateur and the enforcement of the closed shop in the West End and subsequently in the provinces. Reinforced by present-day mechanisms such as the Casting Agreements and the limitation of annual Equity cards, the closed shop is a vital means of checking the potentially soaring numbers of entrants who would completely debauch any claims to professionalization in even worse unemployment and poverty.

Professions must also have some mystery, craft, art or skill not understood by the layman outside the charmed circle. This is most obviously so with professions firmly grounded in learning. The problem of the actor in this regard is that his is an art that disguises art. In the striving to appear natural and to avoid any attention being drawn to technique, the actor's skill is actually in deluding us into believing there is no special skill displayed. This masking of skill has actually increased in the twentieth century with stylistic change. Everybody knew that Victorian actors like Irving and Tree were acting, with rhetorical voices, grand gestures and disguising makeup. But it had to be explained in the 1920s that du Maurier and his followers were acting also and not merely behaving naturally as gentlemen in their drawing rooms. This art-disguising art has become more necessary with the advent of the new media of films and television, where restrained economy of effort and a striving for total naturalness have been even more necessary than in stage acting. This has always made acting appear easier than it is. The unfortunate paradox is that the more skilful the actor the more he can disguise his art, to the extent that the uninformed observer should underestimate the subtlety involved. Whatever the observer's deliberately deceived misperception, the professional craft is certainly there.

As regards remuneration, actors are more genuinely professional than many of the more established groups. Whereas doctors and teachers have become in effect salaried civil servants most actors, like the private doctor and barrister, still take their fees for a one-off engagement and fall back into unemployment until the next client comes along. In this way they retain something of the self-employed characteristics of the older professions, giving a special tailored service intermittently to irregular employers who make a once-for-all payment. In levels of remuneration the leading actors can match the earning power of the wealthiest in the old professions. Before 1914 the leading actor-managers were already able to amass large fortunes, and from the 1930s these could be boosted even massively by earnings in the film studios.

In these various ways – in its education, social background and lifestyles, creation of a controlling organization, deployment of a skill, capacity to earn high levels of remuneration in a client–self-employed professional relationship – acting has taken on many of the characteristics of the older professions in the last hundred years. Yet the assertion of professional status by actors has not been without its dilemmas and drawbacks. Actors' trade unionism at various stages of its development has tended to polarize actors into those with 'professional' pretensions and those who rejected such claims in preference for an emphasis on 'craft' or working-class solidarity. This was so in the conflict between the pioneer trade union the Actors' Association and its breakaway proletarian Actors' Union before the First World War. The rifts continued through the 1920s with the hostility of the professionally-minded West End elite to the Association's attempt to be a working-class trade union. It continued even after the beginning of Equity. The first president, Godfrey Tearle, continually emphasized the professional character of the actors' work and of their trade union, and he felt obliged to resign the presidency of Equity when it joined the TUC in 1940. The rifts underlay disputes of the 1970s with, among other issues, the morning coat and Buckingham Palace Garden Party elite rightly defending their hard-won professional status against the claims of the Left to co-operate in solidarity with striking miners and admit into membership strippers and night-club hostesses.

These long-lasting rifts, and the equally long-lasting claims for professional status, have had weakening effects on the profession. It has fractured the body of actors and prevented a common interest over matters like strike action (including the General Strike most

5

notably), co-operation with other theatrical workers, and so forth. Also, the whole 'professional' psychology in itself can be debilitating for those who make such claims prematurely without having the financial strength to be able to sustain them. Consultant surgeons and barristers are professional people and are accorded public regard as such not only for their attainments but for their high incomes and consequent lifestyles. The leading actors can match this but most actors are somewhere in the lower-middle to working-class range of incomes, and there are certain dangers for them in clinging too fiercely to the notions of a 'profession'. The danger for such groups is that their perception of their professionalism can blind them to a clear view of their own best interests and blunt a properly commercial attitude to their activities. With over 20,000 members in Equity, ranging from the very wealthy and titled down to the chronically unemployed and impoverished, the spectrum of attitudes to professional respectability are as wide as those of expectations and rewards.

Notwithstanding these difficulties the occupation of acting is one infinitely more professionalized, self-organized and able to advance its own interests now in the 1980s than it was when Irving was knighted in 1895. It is the emergence of the disorganized and disreputable body of 'vagabonds' of Victorian times into the profession of the present which is the theme of this book.

NOTES

1 'X', 'Employment in the Theatre', *New Statesman Special Supplement on the Modern Theatre*, 27 June 1914.

1 Escaping the Victorian Legacy

One summer morning in 1895 Max Beerbohm, the novelist, critic and half-brother of the actor–manager Herbert Tree, was crossing the road opposite Marble Arch. As he did so he was passed by a brougham conveying an acquaintance, his hat rakishly tilted, a long cigar in his mouth, and on his face 'a look of such ruminant, sly fun as I have never seen equalled'.[1] It was Henry Irving going from his rooms in Grafton Street to Paddington Station en route for Windsor, where he was to be knighted. While Beerbohm had seen the Bohemian side of the actor's character, the Queen later in the day saw nothing but his grave dignity and presence, as the responsible head of his profession. On bestowing the first accolade ever accorded to an actor, she broke her normal silence on such occasions and spoke to him: 'I am very, very pleased, Sir'.[2]

Actors had not always been so favourably regarded, for Irving's knighthood was a step in the escape from a legacy of low esteem accorded to the actor and the theatre. The Victorians took a low view of the stage, and the early Victorian actor was 'a social and artistic outcast'.[3] Even prominent mid-Victorian actors did not rate their work highly. Macready despised his fellow-players and the actor Samuel Phelps called it an 'ill-requited profession'.[4] Sir Squire Bancroft similarly reflected that around the 1860s most of his fellow-actors were 'deficient in tone . . . unhappily lacking the marks of breeding and education'.[5] If actors themselves held a low view of their calling, this was more than shared by parents and relatives of children hoping to enter the profession. Mrs Patrick Campbell in 1889 was written to by solicitous Aunt Kate: 'Poor unfortunate child . . . you have yet to learn the shame, the humiliation of seeing yourself despised by decent people'.[6] The parental reaction on hearing of the offspring's decision to go on the stage may be gathered from the memoirs of seventy-nine actors and actresses playing in the period 1890–1914. Over half the parents of future actors thoroughly disapproved of their choice of career, and just under half of those of actresses.[7] More parents disapproved of their sons' than of their daughters' wish to go on the stage, since girls had much less to lose. Unlike sons, they could then rarely be expected to follow on in the family firm or profession. In any case it might be hoped that they would marry and leave the stage after a short time.

What were parents afraid of that they felt such suspicion of the late Victorian stage? Since the days of David Garrick there had been a succession of players dedicated to the purification and elevation of the Georgian and Victorian theatre. Such were the Kembles, William Macready and Samuel Phelps, who variously at Drury Lane, Covent Garden and Sadlers Wells sought to make the drama a respected part of the national culture. Yet they were aware that they were but a top layer overlaying various strata of seediness, vulgarity and even squalor. To an extent this difference of layers between those who saw the theatre as an elevating art and those who had no such pretensions also reflected their audiences. The audiences of Covent Garden and Drury Lane were far from 'popular' or working-class in the eighteenth and early and mid-nineteenth centuries. Phelps at Sadlers Wells was unusual in presenting high art theatre, based on Shakespeare, to large working-class London audiences. The popular theatre lay elsewhere, more directly shaped by commercial considerations and likely to reflect the taste of common people.

Beyond the old patent theatres of Drury Lane and Covent Garden, which had enjoyed a metropolitan monopoly of legitimate drama until the Theatres Act of 1843, were less glamorous and more vulgarly popular venues. There were the minors, theatres which being debarred from legitimate drama had developed lurid melodrama and burletta. Among such were the Surrey, Pantheon, the Coburg (the later Old Vic but then a 'blood tub') and the Olympic where Madame Vestris, for all the notorious promiscuity of her private life, sought to refine the entertainment of such establish-

8

ments. Lowest in London were the penny gaffs of the East End.[8] These were often converted shops, warehouses or stables providing crude short plays to impecunious working-class audiences. The plays were usually ones of horror or sexual licence – *Maria Martin or the Murder in the Red Barn, Sweeney Todd the Demon Barber*, and twenty-minute versions of the bloodier Shakespearian tragedies. The audience was well lubricated with drink and laced with the criminal and prostitute classes. The police and magistrates disapproved of the gaffs. But they preferred to have their young savage audiences confined there, absorbed by the play and kept off the streets. For the actor the gaff was often the last resort in a decline before entering the workhouse, or a starting point for many who would never rise much higher.

An actor's life in the provinces could be little better. At the lower end of the touring scale were low-class melodrama companies. There were hundreds of 'blood and thunder' plays presented by companies which could make good money for most of the year by touring provincial theatres. But the acting was crude and regarded as a last resort by the out of work. Maud Gill, who joined one in desperation, remembered that 'hundreds of actors and actresses stayed with the same companies for years, and hundreds who suited melodrama could not have got engagements in any other kind of stage work'.[9] They survived because small theatres needed to attract any kind of touring company to play in them to keep open. Both theatres and companies relied on each other in their common battle for survival until both were wrecked by the competition of the cinema in the interwar years. At least these poor companies were playing in theatres, but below them were the 'fit-up' companies. These played 'in public halls, corn exchanges, assembly rooms and the like, in towns that do not possess a regular theatre'.[10] The companies accordingly carried the stage equipment with them, since their venue was unlikely to have it already. Since such fit-up tours went to small towns and villages without a permanent theatre, such places were not normally large enough to muster an audience for more than a night or two. This entailed perpetual movement from place to place, dismantling and erecting the stage as they went.

A former touring actor described the 'theatre' he encountered in a market town in Yorkshire:

9

'the theatre was a long, low ramshackle building, with a partition open at the top, running down the centre. On one side of this partition was the theatre, on the other side were a number of pens and stalls where unsold cattle were kept on market days . . . I shall never forget the smell which greeted us on entering this filthy den.'[11]

At the very lowest end of the scale were the travelling booth actors. Not for them the luxury of a theatre building, however primitive. They carried round their tented theatre, living in caravans and playing crude melodrama to poor audiences in out-of-the-way places. Mark Melford described a booth which he joined as a young actor:

'I found it amid the living vans with the smoke lifting lazily from the chimneys . . . the booth was canvas topped and in shape an elongated square. The front was surmounted by a stage at the corner of which was the big drum.'[12]

Collier lads and cotton-mill lasses variously made up the audiences. In spite of its picturesque jollity, it was scarcely the ambience of an elevated profession.

Actors also risked being regarded with social revulsion or condescending pity by others. Macready, while visiting Norwich, was asked his view of the stage as a profession and replied that he 'would sooner see a son of mine coffin'd at my feet than that he should take to acting and the stage'.[13] It must have been with such an awareness of his father's prejudices against his own profession that Macready's son in fact became a general in the army. Samuel Phelps's daughter was expelled from school when it was found that her father was an actor. Irving separated from his wife because she despised his profession and taunted him over it, and a generation later their grandson Laurence was reviled as the 'son of a dirty actor' on his arrival at Wellington in 1910.[14] Lesser actors suffered from attitudes ranging from the patronizing to the hostile. Sir Frank Benson's company, which included several public school and Varsity men, was shabbily treated by a host for whom they had been performing on the grounds that 'he imagined they lived on the poorest fare and frequently slept in barns'.[15] Touring with Benson around 1910 was

10

the scientist Thomas Watson, who was Alexander Bell's research assistant in the invention of the telephone. He was acting as a hobby-cum-holiday in England and was dismayed and surprised to find that non-actors he met on his travels, and who were unaware of his true identity, 'pitied me for having to do such degrading work'.[16] The message was clear. The actor was a social outcast without status and public respect.

Acting was also thought to have morally corrupting effects on its practitioners. In men it encouraged excessive egotism and vanity inflated by the adulation of their admirers. It also predisposed men to a life of self-indulgence encouraging 'lax principles' and 'complaisant tolerance' of a low morality.[17] Even worse, a strong element in the low opinion held of actors was the recurrent suspicion of sexual immorality in their lifestyles. At worst there was a shadowy overlap between the theatre and prostitution. Some theatres had promenades and foyers where prostitutes paraded and solicited openly, while 'prostitutes and actresses were still not in wholly separate categories. Until late Victorian times "actress" was a disreputable description'.[18] Guardians of morality were concerned not only with actresses' private lives but with what they depicted on stage. The critic of the *Westminster Gazette* deplored the fact that the theatre tended 'to preach a kind of conventional morality somewhat below the standard considered admissible by serious people'.[19]

The two most serious attacks on the actor and his morals came from two journalists: Clement Scott in 1898 and W. T. Stead in 1904. Scott was the theatre critic of the *Daily Telegraph* and had been a beneficial force, notably in his support of Irving's work at the Lyceum. Yet many years of influence had begun to warp his judgement and widen personal flaws of opinionated vanity. In 1898, Scott launched an attack on actresses and their morality, claiming that 'It is nearly impossible for a woman to remain pure who adopts the stage as a profession . . . There is no school on earth so bad for the formation of character'.[20] This preposterous outburst from a drama critic whose own wife was actually trying to become an actress caused consternation, and it fell to Irving to complain formally to the *Daily Telegraph*. Scott was obliged to resign from the newspaper after writing a retraction[21] and a perso-

11

nal apology to Irving. It was ironic that Scott, the guardian of theatrical sexual morals, followed the recently departed Oscar Wilde into exile in France.

The public, however, continued to be worried about the morals of actresses. In 1904 W. T. Stead, the editor of the *Review of Reviews*, took a belated interest in the matter. He was best known for publicizing the problem of child prostitution, and regarded the theatre with an almost similar moral distaste. He was urged by Irving to make a 'pilgrimage of investigation' to remove these prejudices.[22] This did not have the desired effect. With gross unfairness he quoted Scott's attack on actresses, totally ignoring the latter's retraction, and denied that theatre-going provided any 'moral or intellectual impulse towards higher things'. Stead's relatively ill-informed foray into theatreland and unfair repetition of the Scott libel reinforced the middle-class prejudice against the stage as a career.

II

Yet in spite of the low public view of actors there was both a sharp increase in their numbers and a revolution in their social origins before 1914. Actors in the census increased.

	Actors	Actresses	Total
1881	2197	2368	4565
1891	3625	3696	7321
1901	6044	6443	12,487
1911	9076	9171	18,247

This represented a fourfold increase over the period at a time when the population as a whole grew by 39 per cent. Other leisure –entertainment workers such as musicians (whose numbers doubled) and authors (who tripled) also experienced a far more than average expansion at the time, while the entertainment centre of Blackpool was the fastest-growing town in England in the 1890s. The census figures combine together as 'actors' both legitimate dramatic players and variety artists in music halls. The 1911 census made a distinction between the two:

12

		Actors	Actresses
1911	in theatres	5863	6726
	in music halls	3213	2445

Accordingly about two-thirds of 'actors' were working in legitimate drama. The Report on the 1911 census observed that 'the increase in the number of persons earning a livelihood as public entertainers is one of the most striking features of the occupational table'.[23]

This boom in the supply of actors was also reflected in theatre building in London.[24] The twenty-one West End theatres existing in 1892 had risen to thirty-three by 1914. Twenty-four new London theatres were built in the West End between 1880 and 1914 and seven more were rebuilt or remodelled in the same time. Expressed in another way, of the forty-seven London theatres existing in 1970 nearly half – twenty-one – were opened between 1880 and 1914, mostly in three clusters: 1887–92 (including the Garrick, Wyndham's and Duke of York's), 1903–7 (including the Aldwych, the New [now the Albery] and the Hicks [now the Globe]), and 1910–13 (including the Ambassadors'). London theatreland as we know it is chiefly the product of these years.

There was not only a marked increase in the numbers of actors but a decisive change in their social background.[25] There was a very marked increase in male actors, and especially actresses, coming from a professional background. This was coupled, though to a much weaker degree, with an increase in actors coming from landed, squirearchy and even titled families. The rise in actors from backgrounds of such high status was offset by the relative decline in actors coming from families already in the theatre – the most common source in Victorian times. Indeed, if we focus on actors and actresses whose fathers were themselves actors, we find that they declined sharply over this period.

Having an actor as a father

Actors acting 1890–1913	Actors	Actresses
Starting pre-1880	32.3%	61.8%
Starting 1880–9	25.2%	28.7%
Starting 1890–1913	15.9%	17.7%

As the stage became more 'respectable', so it attracted entrants from the higher ranks of society, which in turn reinforced its respectability. As this happened the theatre did not need so much to recruit internally from existing theatrical families who in an earlier generation would have had nothing to lose by going on the stage. Very few actors came from a working-class or even lower-middle-class background. They lacked the command of good-accented speaking voices, they had no wardrobe of good stage and walking clothes, they were without the social contacts that would have helped a career, and their families could not afford to support them financially in the lean years before they became self-sustaining on the stage. Going on the legitimate stage was an unrealistic goal for all but a handful of working-class aspirants.

Contemporary actors would not have been surprised by these conclusions. Indeed, several comments along these lines were made by observers at the time. In 1905 Sir Squire Bancroft noted that the stage had for some time been 'strongly recruited from the ranks of culture and refinement'[26] and a few years later reflected that most of his actor friends had not come from theatrical families.[27] An *Era* leader hit this nail explicitly on the head around this time:

'In the old times, a man had either to be born of a dramatic family or to be genuinely stage-struck to face the life with its vicissitudes and its slavery. The stage is now taken to by hundreds who would never have dreamt of doing so in the early eighties.'[28]

It is interesting that that commentator agreed with the sharpness of the change over a relatively short time. Seymour Hicks in 1910 also agreed with the time span: 'Five and twenty years ago a gentleman was rare on the stage. Nowadays gentlemen hover round it thick as May-flies on a Hampshire stream.'[29]

The increasing respectability of the profession was also reflected in the educational background of entrants.

There is, of course, no one definition of a public school, so we present here two definitions. The first is 'The Nine', that is those undoubtedly elite and ancient schools recognized by Victorians and the Clarendon Public Schools Commission of the 1860s as public schools.[30] This is a rather narrow definition and omits the newer Victorian public schools often created in the 1840s and 1860s.

Actors coming from 'public schools' and acting 1890–1914

	The Nine		Honey/Gathorne-Hardy (113 schools)	
Starting pre-1880	5/33	15.2%	16/33	48.5%
Starting 1880–9	9/73	12.3%	37/73	50.7%
Starting 1890–1913	44/260	16.9%	143/260	55.0%

Accordingly we include a wider definition based on 113 schools, that is those in Professor Honey's careful analysis of public schools plus a few others included in Gathorne-Hardy's study.[31]

In both cases, for the sample of actors of whose education we have record, we find a sizeable and slightly increasing proportion coming from public schools, of whatever definition. Indeed, in 1914 the principal of the Academy of Dramatic Art told a parent that 'the right kind of aspirant for the stage is a boy 18–24 who has just left a Public School or University'.[32] In the same way we find an increase of actors who came from university backgrounds.

Actors having attended universities and acting 1890–1914

Starting pre-1880	5/33	15.2%
Starting 1880–9	24/73	32.9%
Starting 1890–1913	69/260	26.5%

Similar trends, though to a much lesser extent, are evident in the educational backgrounds of actresses. As there is no single definition of a boys' public school, still less is there one simple list of leading girls' schools. For our purposes we have selected fourteen 'notable' girls' schools.[33] Some were founded after 1914, but these are included for comparability with later decades in subsequent chapters.

Actresses 1890–1914	*from 'notable schools'*		*from universities*	
Starting pre-1880	0	0%	0	0%
Starting 1880–9	5/28	17.8%	1/28	3.6%
Starting 1890–1913	10/97	10.5%	3/97	3.1%

15

No actresses could have been as well-educated as this in the mid-nineteenth century for the obvious reason that public schools, universities and even grammar schools for women were virtually unknown before the 1870s. By 1913 there were a fair number from such well-nurtured backgrounds, though very few became prominent except Lady Maud Tree (Queen's College, Harley Street), Marjorie Fielding (Cheltenham) and Athene Seyler (Bedford College, London).

As the actor in reality came increasingly from good social and educational backgrounds, so leading actors, and notably Irving as the head of the profession, increasingly made high claims for the status of the player and the theatre. Irving often pointed out that it was absurd to venerate 'the drama' and to despise 'the theatre', to regard it as culturally enriching to read Shakespeare in the study and degrading to attend or act in his performance on the stage.[34] The drama enables people to understand the habits, manners and customs of other countries and ages, it gives insight into 'passions and sorrows and ambitions outside the narrow scope of their own lives . . . All this is education – for it broadens the sympathies and enlarges the intellectual grasp'.[35] All subjects of human thought deemed ennobling could be, and had been, represented in the drama and the ultimate aim of the art of acting was truth and beauty. This was an antidote to 'morose and hopeless dissatisfaction' which is corrosive of the national life.[36] The stage was accordingly 'an elevating instead of a lowering influence on national morality'; its intention may on the surface be to interest and amuse, 'but its deeper purpose is earnest, intense, sincere'.[37] The essential duality in the position of the theatre, and of the actor within it, had been posed. How far was it for entertainment, fun, commercial showbusiness, and how far part of some national high culture, ennobling and elevating, even equatable with education? Leading actors put the greater emphasis on the latter values prior to 1914, as part of their claims for higher status.

The actors' claims for social recognition were increasingly taken seriously by those in a position to accord patronage. The breaking down of barriers, with Irving often leading the spearhead, may be seen clustering in the late 1880s and 1890s. In 1882 the Prince of Wales gave a dinner at Marlborough House for leaders of the acting profession. Five years later his mother called the first Royal Command performance since the death of Prince Albert and for the first time received an actress (the later Dame Madge Kendal) in her drawing room. The first Royal Command performance at Windsor was held in 1891 with Irving in *Becket* and the Queen knighted Sir Henry, with personal words of congratulation, four years later. Academic institutions likewise made some unprecedented courteous gestures to the actor and the stage. Irving addressed Oxford University in 1886, and the Royal Institution in 1895. More prestigiously, he received the first honorary degree accorded to an actor, a D. Litt from Trinity College Dublin in 1892; followed by a Cambridge D. Litt in 1898. The Royal Academy Dinner, already used to toasting sister arts of Music and Literature, included Drama in its toasts from 1891 and removed a minor grievance which had rankled. The Churches too abated some of their deep suspicion of the theatre as Cardinal Vaughan invited Irving to lecture at his residence in 1898 and the Church of England received his ashes for burial in Westminster Abbey in 1905.

Virtually every leading establishment institution made some gesture of favourable recognition towards the stage in those years – the Crown, the Churches, the Universities and other academic institutions. It gave weight to claims that the stage could have educational and religious values. Secondly, Irving had been offered a knighthood in 1883 by Gladstone, and yet did not feel the time was ripe for an actor to receive such an honour without incurring a certain amount of scorn from some quarters. This was nicely judged and it took another twelve years of propagandizing, achievement, recognition and change in the public mood – marked by the instances above – before he felt able to accept the accolade proffered by Rosebery. By then it occasioned no surprise; indeed, it would have been absurd to have left Irving undubbed.

Were this merely the recognition of the achievements of one quite outstanding genius of vision and personal magnetism, this would reflect little of changing attitudes to the profession as a whole. More telling was the spate of knighthoods that quickly followed Irving's – Sir Squire Bancroft in the Diamond Jubilee Honours in 1897, Sir Charles Wyndham in the Coronation Honours of 1902, Sir John Hare in 1907, Sir Herbert Tree in 1907, Sir George Alexander in

1911, Sir Johnston Forbes Robertson in 1913, received the accolade before the War. There was no equivalent honour for actresses before 1918 and it is worth noting that all the actors so honoured were actor-managers, businessmen as well as artists.

The giving of such honours was facilitated by the fact that not only did the monarchs have a very keen enthusiasm for the theatre – Edward VII even more than Victoria – but leading politicians shared these enthusiasms. Rosebery was a keen theatre-goer, Gladstone was positively obsessed by it, having his private seat in the wings of the Lyceum. Asquith loved it, partly through his close friendship with actress Lillah McCarthy. He first had drama performed at Downing Street, and his son Anthony Asquith became a leading film director. The positively favourable disposition of leading prime ministers of the day towards actors and the theatre further helped the enhancing of their status.

III

Why then was there this social change in the nature of actors and their increasing recognition? Several factors will be dealt with in subsequent chapters – their education, changing conditions of work, financial attractions, social life and so forth. But here I wish to focus on three elements – the change in the nature of plays and characters depicted, the ambience of amateur theatricality among the upper classes, and the diminishing attractiveness of other careers that actors had left behind.

The change in the social origin of the actor was closely related to the nature of the plays in which he was called to perform. Irving, and before him Phelps, Macready and Kean, worked in the theatre of romantic costume drama and Shakespeare. The grand gesture, torrential rhetorical style, elaborate costume and disguise, characterization far remote from the experience of the audience, the very chiaroscuro of limelight and shadow, distanced the players from the audience. The rise of naturalistic drama from the 1860s, with the Bancrofts' espousal of the work of Tom Robertson, began the subtle change. Now the characters wore modern dress, inhabited recognizable interiors and spoke in the educated parlance of the day.

18

Actors from an upper-middle-class background were needed on the stage because most of the characters depicted in plays came from that milieu. As one critic put it, 'there is and during a long time has been a mania among playwrights for putting aristocratic characters on the stage',[38] and another, 'a large part of the actor's energy is spent in depicting contemporary character in the upper class'.[39] To sustain Society roles convincingly before an audience, many of whose members would move in such circles, an actor needed at least a nodding acquaintance with its style and *mores*. *Era* asked: 'How is he to collect the many little personal details of gesture, speech and deportment which go to make up the manners of modern Society unless he frequent that Society?'[40] For actor-managers putting on such plays the solution was to employ not the actor who had sweated his way round the provinces, but those who could step from the drawing room on to the stage.[41]

This 'gentrification' of the stage was also connected with the social origins of playwrights and the kinds of characters they depicted from their own experience. As in the later nineteenth century, dramatists were rewarded by royalties rather than flat fees, so it became potentially an occupation sufficiently lucrative to attract men from well-to-do backgrounds.[42] The leading playwrights of the pre-1914 period were predominantly sons of professional men.

doctor	– Oscar Wilde, R. C. Carton, Alfred Sutro
solicitor	– Arthur Pinero, Somerset Maugham, John Galsworthy
accountant	– A. E. W. Mason
architect	– Granville Barker
farmer	– H. A. Jones
clergyman	– Anthony Hope Hawkins
headmaster	– St John Hankin
corn merchant	– G. B. Shaw

J. M. Barrie, the son of a Scottish weaver, was the odd man out among his contemporaries, though Shaw's father was much more of a lower-middle-class 'downstart' to use Shaw's own expression, than his occupation implies. Playwrights coming from such backgrounds tended also to create dramatic characters from much the same levels.

19

Pinero said frankly that the materials for English drama could be looked for only in the upper ranks of Society.[43] This was evident with plays whose casts were usually of well-bred, not to say aristocratic, characters. Plays like *The Importance of Being Earnest*, *An Ideal Husband*, *Pygmalion*, *The Voysey Inheritance*, *The Admirable Crichton*, to take but a few examples, required numbers of actors of high social polish, naturally at ease with hunter pocket-watches, parasols and silver tea-pots.

A further factor drawing the respectable classes into the ranks of the professional stage was the tradition of amateur acting. This gathered momentum from the mid-nineteenth century and proved valuable social education for young men invited to country house parties where putting on a play became part of the activities of the weekend. Out in the provinces cultured towns commonly began their own amateur groups, such as the Brighton Green Room Club, Newcastle's Clarion Dramatic Society, and Nugent Monck's Norwich Players, the last two both beginning in 1911.[44] In London there was a plethora of drama clubs in the 1890s, and by 1898 a sympathetic observer noted that amateur dramatic clubs 'now abound in every country town; in London their number is almost beyond computation'.[45]

Amateur dramatics brought amateurs with half a thought of turning professional into contact with established actors. For example, Irene Vanbrugh and Sybil Thorndike worked as professionals with various amateur companies in the 1900s.[46] Conversely the experience of amateur work was often a crucial factor in the decision to turn professional. It was so in the careers of Beerbohm Tree, George Alexander, Playfair, Benson and Aubrey Smith among many others. Leopold Wagner held that 'there is not the slightest doubt that amateur theatricals, in one form or another, have been largely instrumental in raising the stage to its present position'.[47] They gave middle- and upper-middle-class amateurs a direct experience of the theatre and sometimes of professional players, and served as an attractive channel drawing such respectable amateurs on to the commercial stage.

Especially important was the development of amateur dramatics at Oxford and Cambridge. The Cambridge ADC was founded in 1854[48] and from the 1870s and 1880s their repertoire took on a serious character as they produced their first Shakespeare in 1886.[49] Similarly at Oxford University the modern OUDS was formed in 1884.[50] Accordingly the ADC and the OUDS acted as a force directing well-to-do, upper-class, well-educated undergraduates towards careers as professional actors. Actors and managers Sir Aubrey Smith, Sir Nigel Playfair, Sir Frank Benson, Sir Felix Aylmer, authors A. E. W. Mason and Compton Mackenzie and the West End impresario H. M. Tennent were but a few of the noted men of the theatre who owed an early impetus to ADC, OUDS or the Oxford Greek Play before 1914.

These developments in the OUDS and ADC were underlain by a change in attitude within the unversities to the study of English literature. As English, including drama and Shakespeare, came to be regarded as worthy of serious academic attention, so this validated the activities of the amateur societies in the universities. Nor did it fail to cast reflected prestige on those performing the classics in the commercial theatre. At Oxford the Merton Chair of English was created in 1885 and the English degree examination, which included courses and papers on Shakespeare,[51] in 1894. An English examination had started at Cambridge University in 1886, and reforms in 1900 and 1909 created a more genuinely literary course, including drama.[52] It is noteworthy that one of the early teachers of English at Cambridge was F. L. Attenborough, the father of the actor Sir Richard Attenborough. The increasingly favourable attitude towards literature and drama of the prestigious ancient universities in the 1890s helped the stage and the actor on the road to respectability.

Whereas, firstly, the change in the nature of plays and their characters and, secondly, the upper-class amateur tradition were two factors making the stage attractive, there was a third factor 'pushing' many middle-class people there – the escape from alternative professions. Very many actors had had professions before going on the stage; indeed it was an important function of the amateur tradition to serve as a period of transition and try-out for such people. Of 282 actors in the Green Room Book of 1907, 121 had had a previous career or training for such a career, i.e. 42 per cent. Of these 121 the following were the chief careers they were leaving:

Commerce (including 'commerce', 'city', 'mercantile pursuits', accountant, stockbroker, co. executive, shipbroker, bank, insurance)	26	21.5%
Law	23	19%
Army & Navy	17	14%
Engineering	9	7.4%
Artist	8	6.6%
Clerk	6	4.9%
Schoolteacher	6	4.9%

The very high proportion coming from business may reflect the generally depressed condition of such economic activity in the 1880s and 1890s, which may have lowered the expectations of young men in occupations dependent on it. Secondly, this was a time of much complaint about the 'overcrowding of the professions'. Law was, as ever, notoriously overcrowded and the armed forces, after decades of peace and before the naval build-up and increase of tension with Germany in the 1900s, must have seemed a dead end. Lawyers and military men of good bearing, looks and physique, with confident well-modulated voices of acceptable accent, a strong sense of self-projection and a good wardrobe, could look to the stage as an occupation not too dissimilar from those they were already following. It was scarcely more risky, and potentially more lucrative. The desire to act is a compulsive urge barely explicable in such rational terms. But the fact that, at that time, the alternatives of depressed business and the overcrowded professions offered but weak power to retain many of their adherents with theatrical aspirations, increased the attractiveness of the stage.

For women this was probably even more true. The long-term predominance of female over male births throughout the century, coupled with the emigration movements, had left a considerable surplus of women. Many of these were not likely to get married and would need careers to support themselves independently of a husband or their families. Such occupations for middle-class women around 1890 or 1900 were very few indeed. Secretarial work, teaching in a Board School, shop work, or a governess's post presented the obvious outlets for women who did not wish, or were unable, to go to university. These were not attractive alternatives to going on the stage; indeed the alternatives were much less attractive for women than for men. The possibility of becoming a leading actress was one of the few high-status occupations open to middle-class women before 1900.[53]

IV

What then was the nature of the theatre which aspirants sought to enter before 1914? At the top of the theatrical tree was the London West End, with its thirty-two theatres in 1914. Dominating these prior to the War were the actor–managers. In May 1909 no fewer than twelve West End theatres were conducted by managers who were also actors, while others, like Forbes Robertson, Martin Harvey and Fred Terry, who made visits to London, were part of the actor-manager system.[54] At their head were the grandees of the profession closely associated with one particular theatre: Irving at the Lyceum, Squire Bancroft and later Herbert Tree at the Haymarket, George Alexander at the St James, Tree at His Majesty's, Charles Wyndham at the Criterion, John Hare and then Arthur Bourchier at the Garrick. Most of them were knighted and made good fortunes.

Out in the provinces theatre was provided partly by old stock companies, now diminishing and disappearing. The stock company was a group of actors fixed in one theatre in a town where they stayed more or less permanently, or at least for a longish summer season. They were regarded as useful places in which to start one's career and in which to learn the rudiments, the necessity of studying new parts quickly week by week being a good discipline for the tyro.[55] Summer stock especially survived for practical reasons, since for most theatres in the country there were not sufficient first-class stars or companies, or even lesser ones, to fill half the vacant weeks of the year.[56]

By the later nineteenth century, however, stock companies were being replaced by travelling companies. The speed of rail traffic, with its dense network providing easy accessibility to small towns, brought the travelling company to most centres of population. Audiences now benefited from the interest of seeing a constant

23

succession of fresh faces usually led by some well-loved, familiar hero figure such as Frank Benson, Fred Terry or Matheson Lang. The attraction of such national stars far outweighed that likely to be exercised by the local leading man of a small-town provincial stock company. *Era* noted in 1900:

'The stock company is a dead horse . . . to dream that we can turn the clock back and substitute for a polished repertoire of excellent travelling organizations the hurriedly rehearsed, poorly mounted and cheaply dressed productions of a resident company of necessarily second-rate artists is absurd.'[57]

The touring companies comprised a wide spectrum of quality and prestige. Indeed, in 1919 the Touring Managers' Association consisted of some 250 companies employing 3000 actors and actresses.[58] There were various leaders in the field. Sir Frank Benson toured the country from the 1880s to the 1920s playing Shakespeare to generations of schoolchildren. Sir John Martin Harvey, having found great success in 1899 as Sydney Carton in *The Only Way*, a version of *The Tale of Two Cities*, increasingly turned himself, in the 1900s, into a provincial touring actor exploiting this and other roles. Ben Greet ran about ten touring companies in Britain and America, appearing himself in Shakespearian leading roles. He also pioneered the pastoral play, producing Shakespeare in gardens and woodland glades at Kew in London and in the provinces (in Bracondale Grove in Norwich, for example). The Compton Comedy Company under Edward Compton (father of Fay and Sir Compton Mackenzie) specialized in taking Old English Comedy through the provinces, while Fred Terry and his wife combined London production with long provincial tours, notably in *The Scarlet Pimpernel*.

A new form of theatre was emerging in the provinces in the years before the War, namely the repertory. The new repertory theatres usually ran a few plays at a time, alternating them every three or four weeks. This was less hectic than the new play every week of the old stock company and led to more considered and polished production, while also avoiding the dulling long runs of commercial production. Secondly, there was less typecasting in repertory. Unlike old stock, with its actors fitting into much the same kind of roles play by play, the rep changed its players round, avoiding the star system and hierarchy of types. Thirdly, the reps had a more high-minded approach to drama, often espousing advanced modern plays, the theatre of ideas and work of cultural value. As such they came to be valued, like civic universities, libraries, galleries and museums, as ornaments of Edwardian civic pride.

The repertory movement had two chief originators: the Court Theatre in London and Miss Horniman's Gaiety in Manchester. The manager J. E. Vedrenne and the actor-dramatist Granville Barker took over the Court (now the Royal Court in Sloane Square) in 1904. They became virtually a repertory theatre for the works of Shaw, Galsworthy, Masefield and Barker himself. Moreover, it paid financially and set up a realistic alternative strategy to the long runs of the commercial West End. In the provinces the pioneer of the repertory movement was Miss Annie Horniman, the tea heiress.[59] She had developed repertory from 1903 at the Abbey Theatre, Dublin, whose lease she acquired for the Irish National Theatre Society. She then started repertory in Manchester, in 1907 at the Midland Hotel and in 1908 at the Gaiety Theatre. Under her theatre directors, Ben Iden Payne and then Lewis Casson from 1911, the theatre was noted for its fostering of naturalistic Lancashire drama, notably the plays of Houghton, Brighouse and Monkhouse. It stressed ensemble playing and developed many noted actors, including Lewis Casson, Sybil Thorndike and Basil Dean.

Not to be outdone by Manchester, the Liverpool Repertory Theatre began in 1911 on the initiative of two professors from the university.[60] Birmingham followed suit in 1913, the Repertory theatre here arising out of the amateur dramatics of Barry Jackson of the Maypole Dairies.[61] His wealth enabled him to run the Pilgrim Players, who became semi-professional, then to build his own theatre and engage a fully professional company in 1913. Birmingham, like Manchester, depended on the business wealth of one individual; both theatres were keen on using actors with Bensonian experience; they and Liverpool benefited from the friendly interest of their local universities. Other noted reps were Glasgow from 1909, and, in London, Charles Frohman's Repertory season at the Duke of York's in 1910. After the War came Bristol Little Theatre in 1923, Hull Repertory Theatre in 1924, Leeds Civic Playhouse in 1925,

25

Cambridge Festival Theatre in 1926. By 1935 there were fourteen repertory theatres in Britain.[62] An early sympathetic observer noted: 'The proud predominance of London itself as the centre of the theatrical world has been rudely shaken by a growing disposition on the part of the provincial capitals to provide a drama for themselves.'[63]

Slightly to one side in the structure of theatrical employment were the two theatres which were to become major cultural centres – the Old Vic and the Shakespeare Memorial Theatre at Stratford. The Old Vic had originated as the Royal Coburg Theatre in 1818 and operated as a rather boozy old melodrama house with occasional Shakespeare until 1880. In the latter year it was taken over for philanthropic work and renamed the Royal Victoria Coffee and Music Hall, providing purified entertainment and non-alcoholic refreshment for poor working folk. It was run by the remarkable Emma Cons, a disciple of the Christian Socialists, suffragette, LCC alderman and social worker. With her niece, Lilian Baylis she put on a range of concerts and opera, but on her aunt's death in 1912 Lilian Baylis took over and turned the theatre into an institution for drama. Initially they reverted to melodrama but in 1914 the Vic began to focus on Shakespeare, and was set on its course as one of the national centres of Shakespearian drama.[64] Stratford and its Memorial Theatre was already well established.[65] The tercentenary of Shakespeare's birth was held in 1864, and following it Charles Edward Flower of the local brewery firm gave a site for a theatre, which was opened in 1879.[66] From the 1880s the festival became an annual event. Leading touring actor–managers took charge of the festival at various times, but above all it was Sir Frank Benson who maintained the quality and prestige of Stratford and its Theatre. In the 1900s leading London figures like Forbes Robertson and Tree were attracted there. By 1914 all but two of Shakespeare's plays had been performed, and Stratford was established as one of the major centres of national theatrical life.

Beyond the actor–managers of the West End and the provincial touring companies, the reputable stock companies, the reps, Stratford and the Old Vic lay the fit-ups, gaffs and booths of which we have seen something earlier. Many actors accordingly worked in the provinces rather than in London. The extent of provincial activity

26

was evident from the 1911 census, which gave a detailed breakdown of the location of legitimate stage actors (excluding music hall and variety) on the night of the census. Nearly a half of all actors (43.6 per cent) were in London. This was not only because they were playing there but because this was where the unemployed actor rested while taking steps to get back on the boards. Outside London the greatest number were in Lancashire (12.4 per cent), with its large industrial population clustered in many sizeable urban centres. Fewest actors were in the extremities, the northern Lakeland counties, the far West and in the large, empty rural counties of East Anglia and Lincolnshire. If we relate the numbers of actors in an area to the total population of the area, its potential audience, we find a similar spread. The greatest density of actors is found in the industrial areas of Lancashire (3.13 per 10,000) and Worcestershire and Warwickshire (including Birmingham) (3.38 per 10,000). Then there were areas in the immediate environs of the metropolis: Kent, Surrey, Sussex and Middlesex. In the middle range there were commonly 1.5 and 2.5 actors per 10,000 of population, but in the sparsest areas barely more than one actor per 10,000. In Lincolnshire, East Anglia and the far West there were relatively few sizeable towns, with populations scattered over very large areas and probably little opportunity to acquire much interest in the drama.

From the 1890s and 1900s something of the Victorian legacy of hostility to the actor was beginning to be shed. A change in attitude was reflected in the expansion of theatreland and the profession, whose educational and social origins rose markedly. These developments were partly helped on by the change in roles depicted on stage, the amateur tradition and diminishing prospects of alternative careers. By 1914 the structure of the theatre was amply varied, with a large commercial West End and a wide range of provincial work of varying degrees of artistic seriousness. By the 1900s scores of young people were influenced by these factors in their desire to go into the theatre. But how were they to start and gain an education and training for the stage? This was the next problem in the elevation of the profession.

NOTES

1 Max Beerbohm, 'Henry Irving', *Around Theatres* (London, 1924), pp.179–80.
2 Laurence Irving, *Henry Irving* (London, 1951), p.580.
3 Michael Baker, *The Rise of the Victorian Actor* (London, 1978), p.18.
4 Irving, *op.cit.*, p.58.
5 Sir Squire and Marie Bancroft, *The Bancrofts, Recollections of Sixty Years* (London, 1909), p.76.
6 Mrs Patrick Campbell, *My Life and Some Letters* (London, 1922), p.33.
7

	Actors	Actresses
parents approve	8 (15.4%)	9 (33.3%)
parents disapprove	27 (51.9%)	12 (44.4%)
parents no special reaction	17 (32.7%)	6 (22.2%)

8 Paul Sheridan, *Penny Theatres of London* (London, 1981).
9 Maud Gill, *See the Players* (London, 1938), p.69.
10 Leopold Wagner, *How to Get on the Stage* (London, 1899), p.77.
11 F. C. Vernon Harcourt, *From Stage to Cross* (London, 1901), pp.169–70.
12 Mark Melford, *Life in a Booth* (London, 1913), p.16.
13 Elizabeth Grice, *Rogues and Vagabonds* (Lavenham, 1977), pp.162–3.
14 Laurence Irving, *Precarious Crust* (London, 1971), p.182.
15 Constance Benson, *Mainly Players* (London, 1926), p.127.
16 Thomas Watson, *Exploring Life* (London, 1926), p.280.
17 J. F. Brent, *Memories of a Mistaken Life* (London, 1897), p.15.
18 Kellow Chesney, *The Victorian Underworld* (London, 1972) pp.368–9.
19 E. F. S., *Our Stage and its Critics* (London, 1910), p.160.
20 *Great Thoughts*, 1 January 1898, pp.228–30.
21 *Daily Telegraph*, 7 April 1898.
22 *The Review of Reviews*, July, August, September 1904.
23 Parliamentary Paper 1917–18, XXXV, p.105.
24 1892 XVIII *Report of the Select Committee on Theatres and Places of Entertainment*, p.451. *The Green Room Book*, 1907. *Who's*

Who in the Theatre, 1914. Diana Howard, *London Theatre and Music Hall 1850–1950* (London, 1970).

25 See Appendix I for the table of Social Origins of the Acting Profession 1880–1980.

26 Sir Squire Bancroft, 'Dramatic Thoughts', Address at the Royal Institution, 17 March 1905. *Era*, 25 March 1905.

27 Sir Squire and Marie Bancroft, *op.cit.*, p.33.

28 *Era*, 9 February 1907.

29 Seymour Hicks, *Twenty-Four Years of an Actor's Life* (London, 1910), p.11.

30 Eton, Winchester, Westminster, Charterhouse, St Paul's, Merchant Taylors', Harrow, Rugby, Shrewsbury.

32 J. R. de S. Honey, 'Tom Brown's Universe', in Brian Simon and Ian Bradley (eds), *The Victorian Public School* (London, 1975). Jonathan Gathorne-Hardy, *The Public School Phenomenon* (London, 1977).

32 Letter, Kenneth Barnes to Rev. G. H. Williams, 1 January 1914, in Administrator's Letterbooks, Academy of Dramatic Art.

33 Queen's College, Harley Street; Cheltenham Ladies' College; North London Collegiate; Roedean; St Leonard's; St Felix, Southwold; Sherborne; St Paul's; Wycombe Abbey; Westonbirt; Benenden; Cranborne Chase; Godolphin and Latymer; Mount School, York.

34 Henry Irving, *The Stage as it is*, Address to the Edinburgh Philosophical Institution, 8 November 1881.

35 Henry Irving, *The Art of Acting*, Address to the Edinburgh Philosophical Institution, 9 November 1891.

36 *Op.cit.*, 1881.

37 *Op.cit.*, 1891.

38 E.F.S., *Op.cit.*, p.6.

39 *Era*, 24 February 1900.

40 *Ibid*.

41 Percy Hutchison, *Masquerade* (London, 1936), p.31, quoting Sir Charles Wyndham.

42 George Rowell, *The Victorian Theatre 1792–1914* (Cambridge, 1978), Chapter 4, 'The Era of Society Drama'.

43 Hamilton Fyfe, *Sir Arthur Pinero's Plays and Players* (London, 1930), p.18.

29

44 *The Maddermarket Theatre, Norwich* (Norwich, 1975); George Taylor, *History of the Amateur Theatre* (Melksham, 1976).

45 Leopold Wagner, *op.cit.*, p.25.

46 Russell Thorndike, *Sybil Thorndike* (London, 1929), p.203.

47 Leopold Wagner, *op.cit.*, p.30.

48 F. C. Burnand, *Personal Reminiscences of the A.D.C. Cambridge* (London, 1880).

49 W. G. Elliott, 'The A.D.C. Cambridge' in *Amateur Clubs and Actors* (London, 1898).

50 Alan Mackinnon, *The Oxford Amateurs* (London, 1910) and Claude Nugent, 'The OUDS', in *Amateur Clubs, op.cit.*, on OUDS generally.

51 D. J. Palmer, *The Rise of English Studies* (Oxford, 1965).

52 E. M. W. Tillyard, *The Muse Unchained* (London, 1958).

53 Christopher Kent, 'Image and Reality, the Actress and Society', in Martha Vicinus (ed.), *A Widening Sphere* (Indiana, 1977).

54 Horace Wyndham, *The Magnificent Mummer* (London, 1909), p.25.

55 Louis Calvert, *Problems of the Actor* (London, 1919), p.31.

56 Robert Courtneidge, *I was an Actor Once* (London, 1930), p.180.

57 Cited in Lou Warwick, *The Mackenzie's called Compton* (Northampton, 1977), p.126.

58 *Era*, 9 April 1919.

59 Reg Pogson, *Miss Horniman and the Gaiety Theatre Manchester* (London, 1952). Whitford Kane, *Are We All Met?* (London, 1931), pp.21–2.

60 Grace Wyndham Goldie, *The Liverpool Repertory Theatre 1911–1934* (Liverpool, 1935).

61 J. C. Trewin, *The Birmingham Repertory Theatre 1913–1963* (London, 1963).

62 *Theatre World*, June–Nov.1927. *British Equity*, 1934, have useful articles on the repertory movement.

63 P. P. Howe, *The Repertory Theatre, a Record and a Criticism* (London, 1910), p.12.

64 Richard Findlater, *Lilian Baylis* (London, 1975). Peter Roberts, *The Old Vic Story* (London, 1976).

65 M. C. Day and J. C. Trewin, *The Shakespeare Memorial Theatre* (London, 1932). T. C. Kemp and J. C. Trewin, *The Stratford*

Festival, a History of the Shakespeare Memorial Theatre (Birmingham, 1953).
66 The 1879 theatre was destroyed by fire in 1926 and the present one opened in 1932.

2 The Training of the Actor before 1914

One of the most important developments in the professionalization of the actor in the 1900s was the creation of new, better organized forms of drama education. However valuable amateur experience was as a preparation for the stage, dissatisfaction was expressed with the lack of opportunities for formal training. F. C. Burnand complained, 'It is called a "self educating profession" and . . . it is evident that the theatrical profession, left to itself for education, is a very indifferent, if not absolutely bad school'.[1] Victorian actors had learned their craft on the job by imitating fellow-members of their company. At the worst old faults would be perpetuated and even at best the tyro was gaining his training at the expense of the public, who were expected to pay for the barely trained and inexperienced performer. This was hardly the mark of a profession. In 1879 an acting academy was proposed as part of the new Shakespeare Memorial Theatre but this came to nothing, as did further proposals in 1882.[2] There was a tradition of private tutors in the later nineteenth century, but it was in the 1900s that the two major academies emerged – Sir Herbert Tree's Academy of Dramatic Art and Elsie Fogerty's Central School. These changes brought about a revolution in the training of the actor, a raised level of seriousness and professionalism.

Various factors gave greater urgency to the need for more formal training. For example, upper-class, public school and university men who were coming on to the stage spoke the language of their social class. It was complained that 'they don't pronounce half their words at all', pronounced 'hyah' for 'here', 'thah' for 'there' and, adequate as this may have been in the drawing room, it did not project in the theatre.[3] This problem was exacerbated by the increasing size of theatres. The three surviving unremodelled theatres of the 1880s (Comedy, Lyric, Garrick) have an average capacity of 850 and a mean proscenium width of 27 feet. Those built in the 1903–7 cluster have an average capacity of about 1018 and a remarkably uniform 30–31-foot proscenium, and accordingly made greater technical demands on the actor. Even experienced players appreciated their defects. Mrs Campbell had to go into a nursing home in 1897 with fatigue and overstrain. She reflected that if she had had a proper training, 'I would have known how to spare my emotional temperament and to depend a little on skill technique'.[4] If even Mrs Pat felt that she would have benefited from a drama school, it was evident that such training would have been even more valuable for actors of more modest endowments.

Before the foundation of the two leading drama schools in the 1900s – Tree's Academy and Elsie Fogerty's Central School – there were already several individual tutors and 'schools' purporting to teach drama and elocution. These varied greatly in quality and staying power, and some were of an incompetence verging on the fraudulent. In the 1880s John Martin Harvey answered an advertisement in the *Daily Telegraph* purporting to teach 'the whole art of acting' with 'engagements guaranteed', for 2 guineas. This turned out to be an 'inoffensive little man' reading from a penny number in a sordid room. When tackled about the guaranteed engagements his tutor blandly replied, 'Ah, you buy a copy of the *Era* and we will look at the advertisements'.[5] With so many so desperate to go on the stage and with no clear standards, such as in other professions could be guaranteed by the older universities, drama training was an area wide open to the ill-qualified charlatan.

Yet what is remarkable is not so much this aspect as the lively culture of private tuition for the stage provided by a wide variety of tutors and small schools of high reputation. These were of various types – schools associated with acting companies, individual coaches, private institutionalized academies and, finally, elocution taught in officially established public colleges chiefly concerned with other matters.

33

Especially valuable were schools or facilities for training attached to working theatrical companies. To some extent the old stock companies had served as schools, even if informally, with the older actors passing on their experience to the newcomers. However, quite pre-eminent among stock companies giving training was that of Sarah Thorne at Margate. She ran the Theatre Royal, as her father had before her. Margate, as a healthy seaside town, had many private schools for various purposes, and Sarah opened her School of Acting there in 1885. She received pupils who were charged £20 for three months or £30 for six months,[6] boarding at Sarah's house, 'The Towers', in the Square. George Arliss, who was one of her company, recalled that 'her method was to engage about half a dozen experienced actors and actresses for the leading parts and use her students for the rest of the cast so that the pupils were continually playing before a paying audience'.[7] The pupils attended daily classes in acting, voice production, gesture and mime, dialects and makeup, took part in rehearsals and either watched or participated in performances in the evening.

The pupils, in view of the cost of the fees and boarding, were fairly affluent. In Arliss's day 'The pupils were sons and daughters of prosperous businessmen, of well-to-do actors, of lawyers, authors and clergymen'.[8] Miss Thorne was indeed tapping that flush of children from business and professional families who entered the profession between 1890 and 1914. Her school was also taken seriously by leading London theatre people who either sent their children to study there, as did Ellen Terry, or attended performances, as did Irving and Granville Barker. Among the actors and actresses who passed through Sarah Thorne's hands were Irene and Violet Vanbrugh, and Ellen Terry's son Gordon Craig. Sarah Thorne died in 1899 and the School ceased, but during its life in the eighties and nineties it trained more actors and actresses who were to achieve success in the 1900s than any other school.

Ben Greet was a noted actor-manager (and a former pupil of Sarah Thorne's) who ran several touring companies, presenting Shakespeare in the provinces and pastorally in Regents Park. At Irving's suggestion he started his Academy of Acting in 1896.[9] It was held in Bedford Street, the Strand and had the advantage of a large room at the top of the building used as a theatre, the 'Bijou Theatre', where tuition could be given. It was scarcely less an advantage that the premises were over the Bodega, a leading pro's job-finding pub. Here the students were given the usual curriculum of acting, voice production, dancing, fencing and play production. Ben Greet, on returning from his tours, rehearsed the pupils carefully, and public performances were given at the end of term. On the results of these and their general progress the best pupils were invited to join one of Greet's companies. Accordingly Sybil Thorndike played her earliest parts as a student with Ben Greet's Pastoral Players in productions staged in Cambridge and Oxford college gardens in 1904. As well as the Thorndikes, H. B. Irving and Mrs Patrick Campbell both owed some of their early training to Greet's Academy.

The third major company school was that attached to Frank Benson's troupe. Whereas there would always be a certain amount of informal help from the experienced to the newcomers in his company, Benson decided to formalize this as a school from 1901. Whereas the Thorne company was based on Margate and Ben Greet's school remained fixed in London, Benson's school was unusual in being itinerant and travelling with the company. On joining a student paid about fifty or sixty pounds,[10] 'for his tuition during a tour of forty weeks. The sum he paid was in no sense a premium. It was the ordinary school fee, to defray the necessary expenses incurred for the services of experienced professors . . . All travelling expenses were paid by the management'.[11] The teachers included Constance Benson, Paul Berton - who had trained at the Paris Conservatoire and who brought French methods of elocution that Benson especially admired[12] - and Genevieve Ward, the distinguished tragedienne who played guest roles with the company.[13] Their curriculum was common for the time. Benson described it as 'Elocution, Dancing, Fencing, Callisthenics, Rehearsal and general technique', while Norah Nicholson recalled: 'We travelled with the Company, spent our mornings in class (drama, diction, dancing and fencing), attended rehearsals, when needed, and walked on at night – usually seven plays per week.'[14] Reflecting Benson's own interests and aptitudes, there was considerable emphasis on physical skills to induce a graceful and noble stage bearing. The pupils took part in games of hockey and cricket and other sports that were an integral, and unfairly mocked, part of Bensonian life. Pupils looked back with

35

affection and gratitude to the School. Norah Nicholson thought 'our training was first class' and Desmond Chapman Houston that 'never was time or money better spent', as talent 'flowered in the happy, congenial, enthusiastic background'. It may be noted, for clarity, that the Benson company's touring school was distinct from the later Lady Benson's School, which began successfully in London in 1919 when Frank and Constance began to part.

Apart from these companies with their own form of training, there were several individual tutors of high reputation who taught pupils privately. Hermann Vezin was one of the doyens of the breed, 'the best known teacher of acting in England'.[15] He was American-born and educated at the University of Pennsylvania, but had had a long successful acting career in England. By the 1890s he was in his sixties, and devoted himself to teaching in his studio by Waterloo Bridge. He laid stress on the capacity for rapid speech with very clear enunciation.[16] He would make a pupil 'repeat each letter of the alphabet until I was able to set them all slipping off my tongue or through my teeth with amazing rapidity'.[17] He also appreciated the connection between physical training and the voice, making his pupils glean and pitch imaginary sheaves to strengthen the shoulders, extend the lungs and cultivate rounded gestures.[18] Sir Frank Benson, who studied with him, admired Vezin as 'an exceedingly well-read cultivated man . . . an encyclopedia of dramatic acting experience, exercise and training'.[19] Certainly he was the most important single private tutor training actors in the 1890–1914 period.

The foremost woman teacher of drama was Rosina Filippi, who had trained with Vezin and enjoyed a successful career with Benson and Tree. A 'wildly energetic, gypsy-like and exciting actress',[20] she was a half-sister of the great Eleanora Duse. She taught her groups in rehearsal classes in Chandos Hall, Maiden Lane and then in King Street, Covent Garden.[21] Miss Filippi's classes were well-known in London and playwrights like Shaw would come to watch their own pieces being rehearsed by her. Most of her teaching was in speech, with emphasis on 'full vowels and sharp consonants', but she also paid attention to stage movement and dancing.[22] Most importantly, each term was concluded with a public performance at the Court Theatre for parents and friends and, especially in London, managers

36

who were prospective employers. Sir Lewis Casson and Sir Felix Aylmer (whose speech reflected something of the Vezin and Filippi concern for precise diction) were among Miss Filippi's pupils, and she also taught at the new Academy of Dramatic Art. In a wider context, she was unwittingly the originator of the modern Old Vic Shakespearian tradition. She preceded Lilian Baylis in experimenting with bringing Shakespeare to the people after Emma Cons's death in 1912. A third leading private tutor was Walter Lacey, who had acted with Samuel Phelps. His significance was that Irving sent actors in need of further training to him. Ellen Terry also deferred to him on speech matters, while Violet Vanbrugh was sent to Lacey by Baroness Burdett-Coutts (one of Irving's close friends) to learn the 'grand manner' and the speaking of Shakespearian verse.[23]

As well as these freelancers, more formally established colleges in London provided some education for intending actors. The City of London College at Moorgate taught elocution, and Robertson Hare attended Edward Minshull's classes there around 1906.[24] Academies originally or primarily devoted to music also often taught drama and elocution. This training was valuable for singers, especially in opera, but was also useful for non-singing actors. The London Academy of Music was founded in 1861 and taught elocution from the 1860s. A later tutor was Gustave Garcia, who published *The Actor's Art* in 1882, incorporating his version of François Delsarte's system of teaching forms of gesture and expression to convey emotion. It was an early attempt at a scientific approach to the training of actors and was embodied in Garcia's teaching at the London Academy from 1882 to 1904.[25] Finally the Guildhall School of Music was founded in 1880. Reginald Denham, who was there in 1910, recalled that 'It had splendid courses in "Voice, Speech and Gesture" and a list of famous teachers.'[26] Best-known was Kate Rorke, a leading lady with Sir John Hare, who went to teach at the Guildhall on her retirement from the stage in 1907; while Paul Berton also taught elocution and drama, embodying much of the technique of the Comédie Française.[27]

In addition to these chartered academies there were several private enterprise colleges of varying degrees of stability and repute, usually run by retired actors. Well-regarded was Henry Neville's Dramatic Academy, founded in 1884. Neville, with over twenty-five years'

37

stage experience before he began his academy with his brother, was a former actor–manager and playwright noted as a melodramatic comedy hero. As a member of the Garrick Club he had a status and accessibility to contacts rare among academy proprietors.[28] Especially well loved by its pupils was Cairns James's Academy in Oxford Street. Cairns James had been a noted comedian with the Gilbert and Sullivan Operas at the Savoy, and his partner Ernest d'Auban had been stage manager at Drury Lane. Leslie Henson recalled the curriculum. Cairns James 'taught elocution and gave expert instruction in scenes from plays . . . Ernest d'Auban taught singing; and fencing lessons were given as part of our regular curriculum . . .'[29] Gerald du Maurier devised and adjudicated improvisation exercises for them. The School trained Leslie Henson, Robertson Hare, Clemence Dane and Reginald Denham, its happy and hard-working atmosphere proving successful in nurturing comic talents.

It is remarkable that there were so many valuable opportunities for elocution and drama training even before the founding of RADA and the Central School. In a field that one might expect to have been wide open to all kinds of charlatanism and quackery, there was a good deal of serious work in a quite new area of private education. This may be due to three factors. Firstly, a great many of the new aspirants to the stage came from middle- and upper-middle-class backgrounds with parents well used to evaluating private education, less easily hoodwinked and confident enough to see they were getting value for money. Secondly, the fact that many teachers taught in more than one institution maintained a roughly common standard. For example, Kate Rorke and Rosina Filippi not only taught privately but at the Guildhall and ADA respectively. Thirdly, many of these teachers had had long and successful careers on the stage before taking up teaching. The ready availability of tutors of good quality, whom the serious aspirant could contact with a little judicious enquiry, helped to counteract the potential growth of a semi-fraudulent sector, which would have brought discredit on the stage. It is remarkable that actors' memoirs which recall these early forms of training depict them with affection and gratitude as valuable places of hard work and enthusiasm.

38

II

It was in this context that the two major drama schools of today were founded in the 1900s, Sir Herbert Tree's Academy of Dramatic Art (RADA) and Elsie Fogerty's Central School. The concern to have a dramatic academy of some national standing was undoubtedly influenced by foreign example. As the contemporaneous concern over technical education was influenced by Germany and commercial higher education by the United States, so the ideas of acting education owed something to the Continent and America. In particular the French stage and the Paris Conservatoire were much admired.[30] Some bi-lingual English actors, notably Genevieve Ward and Esme Percy, had studied at the Conservatoire prior to 1914 and viewed it with enthusiasm. Austin Trevor, who was fluent in French and German, had actually intended to develop a career as an actor in France, and was to have had coaching in Paris to enter the Conservatoire in 1914. His plan thwarted by the outbreak of war, he went to ADA instead.[31] He recalled that the Paris Conservatoire was well appreciated in England as the major centre of theatrical training. Some devotees of the Conservatoire wanted a proper state-aided school and doubted whether Tree's proposed academy would measure up to the French exemplar.[32] However, Jules Claretie, the Administrator of the Comédie Française, congratulated Tree on his Academy as the English analogy to the Conservatoire.[33] This was premature praise, but pleasing to Tree as recognizing his true hopes and intent.

The awareness of the European Conservatoire tradition continued after the Academy had started. In 1912 Kenneth Barnes had been gathering information from Leipzig Conservatoire,[34] and on the eve of the War was about to embark on a tour of European theatrical capitals.[35] Theatrical circles, and Tree especially, would also have been well aware of the American Academy of Dramatic Arts formed in New York in 1884 with a full and rigorous curriculum, recognized by the University and closely associated with the great impresario Charles Frohman.[36] Why could London, with the greatest theatre in the world, not do what Paris and New York did for the training of its actors?

Tree initially began his Academy in his own His Majesty's

Theatre. Lectures were given in the famous Dome of the Theatre, and the foyer used for rehearsals. The sheer inconvenience of this became evident as pupils increased. The first principal sympathized: it 'must have been a terrible nuisance to the various heads of department in a busy theatre like His Majesty's, young creatures of both sexes emerging scuttlingly from half-lit corners . . . the place was like a rabbit warren'.[37] This was clearly unsatisfactory and could prove no permanent solution to the location of the Academy. In 1905 it was moved to 62 Gower Street, the old home of the playwright St John Hankin. In 1906 control passed from Tree to a formally constituted Council of distinguished men of the theatre, including the founder.

One of the strengths of the Academy was the distinction and interest of the Council. Sir Squire Bancroft, Sir John Hare, Sir Herbert Tree, Sir George Alexander, Sir Johnston Forbes Robertson, Cyril Maude, Arthur Bourchier, Sir Arthur Pinero and Sir James Barrie – seven actor–managers and two playwrights – served from 1906 to the War. They were joined in 1908 by actors Edward Terry, E. S. Willard and Sir W. S. Gilbert, and in 1912 by Shaw and the principal's sister, the actress Irene Vanbrugh. It was of the greatest value that the Academy had such direct contacts with the most successful figures in the West End. This was not merely nominal. Playwrights like Shaw and Pinero came to the Academy to conduct rehearsals of their plays. The Academy also benefited financially from its Council members. Tree continued to support the institution on its move to Gower Street, giving over £600 to help with furnishings and fittings.[38] Sir Squire Bancroft gave £1000 towards the building of their theatre in Malet Street.[39] In the raising of a building fund leading figures on the Council took up substantial amounts of debentures, Bancroft £700 worth, Shaw and Forbes Robertson £300 each and Pinero and Alexander £200 each. Shaw gave it the copyright royalties from *Pygmalion* (and hence from *My Fair Lady*) while, to ease a financial crisis during the War, Forbes Robertson and Miss Vanbrugh took the initiative of making and appearing in a film of *Masks and Faces* to raise £2000 for the Academy.[40]

What kind of students attended Tree's Academy before the War? Firstly, most of them were women. Girl applicants outnumbered

40

men in the ratio of four to one.[41] This imbalance was also reflected in the ratio of graduates. Of 334 students who were at the Academy from 1910 to 1914 and whose employment is recorded, 108 were men and 226 women, a ratio of 1 to 2.1. That the disparity between men and women attending and leaving the Academy was much less than that of applicants reflects Barnes's policy of admitting men more easily, since a certain balance of the sexes was necessary for casting and operating the curriculum. The total number of students rose quickly from about fifty in 1908, to seventy-seven in 1909[42] and 100 by 1910.[43] Secondly, many of the students were clearly quite well-to-do. In 1914 Dodie Smith was awed by 'handsome young women, with their well-cut, up to date clothes plus their Marcel waved hair and lipsticked mouths'. In another term she encountered a new set, but of much the same type, 'the wealthiest and best dressed girls'.[44] Athene Seyler, who was there in the 1900s, remembered her fellow-students as being all of good education and manners.[45] Fabia Drake, who was there just before and after the War, thought that the pupils came often from 'artistic and professional' backgrounds.[46] Working-class pupils were not at all evident. Thirdly, the bulk of the students were seriously hard-working. Miss Seyler and Miss Drake were clear that the pupils had serious intentions of going on the stage and did not regard the Academy as a mere social recreation, while Miss Kathleen Harrison thought her year a good and studious one. The picture that emerges is of a student body of a well-to-do social background (some girls especially so), hard-working and genuinely concerned to go on the stage, though relatively few would make a lasting success there.

The essential purpose of the Academy was training for the stage. Yet girls who did not prove capable of a stage career could still derive social and personal benefit from the training. Barnes told two parents that although their daughters would not be good enough for the stage, yet one had 'an improvement in her general deportment and I think a keener interest in things that are going on around her' and another was 'a brighter and more hopeful personality than when she first came'.[47] At a time when higher education for women was so limited, the Academy must have served a very valuable purpose in broadening the experience of girls, giving them lively and interesting activity to counteract the stultifying effects of limited, if comfortable, backgrounds.

41

Eva le Gallienne gives a vivid description of the layout of the Academy in those days.[48]

> Three old houses had been thrown together forming a rambling building in which there was one small auditorium with a raised platform as a stage – very little equipment, in no sense a 'theatre'. Then there were many small and large rehearsal rooms, a dancing hall where the fencing was also taught, dressing-rooms, and, in the basement, a long, low dining-room, with a counter on which sandwiches and buns were displayed . . . the place always seemed to me like a busy bee-hive.

Dodie Smith is more explicit on the old theatre, the heart of the Academy:

> This had been made by knocking down the dividing wall between the two houses and replacing it with a curtain. The stage was raised in the drawing-room of one house, the auditorium was in the drawing-room of the other; and beyond this another wall had been knocked down so that a little back room could serve as what was known as the Royal Box, for the Administrator and distinguished guests.[49]

What did the Academy teach? Interviewed on the eve of its opening, Tree said that the principal subjects would be voice production, elocution, blank verse, Shakespeare, dancing, fencing, acrobatics and mime, gesture appropriate to periods (minuets, the use of the fan) and the acting of plays.[50] The structure of the curriculum had taken a clear shape by 1906. There were three terms of eleven weeks in the course of a year: January to March, April to July and October to December. The course consisted of four terms: A, B, C and Final School, and accordingly could last about fifteen months. The content was:[51]

Section A. – Voice Production, The Art of Expression, Elocution, Pantomime, Dancing and Callisthenics, Fencing, History of English Theatre and Drama.

Section B. – The Art of Expression, Rehearsal Class, Pantomime, Dancing and Callisthenics, Fencing.

Section C. – The Art of Expression, Rehearsal Class,
Pantomime, Dancing, Fencing.

Final School. – Fencing, Pantomime, Make-up and Rehearsals,
special rehearsals with distinguished actors and
authors.

From 1908 or 1909 the curriculum was enriched by the teaching of
the Delsarte system. This was a system of physical exercises especially
valuable for relaxing the body, giving it flexibility of movement and
loosening up the stiffness of everyday carriage. It was particularly
important for girls of the day, who were brought up to cultivate a
rather rigid reserve as part of their modesty. Their elaborate clothing
and relative lack of participation in sports reinforced this. The
Academy realized that it had to break down these inhibitions and the
physical limitations that were their consequence if it was to turn its
rather well-bred students into actors capable of expressing emotion.

The fees were initially 6 guineas a term in 1905 and then 12 guineas
from 1906 until the War, though children of actors were admitted for
half-fees.[52] Some scholarships were available from the autumn term
of 1910, and twenty-two were awarded between then and the War.
However, Tree was careful to stress that he took no pecuniary gain
from the Academy, quite the reverse: 'The Academy is not conducted
for the purpose of profit. Indeed since the fees may be considered
practically nominal for the amount of tuition given, there must
necessarily be a deficit on current expenses' – expenses which Tree
met himself.[53]

What of the teachers? At the outset Tree seems to have used
working actors like Fred Kerr and J. H. Barnes, who stayed only a
short time. Within a few years, however, the Academy had assembled
a valuable team of tutors, perhaps better known in that capacity than
as stage stars. Gertrude Burnett was highly regarded, especially as a
producer and an excellent teacher. She had been a distinguished
actress with Alexander and Wyndham, among others. Rosina Filippi,
whom I have discussed earlier, was a second leading woman ADA tutor.
A third was Elsie Chester: 'a fierce Jonsonian creation',[54] 'stout,
untidy and excitable';[55] her stage career had been curtailed by the loss
of a leg. Alice Gachet was especially beloved for her teaching of
French and of French plays in the original language.

43

Of the men A. E. George, 'a small man with a tremendous voice' and a veteran of His Majesty's, taught elocution.[56] Other male teachers were Lyall Swete, who had had experience with Benson and Alexander. 'Amiable and enigmatic', as Kenneth Barnes found him, he continued an active stage career while teaching at the Academy. So too did Fisher White, on whom Barnes relied for much good advice. White, in fact, had been with Tree for ten years before diversifying his career by teaching at the Academy. Dancing was taught by Louis Hervey d'Egville, one of the last of a family long associated with instruction in the social graces. The d'Egvilles' private studio at 44 Conduit Street was one of the most important centres in London for the teaching of dancing, deportment and carriage.[57] Their teaching of bowing, dancing and deportment was an essential part of the finishing education of young ladies entering Society. At one level d'Egville provided a training in social graces for well-to-do students whose future lay in Society rather than on the stage. More importantly, his instruction enabled young people to simulate and depict the upper-class styles called for in so many of the characters of the contemporary drama and in classic Old Comedy. Kenneth Barnes had a high opinion of his staff. 'These were all teachers anxious to maintain the artistic traditions of the English-speaking stage, and to pass on to their students the benefits of their own hard-won experience.'[58]

As well as the formal teaching by permanent tutors, lectures were given by outside speakers. Bernard Shaw on 'Elementary Economics for Actors' and William Archer on 'Blank Verse' were among the first. Shaw was especially keen to broaden the students' tuition in this way. On becoming a member of the Council in 1911, he stressed that it was the Academy's duty 'to give the students as liberal an education as possible in subjects required for an Arts degree at a university'.[59] It posed for drama education a dilemma of the balance of technical vocational training and more liberal education. In practice the balance was firmly towards the former emphasis, but these outside lectures provided a leavening influence.

A very important part of the curriculum was the special rehearsals conducted by distinguished actors and playwrights from outside. For example, in 1910 they were taken by W. S. Gilbert, Irene Vanbrugh, Pinero, Granville Barker, Forbes Robertson, and

44

others.[60] The insights such figures could bring were a great privilege for the Academy students, and well appreciated. Further contact with the professional stage could be gained by students who were allowed to take walk-on and even small speaking parts in West End productions. The course culminated in the Annual Public Performances given under full professional conditions in leading West End theatres, usually those of Council members – His Majesty's in 1905 and 1906, the St James in 1907 and 1910, the Playhouse in 1908 and 1909, for example. Here the students were judged by distinguished actors from outside, who awarded the Bancroft Gold Medal to the most accomplished. It speaks well of the ability of the students and the perceptiveness of the judges that three of the ten recipients from 1905 to 1914 went on to distinguished careers, Robert Atkins (1905), Athene Seyler (1908) and Gladys Young (1914), the first two ultimately becoming CBEs and Miss Young an OBE. It is also noteworthy that in those days the Gold Medal really was of pure gold.

What happened to students when they left the Academy? Barnes thought that the great majority of students were able to find engagements on leaving: 'Provided a student has talent and works assiduously the probability is that he will get an engagement after a course here';[61] indeed, 'the exception is when a man does not get an engagement to start him from the Academy'.[62] Where then did they go? The first occupations of students leaving between 1910 and 1914 may be calculated from the Academy's reports.[63] They show the following pattern of first employment:

	Men		*Women*	
West End	72	(66.7%)	82	(36.3%)
Other London	3	(2.8%)	12	(5.3%)
Provinces	1	(0.9%)	13	(5.7%)
Tour in Provinces	26	(24.1%)	118	(52.2%)
Tour abroad	6	(5.6%)	4	(1.8%)
Film	0	0	4	(0.4%)
	108	(100)	230	(100)

Men, being in shorter supply, found it much easier to find initial work in the West End than did women. Women more usually had to settle for a tour into the provinces. In proportion men stood nearly twice the chance of women in getting a West End engagement; women were twice as likely as men to go on a provincial tour. The West End engagements were not especially glamorous, most people having to start as walk-ons, understudies or chorus dancers. But to go straight from the Academy to paid employment on one of the major West End stages was a good and exciting first step. The actor or actress on tour was more likely to start playing more substantial roles more quickly. The repertory movement was beginning to make a slight impact on the Academy's employment scene with the Liverpool Rep., then Glasgow and Croydon taking women from 1911. The thin end of the wedge of film employment is also evident. In fact three ADA students made films before 1914, the best-known being Cedric Hardwicke. They all worked for the British and Colonial Film Company.

But the major employers were the big West End actor–managers. In this ADA was fortunate in having several of them on the Council, and they certainly showed a loyalty to their own institution. Bancroft and Hare had retired and did not control theatres, but the rest provided the following jobs for students leaving the Academy:

Sir Herbert Beerbohm Tree (His Majesty's)	40
Sir George Alexander (St James)	12
Sir Johnston Forbes Robertson (Drury Lane)	10
Arthur Bourchier (Garrick)	25
Cyril Maude (Playhouse)	11

It is pleasing to note that Tree was a major employer of the products of his own Academy. It was natural that these leading actor – managers should have been significant employers. They took the Academy seriously, they visited the place regularly, in rehearsal rooms and at termly productions. Accordingly they were in an advantageous position to spot emerging talent and, as shrewd businessmen, to garner it to their own companies. The influence of Tree and his fellow-members of the Council forged the links between ADA and the prestigious, glamorous and lucrative stages of the West End.

46

III

The second major school created in these years was the Central School of Speech and Drama, founded by Elsie Fogerty in 1906.[64] Miss Fogerty, the daughter of an architect who strongly disapproved of the stage, studied at the Paris Conservatoire in the 1880s and on her return began teaching elocution, producing drama and dealing with speech therapy problems at various girls' private schools. She also gained practical experience of the stage by acting with William Poel's Elizabethan Stage Society. From 1898 she took over some speech training classes formerly held at the Albert Hall. Fogerty's building-up of this clientele proved to be one of the bases of her later School. The other arose from a project of Frank Benson's for a fixed school in London to prepare actors for touring, as an equivalent to the Paris Conservatoire. Miss Fogerty taught diction for Benson's new school at Hampstead, but on its failure she took the remaining pupils back to the Albert Hall. They formed the origins of the Central School of Speech and Drama in 1906.

The curriculum of the Central School between 1908 and 1914 consisted of Elocution and Speech Training (taught by Miss Fogerty herself), Dancing (to which Classical Dancing was added in 1914), Fencing, Physical Training, Voice Production (from 1912) and Rehearsal. Winifred Fortescue, who was there at the beginning, recalled her early tuition:

> I learned that I should have lessons in Voice Production from the famous Professor Hulbert, dancing lessons from Theodore Filmer, who taught the Empire ballet, fencing lessons from a renowned Frenchman, Elocution lessons from herself, and be trained to act by Paul Berton, an ex-stage-manager of Frank Benson who, himself, examined the students at the end of every term.[65]

This cost initially 11 guineas a term in 1908, rising to £36 a year for the first year and £30 for the second from 1912.

The very special characteristic of Fogerty's approach to drama training was the emphasis on a scientific approach to speech and voice. She was fortunate in having the services of Dr H. H. Hulbert, MRCS, LRCP, the father of Claude and Jack Hulbert. He initially

47

taught physical training, then voice production in conjunction with it, before focusing his attention entirely on the voice. This conjunction was important in Hulbert's thought. He stressed the importance of physical training and dancing for relaxing the body and helping the breathing necessary for vocal culture. He also emphasized the value of the physical perception of rhythmic movement as an aid to the development of coherent speech.[66] Medical doctors like H. H. Hulbert, William Pasteur and W. A. Aikin were taking an interest in the voice and physiological aspects of speech. Fogerty was concerned to give publicity to this new interest and bring it to the attention of the universities and other areas of the education system.

After unsuccessful pressure on the Board of Education, Fogerty persuaded the University of London to hold a conference on Voice and Speech Training in 1910. In the following year, 1911, the momentum of scientific interest in these matters was increased by the publication of two major works, F. W. Mott's *The Brain and the Voice in Speech and Song* and W. A. Aikin's *The Voice*. Aikin taught both for ADA and the Central. He was rather more appreciated at the School than at the Academy, where Kenneth Barnes thought his approach to elocution 'too definitely scientific' rather than theatrical.[67] It pointed up the contrast between the two institutions: the Academy concerned with craft training for the commercial West End, the School having wider links with medicine and higher education.

These links were further forged in the summer of 1911 when the Central introduced a new, thorough theoretical examination in voice and speech training. In January 1912 the principal helped to organize the important LCC Conference on Speech at Bedford College with the usual figures, Hulbert, Aikin and Benson. They held sessions on the national need for speech training and its influence on physique, on medical aspects of speech training, on stammering and the need for a National Theatre.[68] The Conference was accounted a great success and further widened the sphere of Fogerty's influence. It awakened teacher-training colleges to the need for this kind of training. In 1913 the bishops of Birmingham and London persuaded Fogerty to train new ordinands in speech, and in 1914 she started her Speech Clinic at St Thomas's Hospital for treating speech defects.

48

What kind of pupils went to Elsie Fogerty's school? Firstly, they were predominantly girls, with a very small minority of men. Medal and certificate winners traceable between 1910 and 1913 were ninety-nine girls and fifteen men.[69] Secondly, there are indications that they were quite well-to-do young women. Norman MacDermott, who taught there in 1918, had a class of 'eight or nine charming young ladies. They were among the year's debutantes and were at the school really to learn deportment and similar graces'.[70] An advertisement in the School's magazine arranging a private party for a leisurely tour of Germany, Austria and Italy in first-class hotels also reflects something of the School's clientele.[71] Many of the girl students accordingly had little serious intention of a stage career, or had little success at it. A pupil of the time considered that 'of my fellow students . . . only a few have made any position on the stage'.[72] About half the men, but only about 13 per cent of the women, were actively pursuing stage careers, since most women probably went back into private life or married. There was admittedly a certain 'girls' private school' ambience about the Central. This arose partly from the clientele and also from Fogerty's previous experience as a visiting speech-training teacher to various girls' boarding and finishing schools. She was still teaching at Roedean, for example, while principal of the Central. As Winifred Fortescue's experience suggests, she must have obtained several of her Central girls from well-to-do private schools where she was a visiting teacher. It was no coincidence that in 1914 the Central mounted a production of *Electra* at the Scala for the funds of the Girls' Public Day School Trust.[73]

What then became of the Central School pupils of whose careers (before 1914) we have record? The seven men were respectively with Miss Horniman, Benson, Alexander, the Liverpool Repertory Theatre, the Lyceum, the Savoy, while Jack Hulbert, who was the best-known, had his own show, *Cheer Oh Cambridge*, at the Queen's. Two women took up teaching posts at Roedean and in Edinburgh. The twelve girls who went on the stage went respectively to the Liverpool Repertory Theatre (3), Her Majesty's Theatre with Tree, William Poel (3), Miss Horniman, the Court, Wyndham's Theatre, Denis Eadie, and one went to play in Newmarket. This is quite creditable; the students were clearly making the right kind of

49

contacts, and their training was being taken seriously by significant employers in the theatre. There is an evident bias to the rather high-minded sector – the Court, Horniman, Poel, Benson, the Liverpool Rep – rather than to the more commercial side represented by Alexander, Tree and Wyndham. This may partly reflect the ethos of the School itself, though more probably the unwillingness (and lack of need) of the more glamorous West End managers to take youngsters straight from college.

The importance of Elsie Fogerty and the Central even before 1914 far transcends the limitations of her early pupils and their initial careers. It will have been evident that Fogerty's bustling energy placed the Central literally at the centre of a wide network of cultural contacts that greatly enriched theatrical training. She reached out to involve the universities and was eager to establish her School as one of the received forms of higher education. Her involvement with doctors stimulated the remarkably intense attention paid to the voice and its physiology in the immediately pre-war years. This interest of the medical profession was an important element, enhancing the status of speech and stage training as a serious and skilled part of higher education. Her links with the Church, the poet laureate, the public schools and St Thomas's Hospital also had the same effect. The actor's training was being raised, retaining the core of craft skill but placing it in a wider cultural and educative context. The fact that the Central trained both teachers and actors with a substantial common curriculum further established that the training of actors was at least as rigorous and serious a matter as that of schoolteachers.

The rise of an efficient form of training for the stage was a powerful force in the professionalization and increasing respectability of the actor. The creation of institutions like the Academy helped to make going on the stage attractive to men and especially women of good social background. The new training set high and verifiable standards, and it could with some credibility be regarded as part of the general expansion of higher education of the period. Fogerty's work at the Central especially associated the training of the actor with that of the teacher, the clergyman and the doctor. All this elevated the profession and its practitioners in their own and others' estimation. With such high ideals, the new would-be actors and actresses left Gower Street and the Albert Hall. But how were they

50

actually to get on to the stage, and what conditions of life would they find there?

NOTES

1 F. C. Burnand, *Personal Reminiscences of the A.D.C. Cambridge* (London, 1880), p.238.
2 Hamilton Aide, 'A School of Dramatic Art', *The Nineteenth Century*, April 1882.
3 *Era*, 5 January 1895. Letter from I.L.C.
4 Mrs Patrick Campbell, *My Life and Some Letters* (London, 1922), p.120.
5 Sir John Martin Harvey, *Autobiography* (London, 1933), pp.44–5.
6 Malcolm Morley, *Margate and its Theatres* (London, 1966), Chapter 12, 'The School'.
7 George Arliss, *On the Stage* (London, 1928), p.141.
8 *Ibid.*, p.155.
9 Winifred Isaac, *Sir Philip Ben Greet and the Old Vic* (London, 1964), p.234. Russell Thorndike, *Sybil Thorndike* (London, 1929), pp.111–120. Henry Kendall, *I Remember Romano's* (London, 1960), p.34 on Ben Greet's Academy.
10 Desmond Chapman Houston, *The Lamp of Memory* (London, 1949), p.107.
11 Constance Benson, *Mainly Players* (London, 1926), p.248.
12 Frank Benson, *My Memoirs* (London, 1930), Appendix C, 'Concerning our Travelling School', p.322.
13 J. C. Trewin, *Benson and the Bensonians* (London, 1960), p.132.
14 Norah Nicholson, *Chameleon's Dish* (London, 1973), p.38.
15 Elisabeth Robins, *Both Sides of the Curtain* (London, 1940), p.103.
16 Constance Benson, *op.cit.*, p.186.
17 Lillah McCarthy, *Myself and My Friends* (London, 1933), p.27.
18 Sir Frank Benson, *I want to Go on the Stage* (London, 1931), p.39.
19 Sir Frank Benson, *My Memoirs* (London, 1930), p.154.
20 John Casson, *Lewis and Sybil* (London, 1972), p.80.
21 Owen Nares, *Myself and Some Others* (London, 1925), pp.57–8.

22 Cathleen Nesbitt, *A Little Love and Good Company* (London, 1975), p.47.
23 Violet Vanbrugh, *Dare to be Wise* (London, 1925), pp.46, 73.
24 Robertson Hare, *Indubitably Yours* (London, 1956), p.40.
25 Stephen R. Macht, 'The Origin of the London Academy of Music and Dramatic Art', *Theatre Notebook*, Autumn 1971.
26 Reginald Denham, *Stars in My Hair* (London, 1958), pp.37–9.
27 The *Genesian* 1965, pp.4–5. Molly Veness.
28 *The Dramatic Peerage* 1892, p.162.
29 Leslie Henson, *My Laugh Story* (London, 1926), pp.60–77 on Cairns James.
30 Arthur Hornblow, *Training for the Stage* (Philadelphia, 1916), pp.128–9.
31 Mr Austin Trevor, interviewed 13 September 1976.
32 Richard Whiteing, 'How they train actors in Paris', *The Nineteenth Century*, June 1904.
33 H. Beerbohm Tree, 'The Academy of Dramatic Art', *Review of Reviews* XXIX, Jan–June 1904, pp.509–10.
34 Letter, Barnes to Dr Aikin, 25 July 1912. Administrator's Letterbooks, ADA.
35 Irene Vanbrugh, *To Tell My Story* (London, 1948), p.113.
36 Arthur Hornblow, *op.cit.*, pp.132–143.
37 G. P. Bancroft, *Stage and Bar* (London, 1939), pp.169–70.
38 Sir Herbert Beerbohm Tree's Papers. Private Ledger September 1904–July 1906. Items 26 June 1906 £284.11.3; £357.8.10.
39 The foundation stone, which was laid in 1913, may be seen in Malet Street. The theatre was destroyed in World War II and replaced by the present Vanbrugh Theatre.
40 Irene Vanbrugh, *op.cit.*, pp.113–17.
41 Sir Kenneth Barnes, *Welcome Good Friends* (London, 1958), p.72.
42 Letter, G. P. Bancroft to Miss Bradley, 21 December 1909.
43 Sir Kenneth Barnes, *op.cit.*, p.77.
44 Dodie Smith, *Look Back with Mixed Feelings* (London, 1978), pp.34, 62.
45 Miss Athene Seyler, interviewed 23 August 1976.
46 Miss Fabia Drake, interviewed 20 August 1976.

47 Letters, Barnes to Mr Badshah 20 December 1912 and Mrs Thompson 27 March 1913. There are other letters in this vein.
48 Eva le Gallienne, *At 33* (London, 1934), pp.77–8.
49 Dodie Smith, *op.cit.*, p.36. This was, of course, the theatre preceding that in Malet Street, whose building began in 1913.
50 'School of Acting, a Chat with Mr Tree', *Era*, 27 February 1904.
51 ADA 1906 Prospectus.
52 Letter, Barnes to Kate Beesley, 3 February 1910.
53 ADA 1905 Prospectus.
54 Fabia Drake, *Blind Fortune* (London, 1978), p.25.
55 Dodie Smith, *op.cit.*, p.37.
56 *Ibid.*, p.40.
57 Alan d'Egville, *Adventures in Safety* (London, 1937).
58 Kenneth Barnes, p.69.
59 Sir Kenneth Barnes, 'G.B.S. and the RADA', in *G.B.S. at 90*, ed. S. Winsten (London, 1946).
60 ADA Annual Report 1911.
61 Letter, Barnes to C. C. Burbridge, 4 May 1910.
62 Letter, Barnes to D. P. Whitmarsh, 27 May 1910.
63 Calculated from Lists of Professional Engagements in Annual Reports 1910, 1911, 1912–13, 1914, 1915–16 for engagements October 1910 to November 1914.
64 Marion Cole, *Fogie, the Life of Elsie Fogerty CBE* (London, 1967).
65 Winifred Fortescue, *There's Rosemary . . . There's Rue* (London, 1939), p.38.
66 For example his talk 'Eurhythmics in Speech' *Viva Voce*, January 1914 and Fogerty on 'Rhythm', *Viva Voce*, January 1915. *Viva Voce* was the magazine of the School.
67 Letter, Barnes to Aikin, 9 August 1910.
68 *Viva Voce*, December 1911, March 1912.
69 *Viva Voce*, August 1910; October 1911; December 1912; July 1913; January 1914.
70 Norman MacDermott, *Everymania* (London, 1975), p.9.
71 *Viva Voce*, August 1910.
72 Winifred Fortescue, *op.cit.*, p.45.
73 *Viva Voce*, May 1914.

3 The Actor's Conditions of Work

After leaving drama school the would-be actor began to encounter the real stuff of life on the professional stage. It was a mixture of the tawdry and tedious enlivened with good fellowship, some flashes of glamour and simple comforts. On the adverse side were the appalling dealings with indifferent agents and the constant anxiety of finding work. Although there was far more theatrical work available then than now, it was still a market in which the actor was at a disadvantage. This reflected itself in the unpleasantness of dressing rooms behind the stage and the potentially rough relationships with rowdy audiences in front. For the child actor the constant visits to the magistrate seeking weekly permission to work could be as baulking as the visits to the agent could be for the adult. Yet on the brighter side there was much to enjoy for those with sociable or bohemian tastes. If visiting agents was painful in the search for work, going between theatrical pubs for the same purpose was more pleasurable. Travelling in the railway trains on tour could be luxurious for leading actors in major companies, but full of fun and good fellowship for even humble players. Staying in digs with 'Ma', the theatrical landlady, was an experience more often valued for its warmth than remembered for its loneliness. Nor was the job itself without a pleasurable glamour. Costumes and makeup improved and became more professional, while the quality of the audience became more refined and appreciative. On balance there were more attractive features than repellent ones, and by and large many aspects of life actually improved. The perception of this by actors and outsiders helped to swell the increasing numbers entering the profession before 1914.

54

I

How to find employment, or get a 'shop', in the parlance of the time, was a perennial problem for the actor. Many youngsters starting out from drama schools found their first engagements through their school. But for the young actor who had not been to drama school and for those who were seeking their third or fourth employment, looking for work was a skilled and arduous task in itself.

The formal way of getting a job was through a theatrical agent. These took the form of somewhat primitive labour exchanges carried on in a rather nasty atmosphere. They had started from about the 1820s, and there were nine in London by 1871.[1] The best-known, the biggest and perhaps the oldest was Blackmore's, established in 1869, at 11 Garrick Street. It was remembered with uniform loathing. The anxious job-seeker had to give his name to an obnoxious youth, variously known as 'Spotty-Face' or 'Horrid Boy', employed, it seemed almost calculatedly, to depress the client with curt, offhanded rudeness. After giving his name to the clerk the actor 'squeezed through a wooden barrier to join ladies and gentlemen of the profession, packed together like sheep in a shearing pen'.[2] Ironically, however impoverished they were, they were immaculately dressed, partly to boost their own confidence and partly to deceive the prospective employer, who might offer too low a salary. In the meantime they sat amid the 'sooty window panes, blackened wallpaper and bare dusty floorboards'[3] of Blackmore's waiting room. They might sit there all day from very early in the morning, possibly most of the afternoon as well, with a bun and cup of tea for lunch at a nearby Aerated Bread Company tea room. There were also registered clients permanently on the firm's books and others who turned up speculatively, possibly hoping, at most, for an interview. Both kinds seemed to be equally badly treated, though the registered clients probably stood a better chance of work. A. E. Matthews, who was a registered client, did at least secure a tour of South Africa as a result of an interview with Lionel Brough in Blackmore's office.

The unpleasantness of the task of finding work was multiplied by the fact that fruitless sojourns at Blackmore's had to be followed by prolonged tramping around the other agencies, many of which followed Blackmore's repellent style. At least the agencies were concentrated in various adjacent localities – Garrick Street (Blackmore's), Leicester Square and environs (Denton and Hart; Ralland and Bay Russell; Enterprising Agency), Maiden Lane (Balsir Chatterton), King Street Covent Garden (Arthur Gibbons) – all these were in reasonable walking distance, while a step away were those in Panton Street and the Haymarket (Adams Agency, George Lestocq), all operating before 1914.

So damning were some of the contemporary observations against agents that they mask the fact that agents actually performed a positive role. No organization could have behaved as obnoxiously as Blackmore's and yet have grown so large, had it not been providing some useful service to its reluctant clientele. Agents were especially useful for provincial tours starting from London; they were important in pantomime recruitment and essential for music hall, where there was a rigged agreement between music hall managers and agents.[4] A good agent would also draw up a standard contract bearing his letterhead.[5] In return for all his services he took 10 per cent of his client's earnings.

II

Resorting to agents was only one of the ways of seeking work, and to overestimate the importance of their function is to suggest that the profession was more organized than was the case. Quite as important were informal methods of getting one's first few parts. These were use of the theatrical press, writing direct to managers, using personal contacts and family influence, and finally the haunting of pubs in the vicinity of the Strand.

The theatre was served by two main newspapers, *Era* and *The Stage*. The former began in the 1830s and the latter in the 1880s. Both carried a great deal of advertising, with actors notifying that they were free and employers advertising for casts or theatres. Accordingly the most straightforward way of finding a job was to watch *Era* and *The Stage*, weekly. Those who could afford it took the initiative and had permanent advertisements in the newspapers. Sydney Paxton noted, 'I had always believed in a card in *The Stage* or *Era* to let my name be known, and where I could be found'.[6]

56

An Actress Seeks a Job (*Punch*, 3 November 1909)

Many actors started by putting more faith in some kind of supported – and supposedly influential – approach to an employer. Some obviously had a head start by having a family contact with a theatrical personage. When Fay Compton wished to go on the stage, 'influence was brought to bear, introductions effected, interviews arranged'.[7] Faith Compton Mackenzie was able to join Charles Hawtrey's company because her father had known the Hawtreys at Eton.[8] Henry Kendall gained employment with Sir Alfred Butt, a racing chum of his uncle Bill.[9] O. B. Clarence's brother knew Frank Benson;[10] even better, Basil Rathbone was Benson's cousin. Harold Child (with Bancroft), du Maurier (with Hare), Sydney Fairbrother (with Kendal) were others who started with some family connection of this nature.

A further important way of finding work was to haunt various pubs and bars around the Strand specializing in theatrical clientele and information. After trying the agents, an actor would go down the Strand and up and down Bedford Street and Wellington Street. A. E. Matthews recalled, 'For small fry such as myself, the Marble Halls had to combine the amenities of club, restaurant and even place of business.' Dallying over drinks, they were 'keenly alert to catch the first whispered news of a job going of any kind, anywhere'.[11] Henry Kendall favoured the Bodega, where free beer was sometimes available. He had no doubt of the importance of the pub network:

> There were very few theatrical agents in those days [1914] and most actors used to patronize certain pubs . . . By doing the rounds of these pubs each morning one heard about new shows going into rehearsal and most of us small fry obtained our engagements in that way.[12]

One way of getting on the stage, though of diminishing importance, was by paying a premium. At first sight it seemed quite reasonable for the premium apprenticeship system, so common in other crafts, to be extended to the stage and 'certain theatres have sometimes been open to receive a certain limited number of aspirants and teach them their business on payment of a premium'.[13] Yet the system was falling into disrepute, due to abuse on both sides. There were a number of court cases in the 1890s in which bogus managers decamped with premium money from stagestruck applicants expecting to be put into a show.[14] The system was also unsatisfactory in giving unmerited and short-lived openings for the lazy and talentless.[15] The rise of efficient drama training largely removed this older mode of getting on the stage.

III

The actor was often responsible for his own costume. Men certainly had to provide modern dress, and this gave an advantage in the early stages of his career to the actor from a comfortable background who actually owned good clothes and appreciated points of fashion. Max Beerbohm observed that contemporary dramatists most usually created characters 'who spend a great deal of money at their dressmakers or tailors' and actors had accordingly to be well dressed to represent them.'[16] Benson had his own Bond Street frock-coat when he started;[17] Harold Child, a former lawyer, found it an advantage that he had his wardrobe from his previous career.[18]

Actresses also would often provide their own costumes. In their case, they were sometimes expected to make them. Mrs Patrick Campbell recalled that early in her career, around 1889, 'My friends gave me some dress materials and I sat up at night making my frocks',[19] while Maud Gill also made her own dresses, not only when in portable rep. but also when playing small parts for Tree.[20] For very well-paid or highly fashion-conscious actresses like Marie Tempest, Lillie Langtry, Mary Moore and Gladys Cooper, ordinary dressmakers were not quite smart enough and they went to Parisian *haute couture* houses for their stage dresses.

Not all costumes, however, were provided by the actors wearing them. Permanent companies like those of Irving, Benson, Alexander and Tree had their own wardrobes for costumes. Indeed, it was a disaster to the first two when their company wardrobes were destroyed by fire in 1898 and 1899. As well as relying on the company wardrobe, managements would hire costumes from specialist theatrical costumiers. The Old Vic hired theirs from Rayne's nearby in Waterloo Road.[21] Berman's, Redfern and Madame Frances were other leading suppliers and most managers were content to deal direct with them.[22] Perhaps the chief firm was

59

Nathan's, who had begun supplying amateurs in the 1790s. Under John Lewis Nathan they especially expanded their professional activity and from the 1880s dressed many of the productions of Irving, Tree, Alexander and others as well as the Gilbert and Sullivan operas.[23] Following the decline of the actor–managers and their permanent establishments, and with less playing of Shakespeare with its predictable repertoire of stock costumes, reliance on costumiers increasingly replaced the company wardrobe. By 1933 'Few theatres today maintain a wardrobe department – the costumes . . . are usually hired from establishments which specialize in these articles.'[24]

Just as the actor bore some responsibility for his costume, so he had even greater control over his makeup. 'To be able to make up is part of the actor's stock-in-trade, and all professionals must be fairly proficient at it.'[25] Old actors used a variety of nostrums – powdered chalk, rouge, Indian ink, chrome, and a rust-coloured powder called Armenian Bole for darkening flesh tones.[26] A base could be made with Fuller's Earth, rice powder, powdered antimony, dry rouge and burnt cork.[27] However, these dry constituents were harmful to the actor's skin, drawing moisture from it. With the advent of very hot gaslight the use of such materials became increasingly uncomfortable, and were deleterious to the face.[28]

The first change was the replacing of these unsatisfactory substances with greasepaints.[29] Greasepaints were invented by the Bavarian opera singer Ludwig Leichner, who began his firm to manufacture them in 1873. Other makeup firms like Miners, founded earlier in 1864, followed suit. The greasepaints, unlike earlier makeup, were positively good for, rather than harmful to, the skin. As well as the greasepaint an array of nose paste, Bardolph noses, bloated cheeks or cotton wool used as pimples was available. Most important was the wig. An actor could make this himself using an old stocking as a foundation on to which to stitch crepe hair. Best of all, he would procure his wigs from Willy Clarkson, the chief theatrical and court wig-maker, who supplied wigs for all kinds of professional and amateur dramatics, fancy dress balls, practical jokers and (unwittingly) criminals.[30] Clarkson also gave makeup classes at the Academy of Dramatic Art.[31]

Gas and limelight made heavy greasepaint necessary and convincing. A second change came with electric light from the 1880s, the Savoy Theatre being the first electrically lit theatre in 1881. George Arliss came to realize that 'electricity had so changed lighting conditions in the theatre that paint was very apt to look like paint and nothing else . . . since that time I have always tried to eliminate paint wherever possible'.[32] The move to a simpler and minimal makeup was in keeping with more modern styles in acting. With the exception of Tree, whose brilliance was as a character-actor, most of the leading post-Irving actors – Alexander, Wyndham, du Maurier, Hawtrey, Forbes Robertson, for example – were noted for their own faces. They may have been lightly greased, indeed, but with makeup that enhanced rather than masked their own personalities.

Costuming and making-up took place in dressing-room conditions which were of an awfulness that was recalled with affectionate relish. In the 1890s an actress in the provinces might try to dress with nine or ten others: 'my dressing table a dress basket, my chair the floor and the light so bad that each of us had a candle stuck in a beer bottle'.[33] In 1914 Lena Ashwell thought, in fairness, 'There has been latterly a great effort to improve the dressing-rooms in the new buildings,' but yet 'there is a great deal to be remedied'.[34] Bad conditions for the lowest in the profession became a perennial concern of actors' trade unions well into the interwar years.

IV

One of the inevitable features of the actor's life was travelling, either as a humble provincial tourer or as part of a grand West End company. Charles Brookfield, touring with Ellen Terry in 1879, presents an attractive picture of theatrical rail journeys – third-class for most of the company, the leading man travelling in carpet slippers, the group playing penny nap on an imitation leopard-skin rug over the knees, nipping out to the bar at station platforms, joking with the porters.[35] Travelling in a company on tour, the actor's train fare was usually paid for him. However, if it was not, he could cushion his costs by being a member of the Music Hall Artistes' Railway Association. This was founded in 1897, and for a subscription members obtained a 25 per cent discount on rail fares and travel insurance benefits. The fact that there were over 7000

61

members in 1907 suggests that in spite of its name many legitimate actors must also have been members of it.[36]

Train travel, changing trains and waiting at junctions, notably the great theatrical junctions of Crewe and Normanton, also served paradoxically to keep members of the profession in touch with each other. This was especially valuable for provincial touring actors who might not be based in London for long. Such was the thronging of actors' companies at junctions that they could even serve as labour exchanges. At Normanton Junction one day the Bensons, the Comptons and the Tearles were all there and Whitford Kane, a young actor changing trains and looking for an engagement, was able to encounter some old friends who took him to the Bandmann-Palmer Company train, where the redoubtable Mrs B-P interviewed and hired him.[37] The trains and junctions were very much part of both the bonhomie and chanciness of the touring actor's life.

For the grand West End companies, and those who wished to emulate them, travelling by train was part of the ritual by which they expressed their dignified status and exclusiveness. Lena Ashwell remembered of Sir George Alexander in the 1890s, 'When these great actors went on the road the company travelled in a special train with the name of the manager and the names of the occupants of each carriage printed in large type and pasted on the windows'.[38] Constance Collier recalled of Tree, 'We were very magnificent with a private train and the royal coach attached. I had the Queen's suite . . .'[39] The Terrys imitated Alexander's policy.[40] Slightly down the scale, Wilson Barrett's company took special carriages with guarded compartments for their hampers because Barrett 'believed that an actress should maintain an air of reserve and aloofness'.[41] Some railway companies, notably the LNWR, went out of their way to facilitate the travel of theatrical people. James Wright became the theatrical traffic manager of LNWR in 1893 and made friends especially with Irving, Hare and Tree. He usually had forty theatrical special trains running on Sundays, and personally arranged and escorted some difficult, long journeys undertaken by Irving, notably to Command Performances.[42]

One of the joys of the touring actor was the theatrical digs he encountered en route. The stars and wealthy of the profession stayed in good hotels: the Midland in Manchester, the Imperial in Blackpool, the Shelbourne in Dublin, and so forth. The more expensive hotel could provide room service and cater for the peculiar meal-times of the theatre. But if the actor, though comfortably off, could not afford such expensive establishments, there was no point in staying in a modest hotel, whose more limited and less flexible regimen did not fit his or her life.[43] Accordingly, all but the richest had recourse to the theatrical landlady, the universal 'Ma'.

The theatrical landlady had emerged partly as a result of the formerly low position of actors. Seymour Hicks recalled that in the 1880s 'the actor was looked upon with absolute contempt by the majority of the landladies whose custom it was not to take in "professionals"'.[44] However, the sheer increase in the number of actors in the 1890s, and the extent of their touring, provided a lucrative market for landladies willing to accommodate their needs. The organizer of a tour did not usually book accommodation for the ordinary members of the company, still less did he meet the expenses of it in addition to salary. The actor was thus left to his own devices. Older touring actors with some experience kept their own records, and accordingly the actor with this information would write ahead to his favourite address. This idea of the address book became systematized by the Actors' Church Union and the Actors' Association, who both began to publish their own lists of recommended addresses for members. The list alone was good enough reason for joining either organization.

The costs of these lodgings were regarded as 'moderate'[45] or 'remarkably inexpensive'.[46] Taken as a class, Cicely Hamilton thought, the theatrical landlady 'was anything but grasping'.[47] The prices which actors found so reasonable were fairly uniform in the range of 10/- to 14/- a week but with 12/- or 12/6d most commonly cited.[48] For this the lodger was given a bedroom, sitting room (possibly shared), fire and the cooking and serving of his own food. The theatrical landladies seem to have served the profession well and were usually recalled with affection. Norah Nicholson found the digs 'for the most part excellent',[49] Faith Compton Mackenzie found the 'cosy fire-lit rooms' with their photographs lingered in her memory.[50] The landladies themselves were variously characterized as 'friendly genial souls',[51] 'kindly, hard working, motherly'[52] and 'hard working, scrupulously honest and kindly disposed'.[53] Sup-

63

In the Stalls (*Punch*, 22 March 1899)

porting actors on tour and theatrical landladies were both groups of people not too well endowed with riches or social position, but blessed with a certain outgoing interest in people and warm generosity of spirit. In their shared deficiencies, qualities and mutual dependence they seem to have got on well together.

V

When all the travelling, finding digs, costuming and making-up was done, the core of the actor's work was in facing an audience and giving a performance.

The actor had to establish a relationship with his audience, and as his own social class, background and status improved, this created some problems. Not the least of these arose from the fact that the audience itself was sharply divided in class terms and in location. The stalls and circle held the wealthiest patrons, 'remarkably frigid'[54] and rarely revealing emotion of pleasure or disapproval. Perhaps the pleasantest part of the audience was the middle range, in the cheaper stalls, upper circle or parts of the pit. These were rather nicely delineated by an Italian observer:

'It is a mixed crowd, formed for the most part of small parties and courting couples. There are shopmen, clerks, and spinsters in pince-nez; but more numerous still are the shopgirls, milliners, dressmakers, typists, stenographers, cashiers of large and small houses of business, telegraph and telephone girls.'[55]

Indeed, the preponderance of women in audiences was often noted, especially where the cast of the play was predominantly male.[56] The socially mobile actor could endure the coolness of the stalls, probably not socially very distant from himself, enjoy the good humour of the petty bourgeois shopmen and clerks and bask in the adulation of the girls. But the real problem was the gallery and (in some of the less genteel, unreformed theatres) the pit.

Before the First World War there had been a pernicious tradition of rowdyism in theatre audiences and in London, from 1902, there was an outbreak of organized first-night wrecking. The managers of theatres accordingly adopted a number of devices to control and discipline their audiences. At the crudest level a sprinkling of

65

The Gallery Audience (*Punch*, 29 June 1910)

'bruisers' could be hired in the pit and gallery to intimidate the rowdy element.[57] Alexander and others also closed galleries, especially on first nights, following rowdyism in 1900.[58] Other devices of a more subtle nature were adopted. Martin Harvey insisted on audience punctuality at the Adelphi. Latecomers had to wait in a corridor while the first piece was played. By 1907 seven London theatres presented short introductory pieces before the main play, which served as a useful trap for the unpunctual.[59]

The most radical means of disciplining the audience was through the layout of the theatre. The most important of these changes was the abolition or diminution of the pit and its replacing by rows of more expensive, socially exclusive stalls. Sir Squire Bancroft abolished the pit at the Haymarket during his tenure there from 1879 to 1885,[60] and replaced the 3/6d pit seat with the ten-shilling stall, of which he was the pioneer. He faced riots over the abolition of the pit, but as his perseverance succeeded, his example was followed by other theatres. New theatres like the Duke of York's (1892), Daly's (1893) and Her Majesty's (1897) had no pits. Between 1866 and 1900, pit and gallery seats as a proportion of all seats in West End theatres declined from 56 to 40 per cent, while stalls rose from 20 to 36 per cent accordingly.[61] Cause and effect reinforced each other. The Bancrofts' concern to raise the status of the actor by paying higher salaries forced them to increase their takings from the audience by displacing the lower-class patrons of the pit by the wealthier stalls, and so trebling the income for each seat. This further had the effect of bringing well-dressed, well-to-do and orderly theatre-goers nearer to the stage and in proximity with the actor, removing *hoi polloi* to the back of the floor or to the gallery. In fact the actual capacity of theatres fell during this time. That of the Adelphi, Criterion, Comedy, Haymarket, Savoy, St James (to take a sample) fell from 7269 in 1892 to 3601 in 1907.[62] Polite society 'cup and saucer' drama drew the middle classes into the stalls. At the St James in the 1890s, Sir George Alexander was drawing in 'people from the big houses in the suburbs as well as the artists, doctors, judges and dwellers in inner London who filled the stalls and the dress circle.'[63] All these interconnected factors – raised salaries, a politer audience immediately beyond the footlights, higher-class characters to portray in the plays – enhanced the status of the actor,

67

now more distanced both socially and spatially from those who had jeered and cheered in the boisterous pit.

The concern to divide the social classes and their assumed behaviour styles reached considerable degrees of elaboration and was actually helped by the concern for safety.[64] For example, for fire security reasons there was a concern to have passages down either side of the exterior or all around the building. A theatre on an open island site was ideal, so that fire could not spread across blocks of buildings. This also had social implications, since the holders of the cheaper tickets could now be made to enter through different entrances in different streets, rather than through the same front façade. More subtly, many theatres were now built with the stalls sunk below the line of the street; this lowered the whole elevation of the theatre and facilitated the playing of firemen's hoses on the upper storeys. It was also argued that panic was diminished in audiences making an emergency exit by rushing *up* stairs rather than down. Important as these arguments were on safety grounds, the sunken auditorium had social implications. The dress circle could now be on the street level and both circle and stalls patrons could enter through the same entrance and use the same foyer and bars. The stalls patrons had access to the circle corridors by a short exclusive staircase and could completely bypass the pit folk, who could probably be made to enter through a separate exterior door. Theatre layout, especially with the rebalancing of stalls and pit, was highly class-conscious. The increasing privileges and prominence given to the wealthy classes and the progressive segregation and degrading of the lower class of patrons had the further effect of enhancing the status of the audience's servant, the actor. As his social origins rose, the new forms of layout and audience disciplining gave him the opportunity to perform his craft in the dignity of being surrounded by that part of the audience nearest in social class to his own, rather than by those markedly below him.

Further disciplining methods came in the 1880s with some innovations by Sir Charles Hawtrey. He started the practice of printed books of tickets with the date, seat number and counterfoil.[65] This quickly became the general practice in theatres. Where the pit remained, there was always an unruly rush to scramble for unticketed seats. Hawtrey claimed to have inaugurated the system of the queue to the pit and gallery, forcing the lower-price patrons to wait in an orderly fashion and inducing in them a sense of controlled order before entering the theatre.

The final development in the audience which affected the position of the actor was use of the matinée. The matinée came into current use in the 1880s, possibly with Bancroft's production of *Diplomacy* in 1878, which started the idea of regular afternoon performances of the same play as that presented in the evening.[66] The increasing size of theatres, and their electrification and increasingly complex and expensive stage machinery, raised their operating costs. Accordingly the theatres had to be made to pay by being kept working day and night. This was made possible by the London suburban transport extensions – the London electrified 'tube' railway from 1890 brought women from the suburbs to shop in the city.[67] Harrods, for example, took its modern multi-departmental form from the late 1880s. They could take lunch in the increasing number of restaurants, some of which, like the Savoy and Criterion, were associated with theatres. It is significant that restaurant chefs increased almost *pari passu* with actors in the censuses between 1881 and 1911. There is no doubt that matinées paid well. The largest sums Tree ever drew at His Majesty's Theatre were for Wednesday matinées of *Henry VIII*, *Drake* and *Macbeth*.[68] The matinée ladies were clearly drawn to lusty historical men with beards on their chins and blood on their hands. They wanted their matinée idols, Lewis Waller, E. S. Willard and the Gerald du Mauriers, Godfrey Tearles and Owen Nares of the next generation. These leisured, post-prandial ladies from the Home Counties brought a new dimension of civilized gentility to the stalls.

VI

A special group within the profession was the child actors. The increase of child actors and their relation to the overall rise of actors as a whole before 1914 was as follows:

	Actors aged 10–14 inclusive		Total actors	
	boys	girls	male	female
1881	17	84	2197	2368
1891	39	131	3625	3696
1901	50	173	6044	6443
1911	74	195	9076	9171

Boy child actors thus rose about fourfold in the period 1881–1911, which was the same proportion as the rise in male adult actors. Girl child actors, of whom there were far more, doubled over the same period. This was somewhat less than the 387 per cent increase of female adult actresses.

The position of the child actor was subject to increasing regulation from the 1880s. Agitation about the employment of children in theatres was stimulated by Ellen Barlee's book on *Pantomime Waifs* in 1884. There was the suspicion that children were overworked for long, late hours or might encounter unsalubrious adult influences backstage. Worst of all was the suspicion that child actors were fed on gin and vinegar and denied sleep in order to stunt their growth to enable them to continue playing children's parts.[69] By the 1889 Children's Act children under the age of seven were forbidden to act on the stage, and employers of children over seven and under ten were required to obtain a licence from the Petty Sessional Court. A separate licence was needed for each child and licences were applicable only within the district of the issuing authority. Factory inspectors were to inspect places of entertainment. In 1894 the Prevention of Cruelty Act raised the age below which a licence was required to eleven.[70]

Redgrave, the Chief Inspector of Factories, was concerned that the legislation should not remain a dead letter, although he found courts differed in the stringency with which they issued licences. He drew up a model licence which required the production of a medical certificate, birth certificate, the allowance of four hours' rest, the provision of a matron and suitable dressing rooms. By the Employment of Children Act of 1903 the minimum age for employment of children in theatres was raised from seven to ten. However, theatre children were exempt from a general regulation of the Act that no children should work after 9 p.m. If they could gain such permission by local licences they were allowed to appear on stage after this hour. In the following year a Prevention of Cruelty to Children Act removed the duty of enforcing the regulations concerning theatre children from the factory inspectors and placed it with the local authorities. Finally, the Children's Act of 1908 required that applications for licences for theatre employment should be made in Juvenile Courts.

Such was the national framework of regulation surrounding the child actor, though there could be local styles of enforcement.[71] Manchester was regarded as one of the best towns in England for the regulation of theatre children. When applications for licences were received, certificates concerning parental consent and the birth of the child were required. Most importantly, the Manchester police made enquiries of the police in the town where the child had last performed as to the satisfactory nature of the company. When the child appeared in the Children's Court a school attendance officer directed which school the child should be sent to, and no children were allowed to perform in school hours. A police inspector devoted all his time to matters arising from children's regulations and plain-clothed police visited theatres in the evenings to see that the conditions of the licence were carried out, including any local concessions and time limits on work after 9 p.m. Such, with slight local variations, would be the normal pattern of dealing with child actors in the provinces.

In the metropolis, by contrast, the surveillance of theatre children fell more within the orbit of the education authorities. For example in 1889, when the minimum age for stage work was set at seven, the London School Board was pressing the Home Office to raise it to ten.[72] The education authorities in London had not only positive views about the theatre but wider powers and responsibilities than in the provinces. In London the police who received applications for licences were, uniquely, not controlled by the local authority which had the duty of seeing that the conditions of the licences were observed. Accordingly it was the School Attendance Department which not only appeared before the magistrates when licences were applied for but also carried out the inspection of theatres. As Keeling

71

noted, 'the police [in London] do little to assist in the protection of the children, which depends solely upon the persistent efforts of the School Attendance Department'.[73]

The need for licensing brought the child actor and the Authorities face to face in edgy circumstances. From the actors' and managers' viewpoint this could be troublesome and distasteful. Noel Coward recalled an incident of 1911:

> The bugbear of the child actor is the business of being licensed. The law insists that no child under fourteen may appear on the professional stage without the sanction of a Bow Street magistrate; consequently, before each production, a miserable morning is spent by the business manager, the Mother, and the child, standing about tortured with anxiety in draughty passages, oppressed by an atmosphere of criminality and surrounded by policemen. The magistrates vary. Some are easy-going and give the licence without any fuss, others are obtuse and disapproving, seemingly obsessed with the idea that the child is being forced against its will to act in order to support idle and dissolute parents.[74]

Their mode of life created problems in the education of child actors. The Actors' Church Union chaplain thought that such children usually attended a local public elementary school, though this was not totally satisfactory since they attended a different school every week and usually missed Mondays in any case.[75] Constance Collier, touring as a child with her parents around 1890, recalled: 'the school authorities were very insistent that travelling children should have a proper education and as we reached each new town Monday mornings were spent finding a school for me to go to'.[76] She hated being stared at by the permanent pupils as 'the acting child'. More rarely, the theatrical companies provided their own school-masters and governesses. There were various instances of this. Sir Augustus Harris of Drury Lane told the Home Office in around 1890 that all his children attended a school in connection with the theatre.[77] Various other companies claimed similar arrangements. Bert Coote told the London School Board that he had two companies on tour 'and in each case we have gentlemen who have been educated at college to look after the instruction of the children' for

72

two-and-a-half to four-and-a-half hours a day. Another company employed a lady to teach a ten-year-old boy for three hours a morning.[78]

As the child actor became a significant part of the theatrical scene, so a specialist form of training for stage children emerged in the 1910s. This was Italia Conti's school, started in 1911.[79] Italia Conti was a great-niece of Madame Catalani the opera singer, and had acted with Benson and Forbes Robertson in the 1890s. She remained an active working actress until 1911. Sir Charles Hawtrey engaged Miss Conti and her sister Bianca Murray to train, discipline and look after the large number of children in the cast of *Where the Rainbow Ends*. From 1911 she devoted herself to the stage training of children.

The children continued at their normal schools for their academic education but attended Conti's dancing, elocution and fencing classes three afternoons a week at six guineas a term. The classes were held in the basement of the Bay Malton public house in Great Portland Street, 'a large room with a lot of mirrors and a slippery floor that was white with french chalk; against the wall were a lot of chairs, some of which were occupied by rather smartly dressed ladies'.[80] Italia was the dancer and elocutionist and her sister Bianca taught character acting.[81] The vast majority of pupils were small girls. Unlike most adult drama schools, here the tuition was linked with paid work. Most importantly, Miss Conti used her children for her annual productions of *Where the Rainbow Ends*, providing armies of nymphs, sprites, gnomes and moths. This was financially worthwhile; Jack Hawkins, a Conti juvenile in 1923, received 30/- a week for his work. Apart from her own productions Miss Conti acted as the agent of her children, securing them engagements elsewhere. Early alumni of the Italia Conti School included Harold French, Gertrude Lawrence and Noel Coward, Anton Dolin, Brian Aherne and Jack Hawkins.

There is no doubt that the life of a child actor could provide many pleasures. In 1913 young Harold French enjoying a good run in *Where the Rainbow Ends*, found himself plied with boxes of chocolates on most afternoons, and was regularly taken out to tea by doting parents of children who had come to see the play.[82] Nobody remembered or conveyed the longings and thrills of the child actor of this time better than Noel Coward.[83] He loved

73

> . . . the months of high romance
> When destiny waited on tip toe
> When every boy actor stood a chance
> of getting into a Christmas show.

Since those days when the child actor became the object of government regulation the situation has changed little. The child actor at present (1983) works under the Children Performances Regulations of 1968[84] following the Children and Young Persons Act of 1963. Children of school age may still not take part in performances without licences granted by local authorities who have to ensure the health, 'kind treatment' and education of the child actor. Children of thirteen and over are not granted licences if they have performanced seventy-nine theatre days' work in the previous twelve months, or thirty-nine days for children under thirteen. They must all receive three hours' education a day from a private teacher on those days when the child would otherwise be at school. The restrictions on length of work are quite stringent and precise. Children may not play for more than eight consecutive weeks without a fortnight's break. Those over thirteen may not work more than eight hours a day (seven-and-a-half for those aged five to twelve); the duration of a child's appearances on stage may not exceed two-and-a-half hours and the older child must be out of the theatre by 10.30 p.m., the younger by 10.00 p.m. Detailed regulations have accordingly been adjusted since 1914. Also more child stage schools, such as the Corona and Aida Foster, have been created alongside the Italia Conti. Yet the essential improvement in the condition of and the professionalization of the child actor chiefly came about between the mid-1880s and 1914.

By and large the conditions of work for actors markedly improved in these years. This was evidently so in such matters as costuming and makeup, travel, audience behaviour and the protection of the child actor. Relations with agents and dressing rooms seemed to remain generally unpleasant; landladies and lodgings generally acceptable. This perception that the circumstances surrounding the actors' work were improving, and even gave opportunities for a lot of fun, was a further factor drawing large numbers into an ever-swelling profession before 1914.

74

NOTES

1 James de Felice, 'The London Theatrical Agent', *Theatre Notebook*, Spring 1969.
2 A. E. Matthews, *Matty*, p.31.
3 *Ibid.*
4 Cecil Armstrong, *The Actor's Companion* (London, 1912), pp.29–31.
5 Gladys Cooper, *Gladys Cooper* (London, 1931), p.48, reprints a Blackmore contract of 1906.
6 Sydney Paxton, *Stage See Saws* (London, 1917), p.129.
7 Fay Compton, *Rosemary* (London, 1926), p.89.
8 Faith Compton Mackenzie, *As Much as I Dare* (London, 1938), p.122.
9 Henry Kendall, *I Remember Romano's* (London, 1960), p.31.
10 O. B. Clarence, *No Complaints* (London, 1943), p.39.
11 A. E. Matthews, *op.cit.*, p.25.
12 Henry Kendall, *op.cit.*, p.30.
13 Cecil Armstrong, *op.cit.*, p.31.
14 Leopold Wagner, *How to Get on the Stage* (London, 1899), pp.17–18. Joe Graham, *An Old Stock Actor's Memories* (London, 1930), p.107 for abuses in Rotherham in the 1880s.
15 Maud Gill, *See the Players* (London, 1938), p.111 for such an encounter.
16 Max Beerbohm, 'The Vesture of Mimes', 12 January 1901, in *Around Theatres*, vol.I (London, 1924), p.202.
17 Sir Frank Benson, *My Memoirs* (London, 1930), p.196.
18 Harold Child, *A Poor Player* (Cambridge, 1939), p.29.
19 Mrs Patrick Campbell, *My Life and Some Letters* (London, 1922), p.38.
20 Maud Gill, *op.cit.*, p.37.
21 Winifred Isaac, *Sir Philip Ben Greet and the Old Vic* (London, 1964), p.132.
22 Louis Calvert, *Problems of the Actor* (London, 1919), p.215.
23 Archie Nathan, *Costumes by Nathan* (London, 1960).
24 Philip Godfrey, *Backstage* (London, 1933), pp.43–4.
25 Cecil Armstrong, *op.cit.*, p.115.
26 Robert Courtneidge, *I Was an Actor Once* (London, 1930), p.90.

27 Marguerite Steen, *A Pride of Terrys* (London, 1962), pp.156–7.
28 Sydney Fairbrother, *Through an Old Stage Door* (London, 1939), p.61.
29 Leopold Wagner, *op.cit.*, p.156.
30 H. J. Greenwall, *The Strange Life of Willy Clarkson*, (London, 1936), p.161.
31 Letter, G. P. Bancroft to Willy Clarkson, 13 May 1908.
32 George Arliss, *On the Stage* (London, 1928), p.208.
33 Constance Benson, *Mainly Players* (London, 1926), p.41.
34 Lena Ashwell, 'Acting as a Profession', in Edith Morley, *Women Workers in Seven Professions* (London, 1914), p.309.
35 Charles Brookfield, *Random Reminiscences* (London, 1902), pp.96–7.
36 *The Green Room Book*, 1907, p.472.
37 Whitford Kane, *Are We All Met?* (London, 1931), p.58. Normanton near Wakefield was a junction of lines to Lancashire, the North East, and South Yorkshire.
38 Lena Ashwell, *Myself a Player* (London, 1936), p.60.
39 Constance Collier, *Harlequinade* (London, 1929), p.177.
40 Julia Neilson, *This for Remembrance* (London, 1940), p.151.
41 Lillah McCarthy, *Myself and My Friends* (London, 1933), p.43.
42 *The Star*, 20 January 1921 on Mr Wright's retirement.
43 Naomi Jacob, *Me* (London, 1933), p.65.
44 Seymour Hicks, *Twenty-Four Years of an Actor's Life* (London, 1910), p.40.
45 Sydney Fairbrother *op.cit.*, p.106.
46 Ben Iden Payne, *Life in a Wooden O, Memoirs of the Theatre* (Yale, 1977), p.16.
47 Cicely Hamilton, *Life Errant* (London, 1935), p.36.
48 Derwent, Benson, Nicholson, Payne cite sums in this range.
49 Norah Nicholson, *Chameleon's Dish* (London, 1973), p.40.
50 Faith Compton Mackenzie, *op.cit.*, p.149.
51 Ben Iden Payne, *op.cit.*, p.15.
52 Elizabeth Fagan, *op.cit.*, p.89.
53 George Arliss, *op.cit.*, p.92.
54 E.F.S., *Our Stage and its Critics* (London, 1910), p.245.
55 Mario Borsa, *The English Stage of Today* p.247.
56 E.F.S. *Op. cit.*, p.247.

57 Gertrude Kingston, *Curtsey While You're Thinking* (London, 1937), p.185.
58 A. E. W. Mason, *Sir George Alexander and the St. James Theatre* (London, 1935), p.144. Alexander Papers, letter W. L. Courtney to George Alexander, 10 May 1904, referring to joint action of Wyndham and Alexander over gallery booing.
59 *Era*, 29 June 1907.
60 Sir Squire Bancroft, *The Bancrofts, Recollections of Sixty Years* (London, 1909), pp.248–9.
61 Brian Crozier, 'The Theatre Audience 1880–1900' (unpublished typescript).
62 1892, XVIII *Report of the Select Committee on Theatres and Places of Entertainment* p.451 compared with seating plans in the *Green Room Book* of 1907.
63 A. E. W. Mason, *Sir George Alexander and the St. James Theatre* (London, 1935), p.97.
64 Richard Leacroft, *The Development of the English Playhouse* (Cornell, 1972).
65 Sir Charles Hawtrey, *The Truth at Last* (London, 1924), pp.141–4.
66 William A. Armstrong, 'The Nineteenth Century Matinée', *Theatre Notebook*, Winter 1959–60.
67 Sir Henry Irving's address at the *Annual Dinner of the Actors' Benevolent Fund*, 1902, is a perceptive analysis of the rise of the matinée.
68 Calculated from Receipt books, Sir Herbert Tree's Papers. *Henry VIII* £396 on 21 September 1910; *Macbeth* £388 on 13 September 1911; *Drake* £386 on 25 September 1912.
69 This belief was fostered by Dickens's *Nicholas Nickleby*, which contained the character of the Infant Phenomenon, who was so treated in Vincent Crummles's troupe.
70 Frederic Keeling, *Child Labour in the United Kingdom* (London, 1914), pp.11–16. 1919 XXX Cmd. 484. *Report of the Committee . . . Licences to Children to take part in Entertainments* describe the system.
71 Frederic Keeling, *op.cit.*, pp.37–9.
72 D. Rubinstein, *School Attendance in London 1870–1904, a Social History* (Hull, 1969) p.63.

73 Frederic Keeling, *op.cit.*, p.39.
74 Noel Coward, *Present Indicative* (London, 1937) pp.28–9.
75 Actors' Church Union Quarterly Papers. Report on the Education Problem, 15 July 1913. Rev. W. E. Kingsbury.
76 Constance Collier, *Harlequinade* (London, 1929), pp.8–9.
77 'Employment of Children on the Stage' n.d., Fitzgerald Collection, Garrick Club, vol. XI fol. 51.
78 'School Board and Stage', *Era*, 7 March 1903.
79 Joan Selby Lowndes, *The Conti Story* (London, 1954).
80 Harold French, *I Swore I Never Would* (London, 1970), p.39.
81 Jack Hawkins, *Anything for a Quiet Life* (London, 1973), p.14.
82 Harold French, *op.cit.*, p.61.
83 Noel Coward, 'The Boy Actor' in *Not Yet the Dodo and Other Verses* (London, 1967), pp.51–2.
84 *Children (Performances) Regulation* 1968. Statutory Instrument 1968 No. 1728. A 'child' is a person of compulsory school age.

4 Financial Rewards and Safeguards 1890–1914

In spite of the attendant pleasures of some aspects of life on the stage, the actor's real business was making a living. For a few acting could be a 'jackpot' profession leading to great riches. This was especially so for that small elite of actor–managers. Several hundred employed actors of the middle rank could earn a decent living, even keeping pace with the inflation of the Edwardian years. Yet the vast majority of actors were at the bottom end of a very wide spectrum. They could earn as much as, but not more than, manual industrial workers. Due to the expenses of the actor's occupation, and especially of touring, many low-paid actors found themselves poorly off with very little margin for saving. This in turn led to the problem of poverty in old age for many actors unable to continue in their occupation. To meet this a range of institutions was created and expanded either to enable the actor to save or, as a last resort, to relieve his poverty and that of his family. Accordingly the Royal General Theatrical Fund, Actors' Benevolent Fund, Actors' Orphanage and others were developed as significant safety nets and safeguards amid the risks and potential poverty of an actor's career.

I

How much were actors paid? Firstly we may gain some idea of typical actors' incomes from various estimates of the time.[1]

As we may expect the spectrum is very wide, from Mrs Patrick Campbell's £173 and Sir Herbert Tree's £150 a week for *Pygmalion* in 1914 down to the 25/- for the small part beginner, with very few in the upper reaches. This spectrum of earnings may be compared with

Upper Range	per year	per week
Major star (e.g. Tree, Mrs Patrick Campbell)		£150–170
a) A leading comedy actress		£50–60
a) A leading actor		£40–50
b) 200	£2000	
b) 200	£1000	
b) 'some few'	£500	
Medium Range		
c) 250	£250	
Lower Range		
d) heavy or juvenile lead		£5
d) average salary of a subordinate actor in a West End Theatre		£2–5
d) a line of business		£2–3
d) a small part		25/- to 30/-
b) 'vast majority'		£1–4

occupations outside the theatre. The headmaster of a large London Board School in 1900, for example, earned £500 a year, comparable with 'some few' actors in the upper income range. An assistant teacher in mid-career would earn £200–250 a year, in line with the medium range of actors.[2] At the lower end the average male weekly wage cited in 1899 in Rowntree's famous study of York was 24/- a week, or 27/5¼d for the male head of a family[3] and the modal industrial wage was 23/10d in 1906.[4] Thus even very lowly actors in the smallest parts compared reasonably in remuneration with average industrial workers.

The rate of remuneration was fixed in contracts or agreements of varying degrees of formality. Actor–managers would arrange these matters by letter with the artist or his agent. These could be carefully tailored to the status and drawing power of the actor. For example, George Alexander employed Fay Davis (the Princess Flavia in his famous production of *The Prisoner of Zenda*) for £35 a week, having gently beaten her down from £40.[5] Alexander made a complicated agreement with Marie Löhr in 1914, with an initial salary of £25 per week rising to £50 when the production costs had been covered, rising further to her 'normal' £100 when 'good profits' were made.

The agent had the right to study the account books to determine with Sir George when these various points had been reached.[6] Fay Davis and Marie Löhr were established young stars with status to protect. They had also the wasting assets of youth and beauty, which had to be capitalized within a limited time. Actresses like this needed finely detailed and flexible contracts. The unknown tyro could be more routinely dealt with on a printed form with a fixed weekly sum, say the £5 a week that Felix Aylmer accepted from Barry Jackson in 1913.[7] Oddly enough, older stars sometimes did not have any contracts or written agreements at all. When they were well established and working for managers whom they had probably known and worked with for some years, this was not always necessary.[8]

Most seductive for the aspirant to the stage was the possibility of very high earnings and of amassing fortunes at the upper end of the profession. The Bancrofts at the Haymarket in the 1880s had been the first to pay very high salaries to leading players – £60, or up to £100 for a special star.[9] Ellen Terry earned £200 a week in the provinces in the 1890s,[10] George Alexander £250 a week at Drury Lane, while Tree regularly paid himself £150 a week from 1909. Even more striking was the possibility of jackpot earnings and profits accruing to actor –managers. Irving made £62,594 net profit from his London productions at the Lyceum during the period 1880–90 and £66,516 from his American tours between 1884 and 1895.[11] Bancroft made £180,000 profit during his twenty years of management.[12] Alexander made £269,400 out of twenty-six plays at the St James,[13] Forbes Robertson £40,000 profit from his Drury Lane season in 1913,[14] while Seymour Hicks took £2,000 or £3,000 a week at the Aldwych in the 1900s.[15]

Theatrical wills also testified to the wealth in the upper reaches of the profession. The following amounts were left by noted actors of the pre-World War I period who died either at that time or shortly afterwards.[16]

Sir Henry Irving	died 1905	£ 20,527
J. L. Toole	died 1906	£ 79,984
Sir Herbert Tree	died 1917	£ 44,085
W. H. Kendal	died 1917	£ 66,251
Sir George Alexander	died 1918	£ 90,672

Sir Charles Wyndham	died 1919	£197,035
H. B. Irving	died 1919	£ 39,176
Sir John Hare	died 1921	£ 30,066
Sir Squire Bancroft	died 1926	£174,535
Dame Ellen Terry	died 1928	£ 22,231

Amassed fortunes were no necessary indication of artistic worth; Irving, who left the least of those above, noted sardonically, 'I am not here to collect money'.[17] Yet acting was a profession whose prizes were sufficiently glittering to attract swarms of entrants, of whom only few would merit or achieve them.

Most actors settled down to careers in which they were less concerned with earning vast fortunes than with more immediate problems. In particular the period 1900–14 was one in which inflation led to a decline in real wages for the first time since the 1870s.

Did actors' wages keep pace with this inflation or did they suffer the common decline in living standards? References to wages in memoirs tend to be too fragmentary to throw light on this, and probably the only available source giving consistent data over a period of time are the financial accounts of Sir Herbert Tree at His Majesty's Theatre during the 1900s. From these actors' wages were calculated for 20 of Tree's major productions between 1903 and 1914.[18] These are presented in Appendix 2. It was clear that Tree's actors enjoyed a rise in wages considerably more than UK average wages, and a rise almost exactly in line with the rising price level. To highlight one telling detail, when Tree cast the leading ten parts in the 1905 production of *Oliver Twist* it cost £298 14s. 7d. per week. When he cast the same 10 parts for the revival of 1912 the cost was £396 0s. 3d. per week, a 32 per cent increase in wages. This was higher than the overall price level change over the same period and greater than the average movement of his own wage rates.

The sustaining of the real wages of the actor at a time when many other occupational groups were experiencing a sharp decline in real wages must have been one of the further attractive features drawing aspirants to the profession at this time. But how typical was Tree, or rather how untypical could he afford to be? He was thought of as a good employer, a pioneer of paying for rehearsals and quite popular with the Actors' Association when it adopted its trade-union form. Yet the London theatre of the time was a situation of almost nearly perfect competition, with several dozen theatres all within a tiny area for patrons to pick and choose, all using, turn and turn about, much the same body of actors. If Tree had paid too little he would not have attracted the high quality of supporting casts he did. If he paid untypically high wages he could not have sustained himself for twenty-seven years in profitable management without going bankrupt. In none of the many memoirs of actors who served with Tree do we find a suggestion that he paid lower or higher than his colleagues and competitors. Indeed, in 1905 Tree was elected by the latter to be president of the Theatrical Managers' Association, a close-knit body well aware of each other's policies. They clearly did not regard Tree as a maverick. This suggests that London West End salaries for speaking actors were keeping in line, and were attractive, outstripping wage movements in other occupations that actors might have adopted and, unusually, matching price rises.

Tree would seem to have been quite fair and generous to his actors. From his point of view, just how important was their remuneration in the wider context of his costs, and how crucial to his balance of profit and loss? The costs of putting on a play were threefold – the capital production costs (scenery, costumes, etc.), recurrent staging costs (orchestra, front of house, stage staff, etc.) and actors' wages. Actors' wages were the largest element in the total budget, averaging 40 per cent of the whole. Capital production and recurrent staging costs were both about 30 per cent of the whole. Yet high actors' wages costs were very rarely the cause of losses when they occurred. Losses were commonly associated with high production costs and the failure to secure a run long enough to move capital production costs per performance below 30 per cent of the total. Apart from the second run of *School for Scandal* in 1913, Tree never got into financial trouble through costs incurred on actors' wages. It profited him to pay well in order to attract good casts, and the proportion of actors' wages in the total budget remained relatively stable and less fluctuating than capital production or stage costs. Tree's awareness of this may have been an element in his rather fair and generous wages policy.

Two Thirty-Shilling Actors (*Punch*, 8 February 1911)

II

The majority of actors, however, crowded the less affluent end of the profession. The poor actor attracted increasing attention with the rise of socialism in actors' trade unionism and the concern of contemporary social investigators about low-paid groups. Fitzroy Gardner, who had been a business manager with Tree, thought that 6600 actors were at work at any one time and nearly as many unemployed: 'The average weekly earnings of an actor or actress who is willing to work all the year round, including London and the provinces, is not more than £2 and probably less'.[19] Another observer thought that 'there are several hundreds of actors of considerable experience touring the provinces who do not earn more than 30/- or 35/- per week'.[20] In 1914 Lena Ashwell put the average yearly income of an actor at £70, or around 27/- a week.[21] In the same year, another commentator put the wages of actors in a provincial touring company at 30/- a week and of actresses at 25/-. He concluded: 'The Profession is largely a sweated trade; it is a casual trade and it is a seasonal trade.'[22]

These estimates and observations have a broad similarity. However, they are given much more meaning by empirical investigations into actors' budgets, which revealed that the low incomes of actors were matched by onerous expenses which left dangerously little for basic needs like food. The Actors' Association presented a budget in 1908 which throws much light on the poor actor's financial problems. An actor employed for 35 weeks would incur the following expenses:[23]

	£ s d
Clothes, renewing wardrobe	10 0 0
Boots, 2 pairs at 18/-	1 16 0
2 pairs of gloves at 2/6d	5 0
2 hats	1 0 0
Recovering umbrella	6 0
Bedroom, 5/- per week for 52 weeks	13 0 0
Washing, 2/3d per week for 52 weeks	5 17 0
Postage and stationery	17 4
Bus and tube	8 6

Baggage collecting and carting	1 15 0
Tips to dresser	17 6
Makeup	3 0
Haircutting	6 0
AA subscription	15 0
	£37 6 4

For such an actor earning £70 a year – say £2 a week for thirty-five weeks – this left £32. 13s. 8d for food, or 1/9½d per day. Another specimen budget confirmed the picture:[24]

At £2. 5s a week for thirty weeks an actor could earn £67. 10s. 0d but of this £33. 4s. 0d would be spent on

	£ s d
Lodgings	13 0 0
Washing	5 4
Wardrobe	10 0 0
Newspapers and tobacco	5 0 0

leaving a balance for food of £34. 6s or 1/10½d a day. All this was used as evidence in support of demands for a £2 minimum wage and rehearsal payments, which suggest that many actors were trying to live below the £2 level in virtual poverty. The low level of wages led to difficulties of saving – 'Only the forty or fifty pound salaries admit of making any capital possible to retire on.'[25] The competitive increase of actors and the large sector of low-paid necessitated a complex system of financial safety nets. As for so many actors the prizes receded with advancing age; thoughts of financial reward gave way to a more modest concern about financial safeguards, to which we now turn.

III

There was no national old age pension in Britain until 1908, or sickness and unemployment insurance until 1911. Accordingly the aged or unemployed actor whose earnings had been too low to permit adequate saving was often forced into destitution. Vignettes of obscure sadness and distress emerge from these years. Robert

86

Courtneidge, for example, found a former member of his company, and former actor–manager himself, now in his eighties, serving as a night watchman to keep out of the workhouse.[26] Cyril Maude particularized the pathos of a general situation in a noted appeal:

'That old fellow there who used to make you laugh so, is it his fault that rheumatism contracted on a drafty stage laid him low. You recognize him? How he used to cheer you after an unsuccessful day of worry in the City. By Gad, Sir! I should have to stop you from running down the street and begging him to accept even more help . . .'[27]

A powerful and wealthy actor–manager could try single-handedly to relieve poverty in the profession. At Irving's Lyceum, 'several members of the company, though continuously on the salary list, were only called on to play for a few weeks in each summer season'.[28] They were in effect charitable pensioners whose self-esteem was preserved by the feeling that they were still acting with Irving's Lyceum company. As well as deliberately overmanning his company, he also dispensed private charity: 'Sir Henry has a private list of humble pensioners who regularly receive a substantial cheque in recognition of kindness meted out to him in his struggling days.'[29] Likewise Wilson Barrett, the actor and producer of the highly successful *Sign of the Cross*, used to pay old actors a good living wage merely to walk on.[30] Yet no individual, even so powerful and large-hearted as Irving, could be expected to sustain the profession single-handedly. Something of a more organized and less personal character was clearly needed.

One of the oldest ways in which the actor could seek to safeguard his old age was through the Royal General Theatrical Fund. This had started in 1839, and Charles Dickens had presided over its first dinner in 1846. It also attracted royal approval and support from Queen Victoria and was granted a Royal Charter in 1853. The fund was not purely a charity but a provident insurance scheme paying annuities to subscribers. However, the assets of the fund comprised not only the subscriptions of members but donations given by well-wishers from outside. These characteristics of an insurance fund subsidized by charitable donations lay behind the remarkable financial strength of the RGTF. It offered a highly privileged and lucrative perquisite to members of the profession.

The leading actors responsible for the fund in this period were George Alexander, the chairman and president, and Edward Terry, the treasurer. Both were among the ablest of that generation of actors in the wider world of practical affairs. Both were councillors in local government and JPs, and Sir George was perhaps the most consistent financially successful actor-businessman in the London theatre in the 1890–1914 period. Alexander stressed that actors could obtain a financial return from the RGTF 'which they could not possibly get from an insurance fund'.[31] Indeed, *Era*, which strongly advocated the Fund, gave various examples of actors dying around 1890 who had received back in annuities ten times more than they had subscribed in their lifetime.[32] Subscribers also had the right to consult the medical staff of the Fund free of charge.

The assets of the Fund rose from £13,000 in 1891 to over £62,000 by 1914. Subscriptions from members were only a part of the total income, which was also derived from charitable donations, the profits of the annual dinner and their investments. As the sums paid to annuitants were usually less than the total income, the surplus each year went to swell the large and increasing assets which were invested on the advice of Alfred de Rothschild. The assets were swollen over the years as the Fund absorbed various other charities, most notably the old Dramatic and Musical Sick Fund in 1904. This also removed a confusion in people's minds between the excellent RGTF and the feebly mismanaged DMSF. It left the RGTF as the only Provident fund specifically for actors.

The actor who failed to provide for himself through saving with the RGTF or in other ways faced destitution in old age. To meet this problem the Actors' Benevolent Fund was started by Irving, Toole and Bancroft at a dinner party in 1882. They were joined by Hare, Wyndham, Kendal and Wilson Barrett and all agreed to support the fund with annual subscriptions of £100 each. Alexander joined a little later. The objects of the Fund were 'to relieve distress in the dramatic profession . . . to see that the generosity of the profession reaches those whose need is urgent, whose misfortunes are inevitable and whose characters are deservedly respected'.[33] It was hoped that the fund would obviate the embarrassing spectacle of poor actors begging at stage doors. By the time of their first dinner in 1891 they had, in the eight years of their existence, distributed £18,000 in relieving 7000 cases of distress, and they maintained a bed at a convalescent home at Ventnor.

It was from around 1890 that the Fund began to grow wealthy due to various changes in policy. When it began, it was hoped to finance it entirely from within the ranks of the profession, without an appeal to the public. Irving had been among the first to realize the futility of this and in 1891 he had inaugurated the system of public dinners to tap the philanthropy of Society at large. Secondly, it was Irving who had suggested the holding of benefits in various London theatres in 1890, the proceeds to be given to the Fund. They raised £1000 thereby in that year.[34] Thirdly, in 1891 James Staats Forbes, the distinguished railway manager, recommended that they open a capital account,[35] investing a reserve sum which grew to nearly £28,000 by 1912. Most importantly, following legal action by the Actors' Association, the moribund Covent Garden Fund, which had £63,000 lying idle, was broken up, two-thirds of the capital going to the ABF and one-third to the Royal General Theatrical Fund.[36]

The income of the Fund came from some 700–900 subscribers who raised around £1000 a year. These ranged from Irving, who would still give his £100, Tree and Wyndham at £50, down to modest sums. It was always deplored that actors did not support their own fund more. Robert Courtneidge, who was a committee member, recalled that 'the contributions from the rank and file are not very satisfactory'.[37] He attributed this to the precarious nature of the occupation and the fact that, even when actors were in funds, they were paying off their own debts from preceding hard times. Indeed, in 1899 it was found that only one in ten applicants to the Fund had ever contributed anything to it.[38]

The dinner enabled the Fund to tap the benevolence of a wider spectrum of London Society. These included distinguished lawyers like Lord Alverstone, Sir Edward Clarke and Sir Francis Jeune, who tended in their speeches to stress the similarity of the legal and acting professions. An interesting group were the railway directors and managers – James Staats Forbes (who actually was a failed actor still with a hankering for the stage), his colleague on the London, Chatham and Dover board, George Wyndham MP, and the manager

89

of the same railway, Alfred Willis. There was a symbiotic relationship between the theatre and railway managers. The theatres needed railway commuters as audiences and the railway men saw that a thriving social life in the centre of London swelled their traffic. Their support of the ABF was a recognition of this.[39] Another group was the financiers, who were a ubiquitous part of the London social scene. Usually Jewish, often with South African interests, Leopold de Rothschild, Otto Beit, Ernest Cassell, Max Michaelis, Julius Wernher, H. L. Bischoffsheim and Barney Barnato all supported the Fund. With this kind of wealth the annual dinner could often raise twice as much as the ordinary subscription.

What did the actors get out of the Fund? They received a variety of services. The Fund would come to the aid of a company left stranded by a bogus manager,[40] the kind of problem that motivated contemporary actors' unionism. It also had its own doctors who gave their services free and, in the event of death, the committee vowed that it 'would not allow any actor to be buried at the expense of the parish'.[41] Most importantly, the Fund made *ad hoc* grants or loans as appropriate to actors who were down on their luck or who had fallen sick and were temporarily unemployed. Most of their work was concerned with actors who still regarded themselves as in the profession, but increasingly it came to serve as a non-contributory pension fund. The example of the national old age pension in Britain from 1908, then, more directly, the Austrian government scheme of pensions for actors from 1909,[42] prompted this concern. Accordingly, the numbers of aged actors receiving regular weekly pensions rose from forty-four in 1892 to 100 by 1911. Although the Fund ran no Home of its own, it provided funds for sick actors to go to hospitals and convalescent homes at Chelsea, St Leonards and elsewhere.

Alongside the major agencies of the RGTF and the ABF were three more specialized charities. Chief in the public affection was the Actors' Orphanage. This had been started in 1896 by Mrs Charles Carson, a former actress, now the wife of the founder–editor of the theatrical newspaper *The Stage*. In this she was associated with Mrs Clement Scott, the wife of the drama critic of the *Daily Telegraph*. The Orphanage cared for about fifty orphans of actors in the 1900s, sent them to good schools and had them taught trades. Actors and

90

actresses such as Cyril Maude, the president, C. Aubrey Smith, the treasurer, Tree, Alexander and Lilian Braithwaite were noted for their support of it. The general public was aware of the orphanage through the annual Theatrical Garden Party, which was run at the gardens of either Kew or the Chelsea Royal Hospital by Gerald du Maurier with typical panache. It was the policy of the Orphanage to rely largely on the Garden Party for their funds, and enough people each year wished to turn up to mingle with the stars who ran the side-shows to make this financially successful. By 1914, at a cost of £34 per child per year, their outlay of around £1700 was amply covered by an income of around £3000. Under Cyril Maude's presidency (following Irving from 1905) the capital of the fund rose from £1000 to £20,000.[43] With this generous support they were able to buy the fine seventeenth-century mansion of Langley Place in Buckinghamshire, with its fourteen acres of ground. This opened in 1915.

The Theatrical Ladies' Guild was also founded by Mrs Carson in 1891. It was an actors' charity for all other types of non-acting theatrical worker – stage hands, cleaners, all front of the house staff and their families. The Guild assisted 'with clothing for themselves and their families and many other necessities. Several applicants had been sent away for a change of air and others have been provided with surgical and medical aid to fit them for work'.[44] Before the First World War they dealt with about 600 cases a year. It was entirely run by actresses, Irene Vanbrugh being the president, supported by May Whitty, Gladys Cooper, Lilian Braithwaite and Fay Compton, among others – the recurrent stalwarts of theatrical good causes.

The final major actors' charity formed at this time was the King George V Pension Fund. On the accession of George V in 1912 Arthur Bourchier suggested to Prince Francis of Teck that the stage should give a gala performance. On the death of the Prince, Bourchier organized this and the performance duly took place in Coronation Week at Tree's His Majesty's Theatre. The profits of £7000 formed the nucleus of a pension fund, named after the new king. Subsequently a play was performed annually in which the leading London actors played all major and minor roles irrespective of their personal status. The purpose of the King George Fund was not to overlap with the ABF but to provide permanent pensions of a more substantial nature for a smaller select body of retired actors.[45]

The two parts of this chapter, the rewards and safeguards, bear a reciprocal relationship to each other. The concern to develop charitable safeguards for the elderly and less fortunate of the profession was a necessary feature of an occupation which had a wide spectrum of incomes, including a large body of low-paid and underemployed casual workers at the lower end. Yet why should the wealthy actors feel any obligation to look after their poorer brethren in hard times – as they clearly seemed to do? Firstly, acting is the most co-operative of arts. The highly paid star cannot play Hamlet without the support of twenty-four other speaking actors and an indefinite number of attendant lords, ladies, travelling players, and so forth. In the nature of theatre economics, these minor players could be paid a living but hardly a saving wage. A few might rise in the ranks, but the star actor–manager still needed his stage army of low-paid, intermittently employed actors as the wealthy farmer needed his seasonal harvesters. The awareness of this, especially with employers like Irving and Tree, who used large casts as a setting for their own genius, gave added point to the support of the poor by the rich in the theatrical profession. Secondly, to this first generation of knighted actors of high social status, the dignity of the profession was at stake. It was an affront to their newly won pride in the profession of acting to have other actors (and especially those who had once had any kind of name) living in destitution and dying in misery – hence the carefulness of the ABF about funerals. The influx of aspirants to the stage, the wide spectrum of earnings, the limited numbers who could rise to affluence, the need for a large stage army of lowly-paid supporters and the spread of charities run by the former for the latter, were all part of the same integrated situation.

NOTES

1 a) Fitzroy Gardner, 'Actors' Salaries', *Era*, 26 October 1907.
  b) Cecil Armstrong, *The Actor's Companion* (London, 1912), pp.179–80.
  c) Francis C. Philips, *My Varied Life* (London, 1914), pp.85–6.
  d) Leopold Wagner, *How to Get on the Stage* (London, 1899) pp. 152–5.

2 J. S. Hurt, *Elementary Schooling and the Working Classes 1860–1918* (London, 1979), p.178 for teachers' salaries.

3 Seebohm Rowntree, *Poverty* (London, 1899), p.115.

4 William Ashworth, *Economic History of England 1870 to 1939* (London, 1963), p.201.

5 Sir George Alexander's Papers. Letters, Fay Davis to Alexander, 3 and 27 April 1897.

6 *Ibid*. Letter, Theo McKenna (Marie Löhr's agent) to Alexander, 6 December 1914.

7 Memorandum of Agreement Barry Jackson and Felix Aylmer, 30 June 1913. British Theatre Museum 1973/A/150.

8 Fred Kerr, *Recollections of a Defective Memory* (London, 1930), pp.134–5. Kerr explained this as a witness in some litigation between Granville Barker and Mrs Campbell, who likewise had no contract.

9 Julia Neilson, *This for Remembrance* (London, 1940), p.30.

10 M. Bingham, *Henry Irving and the Victorian Theatre* (London, 1978), p.268.

11 Alan Hughes, 'Henry Irving's Finances: The Lyceum Accounts 1878–1899', *Nineteenth Century Theatre Research*, vol I, no. 2, Autumn 1973.

12 Sir Squire and Marie Bancroft, *Recollections of Sixty Years* (London, 1909), p.275.

13 A. E. W. Mason, *Sir George Alexander and the St James Theatre* (London, 1935), p.216.

14 William Poel, 'The Passing of the Actor Manager', *The Thespian*, No. 1913.

15 Seymour Hicks, *Twenty-Four Years of an Actor's Life* (London, 1910), p.277.

16 'Theatrical Wills', *Theatre World*, Dec. 1925, p.64 and Appendix, Theatrical Wills, *Who's Who in the Theatre*.

17 Mrs Aria, *My Sentimental Self* (London, 1922), p.121.

18 Appendix 2. Based on the financial records of Sir Herbert Tree specified in the bibliography.

19 'Actors' Salaries', *Era*, 26 October 1907.

20 E. H. Paterson, *Era*, 2 March 1907.

21 Lena Ashwell, 'Acting as a Profession for Women', in Edith J. Morley (ed.), *Women Workers in Seven Professions* (London, 1914), p.300.

22 'X', 'Employment in the Theatre', *New Statesman* Special Supplement on the Modern Theatre, 27 June 1914. William Poel, 'The Economic Position of English Actors', *Nineteenth Century* LXXVI, September 1914, gave wider publicity to the Ashwell and *New Statesman* articles.

23 *Era*, 7 March 1908.

24 *Era*, 8 August 1908. Survey by Daisy Halling and Charles Lister.

25 Elisabeth Robins, *Both Sides of the Curtain* (London, 1940), p.231.

26 R. Courtneidge, *I Was an Actor Once* (London, 1930), p.115. Also p.255.

27 Cyril Maude, Speech to the Actors' Benevolent Fund, 1908. Tape in Cecil Madden Collection, 1964/A/74, British Theatre Museum. He reprinted this in Cyril Maude, *Behind the Scenes* (London, 1927), pp.195–7.

28 Joe Graham, *An Old Stock Actor's Memories* (London, 1930), p.222.

29 L. Wagner, *How to Get on the Stage* (London, 1899), p.13.

30 J. H. Barnes, *Forty years on the Stage* (London, 1914), p.233.

31 *Era*, 25 March 1893.

32 *Ibid.*

33 Report of the Proceedings of the First Dinner of the ABF, 1891.

34 *Era*, 31 January 1891.

35 Report of the Proceedings of the Ninth Dinner of the ABF 1899.

36 *Era*, 10 March 1900.

37 Robert Courtneidge, *op.cit.*, p.279.

38 *Era*, 28 January 1899.

39 Irving spoke on railways and the theatre, for example, at the Twelfth ABF Dinner in 1902.

40 *Era*, 27 January 1894.

41 *Era*, 28 January 1899.

42 Report of the Proceedings of the Nineteenth Annual Dinner of the ABF, 1909. Tree's speech.

43 Cyril Maude, *Behind the Scenes*, p.177.

44 *Era*, 11 December 1912.

45 *Era*, 21 December 1912, 27 May 1914, 21 September 1927.

5 The Actor in Trade Unionism and Politics 1890–1914

Actors, in the main, were not political animals. Still less were they associated, in the nineteenth century, with radical, Left or trade-union sympathies. Tree once told Gladstone that the politics of the profession was solidly Conservative.[1] One commentator attributed this to the old mutual antipathy of the stage and puritanism. The heirs of the Puritan Nonconformist Conscience – Whigs, Radicals, Liberals and even Socialists – incurred and evinced the same suspicion. 'There must be players, managers, and some playgoers belonging to the Liberals or Radicals, but they are much in the minority . . . we are almost all House of Lords men, and ardent Tariff Reformers.'[2] Where leading actors expressed any political opinions, they were usually to the Right. Bancroft was a staunch Conservative and Royalist, Martin Harvey a strong anti-trade-unionist and George Alexander – who actually was in politics as an LCC councillor – was an anti-Socialist moderate. Yet, thrusting through the political neutrality or Conservatism, the profession formed two strong movements which expressed the grievances of deprived groups. These were, firstly, actors' trade unionism embodied in the Actors' Association and the Actors' Union and, secondly, the Actresses' Franchise League.

I

Actors' trade unionism arose as part of the 'new unionism' of the late 1880s and 1890s. In this period occupations not hitherto unionized adopted this form of organization. They included the relatively unskilled, like gas workers and dock workers, women, like those in

95

match factories, and white-collar employees such as schoolteachers. These were in contrast to the skilled male labour aristocracy which characterized trade unionism in the mid-nineteenth century. The new unionists were more in favour of strike action than their predecessors, and some were more sharply distinguished by their espousal of Marx-influenced Socialism from the 1880s. Various parts of the theatre industry were forming their trade unions at this time. The National Association of Theatrical Employees began in 1889, the Musicians' Union in 1892 and the Concert Artistes' Association in 1897. With almost everyone else in the theatre organizing, it was to be expected that stage actors would be part of this movement.

The Actors' Association began in the early part of 1891.[3] A group of actors in a pantomime in Manchester formed a loose association in February of that year and deputed Robert Courtneidge to come to London to establish a national body. Courtneidge then allied with Frank Benson, who had been associated with an earlier attempt called the Actors' Exchange, and Benson became the Association's envoy in securing the support of the chief managers and actors, and especially in enlisting Henry Irving.[4]

Such was the strength of Irving's position as the leader of the profession that his support was crucial. Yet when he first heard of the proposed Association he denounced it as revolutionary and subversive and 'destructive to our best traditions of comradeship and understanding'. Benson went to see him to explain that the proposed union would have none of these disruptive effects: 'it sought to establish co-operation between managers and artists; that it was an endeavour to *avoid* [my emphasis] the establishment of a trade union in the ranks of our art.'[5] Herein indeed lay the seeds of much later trouble. Was the Association genuinely to be an organization protecting and improving the lot of the mass of actors? Or was it to be dominated by establishment managers who wanted anything but a trade union? After a short reflection, Irving agreed not only to become the president of the new Actors' Association but to lend it his Lyceum Theatre for meetings. The effect was magical. Benson and Courtneidge secured the support of the Bancrofts, the Kendals, Charles Wyndham and Ellen Terry, 'and practically all the leading actors and actresses followed suit'.[6]

Following Irving's gesture, a crowded meeting at the Lyceum

under Benson's chairmanship launched the Association in March 1891. Benson stressed that the AA was 'to promote in every way possible the best interests of actors and managers which were – or ought to be – identical. It was intended that they should not become a union in the narrowest sense of the word.' He pointed out that the interests of actors and managers could not easily be separated since many managers were, or had been, actors and combined both roles. Accordingly there was no profession in which there was less friction between employers and employed. Benson went on to outline the purposes and aims of the Association. It was to be a voice for the expression of the views of the profession on legislative matters. It would act as an agency for registering addresses and be a means of communication between managers and actors. It would have a common hall, meeting place and library as a social centre for actors. Very importantly, it would help actors with legal problems and arbitrations between actors and managers, and would root out the bogus manager who left touring actors stranded or absconded with their pay. Finally, it would campaign against unsanitary conditions in theatres and dressing rooms.[7] The AA embarked on its first decade of steady progress. The membership grew:[8]

	Total actors/actresses England/Wales	AA members	AA members as % of total
1891	7321	320 (1891)	4.37
		750 (1892)	10.24
1901	12487	1669 (1899)	13.36
		1597 (1903)	12.64

Within a year the Association seemed to have unionized about 10 per cent of the profession, and this proportion does not seem to have changed much.

The AA had many positive achievements in the 1890s as it tried to carry out some of the proposals outlined by Benson at the Lyceum meeting. It established club rooms at 36 St Martin's Lane which members could enjoy for their ten shillings a year subscription. Thus established, it set out to rectify some abuses to which the actor was subject. One of the most pressing evils was the bad sanitation of theatres and dressing rooms. In 1893 nineteen theatres were reported to the AA Council and they brought three of these cases before their respective county councils, who revoked their licences.[9] In 1896 they dealt with forty-one such cases,[10] and presumably each year they paid equal attention to the problems without always reporting it in detail. More important, the Association began the long campaign against the bogus manager, a main preoccupation of actors' unionism well into Equity days. Bogus managers assembled companies they could not pay, took them on tour and absconded with the cash, leaving actors to struggle back to London as best they could without train fares. The AA began to use its new muscle against these rogue parasites. In 1895 it got one bogus manager fifteen months' hard labour; 'the first crow has already been nailed to the barnyard door', observed Irving presciently.[11] Of even more practical value to its members, it took up 153 cases to recover money from recalcitrant managers. Most of the cash was recovered without legal action.[12] The AA clearly had a credible threat value, reinforced by the prison sentence of that year.

The AA also established less minatory relations between actors and their employers through running arbitration and agency services. Arbitration was provided by T. H. Bolton, who was not an actor but an MP with a keen interest in the theatre. He had attended the Lyceum Meeting founding the Association, and spoke in Parliament about insanitary theatres. Bolton dealt with arbitration, which both actors and managers found preferable to a trial before a jury ignorant of the theatre. In 1896 Bolton resigned, and at Irving's suggestion a joint arbitration committee was established to meet at the Lyceum and work with the Managers' Association. This seems to have worked successfully, settling 104 cases in the year before April 1897.[13]

Another of the aims set out by Benson at the Lyceum Meeting was the establishment of an agency. It was also keenly desired by many rank-and-file members. 'We have groaned and sweated under this private agency business too long', resolved a meeting of the AA in Manchester in 1893.[14] In 1897 it started an agency with an agency committee, two members attending at the AA offices each day. They submitted names to managers and charged five shillings per engagement, including the preparing and stamping of the contract.[15]

98

Within a year they had 1110 members on the books of the agency[16] and by 1900 they were finding 241 engagements a year and being used by 100 managers.[17]

Although the AA was inevitably based in London yet, to be effective, it had a provincial dimension. Lionel Brough, in response to a suggestion that the AA was chiefly a London organization, claimed that it was 'all over the country. It is extended everywhere'.[18] The first moves to start the Association had come from Manchester. Manchester continued to have meetings, sometimes presided over by one of the Council from London. At one such Fanny Brough presided, bearing letters from Hare, Tree and Alexander. It was made explicit that the idea of this meeting was that the provinces should not feel out of touch with the AA in London, and further provincial meetings were proposed.[19] By 1898 there were AA representatives in sixty-seven provincial towns.[20]

The Association, in this first phase of existence, was not concerned only with the immediate details of the actor's life; it also addressed itself to the broader question of the status of the profession. T. H. Bolton, on resigning his duties with the AA in 1896, said that it was essential for the acting profession to have a corporate existence in the Association, but he advised it to aim to become like the Law Society or the Royal College of Surgeons and to secure a Royal Charter which would give it more authority and public recognition.[21] Bolton's suggestion was taken up, and a committee was appointed to look at the possibilities of a Charter. It met, however, commonsense scepticism on the grounds that it would never be possible for the Association, chartered or not, to start prosecuting 'unqualified' actors.[22] The AA then pursued the issue of professionalism and exclusivity on a different tack. In 1899 it considered the possibility of trying to control the profession through a Central Board for the selection, training and registration of actors.[23] This sounds a remarkably bureaucratic way of producing actors, which would have given extraordinary powers to the Association. However, it was even more unrealistic then than it would be now. These proposals for a Royal Charter or very tight conditions of entry suggest that the profession wished to assert its professional status by the same kind of exclusiveness as that enjoyed by doctors and lawyers. The Association also saw itself as the kind of controlling body similar to those heading the ancient professions.

99

II

From the turn of the century the Association began to run into some trouble, and face up to a central issue. Firstly, there were financial problems. When the agency was set up the AA moved to large and expensive offices in King Street, Covent Garden, but at the cost of raising a loan for £500.[24] By 1903 it had debts of £843 and increased the subscription from 10/- to 15/-.[25] Most importantly, an all-star charity matinée of *The Merchant of Venice* was given in July 1903 which brought together Irving and Ellen Terry for the last time.[26] This raised £800 and rectified the finances.

More important than the financial crisis and its resolution was the growing constitutional problem about the class composition of the membership. From the earliest days actor–managers had played a dominant part in the Association. Courtneidge, Benson and Irving – all employer–managers – had started it. Hare, Wilson Barrett, Alexander, Wyndham and Tree variously lent theatres for meetings and presided. The Council was dominated by actor–managers, entrepreneurs and employers of labour. In the 1900s the rank-and-file actors came to feel that there was no necessary identity of interest between themselves and their employers. Most obviously this was the case over issues like wages or payment for rehearsal time, where the interests of managers and actors were diametrically opposed. With the AA dominated by their bosses, the ordinary players felt powerless to better their position through their own Association. Indeed, had not Benson won over Irving with the argument that the Association would *avoid* trade unionism? In the wider world of industrial relations the 1900s saw a marked increase in industrial unrest, partly occasioned by a sharp decline in real wages in the face of the first period of marked inflation since the 1870s. To these pressures was added the influence of Socialism, virtually unheard of amongst actors before the 1900s. But now Socialist actors like Cecil Raleigh and Granville Barker began to challenge the old system and highlight the areas of class conflict hitherto glossed over by actor–manager paternalism and appeals to Bohemian good fellowship and company solidarity.

There was also one vital personal factor. Nobody represented the paternalist good fellowship ideal more than the AA's president, Sir

100

Henry Irving. While he was alive and attending meetings unity was preserved. Irving's presence invoked deep respect for his past achievements and dominant personality as leader of the profession. Latterly this was turned to something like reverence and compassion for the dignity and courage with which 'The Chief' faced the problems of his last years – his ill-health, misfortunes of fire and accident and grinding touring, when he should have been able to enjoy an easeful retirement. No struggling actor need feel any jealous antagonism against Irving. It was significant that obstreperous and challenging behaviour from the rank and file (in the stalls) towards the officials (on the stage) at AA meetings began only after Irving's death. With Sir Henry presiding this would have been unthinkable.

The issue, and some attendant ones, was raised clearly in 1904. The chairman of the AGM, H. B. Irving, Sir Henry's son, noted: 'many actors consider that this Association should be an association of actors only and because it is not so they withhold from it their support.'[27] Granville Barker proposed, and got, a committee to consider proposals that no actor should be employed in the West End who was not a member of the AA presaging the idea of a closed-shop trade union, and he also demanded payment for rehearsals. At once a polarizing of attitudes became apparent. George Alexander said that if relations in the theatre ever became based on a system of trade unionism then he would cease to be a member of the AA. *Era* too took the managers' part: 'we do not believe that anything like Trade Unionism would answer.'

The row continued to brew up in 1906, when the whole idea that managers could be elected to the Council was challenged, notably by Edward Terry on the grounds that the Association was an actors' Association. At the AGM in this year a new tone of rowdy behaviour began to appear. A deep irritation was beginning to show itself against the bland successful managers who claimed the right to control everything, including their own employees' union. It certainly seems anomalous that Herbert Tree, for example, was president of the Theatrical Managers' Association (the employers) and vice-president of the AA (the employed). Basil Dean, then a young actor, remembered the new mood: 'during my first year on the stage [1906–7] I became involved in an agitation to revitalise the Actors' Association, to persuade it to abandon its attitude of gentility and to

101

adopt the principles of trade unionism.'[28] Irving was now dead, and replaced as president by his friend Sir Squire Bancroft, the embodiment of that 'attitude of gentility' that so antagonized Dean and others. Immensely rich, long retired into easeful affluence, he was almost caricatured by his house in Berkeley Square, silk hat and monocle as the 'heavy swell' capitalist against whom the new militant actor could react. C. Aubrey Smith – Charterhouse, Cambridge, England cricket captain and later Hollywood depictor of countless lords, generals and rulers of Empire – was the Council member who clashed with Terry over the rights of managers on the Council. Both Bancroft and Smith were similar physical types, exuding the aura of the well-bred, well-fed, gentlemanly actor of comfortable authority. They must have been baffled by the rowdy challenges of the 1906 meeting.

III

The next year, 1907, was to be a parting of the ways. The demands for reform were led by Harley Granville Barker, the actor, playwright and producer. He was a Fabian Socialist, and before his later fame had experienced the life of the poor actor in the 1890s. He had joined the AA, and in 1904 made proposals for rehearsal and matinée payments and an AA closed shop in the West End. He was elected to the Council in that year. Ironically, this was the same year in which he began his celebrated partnership with J. E. Vedrenne in running the Court Theatre and became an actor–manager–producer. None the less his sympathies, as a Socialist, lay with the rank-and-file actor, and he emerged as a leader of the reform party to reshape the AA on their behalf.[29] Much less well-known today was his co-campaigner Cecil Raleigh, who was an avowed Socialist and a follower of Hyndman and his Social Democratic Federation. He had been an actor before becoming a playwright, best known as the author of the annual Drury Lane autumn play for twenty years.[30] Raleigh was remembered as 'an agile minded and seasoned journalist . . . [with] a knack of swift banter idiomatic of our British fun'.[31]

At the end of January 1907 Cecil Raleigh gave a talk at an AA social gathering. Taking as his theme the issue of whether acting was a
102

profession, a calling or an industry, he uncompromisingly took the stance that the theatre was an industry with £20 million invested in it. Actors should be entirely professionals with a closed shop enforced by the Association – 'study the models presented to you by the great combinations of working men . . . remember the old days of good fellowship have long gone by when actors were a very small brotherly and Bohemian band. Today entertainment is a vast industry.'[32] He insisted that the Association should be reformed on trade-union lines with an enforced minimum wage. In discussion most speakers agreed with Raleigh. Coming on the eve of the AGM, it foreboded a marked change of mood.

That mood was intensified by parallel events elsewhere in the entertainment industry. In 1906 performers in music halls had formed themselves into the Variety Artistes' Federation. Scarcely had they started than they embarked on a highly publicized and successful strike in January 1907. The keen awareness of this among all actors, and the sympathy with it among the rank-and-file, further intensified divisions within the AA and gave heart to the more radical, reformist anti-managerial group.

The AA's crucial AGM was in the month following the VAF 1907 strike, with Bancroft as president and Aubrey Smith chairman of the Council. Here, amid noisy interruptions and exchanges, the reform party, led by Granville Barker and Raleigh, mounted an attack on the manager-dominated Council.[33] Barker insisted that 'the Actors' Association should be conducted in the interests of actors', and the reform party were all elected to the Council, led by Barker with the largest number of votes.

The reform party having gained control of the Association, the scene was set for radical change. This came in May at a meeting presided over by Sir George Alexander which voted by 164 to 136 to exclude managers from the AA.[34] Although this was not the required two-thirds majority the managers, seeing the strength of feeling, retired *en bloc*. Barker did not resign with them but left at the end of that same year. The resigning managers in turn formed their own Society of West End Managers at a luncheon given by Sir Charles Wyndham on 20 February 1908. The Association, now deprived of its upper-class managerial leadership by expulsion, was greatly weakened in this interim 1907–9 period. Its weakness was twofold.

103

Firstly, its membership fell, new members not offsetting losses from the top and bottom of their spectrum.

1907	February	1,400	1909	unspecified	796
1907	May	1,200	1910	January	837
1909	February	1,044			

Secondly, declining membership entailed financial problems. Indeed, by October 1907 it wondered whether to wind up altogether, having simply run out of money,[35] and it was still £136 in debt in 1909. The financial weakness was reflected in and eased by the change of headquarters from its relatively fine premises in King Street, Covent Garden, to smaller offices in The Strand.

In spite of its weakness, the Association took a positive line on a number of issues of varying degrees of importance and realism. Most unrealistically, it revived the idea of the AA's controlling entry to the profession through a Senate granting certificates of competence.[36] This proposal, coming in the depths of its financial problems, could be nothing more than a dream for the future. More realistically, Cecil Raleigh began its campaign for a £2 a week minimum for speakers of more than three lines, and it began devising a standard contract to this effect.[37]

The AA also represented the interests of actors before public bodies on certain issues of the day, notably on censorship. A Commission under the later Lord Samuel had been appointed by Asquith following the suppression of Maeterlinck's play *Monna Vanna*, in which nudity or rape was suggested. The AA was invited to give evidence and first debated the issue itself, coming to the view, after a vote, that the censor should be retained.[38] The interesting grounds for this, from the AA's point of view, was not moral but a concern for continuity of work for actors. It did not want a play running in Manchester which the following week could be prosecuted for obscenity in Liverpool, with the attendant insecurity for the touring actor. Censorship also protected the actor from having to face the dilemma of whether to accept work in an objectionable play. An interesting alignment arose over the censorship issue. Actors, actor–managers and producers were all strongly in agreement on the need to retain censorship; none wished to be subject to the differing attitudes and vetoes of a myriad of local authorities. This would have

104

made the touring trade a nightmare of uncertainty. Nor did managers wish to invest large sums in a production, only to have it prosecuted after its first night. The chief agitators for repeal of the censorship were the playwrights, not the actors. The AA accordingly found itself in unusual agreement with all the managers' organizations, and opposed by the dramatists.[39]

The most tangibly lasting achievement of the AA in these years was its taking the lead in promoting the Irving Memorial.[40] A committee was set up under Sir John Hare, and Thomas Brock's fine bronze statue of Sir Henry – in theatrically full-cut and trailing doctoral robes – was erected opposite the Garrick Theatre at the foot of the Charing Cross Road in 1910. It was an irony that the AA should be erecting this monument to the greatest paternalist manager at a time when managers were temporarily not part of the Association. Yet without the Chief the AA might never have been effectively started in the first place. The AA was still the only sizeable organization of actors that could organize this kind of enterprise, and the universal reverence for Irving rightly submerged the employing manager – actor–Socialist trade unionist divisions that otherwise split the profession in these years.

IV

For some actors the gaining of control of the AA by the reform party was not sufficiently radical, and they formed the breakaway Actors' Union early in 1907. In London a small group of actors were discussing the music-hall strike of January of that year, and the loyalty of the music-hall performers. At the same time a provincial actor, Fred Bentley, unknown to those in London, was holding a meeting in Manchester to discuss a more trade-union approach to actors' organization. Bentley and the London group then combined at a meeting at the Bijou Theatre, Bedford Street. They had some discussions with the reform party of the Actors' Association, who urged them to support their aims. They determined, however, to form a separate organization, to be called the Actors' Union.[41]

A number of characteristics and policies divided the Union from the Association. The Union refused to have managers in its membership, unlike the Association until the resignation of the managers in

May 1907. The Union had a low entrance fee of 2/6d to appeal to a poorer class of actor. It also had a probably firmer commitment to provincial organization than the AA having some forty-two provincial centres by the end of April 1907.[42] The Union also received performers on the fringe of the legitimate theatre, such as music-hall sketch players.[43] But by far the chief differentiating policy was the AU's decision to be a genuine trade union, and it registered as such in October 1907: 'for the first time in the history of the stage, actors and actresses combined and came into line with the great Trade Union movement.'[44] In other ways it inevitably duplicated many of the purposes of the Association – the minimum salary of £2 a week, decent and healthy conditions backstage, free legal advice for members, the abolition of unfair competition from amateurs and premium players. Indeed, some actors were members of both the AA and AU.[45] The reform party of the AA and AU also met in the same place – , 3 Bedford Street, Strand.

This combination of traditional progressivism with a radical trade-union edge was clearly attractive, and Actors' Union membership rose strongly from 400 in March 1907 to a peak of 910 in the summer of 1908. Throughout October 1907 the Union held a series of mass meetings, both to drum up support from actors and to express solidarity with other working groups.[46] The Manchester meeting was held with typographers and paper-mill workers, while one at Liverpool was presided over by a representative of the Trades Council and attended by other unionists. This deliberate *rapprochement* with proletarian groups was a distinctively AU policy. It was also accompanied by various de-professionalizing statements designed to suggest a solidarity of actors with the working class. Frank Gerald, the AU representative at the TUC, variously stressed this approach. 'Consider us artists, professionals, tradesmen, what you will', he told the TUC,[47] and reminded the Manchester meeting that actors 'should not pretend to be capitalists when they were only workers'.[48] They were subject to questions of capital and labour as much as any other trade; the actor was a workman.[49] These feelings that the actor was only a 'worker' or 'labourer' in an industry controlled by blind investment capital were particularly strong in the Actors' Union. They were reinforced by much contemporary comment about the real or threatened power of American trusts in the English theatre.

106

American financiers were thought to control eight London theatres and were trying to organize a large trust in Britain on the lines of the Theatrical Trust, which controlled most provincial playhouses in the USA. Klaw and Erlanger had designs to buy up and control strings of theatres in England.[50] The example of the music halls, grouped in monopolistic chains like Moss Empires and the de Frece Circuit, was ever-present. This awareness heightened the class consciousness of the lower-paid actor, and his perception of his status as an industrial worker needing a trade union to defend his interests.

From the early part of 1908, however, there were growing indications that a future reunion with the AA was being contemplated. With the AA stripped of managers, the AA and AU were working to virtually identical ends, providing duplicate services. These would be better served by joining forces of their separate memberships.[51] In August 1909 the AU agreed to accept the constitution of the AA in the interests of unity[52] and in November it wound up completely. The Actors' Association then absorbed the remaining members of the defunct Union and resumed its course as the single representative body of actors from 1910.

With the demise of the Actors' Union the AA became again the focal organization for the profession. The next step seemed to be to effect a similar *rapprochement* with the managers. Tree had expressed a willingness to return, and Clarence Derwent proposed a motion that the managers be invited back. He took up a non-trade-union position that 'no form of trade unionism could be even approximately applied to the conditions of their profession.' This aroused a good deal of support, and Derwent's proposal inviting the managers to become members once again was passed.[53] At the time Derwent took the view that the return of the managers 'proved the turning point, and from that day the Association has not looked back.'[54] It is interesting that, reconsidering the episode many years later, he totally changed his mind. He had rightly gauged that actors at that time were not ready for an affiliation with Labour, but 'I was quite wrong in principle . . . I realize now that the bringing of the employer into the employee's organization could never work and was a reactionary step not finally corrected until the establishment of British Equity.'[55]

107

In 1910–11, however, the mood was one of renewed optimism. Tree returned as president of the AA and Sir George Alexander as a vice-president. Tree was greeted with applause at the 1911 AGM, and further delighted his audience by announcing that he was going to pay for rehearsals. The agency was flourishing, and Irving's statue unveiled.[56] The final reconciliation was the coming-of-age dinner of the Association in 1912 when Tree, Alexander, H. B. Irving and Arthur Bourchier made friendly speeches to some 300 diners, including Robert Courtneidge, one of the AA's founders. Derwent, who was employed in Tree's company at the time and who had negotiated the rehearsal payment from him, replied, and all was amicable. The anomaly of the whole situation did not occur to Derwent until many years later.

Derwent gave a clear picture of the AA immediately prior to the War.[57] It had four good clubrooms at the corner of Piccadilly Circus, with a dining room and also a hireable rehearsal room. The agency was still flourishing, negotiating six or eight engagements a week. All members were entitled to free medical advice throughout Britain, and free legal and arbitration services. The Association provided a lodgings list and acted as a permanent postal forwarding address. Its aims remained the same, fundamentally 'the economic emancipation of the worker'. In detail it entailed the improvement of insanitary theatres, the rooting out of the bogus manager, the extension of the practice of payment for rehearsals and matinées and the £2 minimum.[58]

Those who wanted a move to more active trade unionism had some grounds for disappointment with the Association as it was. It had not been able to induce the managers to accept the Standard contract of 1909, which removed the anomaly of managers being able to dismiss actors at a fortnight's notice, while actors did not have the reciprocal privilege. The AA also eschewed the use of strike action to try to enforce the contract. Possibly because of this, the membership did not seem to recover even after the demise of the Actors' Union and the return of the managers. It remained at around 840 from 1910 to 1914.

In spite of the positive achievements of the Actors' Association and the Actors' Union, it must be asked why actors' trade unionism was not more successful than it was in the years before the First

World War? There were certain inherent difficulties in unionizing actors.[59] Unlike, say, bricklayers or locomotive drivers they were not a large homogeneous body of labour doing a common standard of work for a standard pay. There was a vast spectrum of gradation from poor actors up to the major stars. Moreover, the change and increase in an actor's income could be so rapid for the successful that they could quickly lose any sense of identity of interest with actors who had once been their fellows. Most important of all, the profession was rifted into managers and employees. There was always the hope among many actors that they could break through into management, and indeed it was possible for an actor in his career to move back and forth between being a manager and an employed actor. In this Britain contrasted with Germany, for example, with its system of municipal and state theatres as employers, or the USA with its control by private non-actor entrepreneurs. In both Germany and the USA actors' trade unionism was accordingly stronger than in Britain. In England many actors were, in trade-union terms, more like small Birmingham or Sheffield metal-workers who were very difficult to unionize because they expected ultimately to become entrepreneurs in their own right. This lay behind the quite peculiar situation of having both employing managers and employee actors all together in the same union.

Unionization was also weakened by the large influx of actors in this period, many of whom were, as beginners, of little experience and all too happy to accept very low wages. These depressed general wage levels at the lower end; hence the concern of the Union and the Association to aim for a minimum wage. Yet perhaps the chief factor holding back genuine trade unionism among the actors was the change in the social class of the new wave of entrants that we analysed in Chapter I. These sons and daughters of professional and business fathers liked to think that they too were joining a profession. They would have regarded getting involved with a trade union, and still more with a Socialist trade union, as a distinct downgrading of their status, not least in the eyes of their families. Going on the stage at all was *déclassé* for many of them. Becoming a trade unionist along with railwaymen, miners and match girls would compound the social sin.

109

VI

As actors and actresses became more politically conscious in the 1900s, so it was inevitable that actresses should be affected by the contemporary concern with the suffragists' demand for the franchise.

Following the formation of the National Union of Women's Suffrage Societies in 1897, a number of specialist suffrage groups emerged. These included, for example, the Catholic Suffrage Society, and the London Graduates' Union. The Actresses' Franchise League of 1908 was one of these.[60] In July 1908 Janet Steer gave an 'At Home' for actresses, to be addressed by Christabel Pankhurst on the subject of votes for women. They must have been influenced by the great suffrage marches of 13 and 21 June a few weeks earlier. One or two noted stage names attended the July 'At Home', notably Mary Moore, Lilian Braithwaite and Violet Fairbrother. The assembled ladies expressed themselves broadly in favour of women's suffrage.[61]

The first formal meeting was held later that year, in December at the Criterion Restaurant, presided over by Sir Johnston Forbes Robertson.[62] He, like his mother before him and his wife Gertrude Elliott, was a genuine believer in the cause.[63] Mrs Kendal became president of the League, with Gertrude Elliott and Violet Vanbrugh among the vice-presidents. The formal motion approved by the meeting was 'that women claim the franchise as a necessary protection for the workers under modern industrial conditions'. The objects of the League were 'to convince members of the Theatrical Profession of the necessity of extending the franchise to women' and 'to work for Votes for Women on the same terms as they are, or may be, granted to men by educational methods such as propaganda meetings, sale of literature, propaganda plays, lectures'. It aimed to be strictly neutral over suffrage tactics; its members could be in any branch of the stage, though only actresses were admitted to the executive committee.[64]

Actresses could contribute to the cause in the way they knew best, by putting on plays, and the suffragette play became a lively part of the London fringe theatrical scene between 1909 and 1914. A Play Department of the League was organized by Inez Bensusan to

formalize this activity. In 1912–13 it put on thirty-three performances of plays, including a four-act suffrage play, *The Better Half*, at
the King's Hall, Covent Garden, for the Liberal Federation Delegates. In addition it presented concerts at the Empress Rooms
during the ten-days' Fair of the Women's Social and Political Union.
It tried to begin a 'Women's Theatre' movement, taking a London
theatre for a week in the autumn and putting on feminist plays – *La
Femme Seule* by Brieux and Bjornson's *The Gauntlet* in 1912.
Suffragist plays were performed not only in the capital but as far
away as Northampton and Nottingham, though most of the
League's activities were in London and the Home Counties. The
propaganda play was one of the most distinctive ways in which the
Actresses' Franchise League could use its special skills in support of
the cause.

As well as its theatrical ventures, the League engaged in orthodox
political activities. It was especially effective in open-air marches and
demonstration meetings. That many of the actresses were strikingly
handsome figures, and well-known names surrounded with the
magic of the theatre, added to the piquancy of their appearing in so
public a fashion. They took part in the Hyde Park demonstration of
July 1912 and the March to Trafalgar Square in November of that
year, and attended the funeral of Emily Davidson. In Manchester,
too, a contingent attended mass meetings at Platt Fields and Victoria
Park in 1912 and 1913.

Actresses had certain strong moral advantages in their demands
for the franchise. It was often pointed out that there was no
profession in which women were as equal with men as acting. Thus
they seemed especially disinterested. Having little to gain financially
or in terms of status, they could appear to be fighting the cause less
for themselves than for their less fortunate sisters. Furthermore,
though having few substantive grievances, they could yet arouse
more public sympathy than many groups who needed it more. Ellen
Terry, for example, commanded far more public regard than any
comparable lay-woman of the time. Thirdly, the argument that
women were unfit for the vote because their sphere of activity was
confined to the home, and they were sheltered in ignorance of the
world outside, was patently false in the case of actresses. Their work
conditions were identical with those of male actors, and they

111

travelled more than most men outside the theatre. The idea was much bruited that actresses had little to gain from the vote, but that they were supporting the cause on behalf of less fortunate women workers out of a sense of 'generous feeling'.[65]

By 1913 there were 760 members in the League, including most of the leading actresses of the day. It had merited and gained the respect even of those who had been sceptical. *Era* noted in 1910 that 'some of the cleverest and ablest of our actresses' were members and that 'it is therefore beyond dispute that the question of votes for women has been taken up seriously by the female side of the profession'.[66] The League continued with a fine record of (non-political) service in the First World War, which we will examine in Chapter 8. With the ending of the War and the granting of the first measure of suffrage the AFL experienced an inevitable hiatus. The government had passed the legislation it had wanted: the women's right to the vote over the age of thirty, the right to sit in Parliament and equal rights through the Sex Disqualification Removal Bill. The AFL, much of its purpose removed, lingered through the 1920s and finally disbanded in 1928 with the granting of full adult suffrage to women.

This trade-union and political activity by actors and actresses, especially in the 1900s, was important. It is one of the major watersheds between the Victorian and the modern actor. In the activities of this decade lay the roots of some dilemmas and conflicts that have marked the profession in the interwar years and since. They posed the fundamental question of whether actors should regard themselves as a profession seeking, as T. H. Bolton advised them, analogies with medicine and law. Or should they regard themselves as workers in a capitalist industry, using trade-union measures to fight their corner against employers with whom they had a conflict rather than an identity of interest? Many concerned to raise acting to the level of a profession, and to safeguard that status, saw the second strategy as undermining their prior aim. Actors began to wonder whether Socialism had any relevance to their situation or whether they should retain their traditional Conservatism, either because their patrons were Conservatives or because some of them hoped to become employing businessmen. Many of them felt that Conservatism accorded better with their claims for professional status. Was it absurd to have a union including wealthy employers, or could an actors' trade union thrive only with such skilled elite leadership from above? These were all questions raised in this decade for the first time and which still remained lively cross-currents in the attempts of actors' organizations in the interwar years and since. The years also saw the origins of the tradition of the politicized, militant actress, so strongly revived in recent years. Various tactical ideas also stem from this time: the maintenance of wages by minimum wage regulation; the control of professional entry by using the mechanism of controlled entry to drama schools, Granville Barker's proposal of a closed shop; the regarding of rehearsal time as paid work rather than unpaid training. The acting profession was no more immune from the changes in labour and trade-union history at this time than any other occupation. It was never to be the same again, and many of its early dilemmas and issues in the 1900s were to be interwoven with the rise of Equity in the 1930s.

NOTES

1 Hesketh Pearson, *Beerbohm Tree* (London, 1956), p.60.
2 'E.F.S.' of the *Westminster Gazette, Our Stage and its Critics* (London, 1910), p.113.
3 Joseph Macleod, *The Actor's Right to Act* (London, 1981) gives a valuable account of the AA.
4 Sir Frank Benson, *My Memoirs* (London, 1930), p.295.
5 *Ibid.*, p.295.
6 *Ibid.*, p.296.
7 *Era*, 21 March 1891, on the Lyceum meeting.
8 Figures variously reported in *Era*.
9 *Era*, 1 April 1893.
10 *Era*, 4 April 1896. Lionel Brough, in his evidence to the 1892 *Select Committee on Theatres*, laid especial stress on this activity in which they had done 'a good deal', Q.3503.
11 *Era*, 30 March 1895.
12 *Ibid.*
13 *Era*, 24 April 1897.
14 *Era*, 4 March 1893.

15 *Era*, 24 April 1897.

16 *Era*, 2 April 1898.

17 *Era*, 10 March 1900.

18 Lionel Brough at the 1892 *Select Committee*, Q.3502.

19 *Era*, 27 January 1894.

20 *Era*, 2 April 1898.

21 *Era*, 4 April 1896.

22 *Era*, 2 April 1898.

23 *Era*, 10 March 1900. Refers also to earlier meetings, July and December 1899.

24 Clarence Derwent, 'The Actors' Association', in C. F. Armstrong (ed.), *The Actor's Companion* (London, 1912), pp.156–7.

25 *Era*, 4 April 1903.

26 Clarence Derwent, *The Derwent Story* (New York, 1953), p.29. Derwent played a small role in the matinée.

27 *Era*, 27 February 1904.

28 Basil Dean, *Seven Ages* (London, 1970), p.47.

29 C. B. Purdom, *Harley Granville Barker* (London, 1955), pp.24–5.

30 *Era*, 18 November 1914, Raleigh's obituary.

31 Gertrude Kingston, *Curtsey While You're Thinking* (London, 1937), p.185.

32 *Era*, 26 January 1907.

33 *Era*, 23 February 1907.

34 *Era*, 11 May 1907.

35 *Era*, 5 October 1907.

36 *Era*, 14 September 1907.

37 *Era*, 13 February 1909.

38 *Era*, 31 July 1909.

39 1909 VIII *Report of the Joint Select Committee on Stage Plays (Censorship)* Evidence of Clarence Derwent for the AA. 19 August 1909. Evidence of Frank Gerald for the AU, 26 August 1909. Clarence Derwent, *The Derwent Story*, pp.72–9.

40 *Era*, 1, 29 February 1908.

41 Accounts of the founding of the AU are in their First Annual Report in *Era*, 23 May 1908, and Oswald Marshall's account at the Criterion Meeting reported in *Era*, 16 March 1907.

42 *Era*, 20, 27 April 1907.

114

43 *Era*, 29 June 1907.

44 AU First Annual Report, *Era*, 23 May 1908.

45 1909 VIII *S.C. Stage Plays (Censorship)* Q.3502. Derwent said there was 'a small minority who are members of both bodies'. Lewis Casson and Cecil Raleigh were examples.

46 *Era*, 26 October 1907.

47 *Era*, 14 September 1907.

48 *Era*, 26 October 1907.

49 *Era*, 11 January 1908.

50 *Era*, 27 July 1907 and Mario Borsa, *The English Stage of Today* (London, 1906), p.15.

51 *Era*, 10 July 1909.

52 *Era*, 28 August 1909.

53 *Era*, 29 January 1910.

54 Clarence Derwent in C. F. Armstrong, *op.cit.*, p.159.

55 Clarence Derwent, *The Derwent Story*, p.83.

56 *Era*, 11 February 1911.

57 Clarence Derwent in C. F. Armstrong, *op.cit.*, pp.155–67.

58 The AA tried to enlist the support of the Academy of Dramatic Art over the last issue. The ADA Council debated it and, while sympathetic to the AA, was divided over the minimum wage issue. Letter, Kenneth Barnes to Secretary of AA, 18 June 1913.

59 *Era*, 8 August 1908, is perceptive on this.

60 Constance Rover, *Women's Suffrage and Party Politics in Britain 1866–1914* (London, 1967), p.56. Julie Holledge, *Innocent Flowers* (London, 1980), Pt.II, contains a good account of the AFL.

61 *Era*, 25 July 1908.

62 *Era*, 19 December 1908.

63 Eva Moore, *Exits and Entrances* (London, 1923), p.94, on the first meeting.

64 *Report of the Actresses' Franchise League*, 1912–13. (The only existing report of the AFL is in the British Library [pp.3611 mg]).

65 *Era*, 21, 28 August 1909, 22 January 1910, 8 March 1913.

66 *Era*, 22 January 1910.

6 The Actor in the Music Hall

As the profession of the actor improved in status and organization, it faced the problem of its borderland relations with the music hall. This was not merely a matter of living with the neighbours, because in the 1890s and 1900s the legitimate actor was careful to stress his separateness from the music-hall artist. Yet in the 1910s there was much more exploration and crossing of the borderland as the stage actor took to the halls. The purpose here is not to recount the familiar history of the music hall for its own sake but to illustrate how the defining of the relationships between the legitimate stage and the music halls was an important element in helping the actor to come to a more self-conscious view of his own professional status.

The theatres and the music halls were different worlds in Victorian times. The halls had their origins in the early part of the nineteenth century as part of the entertainment of public houses.[1] Taverns had music licences and a singer would sing ballads amid the hubbub of drinking, eating and conversation. In some places a kind of stage might have been erected at one end of the room in some embryonic theatrical form. In 1843, however, the Theatres Act forced a clear distinction between such activities and the legitimate theatre. Theatres (and now not only the patent theatres of Covent Garden and Drury Lane) were allowed to present legitimate spoken drama but were not allowed to serve food and drink in the auditorium. Conversely, music-hall taverns were allowed to continue serving food and drink but were forbidden to present legitimate drama. Most taverns providing entertainment took the latter choice presented to them. They opened concert rooms and song saloons, and some new music halls of the 1850s were converted pubs – the Mogul in Drury Lane, Weston's in Holborn, Wilton's in Whitechapel. Some were newly purpose-built, notably the Canter-

116

bury in 1849 and the Oxford in 1861, both run by Charles Morton, the 'Father of the Halls', who was aiming at a higher degree of respectability than music halls had hitherto enjoyed. In the 1850s the clearing of bookmakers out of the halls, the increase of entertainment advertising due to the abolition of the advertisement tax, and the spread of the horse omnibus all stimulated the growth of the new entertainment. In 1878 the fire regulations of the Metropolitan Board of Works Act required structural features in halls and theatres, notably the proscenium arch supported by thick brick walling. These demands weeded out the smaller music halls which, unable to meet these requirements, reverted to being pubs or billiard halls. It was a further step in the music hall's drawing closer in form to that of the theatre.

In the 1900s the scale of commercial organization in the music hall became much bigger. This was presaged by the new London Pavilion of 1885, a pioneer of the public investment company hall with large audiences, fixed seats, twice nightly performances and a respectable clientele. Entrepreneurs built up chains of music halls in the provinces, and in 1900 Sir Edward Moss, Richard Thornton and Oswald Stoll merged their halls into the giant Moss Empires, with a capitalization of some £1.4 million. Apart from these, Sir Walter de Frece controlled circuits in the North of England and Walter Gibbons his London Theatres of Variety in London. Several of these businessmen then began to build very large 'flagship' music halls in the capital – Moss the Hippodrome in 1900, Stoll the Coliseum in 1904, Gibbons the Palladium in 1910 and Sir Alfred Butt the Victoria Palace in 1911. The scale and respectability of these new theatres were to have important implications for the stage actor and his changing relationship to the music halls.

There were various reasons why the legitimate stage actor would have looked somewhat askance at the Victorian music hall. Firstly, the conditions of work were quite different and far from attractive. Early music-hall audiences sat at tables, eating, drinking, smoking and talking, often not even facing the stage but at right-angles to it. Patrons could stroll off during the acts for a walk around the promenade at the back. In the legitimate theatre lights might be dimmed to focus attention on the stage, especially since Irving's innovations at the Lyceum. In the music hall they remained

117

distractingly on.[2] In the legitimate theatre conditions were increas-ingly designed to enhance the actor's playing. In the music hall the artist more often had to battle with his audience and environment to project his performance.

Secondly, music-hall performers were a quite different sort of per-son from stage actors. Their social origins were much more humble. Lois Rutherford has found that the origins of a sample of fifty-two music-hall artists of the pre-1914 generation were as follows[3]

Professional	5	9.6 per cent
Industrial and commercial	4	7.7 per cent
Literary and artistic	3	5.8 per cent
Theatrical	25	48 per cent
Clerical and lower sales	9	17.3 per cent
Artisan and manual	6	11.5 per cent

Most came from families already on the boards, and there was a large working-class element among the fathers of music-hall performers, while few came from professional families. By contrast, few stage actors came from working-class families and many from professional backgrounds. This status division between the music-hall and stage actors reflected itself in a homely way. There was an increasing tendency for music-hall performers to use familiar diminutives in their names. This seemed to become more usual from around 1890 when Dans, Harrys, Lotties and Gerties took to the boards. Indeed, of 131 committee members of the Variety Artistes' Federation in 1908, fifty-nine used such diminutives. It endeared them to their working-class audiences, many of whose members would be simi-larly named. However, legitimate actors, by conscious contrast, did not accept such familiarity – Henry, Herbert, George and Charles were dignified names inviting some future accolade 'Sir' without incongruity.

Furthermore, a music-hall career provided an escape for the deprived and deformed. Dan Leno and Charlie Chaplin could escape from backgrounds of an alcoholic father in the one case and an insane mother in the other. Little Tich and Wee Georgie Wood could turn their physical disabilities to good account. Such people would have found very little opportunity on the legitimate stage. In any case, most music-hall performers were not actors at all but singers, stand-up comedians, jugglers and acrobats, ballet dancers, animal trainers and nigger minstrels. They could have no share in the literary and educational pretensions which the respectable stage actor increasingly claimed for the theatre.

Thirdly, the music hall was far more tainted with suspicions of immorality than the theatre. It was closely associated with the drink trade, with many songs extolling the virtues of 'Champagne Charlie' and ''Arf a Pint of Ale'. It was part of the Tory–Jingo Imperialist –Drink Trade connection. It also fitted in with the anti-Gladstonian, anti-Temperance outlook which was an important element in certain late Victorian working-class attitudes.[4] From the 1880s the halls faced a sustained attack from Temperance moral reformers. Even worse was the taint of sexual immorality. Prostitutes openly paraded in the promenades of the Oxford and the Empire Music Halls in the 1890s, calling forth the strictures of Mrs Ormiston Chant and her Social Purity League against the immorality of the halls. The erection of a screen in the promenade of the Empire led to rowdy scenes as a mob of posh hooligans (including Winston Churchill) smashed it up as a protest. However dubious were the morals of some of the patrons in the auditorium, those of the performers did not escape criticism either. In 1896 the Empire licence was challenged over the bawdiness of Marie Lloyd's act and certain indelicate references ('she sits among the cabbages and peas'). This all added up to a form of entertainment from whose vulgarities the new style of dignified, gentlemanly actor did well to steer clear.

It was not only a matter of taste, since the stage actor in the theatre and the music-hall artist in the halls were commercial rivals. The conflict of interest between them focused on the increasing tendency of the music halls to include sketches in their programmes. These sketches could easily trespass into becoming short plays, thus threatening competition with the legitimate theatres and flouting the 1843 Theatres Act. The rise of the sketch as a music-hall turn was partly due to the increasing tendency of music-hall artists to be employed in pantomime during the winter. Here they were replacing stock company actors – a further cause of rivalry between the artist and the actor. Being used to playing semi-dramatic sketches in pantomime, the same players carried back this form to the music hall

119

for the rest of the year. The essence of the music hall was variety, and short sketches fitted in well as a contrast with musical and physical acts which were not based on spoken dramatic prose.

In the 1890s and 1900s actors looked with suspicion on these sketches. Lionel Brough, in 1892, said that real actors would not appear in a music hall, where smoke in the air damaged the voice and the opening of soda bottles distracted from the scene. He knew of only one or two who had taken such work, and that purely out of poverty.[5] In the 1900s the antagonism was most intense. By an agreement of 1906 music-hall programmes were limited to a major sketch of no more than thirty minutes in length and six characters, and a minor sketch of no more than fifteen minutes and four characters. Anything in excess of this was liable to prosecution. The sketch activity of the music halls was considerable after the agreement of 1906. It was noted in 1907 that 'the dramatic element in variety entertainments has greatly increased and the number of actors engaged in such entertainments in sketches is now very considerable indeed'.[6] In fact, in 1907 199 sketches were presented in music halls.

These were watched over, hawklike, by theatrical interests. Theatre managers 'would arrange that informers with stop watches would be present at the performances to time the length of these sketches, and to keep a strict account as to how many characters uttered a word'.[7] West End managers turned up themselves or commissioned the agent Blackmore to lurk with pocket watch in hand. Any infringement would be open to prosecution. Between 1907 and 1911 there were thirteen, most brought by the Theatre Managers' Association, one by the Actors' Association and one (in Jarrow) by the police, all under the 1843 Theatres Act.[8] This atmosphere of deep legalistic suspicion between the legitimate stage and the music halls, and the severe artistic limitations on the development of the sketch, both inhibited the movement of the actor to the music halls. Seymour Hicks, who was unusual in making music-hall work a significant part of his career before 1910, noted that his fellow-actors 'shook their heads and predicted the end of all things for us'.[9]

A major personal influence keeping the theatre and music hall apart was Sir Henry Irving himself. Irving, in the last years of his life, resisted the most lucrative offers to appear on the halls. 'It was well known in the profession that Sir Henry had no love for the Music Halls, that he considered they were encroaching on the preserves of the legitimate theatre by producing dramatic sketches and that he never failed to express his dislike of the halls.'[10] The impresario Sir Walter de Frece (Vesta Tilley's husband) seriously upset Irving by pestering him about a variety appearance. For Irving, whose whole life was devoted to raising the status of the legitimate drama with its literary and cultural pretensions, it was particularly important that the actor should distance himself from what he regarded as lower performers. For the actor to appear in the halls, especially before 1900, would seem to him a betrayal of hard-won status and standards. It must also have been doubly galling to have been continually offered large sums to appear on the halls at the end of his life, when the money would have been useful for his old age. Irving did actually once appear on a variety bill, though not as a professional. At a charity matinée at the Alhambra he appeared with Dan Leno. Mindful of his status, Sir Henry intended to insist on being top of the bill. But on being shrewdly advised that Dan Leno's act was an impossible one to follow, he unusually allowed the theatre to defer to the halls.[11] He was prepared to do this for charity, but he would never have put himself in such a position professionally.

It was ironic, in the light of this, that a pioneer in effecting a *rapprochement* between the theatre and the music hall should have been Sir Henry's son Laurence. In 1903 he devised a short play about Garrick's mistress Peg Woffington, which he intended to play with his wife during the summer break from the Lyceum season. To the amazement of his fellow-actors, especially those expecting his father's disapproval, he announced his intention to play it as a turn in London and provincial music halls. 'Here was defection. How could the son of the Elevator of the English Stage drag its hard won status into the vulgar arena of Variety? How could he leap contemptuously the social and artistic barriers that separated the legitimate from illegitimate vaudeville?' Sir Henry expressed no disapproval, and Laurence went ahead. His motive was plain. He intended to make enough money quickly in the halls to enable him to set up in management with his wife. He also hoped to indicate to music-hall patrons the pleasures they might gain from theatre-going. The

121

venture was a success, and in the wake of this a number of legitimate actor-managers 'began to consider the lucrative possibilities of following the trail blazed by Laurence that led to the booking offices of the vaudeville empire'.[12]

It was specifically from 1911 that this closer *rapprochement* came about and many actors, from the highest down, came to be willing to appear on the music halls. Several factors lay behind this shift of attitude. Firstly, from 24 November 1911 the LCC began to grant double licences whereby places of amusement could present variety or drama.[13] The Lord Chamberlain approved of this, and extended his jurisdiction to music-hall sketches. This now meant that sketches were no longer limited to a half-hour, which gave scope for dramatic one-act plays of more substance. A music-hall programme still had to contain at least five other items to prevent its turning over to drama excessively.

The new arrangements, however, freed the halls from the restrictions and petty spying to which they had been subjected, and prosecutions ceased. Most importantly, the new sketches were often one-act plays of some quality, written by writers like J. M. Barrie, A. A. Milne, W. S. Gilbert and Max Beerbohm. These provided vehicles in which the status-conscious stage actor could be seen with dignity in one-act plays akin to those of his legitimate work. The writers saw this as a new market and a source of income. J. M. Barrie initially did not like the music hall, but came to enjoy it and the £50 a week in royalties he could receive for a sketch. It was noted in 1912 that 'sketches now have a recognized place on every music hall programme'; it was no longer *infra dig* for the actor to appear in such sketches, and indeed he should be grateful for the sketch, 'which has so materially widened his market'.[14]

Secondly, such work was clearly lucrative. Irene Vanbrugh was offered a 'very handsome salary' by Oswald Stoll to appear at the Coliseum.[15] Stoll had already offered Irving any price he cared to name. Cyril Maude's salary was so huge that it 'frightened me'.[16] In fact, the whole level of earnings for performers in the music hall was higher than that for stage actors. For example George Leybourne (Champagne Charlie) earned £125 a week,[17] Dan Leno £230 a week, and at his peak £20,000 a year.[18] Marie Lloyd earned £100 a week at the age of 16 and £11,000 a year in her decline in the 1920s.[19] Her

122

mid-career earnings must have been as much as Leno's. These earnings of Leno and Lloyd were considerably in excess even of Tree's £150 a week, which must have been at the top end of the stage actors' incomes of the day. Stoll paid £350 a week to entice Charles Hawtrey to the Coliseum for six weeks[20] and he was actually offering £500–£700 a week to lure top-line West End actors like the Kendals and George Alexander to appear at the same theatre.[21] This was vastly higher than actors would receive in the legitimate theatre, and higher even than established music-hall stars would earn. For the stage actor to move into the halls was thus to move into a lower league of artistic fulfilment but a higher league of income-earning capacity.

Why should the music halls have been so keen to entice the stage actor on to their boards with such lucrative inducements, and how could they afford to pay them? These policies arose out of certain difficulties being experienced by the halls. Stoll himself was in considerable financial difficulty over the Coliseum. The building and running costs had entailed large bank debts which a flagging box office could not liquidate. In fact, the Coliseum closed altogether in 1906 and 1907. When, after financial reconstitution, the theatre opened again, the spoken sketch was part of the gamut of varied attractions designed to sustain it. Stoll used Sydney Blow the writer and Hartley Milburn the agent to approach stage actors to persuade them to come to the Coliseum. However, the problem was not, of course, confined to Stoll. The music hall, in spite of the *élan* of its rise, actually felt itself under a certain commercial threat in the years before the First World War.[22] The rise of the picture palaces was beginning to have an adverse effect on trade by 1911. This was compounded by the hot summer of that year, which had deterred patrons from sitting inside. It was significant that 1911 was also noted as the year when music halls began to resort to nude shows in order to increase trade. Conversely, just as theatre managers defended their rights against the music-hall owners, so the latter were very keen to contest the attempts of cinemas to secure music and dancing licences. In this three-cornered duel of theatres, music hall and cinema the concern of the music halls to win over star names from the legitimate theatre as attractions for their programmes was a tactic in the wider battle for trade. Sydney Blow saw clearly that 'it was

123

only the success of the cinema that made these deadly rivals [theatre and music hall] bury the hatchet'.[23]

If such were their motives, how could the large music halls afford to pay such huge sums to draw the stage actor? The economics of the new music halls operated on a larger scale than those of the drama theatres. The capacity of the Coliseum, for example, was 2200 seating with standing room for a further 500. The median seat price was 3/- and a performer would appear twice daily. In fact, when the theatre opened there were four performances a day with two separate casts.[24] This combination of vast capacity and duplicate shows made possible weekly wages of several hundred pounds for the leading acts, something which the legitimate theatre could not match. Stoll emphasized the wages power of his theatre, as well as the temptation involved, by paying the actors with piles of gold sovereigns heaped on their dressing tables.

From the actor's point of view a third factor making the music hall more attractive was the increasing respectability of the hall itself. During the 1890s the LCC licensing authorities tried to check the use of indecent material in acts, hence the investigating of Marie Lloyd referred to earlier. Also, the new variety theatres like the Hippo-drome (1900), Coliseum (1904), Palladium (1910) and Victoria Palace (1911), all built by the great theatre architect Frank Matcham, provided a new, opulent, totally respectable milieu for variety.[25] Family audiences went to such venues in total propriety, and their scale and pompous dignity enhanced rather than diminished the actor appearing on their stages. In such matters as ventilation and seating they were often superior to many West End theatres, and this further attracted a better class of audience and performer. Moreover, it became evident that there was a latent demand among music-hall audiences for something akin to high-class legitimate drama. For example, from 1896 Bransby Williams developed a successful career on the halls by impersonating leading West End actors of the day.[26] Indeed, his ability to mimic Irving's voice with great accuracy influenced Olivier's choice of voice for the film of *Richard III*. If audiences derived such pleasure from so vicarious an experience as listening to Williams's impersonations, might they not listen with even greater respectful attention to the living presences of some of the original leading actors themselves?

124

The Actor in the Music Hall (*Punch*, 24 April 1912)

This was confirmed by the sensational appearance of the leading French tragedienne Sarah Bernhardt at the Coliseum in 1910. She played one act of a straight drama, *L'Aiglon*, and so successfully was this received that she returned every year up to the War. The improved standing of the music hall at this time was also symbolized by the first Royal Command Performance of 1912. This latter event, coming soon after the Bernhardt appearance of 1910 and the new sketch agreements of 1911, must have been a powerful influence in deciding many actors to participate in music-hall entertainments around this time. Furthermore, many actors who had had experience of work in the United States would have been aware that by that time it was quite usual for leading American stage actors to appear on vaudeville. It was noted that 'by 1912 nearly every prominent American actor or actress had appeared in vaudeville at one time or another'.[27] All these factors made the five years before the outbreak of war an especially fruitful time in the coming together of the stage actor and the music hall.

Irene Vanbrugh claimed to have been one of the first to be approached by Stoll (or his agents Blow and Milburn) to appear at the Coliseum. In 1911 she appeared in *The Twelve Pound Look* by Barrie in a programme including gorillas and an elephant. Irene Vanbrugh's success in this had a significant effect in changing the attitudes of other actors and also of Barrie, who wrote another sketch for her to play at the Hippodrome. Violet Vanbrugh, influenced by her sister's success, moved from playing Lady Macbeth with Tree to do the sleepwalking scene at the Coliseum as a variety turn.[28] The example was contagious as Tree himself followed his leading lady and appeared at the Palace in 1912 in Kipling's *The Man Who Was*. Tree's conversion to the music hall created a 'mild sensation' in theatrical circles. Undismayed at having to follow a performing seal act and at being enjoined by the call boy to ''Urry up 'Erbert',[29] Tree acquired a taste for the halls and subsequently toured provincial variety theatres as Svengali in a condensed version of his great success *Trilby*.[30] Arthur Bourchier and Charles Hawtrey (who was one of the first British actors to appear in American vaudeville) regularly appeared at the Coliseum in short plays and sketches.[31] Frank Benson's wife Constance appeared in Shakespeare at the Tivoli in a programme along with Marie Lloyd and an elephant in a

126

pierrot hat,[32] while Lilian Braithwaite and Ernest Thesiger appeared in sketches at the Pavilion, Glasgow.[33] Fred Kerr, Constance Collier, Henry Ainley, Fay Compton, Mrs Martin Harvey, Sydney Fairbrother were others traceable in music-hall work between 1910 and 1914. Indeed, Blow and Milburn claimed personally to have recruited a dozen or more actors for Stoll. Many of these were, or were to be, fairly prominent actors (several future knights, dames, ladies and CBEs) but the greatest catch of all was Sir George Alexander. No actor of the time more consciously cultivated or expressed the *persona* of the dignified gentleman, and few were wealthier. In 1908 he specifically refused an invitation from Stoll to appear at the Coliseum on the grounds that it would damage his image with his St James patrons. But such was the change of mood within the few short years that in 1913 he appeared in variety for the first time at the Palace Theatre. This was in a short comedy by Max Beerbohm, aptly titled *A Social Success*. What had been impossible for Irving before 1905 had become quite acceptable for his two chief successors in 1912 and 1913. Since then, Vesta Tilley (herself the wife of a music-hall impresario) reflected: 'I can recall very few actors and actresses who have not appeared on the variety stage.'[34]

As Vesta Tilley's comments suggest the interrelation of the music halls and the theatre tradition carried over into the interwar years. Some were established stars lured into the halls. In the early 1920s Owen Nares played in variety at the Coliseum and in other halls of the Stoll tour 'at odd times between other engagements'.[35] Godfrey Tearle similarly played an A. A. Milne sketch about demobilization (which had been originated by Nares) for several weeks on the halls. John Gielgud, following his successful Romeo at the Regent Theatre, was invited by Stoll to perform the balcony scene in a variety show at the Coliseum in 1926,[36] while Cedric Hardwicke played *The Point of View*, a one-act play by Eden Phillpotts, in provincial music halls and the Coliseum in between successful legitimate engagements. He found the experience 'invigorating and salutary'.[37] Nares, Tearle and Hardwicke were stars in the twenties who would bring drawing power into the halls. At a lower level, the variety theatre could be used by struggling unknowns to sustain a regular income and fill in between jobs while getting a start. Donald Wolfit went into a music-hall sketch at the Empire Theatre,

Chatham[38] while between engagements in 1922. Three years later, in 1925, Olivier's first entrance on the professional stage was in a sketch with Ruby Miller at the Hippodrome, Brighton. This was in a music-hall programme, with Harry Lauder and George Robey also on the bill.[39] Anthony Quayle likewise started his stage career in a music hall in 1931.[40]

After the 1920s the phenomenon of legitimate actors playing in music halls sharply diminished. This was partly due to the decline of the music-hall and variety theatre under the impact of the cinema. Equally important, in the 1930s the cinema studio totally replaced the music hall as the alternative form of work where extra very lucrative earnings could be made. Thirdly, the public taste changed with the rise of the revue. In this form some musical, dancing and singing skill was usually required of the performer. Also the revue depended on an ensemble of reappearing players rather than a series of totally discrete acts. In these new circumstances the stage actor (and especially the melodramatist or Shakespearian) with his individual sketch or scene appeared as a heavy, stylistically inappropriate intrusion amid the tapping feet, light high tenors, top hats and tails.

Under these pressures the venues for legitimate actors to appear in music halls began to disappear. The London Pavilion and Hippodrome went over to revue in the 1920s, The Palace and the Alhambra to musical comedy, the Empire and Tivoli to films. Suburban music halls likewise became cinemas. The Coliseum was left fighting a rearguard action trying to sustain music hall including stage actors until it too closed in March 1931. Only the Palladium in the 1930s tried to keep on with variety. It was there, for example, that Bernard Miles developed his 'farm labourer' comedy sketch based on gardeners' talk remembered from his early days as a seedsman's son. Miles at the time was a struggling Shakespearian actor but was happy to do this – at Val Parnell's behest – to supplement an emergent career.[41] However, for actors better established than Miles then was, the new sound film studios of the early 1930s offered a more attractive form of additional lucrative work than the variety theatre.

Since the 1920s the interesting traffic has been in the opposite direction, with music-hall artists going legitimate, if only tempor-

128

arily. An early example was Granville Barker's casting of Wish Wynne, a music-hall comedienne, in Arnold Bennett's *The Great Adventure* in 1913.[42] Her success in this belied the misgivings of those who doubted the capacity of a music-hall artist to make the transition. The most striking example of this in the interwar years was George Robey's essaying a creditable Falstaff in 1935 which he repeated (silently) in the film of *Henry V*. Such unusual temporary movements have been echoed in the post-war years, with Frankie Howerd and Tommy Steele playing Bottom and Tony Lumpkin, both at the Old Vic, in 1957 and 1960 respectively. The forays of Howerd and Steele did not represent major changes in the direction of their careers. But some variety artists in their later years have recently made a more permanent and successful transition into the serious theatre – notably Jimmy Jewel in *The Comedians* and Max Wall in *Waiting for Godot* and *The Entertainer*. Oddly enough, the curious lingering remnants in recent times of the 'legitimate' actor appearing on 'the halls' have been those occasions when Shakespearian actors like Robert Hardy, Glenda Jackson, Vanessa Redgrave and others have happily joined Morecambe & Wise in the comic sketches of their television shows. The *frisson* of incongruity and contrast in such events tells us something of what the Edwardians found attractive in this fusion of the two theatrical traditions.

The close involvement of the legitimate stage actor with the music hall was of relatively brief duration, some twenty-five years between 1906 and 1930. No actor, with the exception of Albert Chevalier, became a significant full-time music-hall star.[43] The music hall was never so important a supplementary part of any legitimate career as the film studios of the 1930s and 1940s or the television studios of the 1960s or 1970s were later to become. Yet the almost magnetic relations of attraction and repulsion between the halls and the actor were important for the latter, especially before 1914. We have already seen in earlier chapters that the unionization of the variety artist positively stimulated trade unionism of the actor in the 1900s. The growth of the halls must also have drawn off the rowdier elements from the galleries of theatres, increasing the respectability of the latter. Most importantly, the emergence of the powerful borderland neighbour of the music hall forced the actor to take a self-aware view of his own increasing status. The cautious attitudes

129

of Irving and Lionel Brough testifying to the 1892 Royal Commission reflected this, as did Alexander's refusal of 1908. It was only when the music hall itself strenuously sought an almost pompous dignity in the 1900s that stage actors felt able to accept work in the new cavernous palaces of variety. Even then they usually did so in the familiar surroundings of the one-act play by reputable authors, not as stooges or competitors to Dan Leno or Little Tich. It was a measure of the increased status of the legitimate acting profession that a clear frontier was maintained between itself and the music hall. It was a reflection of the self-confidence of actors by the 1910s that they were able to cross and recross that frontier on their own terms.

NOTES

1 For the history of music hall generally see Harold Scott, *The Early Doors, Origins of the Music Hall* (London, 1946, 1977); D. F. Cheshire, *Music Hall in Britain* (London, 1974); Samuel McKechnie, *Popular Entertainment Through the Ages* (New York, 1969), Chapter VI, 'The Halls'; Raymond Mander and Joe Mitchenson, *British Music Hall* (London, 1965); Peter Bailey, *Leisure and Class in Victorian England* (London, 1978), Chapter 7.

2 Mario Borsa, *The English Stage of Today* (London, 1906), p.19.

3 I am grateful to Miss Lois Rutherford of Girton College, Cambridge, who made available these early findings from her own work on the variety comedian.

4 Gareth Stedman Jones, 'Working-class culture and working-class politics in London 1870–1900', *Journal of Social History*, Summer 1974; Laurence Senelick, 'Politics as Entertainment: Victorian Music Hall Songs', *Victorian Studies* XIX No. 2, December 1975.

5 1892 XVIII *R. C. on Theatres and Places of Entertainment.* Evidence of Lionel Brough, 11 May 1892. QQ. 3518, 3535.

6 *Stage Year Book* 1908, p.26 (referring to 1907).

7 Sydney Blow, *The Ghost Walks on Fridays* (London, 1935), p.97.

8 *Stage Year Books* 1908–1912 listed court cases.

9 Seymour Hicks, *Twenty Four Years of an Actor's Life* (London, 1910), p.313.
10 Vesta Tilley, *Recollections* (London, 1934), pp.95–6.
11 H. Chance Newton, *Cues and Curtain Calls* (London, 1927), pp.53–4.
12 Laurence Irving, *Precarious Crust* (London, 1971), pp.81–2.
13 *Stage Year Book*, 1912.
14 Cecil Armstrong, *The Actor's Companion* (London, 1912), p.95.
15 Irene Vanbrugh, *To Tell My Story* (London, 1948), p.104.
16 Cyril Maude, *Behind the Scenes* (London, 1927), pp.203–4.
17 Colin MacInnes, *Sweet Saturday Night* (London, 1967), p. 110.
18 Gyles Brandreth, *The Funniest Man on Earth, the Story of Dan Leno* (London, 1977).
19 Daniel Farson, *Marie Lloyd and the Music Hall* (London, 1972).
20 Sydney Blow, *op.cit.*, p.110.
21 Joe Graham, *An Old Stock Actor's Memories* (London, 1930), pp.245–6.
22 *Stage Year Book* 1912 gives the following analysis.
23 Sydney Blow, *op.cit.*, p.101.
24 Felix Barker, *The House that Stoll Built* (London, 1957), pp.15–22.
25 B. M. Walker (ed.), *Frank Matcham* (Belfast, 1980).
26 Bransby Williams, *Bransby Williams* (London, 1954), p.35.
27 Jessie Millward, *Myself and Others* (London, 1923), p.269.
28 Irene Vanbrugh, *op.cit.*, pp.104–5.
29 Jessie Millward, *op.cit.*
30 Tree's obituary in *Era*, 4 July 1916.
31 Arthur Croxton, *Crowded Nights and Days* (London, 1934), Chapter XVIII. Croxton was the manager of the Coliseum, 1912–27.
32 Constance Benson, *Mainly Players* (London, 1926), pp.272–3.
33 Naomi Jacob, *Me* (London, 1933), p.112.
34 Vesta Tilley, *op.cit.*, p.95. This comment was 1934.
35 Owen Nares, *Myself and Some Others* (London, 1925), p.194.
36 John Gielgud, *An Actor in his Time* (London, 1979), p.64.
37 Cedric Hardwicke, *Let's Pretend* (London, 1932), pp.160–5.
38 Donald Wolfit, *First Interval* (London, 1954), pp.86–7.
39 Laurence Olivier, *Confessions of an Actor* (London, 1982), p.27.

40 Anthony Quayle, 'Desert Island Discs', 6 November 1976.
41 Bernard Miles, 'Desert Island Discs', 20 March 1982.
42 Clarence Derwent, *The Derwent Story* (New York, 1953), p.107.
43 Seymour Hicks may be an exception. Around 1910 he divided his year equally between theatre and music hall. This was most unusual.

7 The Actor Off-Stage and in Society

In 1906 an Italian observer of the English stage noted an important difference between the English actor and those of his homeland: 'In Italy actors dwell apart . . . in England on the contrary their aim is to mingle and blend with the great family of the nation.'[1] Accordingly, when the actor was not working he developed certain distinctive forms of leisure. For the more successful and well-to-do these off-stage activities brought them into touch with the kind of fashionable society that composed their audiences. This reception of the actor by polite society further enhanced the profession's status, confirming the respectable and gentlemanly character of its leading practitioners. These contacts took various forms. At the highest level, Queen Victoria and Edward VII had an interest in the theatre which no sovereign has matched since. King Edward actually enjoyed off-stage social relations with certain actors. At a somewhat lower level actors mixed in some aristocratic and London professional circles, either as celebrities in private houses or in the gentlemen's clubs of the West End. The Garrick Club emerged as an especial focus of this social mixing. In a less formal way so did the fashionable restaurants, sometimes linked with theatres, which flourished in London in late Victorian and Edwardian times. In healthier outdoor activities too the actor participated in sports, notably golf, which not only kept him physically fit but brought him into equal association with legal and military men and the like, against whom team competitions were played. The symbiotic relationship of the actress and fashionable society was seen in the way the stage both initiated and reflected changes in dress. Finally, the grouping of actors in religious organizations enhanced not so much

133

their social status as their moral respectability. In all these ways the actor, in his life off the stage, not only enjoyed himself but, by these various associations, presented the profession as socially acceptable, gentlemanly and sporting, fashionable and even religiously moral.

I

At the head of the 'family of the nation' was the Crown, which began to take an interest in the theatre. Queen Victoria had a personal love of the theatre which distinguished her from her Hanoverian predecessors.[2] She was a keen and discerning theatre-goer in her early reign, from 1837 to 1861, and also had professional performances produced at Windsor in the 1850s. On the death of Prince Albert she ceased her theatre visits for twenty years, until the beginning of command performances in 1881. Between 1881 and the end of the reign she attended twenty-eight command performances, eleven of them legitimate drama and the rest opera. They were held in royal residences, and most of the leading actors of the day appeared at them. The Queen had no social relations with these actors, but the fact that the sovereign, from the 1880s, received leading members of the profession in her homes, appreciated and rewarded their work and found that off-stage they were gentlemen, set a seal of approval on the new profession. It made it possible for others, including the Prince of Wales, to be more intimate.

The most important influence drawing the actor into Society, however, was Edward VII, both as Prince of Wales and as King. Sir Charles Wyndham acknowledged the debt: 'the modern English stage has been made by King Edward. His Majesty has made the theatre fashionable and respected.'[3] Edward's love of good food, lively company, bright lights and pretty women gave him a natural, avid, predilection for the theatre. He attended thirty-one command performances of legitimate drama between 1901 and 1909. Apart from these command performances, which were held in royal residences, Edward attended theatres for his own pleasure. Fred Kerr told him, 'I don't believe anyone living sees as many plays as you do.'[4] He was also fond of mixing with actors socially. His relation with Lillie Langtry, and his helping her to start on a theatrical career, is well-known. She started with Bancroft, with

134

whom Edward's relations had been especially close ever since, with permission, the former had called his theatre the Prince of Wales. In February 1882 Edward gave a dinner at Marlborough House for leading actors in London, which was thought to be in gratitude for the profession's goodwill to Mrs Langtry in the early stage of her career.[5] In turn Edward accepted the actors' invitation to dine at the Garrick Club, while actors presented the Prince with a gold and diamond cigarette box in 1891 to mark his fiftieth birthday. Even abroad Bancroft, Pinero, Tree and Hawtrey would meet him on holiday at Marienbad for lunch or dinner.[6] In spite of his reputation as a womanizer, as far as the stage was concerned he most genuinely enjoyed the company of men – clubbable, humorous men about town who did not abuse his friendship and brought no emotional entanglement. Although he had less artistic discernment than his mother, the royal influence of Edward was a most important factor raising the estimation of the theatre in the eyes of Society and in turn drawing leading actors into a wider circle of social acceptance. Sir Squire observed, 'the stage has never found among Royal heads a firmer friend than was the late King; his gracious words and acts went far to conquer a decaying prejudice.'[7]

The actor found himself taken up by aristocratic Society. An early link was Baroness Burdett-Coutts, a financial backer of Irving at the Lyceum and a close friend of the Queen. Another was Lady Greville, one of the first London hostesses to receive actors and actresses at her house.[8] The Duchess of Sutherland was a further Society hostess devoted to the theatre. Irene Vanbrugh stayed with her party at Dunrobin in 1902, later joining the King on his yacht cruising nearby.[9] Sir George Alexander's social circle included the Duke of Fife, Lord and Lady St Helier and Sir George Lewis, the most famous solicitor of the day,[10] while Sir Squire Bancroft enjoyed a circle of eminent legal friends including all the chief justices from Cockburn to Hewart. Sir John Martin Harvey revelled in this kind of aristocratic contact and did not disguise his relish: 'the doors of the mighty are thrown open to us. We meet the leaders of the day in Society, politics, art and fashion.'[11]

Some actors made themselves the centre of a social circle running virtual salons attended by a wide cross-section of intelligentsia. Sir Charles Wyndham 'was very fond of playing the host and his supper

135

parties were popular entertainments in the nineties'.[12] He often held these in the 'yacht room' at his Criterion Theatre, which was furnished in imitation of a yacht cabin and served as an office by day and a supper room by night. Royalty like the Duchess of Teck and the Duke of Cambridge and lawyers like Lord Killanin and Morris, as well as actors, were frequent guests at his 'yacht' suppers. Tree likewise held court in the famous Dome of His Majesty's Theatre. His leading lady recalled: 'All the well known people of the day would be there . . . Winston Churchill and Lloyd George arguing with Maxine Elliott on some political point: The discussions were tremendous! All adored the theatre.'[13]

II

One of the most important ways in which the actor was assimilated into Society was through various gentlemen's clubs which flourished at the time.

The Garrick Club was the leading London club for actors. It had been founded in 1831 'for the purpose of bringing together the patrons of the drama and its professors' and as a place 'in which actors and men of education and refinement might meet on equal terms'. These aims rather implied that actors were not then thought of as men of 'education and refinement' nor likely to meet socially with such people in the natural course of events.[14] In 1864 they moved into their present premises in Garrick Street and the Prince of Wales became a member and a patron of the club in 1867, further cementing the relations of royalty and stage. Irving, after originally being rejected, was finally elected in 1874.

In 1880 there were only 13 actors in the Club, including Bancroft, Hare, Irving, Toole, and Benjamin Webster, who had been elected as far back as 1838. Out of 694 members they were less than two per cent of the membership, somewhat at variance with the original intentions of enabling actors to mix with other professional groups. However, with the increasing respectability of actors their membership of, and influence in, the Garrick Club increased. It was a further measure of their assimilation into polite society.

Increasing numbers of actors and other theatricals (playwrights, critics, managers and so forth) became members of the club.[15]

	Total members	actors	%	all theatricals	%
1880	694	13	1.87	13	1.87
1890	696	21	3.02	25	3.59
1900	606	28	4.62	38	6.27
1910	685	39	5.69	57	8.32
1920	677	41	6.06	57	8.42
1930	686	48	7.00	69	10.06
1940	507	42	8.30	61	12.06
1950	590	59	10.00	80	13.56

Lawyers and gentlemen of leisure were the two largest groups in Garrick Club membership, closely followed, before 1914, by military men and those in the literary professions.[16] Actors were relatively few compared with these, but their influence was considerably greater than this would suggest.

The club's atmosphere and even décor was, and is, decidedly theatrical. The chair in which Irving died adorns a landing of the central staircase, and many David Garrick relics are displayed on the main landing. The Club is uniquely rich in theatrical portraiture, which densely clothes the walls, including several paintings by Zoffany of Garrick and his contemporaries. This sheer physical accretion of memorabilia to the glorification of the actor's art belied the relative paucity of actor members. Also the great actors, by their larger-than-life personalities, seemed to dominate – even in their absence after death. Compton Mackenzie, on being invited to supper at the Garrick in 1902, declined to go to the top end of the table even though the room was completely empty: 'I was sure that his [Irving's] place at the head of the table now belonged to Sir Charles Wyndham or Sir Squire Bancroft.'[17] He had an instinctive feeling for the actor's pride of place in the Club. In this time, the early 1900s, dramatists Pinero and A. E. W. Mason would dine at the Garrick regularly if not nightly, 'and remained until the stage contingent, headed by Beerbohm Tree, John Hare and Dion Boucicault, joined them for supper'.[18] To accommodate the actors, after-theatre supper was served from 10.30 to 1.30 a.m. from the 1890s to the 1920s and the Club closed at 3.00 a.m. and even at 4.00 a.m. on Sunday mornings.

Perhaps most importantly, actors were well represented on the committee of the club. The committee consisted of twenty-four members, and theatrical representation on the committee – rising from one-twelfth in 1880 to usually around one-sixth between 1890 and 1940, to a quarter by 1950 – considerably outweighed the proportion of actors and theatricals in the Club as a whole. In turn the Club was fortunate in having the services of leading actor –managers who brought sound and proven business experience to the committee. As actors began to take a prominent part on the committee, so did they in the trusteeship. The Club had two trustees, and in 1916 Sir John Hare was made one of the pair. This then established a pattern which was followed, of one trustee being an actor or dramatist and the other being a distinguished lawyer.

The Club also served two other purposes, as a sanction of behaviour and as a network of contacts. Election to and acceptance into a club of this nature suggested not only the social status of a gentleman but also certain standards of gentlemanly behaviour. The Club kept an eye on the conduct of members who could be reprimanded for breaches – drunkenness, arrogance to servants or small acts of selfishness to other members, and so forth. These are not common, but it is interesting that actors were not involved in them. That actors were received into the Club in increasing numbers, and not only acquitted themselves honourably but became arbiters of conduct, was an important element in their acceptance into the most polished levels of London Society.

Finally, the Club could naturally serve as a network of friends and contacts who could be useful to each other on a professional basis. There are one or two traces of this that must be typical of many more essentially private arrangements. For example, Sir Patrick Hastings the advocate was a popular member of the Club with many theatrical friends there; his wife ran an interior decorating business and through her husband's contacts moved into designing decor for Basil Dean.[19] It was also at the Garrick that Dean in 1939 re-established contact with his former schoolfriend, the future Lord Tedder, a contact that was to prove important for the latter's support of ENSA during the War.[20] It is also worthy of note that eight of the leading actors in Laurence Olivier's film *Henry V* were members of the Garrick (Olivier, Aylmer, Banks, Hannen, Genn, Robey, Shepley, Laurie).

138

The second actors' club was the Green Room, which was a reconstitution in 1877 of the earlier, bankrupt Junior Garrick. It was a social centre purely for actors and in the 1900s its 415 members enjoyed spacious accommodation in Leicester Square.[21] Regular members included Toole, Pinero, Wyndham, and Tree, and the distinction of these actors and playwrights lent a certain 'Garrick' prestige to the new club. Accordingly actors not (or never) ready for election to the Garrick felt honoured to be elected to the Green Room, in which they took a proper pride.

As well as the prestigious London clubs with permanent premises there was also a plethora of less formal groupings or 'clubs' of actors and others, often focused on restaurants. Several of these were of mixed-membership, mingling actors and other professions. There were the Knights of the Round Table, which met at Simpson's restaurant in the Strand, 'not very much of a club, but rather a coterie of jolly old friends' including Irving and Toole.[22] Rather similar were the Lambs, meeting at the Gaiety Restaurant for 'fun and good fellowship' with Hare, Irving and Bancroft.[23] It was the origin also of the Lambs' Club in New York. Another with American links was the Kinsmen, half English and half American, and a mixture of actors and other artistic people with lawyers and politicians. As usual Irving, Hare, Bancroft and Fred Kerr were active members, and like the Lambs it flourished in New York also.[24] These clubs mixed actors with gentlemen outside the profession, but one or two were created for an exclusively theatrical membership. The Touchstone was for actors only (not managers) who had been on the stage for twenty years.)[25] Of a socially higher class was the Twenty Two Club, limited to a membership of 'some sort of position, not necessarily a big one, on the stage, and a public school or university upbringing'.[26] Its members Forbes Robertson, Charles Hawtrey, Arthur Bourchier and others would meet at Rule's Restaurant in Maiden Lane, which was also a haunt of Willy Clarkson and other theatricals.

Actors also favoured a range of high-class restaurants that emerged at the end of the century. In the London of the 1880s people still entertained in their own homes[27] but with the rise of the new theatres, and a livelier social life in the West End, large restaurants flourished, often in the same area. Theatres and

139

restaurants enjoyed a symbiotic relationship, audiences combining a visit to the theatre with supper and actors and actresses frequenting the restaurants as part of their social life. The Savoy opened in 1889 and the Carlton in 1899, both under the management of Cesar Ritz and with the most noted Grill Rooms in London. The Criterion Restaurant was part of the Criterion Theatre, remodelled in 1903. Charles Wyndham and Charles Frohman, the American impresario, would regularly lunch at the Savoy Grill at the 'Table of the Two Charles' during the latter's visits to London.[28] Going to the Savoy Grill became the mark of the successful actor and actress; it was the place to float ideas, arrange projects and celebrate triumphs.

The Pall Mall Restaurant was also a social focus for 'authors, artists, playwrights and the idle rich who having a flair for the theatre, sought introductions to Marie [Löhr] and Stella [Patrick Campbell].'[29] Gatti's Restaurant was run by two Swiss brothers who were the owners of the Adelphi and Vaudeville Theatres in the Strand and had a strong theatrical clientele,[30] while Romano's under Luigi Naintre was 'the centre of the town'. Fay Compton went there every day and the stars of the Gaiety had champagne drunk from their slippers by earls and maharajahs.[31]

III

These clubs and groupings focused on London were essentially for dining, relaxation and good fellowship. Serving the same purpose, if more strenuous, was the involvement of the actor in sports, and notably golf, both in London and the provinces. One of the problems, especially of the touring actor, was slack time during the day. Far from home and friends, in strange towns and lodgings and with too little to occupy leisure time before the evening performance, the unresourceful actor could too easily fall prey to lethargy or, still worse, to drink. Actors were often enjoined to 'cultivate some rational hobby'.[32] Golf filled the bill. During a tour in 1898 George Edwardes had the idea of encouraging his company out into the fresh air.[33] So successful was this that in 1903 a George Edwardes Golfing Society was formed with 100 members from Edwardes's various companies. This was not unique. On a tour of Peter Pan (probably sometime between 1905 and 1908) Barrie formed a Peter Pan Golf

Club for the 'health and morals' of the company, with trophies presented by himself and du Maurier (the original Captain Hook).[34] This does not seem to have lasted, but Edwardes's club was so flourishing that it was opened to the profession generally in 1908, and membership rose to 200. It is of interest to note that of 142 actors of surnames A–K inclusive in the Green Room Book of 1907 about a fifth (30) claimed golf as a recreation. An Inter-Theatre Shield was presented for competition by leading actor–managers Tree, Alexander, Hicks and others. After the First World War the Club, in keeping with its new catholicity, became the Stage Golfing Society. Throughout its history it was associated with various courses – Bushey Hall, Ashford Manor, Moor Park and Richmond Golf Club, where it is still based. Among the keenest and best players in its early days were the actors Owen Nares, Oscar Asche and Sir Gerald du Maurier, who gave the first President's Cup. A Stage Ladies' Golfing Society was formed in 1922 under the presidency of Sir Gerald's wife.

The value of this activity was well appreciated. Firstly, the decline of drunkenness among actors was chiefly attributed to golf.[35] Actors' Church Union chaplains introduced touring actors to local golf clubs[36] and by 1912 actors were advised that secretaries of almost every club in Britain were 'only too delighted' to welcome them to temporary membership in towns where they were working.[37] Secondly, golf helped to establish the actor as a gentleman; indeed the first resolution of the meeting creating the society in 1903 was that 'members should be expected to play golf like gentlemen'. The society played matches against other clubs, (The Guards, for example) while royalty, lawyers and politicians attended their annual dinner at the Savoy from 1929, all helping to assimilate the actor into respectability. Thirdly, golf obviously made the actor physically fit and helped co-ordination of movement, as did the fencing and dancing of his training. The 'matinée idol' good looks of Alexander, du Maurier and Owen Nares owed much to a physical tone acquired on the golf course.

To a lesser extent cricket, too, provided a focus for actors. The counterpart to the Stage Golfing Society was the Thespids' Cricket Club in London, of which the England cricketer Aubrey Smith and Owen Nares were stalwarts.[38] Wilson Barrett the actor–manager also

141

ran his own cricket eleven; this was so noted that W. G. Grace was kept informed of their fixtures and played for them when he could. This could be as useful for touring actors as golf. For example, the Nottingham Conservative Club offered hospitality to them, arranging local games of cricket and football.[39] All this sporting activity by actors found formal centralized expression in the establishment of an annual theatrical sports in 1903, with athletic and cycling events organized by Matheson Lang, Henry Ainley, Robert Loraine and C. Aubrey Smith[40] – all large, handsome men whose virile good looks and physical presence contributed much to their stage careers.

IV

With actors now moving more easily in fashionable Society, the rise of Society drama, a more discerning audience, the higher social origins, status and wealth of actors and actresses, so there arose an interrelationship between the worlds of the stage and fashion. Fashionable couturiers were employed to produce gowns for the stars equally wearable on stage or in the drawing room. In turn actresses, and the clothes they wore in plays, began to have an influence back on the off-stage fashions of the well-to-do. In an early example the dresses of Mary Moore (the later Lady Wyndham) as Roxane in a 1900 charity performance of *Cyrano* were made by Worth of Paris.[41] But these were essentially historical stage costumes. More important was the making of contemporary or near contemporary clothes for stage work. In 1883 Lillie Langtry ordered gowns in Paris from Worth for use on the stage, consciously using fashion as a drawing attraction.[42] Marie Tempest also broke from tradition by going to Parisian couturiers Doucet, Worth and Felix instead of to theatrical costumiers for her dresses in the 1890s. She was probably the first to use fashion houses so widely.[43]

Actresses at the St James Theatre were expected to dress for stage parts from the theatre wardrobe. Gladys Cooper, finding nothing appropriate to her taste and to her role in *The Importance of Being Earnest* in 1911, had her own dress made by Corot, with Alexander's concurrence.[44] Miss Cooper's action was by that date reasonable. Corot et Cie were already important couturiers for actresses, Marie Tempest, Iris Hoey, Dorothy Minto and Minnie Terry having their stage dresses made there.[45] Martial and Armand and Charles Lee were also fashion houses making stage clothes. *Era* noted in 1912 that 'it is behind the footlights that the new fashions make their début on both sides of the Channel'[46] in preface to a long description of Gladys Cooper's dresses in her current roles. Indeed, it was an indicator of this trend that *Era* in the 1900s and 1910s ran regular features on 'Dresses at the Play' and 'Fashions Across the Foot-lights'.

As fashion invaded a stage which reflected the modes of Society, so in turn the stage became a positive influence on the audience itself. *Era* saw clearly that it was 'an indisputable fact that the stage has a considerable influence upon the prevailing and future modes. The first performance of a Society play at a West End house serves to introduce gowns which are liberally reproduced in the illustrated papers, and copied by the dressmaker'.[47] There were indeed a number of instances of fashion change being influenced by theatrical example. Jessie Millward at the Adelphi in the mid-nineties deplored the 'hideous and exaggerated' fashion of leg-of-mutton sleeves. She appeared in a play wearing a dress of her choice with tightly-fitting sleeves and natural shoulders, which 'in a few weeks was the height of fashion'.[48] The V-neck blouse worn by Lily Elsie (*The Merry Widow*) was another influence on the style of upper garments.[49] In the early 1900s Constance Collier, while playing Roma in *The Eternal City* with Tree, wore a sable stole worth £1000, the first time furs had been made up into a stole. This attracted wide fashionable attention, indeed to the extent of prompting death threats from a maniac who demanded she sell it for the benefit of the poor.[50] In the mid-1900s Marie Tempest was credited with influencing Ascot fashions with a pannier dress worn in a play, and with making mustard yellow and furs fashionable in London. Always an impecc-able dresser, 'Marie Tempest set the fashions which were copied . . . she was a prophetess in dress.'[51] Marie Tempest also gave an impetus to fashionable headgear on stage by wearing the hats of Maison Lewis of Regent Street. Several actresses followed her, and 'Maison Lewis hats are becoming more and more popular behind the footlights.'[52] Underneath the hats actresses sometimes had an influence on hairstyles, notably the curl in the middle of the forehead which Gertrude Kingston claimed to have devised as 'Mrs

143

A Fashionable Actor in the Park (*Punch*, 22 July 1914)

Harkaway' in 1888.[53] Similarly, the fashion of wearing side-combs in the hair was copied from the actresses Zena and Phyllis Dare around 1910.[54] Some serious critics deplored 'the temptation to use the stage as a milliner's shop or a costumier's display room'[55] but audiences loved these delights to the eye as a legitimate part of the pleasures of theatre-going.

A sense of dress and fashion was important also for the male actor. Indeed, the phrase 'dress well on and off' was often used in job advertisements or applications. For the public appearance of the actor reflected not only his own standing but also that of his employer. The actor was warned against appearing in any way démodé, for 'many managers would far sooner have an inefficient actor of doubtful character in their company than a man who appeared off the stage in a frock or morning coat with brown boots'.[56] Since, in the naturalistic drama, stage and street clothes were the same, the fashionable and well-to-do actor patronized the best tailors, who in turn used their clients as informal models and the stage as a showcase. Dennis Bradley, the Bond Street tailor, was frank on this point: 'I have always regarded the stage as the ideal showroom and have for many years used it for the introduction of new styles.'[57] Perhaps the most important male stylistic change helped on by theatrical example was the modern collar and tie pioneered by Sir George Alexander. Nigel Playfair recalled going to Ascot with Alexander in the mid-nineties and the latter wearing 'the first example of the double collar, which is now so universal, and of which . . . I believe him to have been the inventor.'[58] By the 1900s Alexander had a distinctively modern – and comfortable – appearance compared with his fellows.[59] Indeed, he actually appeared in advertisements for flannel collars.[60] Few actors equalled Alexander in his concern for sartorial punctiliousness; his audiences and theatre were among the most fashionable in London. It was accordingly significant that his taste, in advance of its time, helped to establish twentieth-century norms.

V

Important as these sporting and social groups were, none was as widely embracing as the creation of a religious sub-culture within the

145

profession after 1890. In turn, few developments more strikingly indicated and contributed to the increasing respectability of the stage in this time. In the later nineteenth century church and stage viewed each other with a good deal of suspicion. This had long been so. In England the fusion of theatrical productions and religious exposition in the medieval mystery plays was sharply broken by Reformation puritanism and its subsequent Nonconformist tradition. The fierce hostility of the Puritans to the stage on the grounds of its frivolity and immorality seemed not unjustified in the light of the subsequent Restoration, with its licentious plays and actresses thought to be little removed from prostitutes.

This attitude continued well into the nineteenth century. Canon Liddon, in the 1880s, used to attack the stage from his pulpit, while a Methodist minister from Wigan, the Rev. R. Eardley, made an abusive attack which attracted attention in 1891.[61] The Bishop of London attacked Pinero's *The Gay Lord Quex* in 1900[62] and The Church Pastoral Aid Society called on incumbents to regard theatrical performances 'as a serious menace to the spiritual influence of the Church.'[63]

In this climate it took a somewhat eccentric clergyman to try to build a bridge of friendly concern between church and stage. The Rev. Stewart Headlam, a High Churchman and Socialist, had tried such an early venture with his Church and Stage Guild in 1879.[64] His experience in his parish in Drury Lane had brought him into contact with the theatre and ballet, and a lecture which he gave supporting the theatre and music halls in 1877 led to his sacking by Bishop Jackson of London. As if further to reassert his position, Headlam brought his Guild into being.

The aim of the Guild was to 'break down prejudice against theatres, actors, music hall artists, stage singers and dancers . . . to promote social and religious sympathy between Church and Stage' while rejecting the idea that the Guild was in any sense a patronizing mission to outcast actors. It attracted some 470 members within a year, including 172 theatrical members. Headlam was successful in recruiting the later Dames Madge Kendal and Genevieve Ward and (Sir) Ben Greet. Irving held aloof, partly because he was suspicious that clergymen regarded a 'mission' to the stage as an opportunity 'to lay hold of the humbler members of the profession to convince them

146

of the sinfulness of their calling.'[65] The Guild held social events, At Homes, dances, lectures (by Shaw and Poel among others), but it had its difficulties. Headlam was rather more interested in ballet and dancers than in actors, and so the legitimate stage gradually drifted away. His predilection for ballet, his support of Oscar Wilde and his Socialism and Anglo-Catholicism did not endear him to the authorities. He was also too active in other things, notably the London School Board and Fabian politics. Amid this hostility and distraction the Guild faded away by about 1900.

The importance of the Guild, however, was that it put forward the idea and suggested what might be done by less flamboyant, if better organized members. The idea was taken up and brought to fruition by the Rev. Donald Hole and his Actors' Church Union, created in 1898.[66] Hole had been a friend of Headlam and had attended meetings of the old Guild. Moreover, Hole's wife had been a touring child actress and her godmother was also on the stage. Through them Hole became aware of some of the difficulties of the touring actor's life, not least his isolation from parish-organized worship and the wider need of someone to turn to in trouble. The old Guild had not concerned itself with the touring players, but they were to be a special concern of the new Actors' Church Union. Membership did not imply communicant status in the church; the object was simply to get parochial clergy into touch with touring actors. In the Union's first report it described its function as 'for the purpose of organizing the work of the clergy more easily within the reach of members of the theatrical profession, whose lives are spent in travelling from place to place.'[67]

Lacking the antagonizing characteristics of the Church and Stage Guild, the new Union quickly gained support. Twelve centres were established in the first year where clergy were specifically willing to contact actors at the local theatre. One ex-actor priest, the Rev. R. T. Talbot of Sunderland, became Dean of Rochester. He was a keen supporter of the Union and the Bishop of Rochester became the patron, and then president of the organization. Hole thus acquired benevolent approval within the hierarchy, which Headlam had never enjoyed. For all that, Hole maintained a low profile. There was no great appeal to the church or the profession; they avoided self-advertisement, relying on becoming gradually known. The council

147

was 'impressed with the great necessity for caution and for making sure of its ground'.[68]

Prominent actors began to join – Cyril Maude, Ben Greet, Edward Compton, George Alexander, Forbes Robertson, Lilian Braithwaite, Lewis Waller and Edward Terry by 1902, to be joined by Ellen Terry, Charles Wyndham and Irene Vanbrugh in the following year.[69] Frank Benson and Martin Harvey had joined by 1905, so that the Union, within six years, had attracted a sizeable portion of the elite or emerging elite of the stage. The above names contained nine future knights and dames of the theatre. Links were forged with other organizations, for example Mrs Carson, the founder and secretary of the Theatrical Ladies' Guild, and Charles Cruikshanks, the secretary of the Actors' Association, also served on the committee of the ACU. Reciprocally, the AA invited the ACU secretary to its meetings.

The Union also began to discover gaps in the actor's life where it could be useful. It was clearly a problem that the role of the chaplain was somewhat loosely defined. For the non-religious actor the mere fact that a chaplain was available for keeping in touch could have little practical value. By the mid-1900s more tangible functions were being adopted. Chaplains started looking after sick actors left behind on tour, or others abandoned by bogus managers.[70] The most valuable service they began, however, was the list of theatrical lodgings, first published in 1909. For such tourers the lodgings list of the ACU was almost sufficient reason in itself for joining the Union. Most of the thrust of the Union had been in the provinces and in serving the touring actor, but from 1907 to 1910 it seemed to pay particular attention to extending its work in London. It was especially concerned with women, visiting lonely and ill actresses[71] and setting up fifty-four metropolitan centres, with social At Homes and a Conversazione at the Royal Victoria Hall held by Emma Cons and Lilian Baylis.[72] Even for the actor with only slight spiritual interests, the Union was setting out successfully to be a helpful and caring influence in their lives both in London and on tour.

Such activity had to fight against residual suspicion from the actors themselves. It was inevitable, after so long a period of anti-theatre feeling on the part of the church, that so swiftly growing a *rapprochement* should have aroused doubts in the minds of some

148

actors. In the context of a plethora of missions to down-and-outs, prostitutes, colonial heathens and the like, the Union could be misconstrued as classifying the actor as yet another outcast group. The Union was aware of this. At the outset it noted a 'lurking suspicion' that the Union was 'an attempt on the part of the Church to patronize the Stage, or that it implies that actors as a class are worse than other people.'[73] An Italian observer, for example, thought its object was 'to reclaim actors and actresses who have strayed from the right path'[74] and regarded the chaplains as a kind of moral police. Further sniping on these lines had to be endured from *London Opinion* and *John Bull*,[75] which suggested that it was all an excuse for arty curates to take tea with pretty actresses.

The Union thrived, as is indicated by the table below.

	Actor Members	Lay Associates	Chaplains	Centres
1899	5	–	13	12
1913–14	926	553	349	255 (1910–11)

As its work gradually became known, so from about 1904 actors flocked to join at the steady rate of about 100 a year. The lay associates were men who were prepared to help the chaplains 'by showing friendliness and hospitality to members of the profession visiting their towns'.[76] Part of the dynamic of expansion was provided not only by the willingness of actors to join and others to serve them, but also by the virtually uniform approval of theatre managers. The reports refer frequently to their support and their willingness to co-operate. Since it was clear that the chaplains were not clandestine trade-union organizers, they had little to lose. Indeed, the managers must have looked on the chaplains as very useful social worker allies, ready to shoulder awkward problems like the care of the sick and stranded and those without lodgings. Also, the managers were reassured that the Union and chaplains were not concerned to interfere with the moral tone of plays, or to pass judgement on them.[77]

The Union also spread its influence abroad. By 1913 it had centres in Paris, Brussels, Berlin, St Petersburg, Constantinople and Cairo, where British actors and entertainers appeared.[78] From 1907 Father

149

Cardew ran a Theatre Girls' Home in Paris, partly to prevent young British theatrical women being lured into the white slave traffic.[79] Edward Terry established the Union in Canada in 1910,[80] while the USA had its own independent Actors' Church Alliance, founded in 1899.

By 1914 it was possible for the Union to claim that 'the atmosphere of suspicion and misunderstanding which once existed between the Clergy and the Actor, is now almost entirely a thing of the past.'[81] The Union was now firmly entrenched playing a part, primarily spiritual indeed, but also social as an agency of welfare. Not least, it was one of the reinforcements of the respectability of the new breed of Christian, gentlemanly actor.

The Church and Stage Guild and the Actors' Church Union were Anglican institutions but both rather High-Church in leadership. To some degree this was a reaction against Puritan, Low-Church hostility to the stage. Anti-Puritans found it easier to come to an accommodation with it. Headlam was active in the Anti-Puritan League, while secretaries of the ACU used the Anglo-Catholic style 'Father'. If the concern to establish church and stage links tended to be a High- rather than a Low-Church concern, it was not surprising that Roman Catholics themselves should establish their own organization for Catholic actors.

Official Catholic opinion in the later nineteenth century was as suspicious of the stage as was Anglican. But in the wake of the Anglican initiative of the Actors' Church Union it was evident that in those non-ecumenical days the Catholic church would have to follow suit. An early, short-lived attempt was the Catholic Actors' Guild, founded by Charles Brookfield in 1908. Brookfield, a clergyman's son, had enjoyed a moderate acting career and was a minor playwright and sociable clubman.[82] He was also well-known for collecting evidence against Oscar Wilde. It was a curious irony that Headlam, the founder of one actors' religious society, was defending Wilde as Brookfield, the future founder of another, was attacking him. Brookfield acted as secretary of the new Guild, and George Edwardes of the Gaiety was the president. They seemed to gain strong initial support with a charity matinée at Dalys,[83] but the early Guild did not last, possibly due to Brookfield's lack of drive, and it had to be revived in a new form.

The modern Catholic Stage Guild was founded in 1911 by Ethelred St Barbe. She in turn seems to have been influenced by a Jesuit Father, T. Kelly of Preston, well-known in musical circles of that most Catholic town. The intention of both was to carry on an organization on lines similar to those of the Actors' Church Union, to help Catholic artists on tour and put them in touch with the clergy.[84] The Guild began to make an impact quite quickly, and by 1912 complaints about the 'new Romish Guild' posting its notices in theatres began to be made by Anglican chaplains.[85] This contrasts with the lack of impact of Brookfield's Guild in the provinces.

In London the Catholic Stage Guild held meetings at Sodality Hall in Farm Street, and some interesting points of difference from the ACU began to emerge. Firstly, some hoped that the Guild would take a positive line in trying to influence the moral tone and content of plays. Then beyond that it was hoped to use the stage as an instrument for the conversion of England.[86] The stage came in for some moral castigation at a meeting at the Bishop of Southwark's house in 1913 where the decadent nature of some theatre was condemned, notably the Max Reinhardt–Diana Cooper *The Miracle*, to which exception was taken.[87] The Guild was rightly, from its earliest days, making its moral position clear as an act of witness.

It must be admitted that in those times the Catholic church also viewed the stage more severely than High Anglicans did. Priests were not allowed to go to the theatre to see a play, which hindered their activities, and they were more reluctant to go to the stage door or backstage.[88] Bishop Keating, speaking at a session devoted to the Guild at the National Catholic Congress in Cardiff in 1914, referred to the church as the mother of drama. Mothers had to spank 'wayward if brilliant children' and he was 'afraid that most of the spanking had been in the dramatic profession'.[89] He stressed the need for more austerity in art.

This proper moral concern of the Guild, and its suspicion of some contemporary entertainment, led to a wish to provide good religious plays that would have a spiritually stimulating effect on audiences. In this positive activity too it differed from the ACU. Monsignor Benson urged Catholic actors to tour the country putting on old Mystery plays[90] and Patrick Kirwan, perhaps the most distinguished Catholic actor of the pre-1914 years, suggested the Coventry Nativ-

ity Play, which was performed with success in Westminster
Cathedral Hall in 1914.[91] Catholics also supported the Pioneer
Players who put on *Paphnutius* by Hroswitha, the Nun of Gander-
sheim, in the same year. The Pioneer Players were not exclusively
Catholic (Ellen Terry and her daughter were in the cast), but Patrick
Kirwan was again prominent here.

Apart from Kirwan, who was a distinguished man – a London
University civil engineer, actor-manager, lecturer in elocution at
various public schools and consultant to the London School Board –
the Guild did not contain many well-known names of the English
stage before 1914. For example, of the twenty lay members of the
first committee of 1912 only two, Mary Rorke and Harry Paulton
were at all well-known and listed in the Green Room Book of 1907.
This is not surprising; the theatrical elite tended to be English and,
whatever their religious views, espousal of the Anglican Church and
the ACU was the natural allegiance for those who saw religion as a
mark of respectability. Many members must have been Irish men
and girls coming to England to try their luck on the stage.[92] The
Guild thrived like its counterpart, as the secretary's figures
indicate:[93]

	actors	lay associates	priests
June 1913	337	112	500
September 1913	369	162	450
October 1913	393	172	500
July 1914	582	230	550

Within fourteen years from 1900, both Anglicans and Catholics
had created a rich sub-culture within the acting profession, and this
was to continue to flourish in the interwar years.

The actor playing his new real-life parts as churchman, clubman,
sportsman and man about town both reflected the higher social
origins from which he now came, and enhanced the image of the
profession itself. The coming War was soon to draw him into more
and unfamiliar, roles.

NOTES

1 Mario Borsa, *The English Stage of Today* (London, 1906), p.268.

2 George Rowell, *Queen Victoria goes to the Theatre* (London, 1978).

3 Cited by Percy Hutchison, *Masquerade* (London, 1936), p.58.

4 Fred Kerr, *Recollections of a Defective Memory* (London, 1930), p.180.

5 Sir Philip Magnus, *King Edward the Seventh* (London, 1964), p.173.

6 Sir Squire Bancroft, *Empty Chairs* (London, 1925), pp.1–14.

7 *Ibid.*, p.1.

8 F. K. Peile, *Candied Peel* (London, 1931), p.58.

9 Irene Vanbrugh, *To Tell My Story* (London, 1948), p.65.

10 A. E. W. Mason, *Sir George Alexander and the St James' Theatre* (London, 1935), p.124.

11 Sir John Martin Harvey, *Autobiography* (London, 1933), pp.226–7, 232.

12 Percy Hutchison, *op.cit.*, pp.65–6. Hutchison was Wyndham's nephew.

13 Constance Collier, *Harlequinade* (London, 1929), p.134.

14 Percy Fitzgerald, *The Garrick Club* (London, 1904), p.2; also Guy Boas, *The Garrick Club 1831–1947* (London, 1948).

15 Calculated from *Garrick Club Lists of Members* collated with MS Application Forms to the Club.

16 Calculated from Application Forms, Garrick Club 1890–3 and 1910–13 (Lawyers 21.7%; Gentlemen of leisure 16.7%; Army Officers 11.7%; authors and publishers 11.7%).

17 Compton Mackenzie, *My Life and Times, Octave 3 1900–07* (London, 1964), p.116.

18 R. L. Green, *A. E. W. Mason* (London, 1952), pp.161–2.

19 Basil Dean, *Seven Ages* (London, 1970), pp.282–3.

20 Basil Dean, *The Theatre at War* (London, 1956), p.32.

21 'The Green Room Club', *Era*, 6 September 1902. J. H. Barnes, *Forty Years on the Stage* (London, 1914), pp.80–1.

22 J. H. Barnes, pp.62–3.

23 T. Edgar Pemberton, *John Hare* (London, 1895), pp.169–70.

24 Fred Kerr, *op.cit.*, pp.226–8.

25 *Era*, 20 January 1912.
26 Kerr, *op.cit.*, pp.225–6.
27 Hector Bolitho, *Marie Tempest* (London, 1936), p.71, makes this point.
28 Percy Hutchison, *op.cit.*, p.196.
29 Winifred Fortescue, *There's Rosemary . . . there's Rue* (London 1939), p.67.
30 Jessie Millward, *Myself and Others* (London, 1923), pp.211–13.
31 Mario Gallati, *Mario of the Caprice* (London, 1960), pp.46–7.
32 H. B. Irving, 'The Calling of the Actor' in *Occasional Paper* (London, 1906), p.136, for example.
33 A. J. Evans, *The Stage Golfing Society 1903–1953*.
34 A. E. Matthews, *Matty* (London, 1952), p.142.
35 J. F. Graham, *An Old Stock Actor's Memories* (London, 1930) p.114.
36 *Annual Report of the Actors' Church Union* 1907–8. Report of the Wigan Chaplain.
37 Cecil Armstrong, *The Actors' Companion* (London, 1912), p.104.
38 Owen Nares, *Myself and Some Others* (London, 1925) pp.199–200.
39 *Era*, 24 August 1907.
40 *Era*, 26 June 1909.
41 Percy Hutchison, *op.cit.*, p.81.
42 James Brough, *The Prince and the Lily* (London, 1975), p.283.
43 Hector Bolitho, *Marie Tempest* (London, 1936), p.89.
44 Gladys Cooper, *Gladys Cooper* (London, 1931), p.69.
45 *Theatreland*, 29 January 1913.
46 *Era*, 3 February 1912.
47 *Era*, 24 February 1912.
48 Jessie Millward, *op.cit.*, pp.192–3.
49 Dodie Smith, *Look Back with Mixed Feelings* (London, 1978) p.28.
50 Constance Collier, *Harlequinade* (London, 1929), p.127.
51 Hector Bolitho, *op.cit.*, pp.150–1.
52 *Era*, 4 April 1908.
53 Gertrude Kingston, *Curtsey While You're Thinking* (London 1937), p.135.
54 Dodie Smith, *op.cit.*, p.4.

55 Louis Calvert, *Problems of the Actor* (London, 1919), p.216.
56 Cecil Armstrong, *op.cit.*, p.116.
57 *Era*, 7 April 1915.
58 Nigel Playfair, *Hammersmith Hoy* (London, 1930), p.163.
59 *Parts I Have Played* (Abbey Press, Westminster, 1909). A popular series of photographs.
60 Horace Wyndham, *The Magnificent Mummer* (London, 1911), p.18.
61 *Era*, 14 March 1891.
62 Mario Borsa, *op.cit.*, pp.21–2 for Liddon and the Quex incident.
63 E.F.S., *Our Stage and its Critics* (London, 1910), p.158.
64 F. G. Bettany, *Stewart Headlam* (London, 1926), pp.43–4 and Chapter X.
65 *Report of the Proceedings of the First Annual Dinner of the Actors' Benevolent Fund*, 1891.
66 Donald Hole, *The Church and the Stage, the early history of the Actors' Church Union* (London, 1934).
67 *Annual Report of the Actors' Church Union*, 1899.
68 *Ibid.*
69 *Annual Report of the Actors' Church Union*, 1901–2.
70 *Annual Report of the Actors' Church Union*, 1903–4.
71 *Annual Report of the Actors' Church Union*, 1908–9.
72 *Annual Report of the Actors' Church Union*, 1909–10.
73 *Annual Report of the Actors' Church Union*, 1900–1.
74 Mario Borsa, *op.cit.*, p.21.
75 *London Opinion*, August 1904 and *John Bull*, 27 July 1907, cited by Hole, *op.cit.*, pp.54–6.
76 *Annual Report of the Actors' Church Union*, 1899.
77 ACU Quarterly Paper, October 1916 in reply to William Poel, who wanted the Union to use its influence in this way.
78 *Annual Report of the Actors' Church Union*, 1912–13.
79 *Annual Report of the Actors' Church Union*, 1939.
80 *Annual Report of the Actors' Church Union*, 1910–11.
81 *Annual Report of the Actors' Church Union*, 1914–15.
82 Charles Brookfield, *Random Reminiscences* (London, 1902), and *Green Room Book* 1907, pp.47–8.
83 *Era*, 30 May 1908, refers to the CAG as having been established only a few weeks.

84 *Era*, 27 January 1912.
85 *Annual Report of the Actors' Church Union*, 1912–13, for example from Wigan.
86 *The Times*, 28 November 1911. Mgr R. H. Benson and Father Bampton.
87 *The Universe*, 3 October 1913. Patrick Kirwan.
88 *The Universe*, 3 October 1913. George Mozart and Father Kelly.
89 *The Universe*, 17 July 1914.
90 *The Universe*, 3 October 1913.
91 *The Universe*, 9 January 1914.
92 *The Times*, 28 November 1911. This was Father Bampton's experience.
93 *The Universe*, 13 June, 12 September, 3 October 1913, 10 July 1914. The American Catholic Actors' Guild began in 1914.

8 The First World War 1914–18

I

War between Britain and Germany was declared on 4 August 1914. This caught some theatre people by surprise. Sir Herbert Tree, who had been motoring in Belgium, crossed into Germany and, finding his ancestral fatherland at war-fever pitch, quickly returned to England.[1] Marie Tempest learned of the outbreak of hostilities while journeying to Dover (with twenty-two pieces of luggage) for a continental holiday. She abandoned her holiday and, declaring no interest in the War, departed for North America for the duration.[2] Fortunately, most actors reacted less self-centredly than this. Indeed, the War provided opportunities for the profession to prove its worth to the nation through service in many fields of activity.

The ethos of the army was initially far from favourable to actors. Roland Pertwee, on enlisting in 1914, was addressed by the sergeant-major:[3]

'What do you do for a living, Peewit?'
'I'm an actor, Sir.'
'For Gawd Almighty's Sake! Well, we want no acting here!'

Yet actors responded gallantly to the call to military service before the coming of conscription. Among those who volunteered within the first four or five weeks were Lewis Casson, Robert Loraine, Russell Thorndike and Felix Aylmer.[4] By the end of September 1914 170 actors had joined up,[5] but by June 1915 about 1000 actors had enlisted, some 10 per cent of the profession, and by the end of the next month some 1500 actors were with the colours.[6]

When conscription was introduced in 1916, actors enjoyed no special status. By the Restricted Occupations Order actors were

157

The Actor off to War (*Punch*, 17 November 1915)

classed as a non-essential occupation and not eligible for reserve. In practice, however, the conscription probably made little difference and was thought to affect stage staff rather than actors. At Ipswich, for example, it was reported that on the eve of conscription all the staff were women in any case, and only older men were still on the stage as actors.[7] From 1915 managers had been urged to employ only actors not fit for national service and to make this policy clear to audiences.[8] Scarcely any occupation was more vulnerable to public disfavour, and less able to conceal any clinging to civilian life, than the actor. It would have taken a young, fit actor of unusual temerity to continue appearing on stage before audiences of women in 1916, and most preferred not to remain in that position. Attempts by actors to obtain deferment on grounds of indispensability, or to fudge their ages, met with short shrift from Tribunals.[9] Voluntary enlistment and conscription led to a shortage of male actors which necessitated the substitution of women. For example, Sybil Thorndike at the Old Vic in wartime played several men's parts, including Prince Hal in *Henry IV* and Ferdinand in *The Tempest*.

Several actors already well known to theatre-goers, such as Godfrey Tearle, Lewis Casson and Henry Ainley, served with distinction, gaining commissioned rank. Henry Kendall, Ivor Novello, Laurence Irving and Ben Travers were all commissioned in the new Royal Naval Air Service, and knew each other well. A. E. W. Mason and H. B. Irving were both officers in Intelligence, while Cedric Hardwicke was one of the last officers to leave France at the end of the War. Other actors courageously bore injuries. Ernest Thesiger was about to be commissioned when his hands were smashed by a shell. He took up embroidery to facilitate his manual recovery, and ultimately became president of Queen Mary's Guild of Needlework. Herbert 'Bart' Marshall lost a leg and continued acting with an artificial one, while Leslie Banks's face was smashed, though this did not impede his successful film career. Several actors were decorated for gallantry. Richard Lambart won the first DSO in January 1915, and he was joined by Leslie Faber and Robert Loraine. Sir Frank Benson won the Croix de Guerre for his work in France, and Athol Stewart was the first actor to gain an OBE, for his Foreign Office work. The Military Cross was awarded to Lewis Casson, Basil Rathbone, Colin Keith-Johnston and Loraine again,

159

and the AFC to Henry Kendall. The sole Victoria Cross awarded to an actor was posthumously that to W. Dartnell in January 1916.

One form of civilian service for actors too old for the forces was the police. On the outbreak of war Sir Edward Ward persuaded Cyril Maude to form the Actors' Contingent of Special Constables, and between thirty and forty actors joined the scheme.[10] Many actors were enrolled at Bow Street. Sydney Blow recalled, 'It was not an uncommon sight to see half a dozen stellar attractions of the West End theatre at 2 a.m. making their way to Bow Street to go on duty from two o'clock until six in the morning.'[11] Actors also worked part-time in industry. In the early stages of the War, men from the Birmingham Rep used to go to the Birmingham Aluminium Casting Co. to make shell cases on Sunday mornings.[12] Reciprocally, after conscription, men on national work in Britain during the day could work in theatres after 6 p.m.

Keen, younger actors gained some early military instruction in the Artists' Rifles even before enlisting or being called up. There was a long pre-war tradition of actors' participation in voluntary military activity. There had been an Artists' Corps formed in the early 1870s as part of the Volunteer movement of that time,[13] and some thirty years later, around 1900, an Actors' Company was raised with about 120 volunteers.[14] This issue was revived yet again in 1909, partly stimulated by the highly patriotic anti-German play *An Englishman's Home*, produced at Wyndhams. Charles Ommaney, an actor who had served as an officer in the Boer War, proposed a military organization purely for theatricals.[15] He envisaged that touring actors would drill in whatever towns they were staying and would be expected to put in a certain number of parades a year. The idea caught on initially, with Ommaney claiming a large response and theatre-owners lending their theatres for patriotic displays by the theatrical Territorials and Boy Scouts.[16]

This cannot have lasted long since, as international relations deteriorated further, another initiative was made in 1911. In February Tree presided over a meeting at His Majesty's Theatre with the object of forming a theatrical branch of the National Service League. Now the movement attracted the support of high-prestige names. Lord Roberts was the main speaker and among the actors attending, as well as Tree, were Alexander, Maude, Aubrey Smith, and Robert

160

Loraine (a future Colonel DSO, MC). The need for the military training of volunteers for defence was stressed and a branch of the National Service League formed. It is interesting, as a reflection on the mood of the time and the synthesis of patriotism and theatricality, that the report of this in *Era* was juxtaposed to an article on 'Shakespeare's Patriotism'.[17]

The outbreak of war inevitably gave greater urgency and continuity to such endeavours. Accordingly the Artists' Rifles was formed for actors, musicians and artists, under the Presidency of H. B. Irving.[18] A regular sergeant-major was employed to teach drill and bayonet fighting to the members. The organization was not a regiment, and its voluntary members then passed to combatant units. It was, however, a useful form of pre-training and also a way in which those rejected from the forces on grounds of unfitness or age (like Benson) could get some military training that might be valuable later on.[19] Most important, it was a further gesture in which actors could be seen to be 'doing their bit' in the crisis.

II

The War inevitably had a marked effect on theatrical business and the nature of audiences. This was not immediately evident: there were large crowds in theatres on the Saturday night and the August Bank Holiday, when patriotic outbursts and songs marked performances.[20] However, only eight West End theatres were open,[21] not because of the War but because in those days most theatres (like the clubs) normally closed in the hottest part of the summer, when it was unfashionable to remain in London. In the autumn, however, by which time the season should have restarted, the theatre entered its blackest phase of the War. By September people had stopped going to the theatre, and theatres closed or did not reopen. Some 200 touring companies were also taken off the road.[22] Various reasons were given for this. Many people took the view that the sorrow and anxiety of the War rendered inappropriate the pursuit of pleasure at home, and that self-denial was a moral gesture of support for those suffering at the front. The King and Queen held this view and did not visit a theatre, save for charity benefits, during the whole of the War.[23] Their example must have been followed by many in the fashionable Society which provided much of the pre-war audience. Others would have found it distasteful in 1914–15 to applaud an actor who (they might consider) ought already to have volunteered to fight. Many may also have been afraid of the threat of air bombing, which was a serious reality in 1915.

Within a month or two of the outbreak of war the theatre and actors were in a poor state. In response to the crisis, *Era* started a War distress fund to help actors put out of work, which had raised £1062 by the end of 1914 and helped eighty-three actors. By the end of 1915 theatre business seemed not only to have revived but to be flourishing.[24]

In 1916 there was another potential threat to trade with the entertainment tax announced by Reginald McKenna on 4 April.[25] This, however, was no serious blow. Sir George Alexander and the managers had been consulted about it and regarded it as fair.[26] An indication of the healthy state of the theatre by the end of 1916 was the winding up of the *Era* distress fund, which under May Whitty's chairmanship had collected and paid out over £2000.[27] A greater blow was the new more severe entertainment tax, which came into effect in October 1917. This fell heaviest on the popular medium prices[28] and did have an initial effect in reducing business, many claimed by 25–30 per cent.[29] There were also restrictions on rail travel, which made it impossible to plan extensive tours.[30] The Board of Trade, who imposed this, also required theatres to close at 10.30 to save lighting and fuel.[31] This however had no serious long-term adverse effect, and by the end of the War theatre business was booming.[32]

It is evident that apart from the first two or three months, and the initial reaction to the entertainment tax in the autumn of 1917, the theatre was in a flourishing condition during the War. There were several reasons for this. Firstly, it was evident that most people did not continue to maintain the principle of abstaining from the theatre as a moral gesture of self-denial. On the contrary, theatre-going was increasingly welcomed as a proper relief from wartime strains and depression.[33] Secondly, the War brought a new prosperity to the working classes, shopkeepers and the like who benefited from the full employment, high wages and expanding activity of the war effort. Women's working also increased family incomes. Accor
162

dingly, theatre-going was one of the ways in which they experienced a raised standard of living. Thirdly, there was a concentration of population:

> London had now become a sort of gigantic clearing-house, troops passing through . . . men on leave from the front with their wives and relations; innumerable staffs of the gigantic Government departments – all these combined to form a totally different theatre-going public from that of the halcyon pre-war era.'[34]

This larger, pleasure-seeking population, concentrated on London and constantly changing, was ideal for theatre managers and actually better than the relatively static native population on whom they relied before the War. Many people who had not normally been theatre-goers now started attending to accompany their servicemen friends on leave.[35] Finally, many West End managers kept plenty of free seats for wounded soldiers.[36] The improved 'tone' of audiences was also welcomed, the Knut 'in immaculate evening dress, a cigarette and a snigger' was replaced by 'bronzed men with square jaws and shoulders'.[37]

If it was thought that the audiences had improved during the War, the same could not always be said of the fare presented to them. Many complained that there had been a complete decline in any serious purpose in the theatre and a retreat into frivolity. The War indeed initially posed a problem for actor–managers, who had to gauge the potential mood of audiences in the crisis. Alexander, in the early months, was advised by one of his play-readers, 'I doubt whether the War would make a difference, believing that there is little in the general view that at present people want frivolous, gay works . . .'[38] As the War progressed a little, the view of this adviser proved to be increasingly misguided. One observer commented in 1916: 'the drama for the time being may be said scarcely to exist, having been replaced by a species of inanity.'[39] *Chu Chin Chow* flourished, along with *A Little Bit of Fluff*, *Romance* and *Maid of the Mountains*, all of which exceeded 1000 performances. In this the London stage and that of Paris provided a sharp contrast with that of Berlin. London moved to the light and frivolous as a relief from and contrast to the War. In Germany, on the other hand, the serious work of Shakespeare, Goethe and Schiller held sway, in keeping

163

with the atmosphere and as a means of stirring national conscious ness and inculcating a sense of serious moral purpose.[40]

The War actually brought danger to actors and audiences at home. The Zeppelin bombing raids were a grave threat to people concentrated in a confined space, either inside a theatre or queueing, or dispersing after a show. Frederick Harrison, manager of the Haymarket, decided to have only matinée performances except on Saturday to avoid Zeppelin night raids: 'the more I think of the result of a bomb dropping on the audience, the more I dread the responsibility of having them there.'[41] To mislead the Zeppelins the parks of London were brilliantly lit and the streets left in darkness, which added to the hazards of theatre-going. The worst episode took place one evening in 1915 when a bomb fell in the Strand, affecting a number of theatres. It fell right by the Strand Theatre, where Fred Terry was playing in *The Scarlet Pimpernel*.[42] At the Duke of York's Owen Nares was playing a quiet love scene in *Romance* 'with a positive fusillade and crashing of bombs proceeding outside'.[43] The Lyceum was also hit and a call-boy from the Gaiety killed. The second serious incident in the West End came in the late summer of 1917, when a bomb exploded in Piccadilly Circus just as the theatres were emptying.[44] The dangers were by no means as great as those of the Second World War either for audiences or actors, but in a small way the theatre was made to share in the wider peril of the situation.

III

One of the most remarkable initiatives undertaken during the War by members of the profession was the Women's Emergency Corps. In a sense it was the wartime activity of the Actresses' Franchise League, which temporarily set aside its suffrage intentions and concentrated on war work. Within forty-eight hours of the outbreak of war leading figures in the AFL – Decima and Eva Moore, Lena Ashwell and Gertrude Kingston – formed the new Corps. The initial idea was to act as a clearing-house, receiving offers of help from women and allocating them to necessary war tasks. Gertrude Kingston lent it the Little Theatre as a base.[45] One of the founders remembered:

164

'Women enrolled in thousands; trained women were grouped into their proper classes and untrained women were questioned as to what they 'could do'. Weekly lists were sent to the War Office containing full particulars as to the numbers of women we could supply for transport, cooks, interpreters and so forth.'[46]

It quickly proved its worth. The Corps was the first body to deal with the Belgian refugees, finding hospitality, food and clothes. It sent women to training camps to teach French to soldiers, provided blankets for Serbia and canteens in France. It even provided a militant suffragist as a chauffeuse for Lloyd George. Most enterprisingly, it started a toy factory as a deliberate attempt to replace German pre-War dominance in this industry.[47]

This bustling activity outgrew the Little Theatre and it moved to Old Bedford College. Here one of the Corps' offshoots, the Three Arts Employment Fund, was run, under Naomi Jacob: 'We had workrooms, and admitted people who could prove they had been connected with Art, Music and Drama.'[48] In this way some of the theatrical unemployment of the early stages of the War could be absorbed and channelled into war work. Miss Jacob was also secretary to the toy-making department: 'By this time we had a factory, small but quite good, and a staff of about eighty girls, and a knitting department, making Balaclava helmets and things for the troops.' The Corps became 'enormous', and Bedford College was always seething with people.

So vital were the AFL and the Corps that they spawned several other activities and organizations. The AFL administered the *Era* War distress fund. Decima Moore and Eve Haverfield started the Women's Volunteer Reserve, ('Kitchener's Lizzies') the first women's army, long preceding the WAF and WAAC. In 1914 the AFL also founded the British Women's Hospital for sending hospital units to France, financed, maintained and staffed by women. It personally presented £50,000 raised for this directly to Queen Mary.[49] At home it restored the Star and Garter Hotel on Richmond Hill as a home for disabled servicemen, the origin of Star and Garter homes. It raised a further £150,000 for this.[50] Decima Moore also ran the Leave Club for troops in Paris.

As the War brought decorations and honours to actors for their

165

gallantry, so the first similar awards to actresses came for their charitable work during the War. Decima Moore received the CBE and Lena Ashwell the OBE. Most notable of all, Dame May Whitty became the first British actress to be awarded the DBE, in 1918. She was the ubiquitous 'Madame Chair' of the AFL, of the Women's Emergency Corps, The Three Arts Women's Employment Fund, The British Women's Hospital and much else. Though she was honoured not so much for her dramatic art (as Ellen Terry was soon to be) as for her public activities, May Whitty's DBE was a fitting tribute to the work of actresses as a whole in the War effort.

IV

One important dimension of the actors' service was in entertaining, and otherwise ministering to, the troops abroad. In the new style of static trench warfare entertainment was all the more vital to combat the boredom that could be as demoralizing as the danger. This was early appreciated, and the first party of actors was sent to France in December 1914 by the *Daily Telegraph*, including Seymour Hicks, Ellaline Terriss and Gladys Cooper.[51] Visiting the trenches, they 'played between Havre and Rouen, giving performance after performance in twenty-minute relays'. Most fell ill, and Hicks caught pneumonia.[52]

The chief responsibility of organizing entertainment in France, however, was that of Lena Ashwell, one of the founders of the Women's Emergency Corps.[53] As soon as war broke out she was trying to get the entertainment of troops nationally organized and a theatre in every camp. This met with blank refusal from a War Office which was actually abolishing military bands. Then in November 1914 the Princess Helena Victoria, who was President of the Women's Auxiliary Committee of the YMCA, used her influence with the War Office and invited Miss Ashwell to organize concert parties for France.[54]

The first concert party played at Le Havre in the first week of 1915. The work quickly expanded, with bases at Le Havre, Rouen, Boulogne and Amiens. There were permanent parties staying for up to six months at a base, and touring parties moving around the fighting area. By 1918 there were twenty-five concert parties operating in France and some 600 artists, including Ivor Novello and Edith Evans, had taken part. Most, however, would be fairly obscure, like 'the chap in brown . . . jaunty and lean and pale . . . some actor-bloke from town'[55] encountered at a concert by Siegfried Sassoon and immortalized in his poem 'A Concert Party'. Many artists gave their services free, though expenses could be paid, and off-stage they wore a YMCA uniform. On stage, however, the emphasis was on the brightest colours and the prettiest frocks, to boost morale. As Miss Ashwell finely said, 'In the services of the concert parties was the dear and intimate human love which brought back health of mind to lonely men.'[56]

From August 1915 they started taking out plays, notably the one-act plays of Gertrude Jennings, who organized the first dramatic party. After the early stages of the War there was a concern that the troops be given something more substantial than music hall and short pieces of music. More theatre parties went out in 1916 and, following requests for Shakespeare, Miss Ashwell took out a party to perform scenes from *Macbeth* and *The School for Scandal*. These were received appreciatively and the dramatic activity expanded. They started running repertory theatres – the Théâtre Albert Premier in Paris and theatres in Le Havre, Rouen, Abbeville, Etaples and Calais. These were organized by professionals like Penelope Wheeler at Le Havre and Cicely Hamilton at Abbeville, but the actors were serving soldiers. Miss Wheeler started this scheme at Le Havre in 1917. Now full-length plays of quality were produced – *Electra, Candida, The School for Scandal, The Merchant of Venice* and several others. John Martin Harvey, for example, went to France for Miss Ashwell in July 1917, proudly in his YMCA khaki, to 'shout Shakespeare in the midst of a rain of German shells'.[57] Cicely Hamilton described her arrangements at Abbeville:

The huts run by the YMCA were the usual scene of entertainments for the troops. There were several of these huts, six or eight at the least, in Abbeville itself and its immediate surroundings, besides others scattered more distantly about the area . . . Conveyance of the parties to the various destinations was by car, usually of the lorry type, into which was packed a party, its properties and

167

makeshift effects. Make-up and dressing would be got through
before starting.[58]

She was fortunate in having Leslie Banks as a leading man – in the
intervals of his duties as gas officer for Abbeville.

At home just before the ending of the War Miss Ashwell's
organization ran concerts and theatre on Salisbury Plain and in
Winchester, where large numbers of Americans camped before
embarking for France through Southampton. It also provided the
entertainment at Ciro's night-club now run by the YMCA for servicemen. This work did not cease with the Armistice, since demobilization took some time and troops remained in France, as well as in the
Army of Occupation on the Rhine. In 1919 Cicely Hamilton moved
to Amiens as a base and Lena Ashwell, having given up her Paris
theatre to the Americans, moved to the North East of France, to the
devastated industrial area. The Abbeville Repertory Company
moved to Belgium and then into Germany, where they had the
luxury of playing in real, and notable, theatres in Bonn and
Cologne.[59] They did not leave France until their services were no
longer needed to relieve the spirits of the last burial parties. On her
return, Miss Ashwell was honoured with the OBE.

The Bensons also did their bit in France, though not in entertaining. Constance became directress of a *Cantine des Dames Anglaises*
under the French Red Cross, and a staff of workers under Sir Frank
accompanied them:

'I was placed in charge of two canteens, one a station canteen, the
other, a *cantine des éclopés*, a kind of convalescent camp, where the
sick *poilus* are sent before returning to the front. I had also duties
in the hospital attached, and used to dress the wounds of those
poor fellows . . .'[60]

When they returned in 1918 Constance ran a recreation room at
Etaples. Benson himself went to drive a French ambulance in the
most dangerous conditions, rescuing wounded soldiers under fire in
the front line. He was awarded the Croix de Guerre for his bravery,
though it can have assuaged only a little the loss in 1916 of his son,
who had been the youngest colonel in the British army.

Another agency providing entertainment for troops was the

Entertainment Branch of the Navy and Army Canteen Board, under Basil Dean. Dean had acted with Miss Horniman, been director of the Liverpool Repertory Theatre, and worked in management for Tree. Knowing of his background his colonel asked Dean, then a young officer, to get up some shows for the men. A battalion concert party was formed after an inter-company competition. When the battalion moved to Aberystwyth for the winter of 1914/15, an entertainment unit was formed with some professional scenery, wigs and actresses. Generals at the camp approved the idea and demanded organized entertainment for all units in training. There was no shortage of funds. Catering contractors, who at that time ran canteens, paid large sums to regimental funds for soldiers' welfare, and these funds were usually embarrassingly flush. Dean secured approval for a plan by which battalions should make contributions from their funds to build camp theatres. The director of barrack construction was delighted to start theatre-building to designs devised by Dean, and Oswestry was the first garrison theatre so constructed. Sir William Pitcairn Campbell, GOC Western Command, was equally delighted and wanted more camp theatres, so Kinmel Park, Ripon and Catterick followed suit. It had all been done without War Office authority, internally financed from canteen funds. In 1917 this was formalized with the creation of the Army Canteen Committee and the Entertainment Branch of the Navy and Army Canteen Board.[61]

The Entertainment Branch ran its own companies for drama, musical comedy, revues and melodramas, each with its cast of actors and repertoire of plays. Sir Frank Benson toured the camps with his Shakespearian productions. Sydney Blow also worked for Dean: 'We organized musical comedy shows. At one time we had no less than nine Companies touring the camps and provincial towns. It was tremendously hard work writing and organizing under war difficulties.'[62] Dean's activities with the NACB aroused some ill-feeling from the commercial theatre outside. His shows were free of entertainment tax, the theatres could sell drink and they admitted civilians, which provided grossly unfair competition for local theatres nearby.[63] However, following consultations in November 1917, the Canteen Board agreed to restrict the entry of the public.[64] Starting from such casual, *ad hoc* beginnings Dean's initiative had been a remarkable one, and laid the foundations of the ENSA he was to direct in World War II. He was awarded the MBE for his services.

Other actors, especially the very young and the elderly, served at home by giving their talents free to service or distressed audiences. Eva le Gallienne, then only a young beginner:

> 'like all the other people of the Theatre tried to help do my bit by taking part in countless entertainments for the wounded, for the Belgian refugees, of whom there were many thousands in a huge camp at Earls Court, and for young recruits in the training centres.'[65]

Charles Hawtrey performed variety in hospital wards, where his optimistic, pleasure-loving personality was badly needed.[66] Bransby Williams undertook a lot of hospital entertaining, while the Eccentric Club, of which he was a member (with actors like Wyndham and Bancroft), entertained the wounded at the club every Sunday evening.[67] The elderly Bancroft, who had used his retirement to give Dickensian readings in and on behalf of hospitals, now resumed his charitable monologues to the wounded. Troops returning from the front to Waterloo Station would also be greeted by entertainments.[68] As the YMCA had been a chief purveyor of entertainment in France, so too their Shakespeare Hut in Gower Street was an important focus in London. Here as yet unrepatriated Anzac soldiers were treated, in early 1919, to an unusual double bill of Ellen Terry as Portia and a group of children, led by Fabia Drake, in *Henry V*.[69] Miss Drake was a juvenile student at the Academy of Dramatic Art at the time. It was the Academy's policy to have its students provide camp and hospital entertainments rather than fund-raising public performances.[70]

V

Just as the profession had arranged its own charities so effectively, so they turned their special talents for touching heart- and purse-strings in service of the War effort. In this the actors' own generosity matched that of those they solicited, and this brought great prestige to the stage. On the outbreak of war Mrs E. S. Willard started an Actresses' First Aid and Nursing League which provided four beds for wounded men,[71] while Mrs Martin Harvey gave her Isle of Wight cottage as a hospital.[72] Tree and *Era* also ran a scheme to raise funds to buy cigarettes for the troops.[73]

1915 was a great year of charity matinées. The Boer War had already provided recent experience in this form of activity. In that war actors had run twenty-four charity matinées and raised funds for an Actors' Hospital for the troops.[74] In 1915 there was a huge benefit performance at His Majesty's Theatre, organized by Constance Collier for the Red Cross: 'The best-known stars of the London stage took part in it.'[75] In February there was an 'Entente Matinée' in the same theatre featuring leading lights of the French and British stages, and in July one at the Haymarket in aid of Invalid Kitchens, attended by Queen Alexandra. These were but a few among a plethora of activities.[76] In the spring of 1915 there were charity matinées on four afternoons a week on average, and by August 1915 it was estimated that £1 million had been raised.[77] From August 1914 to the end of 1915 matinées at His Majesty's Theatre had raised £7500, and Howard and Wyndham had raised 'huge sums' by providing theatres free for matinées.[78] Indeed, so flourishing were these charity matinées that they were thought to be harming the commercial theatre. Tree, who had been most generous with His Majesty's Theatre, complained that theatres and performers' services were given free for these charity performances, but the public going to them were commensurately not going to normal commercial performances in the evening.[79] The sacrifice of actors and theatre-owners was thus twofold.

Some actors and actresses carried on valuable private initiatives. Ellaline Terriss (Mrs Seymour Hicks) raised £25,000 for disabled soldiers.[80] The Eccentric Club, under the Presidency of Sir Charles Wyndham, raised money for a hostel in Soho Square with wards named after Lady Wyndham and Vesta Tilley.[81] Mrs Martin Harvey raised £30,000 for Lord Roberts's Workshops for the Wounded and, as a result of appeals from the stage, an undisclosed sum that bought 'a small army of ambulances'. She raised enough surplus money to be able to buy a villa in the Isle of Wight (near her cottage, already given as a hospital) which was made into a Seaside Cottage Home for Nurses, especially those worn out by the War.[82] Sir Oswald Stoll was also noted for his generosity, having raised nearly £20,000 by the

171

end of 1915. He ran the War Seal Foundation, one of whose most spectacular enterprises, with the support of the railway fraternity, was a vast concert in the Great Hall at Euston, in which Sir George Alexander took part.[83] Finally, Bransby Williams (whose son was a captain and MC) raised £3000 for blind servicemen by his recitals.[84]

Actors were inevitably drawn into propaganda work for the War effort. Some actors made patriotic speeches or recitations on their own initiative. Lt Philip Ridgeway, who claimed to have been the first actor to enlist on the first day of the War, when invalided out devoted himself to making recruiting speeches in theatres, while Ion Swinley would recite 'The Flag' by Kipling as a patriotic curtain-raiser before the play.[85] Lewis Waller addressed recruiting meetings in Hyde Park,[86] and Sir Frank Benson would appear on variety stages in a programme of patriotic and martial pieces from Shakespeare entitled 'Shakespeare's War Cry'.[87] Probably no actor was more enthusiastic about this kind of activity than Sir John Martin Harvey. In the towns where he toured he would stage a special Sunday evening event of war lectures and patriotic music, supported on stage by civic and military dignitaries, and actually induced young men to file up on stage to enlist there and then.[88] He continued this work for two years, earning the thanks of Asquith and Lloyd George.

An attempt was made to provide formal governmental support and direction for whole productions that could be used to good propaganda effect. A committee was formed under the Ministry of Information for propaganda in theatres and music halls. One manager took a rather jaundiced view of this:

> By December [1914] the Government had put in hand its manu-
> facture of War plays. One Department devised the idea, another
> offered the plays to the poor, unsuspecting, long-suffering mana-
> gers whose intelligence had to give way to patriotism.'[89]

Arthur Croxton of the Coliseum, whose comment this was, thought that the Coliseum got the best of the war propaganda plays. He and half-a-dozen dramatists were invited to write plays to be presented at the Coliseum for the Government Economy Committee. For exam-ple, one of Alfred Sutro's was to persuade the now more affluent working classes to invest in War Loan Certificates. The cast included

172

Athene Seyler, whose character had to give a tirade against spending on luxuries and in favour of saving and Certificate buying.[90] Later in the War, Beaverbrook changed his policy and decided to use the cinema rather than the theatre for propaganda.[91] One of the products of this policy was a 1917 film, *Everybody's Business*, starring Gerald du Maurier and Matheson Lang, dealing with food economy.[92]

As well as these government-sponsored plays and films, now of little note, the ordinary commercial theatre produced plays of unmistakable patriotic or moral content. For example, Tree ran *Drake* with great success in 1914. Also of special note were *The Bells of St Valoir* and *My Friend Thomas Atkins* – 'all with a genuine War flavour, all written to encourage and stimulate a patriotic feeling'.[93] Perhaps the most notable war play was Barrie's *Der Tag* in 1914, starring Irene Vanbrugh as Culture berating the Emperor. Certainly the most powerful moral play was Eugene Brieux's *Damaged Goods*, the famous warning against venereal disease, especially salutary for the troops. By coincidence the censor had lifted his ban on Ibsen's *Ghosts* in the spring of 1914, which enabled wartime productions of the play to depict the same problem.

Actors did not express their anti-German feeling only through such plays but even carried it into their rejection of German makeup. As the Germans had been predominant in the world manufacture of all kinds of chemicals, from dyes to drugs, so Leichner was the leading and original greasepaint. With the War this came to be regarded as unacceptable, as well as unobtainable. As early as 26 August Willy Clarkson declared he would no longer sell German makeup; instead he offered Goulding's, which was British and in every way superior.[94] Boots immediately set their laboratory staff on to the problem and rushed out their 'All British Grease Paint' by December 1914.[95] By 1916 Hovenden's British Grease Paint, endorsed by Martin Harvey, was also on the market.[96] In this, as in many other ways, the discontinuation of German science-based products belatedly forced British industry to find substitutes it could well have devised before. Leichner's did not begin readvertising their wares in *Era* until 1922, when some of the hostility to all things German had abated a little. Then it had to face competition from Max Factor, which came into England from 1927.

The contribution of actors to propaganda was not confined to activities at home. During his visits to America, Sir Herbert Tree would produce his popular success *Colonel Newcome* as a patriotic vehicle for arousing American sympathy for the British war effort. This was taken quite seriously. Lloyd George and Balfour both wrote to Tree thanking him for his contribution in winning American support, and the *New York Times* termed him 'unofficial ambassador extraordinary'.[97] Ivor Novello played a similar role in Sweden. Although Sweden was a neutral country and pro-British, German attitudes and entertainers dominated their popular entertainment. Accordingly Ivor Novello, already the composer of 'Keep the Home Fires Burning' and a naval officer, was sent with a small band of entertainers to redress the balance in 1918. 'Ivor Novello became a species of ambassador . . . and he succeeded completely.'[98]

As the War ended, the authorities were as loth to let the actor go as they had been to grant any deferment. Actors were No. 41 in precedence on the list of occupations due for demobilization. They were somewhat disadvantaged in that preference in the return to civilian life was given to servicemen 'with definite employment awaiting them'.[99] Actors could have no such specific employer awaiting their release, indeed in that respect actors were more like self-employed businessmen. They, at least, were more fortunate than those already released from the War by death. The profession had a right to feel proud of its record in the War, and commemorated its fallen with due solemnity and dignity. A Roll of Honour containing the names of forty-two actors, musicians and writers who had been killed was erected over the stage door of the Old Vic. It was unveiled by the Bishop of Southwark and the names were solemnly read aloud by Lewis Casson.[100] In February 1919 the Catholic Stage Guild held a service for actors killed in the War. A memorial was dedicated by the Bishop of London at Drury Lane, and a great service organized by the Actors' Church Union was held in Westminster Abbey on 18 February 1919.[101]

The mood soon changed. Just as the outbreak of war had seen Sir Herbert Tree quickly motoring back from Germany, so its ending was marked by a riotous Armistice night which neither Tree nor Alexander lived to see. It was, however, enjoyed to the full by a fearsomely precocious nineteen-year-old Noel Coward, who celebrated by driving to the Savoy in a Rolls Royce with two wealthy Chilean men friends.[102] The twenties had arrived.

NOTES

1 *Era*, 5 August 1914.
2 Hector Bolitho, *Marie Tempest* (London, 1936), p.165.
3 Roland Pertwee, *Master of None* (London, 1940), p.141.
4 *Era*, 9, 16 September 1914 for first two lists of volunteers.
5 *Era*, 30 September 1914.
6 *Era*, 28 July 1915.
7 *Era*, 24 May 1916.
8 *Era*, 23 June 1915.
9 Lou Warwick, *The Mackenzies called Compton* (Northampton, 1977), p.267 for some cases.
10 Cyril Maude, *Behind the Scenes* (London, 1927), p.246. *Era*, 12 August 1914.
11 Sydney Blow, *The Ghost Walks on Fridays* (London, 1935), pp.151–2.
12 J. C. Trewin, *The Birmingham Repertory Theatre* (London, 1963), p.36. Photograph, p.17.
13 Sir Johnston Forbes Robertson, *A Player under Three Reigns* (London, 1925), p.61.
14 *Era*, 27 February 1909.
15 *Era*, 13 February 1909.
16 *Era*, 20 March 1909.
17 *Era*, 11 February 1911.
18 Laurence Irving, *Precarious Crust* (London, 1971), p.241.
19 J. C. Trewin, *Benson and the Bensonians* (London, 1960), pp.209–10.
20 *Era*, 5 August 1914.
21 *Era*, 12 August 1914.
22 Eva Moore, *Exits and Entrances* (London, 1923), p.80.
23 *Era*, 9 September 1914. The King declined a request from the Actors' Association to continue theatre-going.
24 *Era*, 22 December 1915.
25 *Era*, 12 April 1916.
26 *Era*, 19 April 1916.

27 *Era*, 22 November 1916.

28 *Era*, 19 September 1917.

29 *Era*, 7 November 1917 presented two pages of reports from theatres around the country.

30 *Era*, 20 December 1916.

31 *Era*, 3 April 1918.

32 *Era*, 11 September 1918.

33 Ronald Adam, *Overture and Beginners* (London, 1938), p.60.

34 W. H. Leverton, *Through a Box Office Window* (London, 1932), p.221.

35 *Era*, 15 November 1916. Comment by George Robey.

36 Henry Kendall, *I Remember Romano's* (London, 1960), p.26.

37 *Era*, 6 February 1918.

38 Sir George Alexander's Papers. Letter, E. F. Spence to Alexander, 18 February, 1915.

39 G. T. Watts, 'The Tradition of the Theatre', *The Englishwoman*, November 1916.

40 *Era*, 22 March 1916. H. R. Barbor, *The Theatre An Art and an Industry* (London, 1924), p.10, points this contrast.

41 Sir George Alexander's Papers. Letter, Frederick Harrison to Sir George Alexander, 17 October 1915.

42 Marguerite Steen, *A Pride of Terrys* (London, 1962), p.315.

43 Owen Nares, *Myself and Some Others* (London, 1925), pp.172–4.

44 *Ibid.*, p.184.

45 Gertrude Kingston, *Curtsey While You're Thinking* (London, 1937), p.191.

46 Eva Moore, *op.cit.*, p.74.

47 Lena Ashwell, *Myself a Player* (London, 1936), p.183.

48 Naomi Jacob, *Me* (London, 1933), pp.117–19.

49 Eva Moore, *op.cit.*, pp.77–8.

50 Margaret Webster, *The Same Only Different* (London, 1969), pp.252–3.

51 *Era*, 17 March 1915.

52 Gladys Cooper, *Gladys Cooper* (London, 1931), pp.100–1.

53 Lena Ashwell's accounts of her wartime entertainment activities are in her books *Modern Troubadours* (London, 1922); *The Stage* (London, 1929), pp.142–51; *Myself a Player* (London, 1936), pp.194–223.

54 *Modern Troubadours*, p.6.
55 Siegfried Sassoon, 'A Concert Party', April 1918.
56 *Myself a Player*, p.199.
57 Sir John Martin Harvey, *Autobiography* (London, 1933), p.481.
58 Cicely Hamilton, *Life Errant* (London, 1935), p.138.
59 *Ibid.*, p.183.
60 Constance Benson, *Mainly Players* (London, 1926), p.292.
61 Basil Dean, *The Theatre at War* (London, 1956), pp.22–9.
62 Sydney Blow, *op.cit.*, p.151.
63 *Era*, 17 October 1917.
64 *Era*, 21 November 1917.
65 Eva le Gallienne, *At 33* (London, 1934), p.87.
66 Sir Charles Hawtrey, *The Truth at Last* (London, 1924), p.314.
67 Bransby Williams, *Bransby Williams* (London, 1954), pp.134, 150.
68 Irene Vanbrugh, *To Tell My Story* (London, 1948), p.110.
69 Fabia Drake, *Blind Fortune* (London, 1978), pp.36–7.
70 Letter, Kenneth Barnes to Viscount St Cyres, 5 March 1915.
71 *Era*, 12 August 1914.
72 *Era*, 19 August 1914.
73 *Era*, 25 November 1914.
74 Gertrude Kingston, *op.cit.*, pp.169–70.
75 Eva le Gallienne, *op.cit.*, pp.87–8.
76 *Era*, 27 October 1915.
77 *Era*, 25 August 1915.
78 *Era*, 1 December 1915.
79 *Era*, 28 July 1915.
80 *Era*, 6 October 1915.
81 *Era*, 8 August 1917.
82 Sir John Martin Harvey, *op.cit.*, pp.449–51.
83 Arthur Croxton, *Crowded Nights and Days* (London, 1934), pp.371–4.
84 Bransby Williams, *op.cit.*, p.67.
85 *Era*, 2 September 1914.
86 *Era*, 30 June 1914.
87 *Era*, 17 January 1917.
88 Sir John Martin Harvey, *op.cit.*, p.448.
89 Arthur Croxton, *op.cit.*, p.233.

90 Alfred Sutro, *Celebrities and Simple Souls* (London, 1933), pp.268–9.
91 Lena Ashwell, *Modern Troubadours* (London, 1922), pp.190–1.
92 *Era*, 30 May 1917.
93 Arthur Croxton, *op.cit.*, p.233.
94 *Era*, 26 August 1914.
95 *Era*, 2 December 1914.
96 *Era*, 22 March 1916.
97 Hesketh Pearson, *Beerbohm Tree* (London, 1956), p.231.
98 W. MacQueen Pope, *Ivor* (London, 1951), pp.148–9.
99 *Era*, 18 December 1918.
100 Winifred Isaac, *Ben Greet and the Old Vic* (London, 1964), p.148.
101 *Era*, 19 February 1919.
102 Noel Coward, *Present Indicative* (London, 1937), p.116.

9 Continuity and Change 1919–39

Between the two wars the actor experienced both a continuity of certain developments already evident before 1914 and several significant changes. The two most important new features were the rise of the new media of film and broadcasting, with the fresh opportunities they provided for the actor, and the revolution in actors' trade unionism that led to the creation and consolidation of Equity. These matters are of such importance that subsequent chapters are devoted to them. Before dealing with these, we need to focus on various other features. In the interwar years there was remarkable stability in the number of actors compared with the surge of the pre-1914 years. There was also little change in the social and educational origins of actors, with professional and commercial family backgrounds being maintained. By contrast, there were important changes in what went on on-stage. The old generation of actor–managers were replaced by businessmen theatre-owners, which entailed the emergence of the professional director, who took over the stage direction functions of the actor–managers. In both ways the actor was placed in a subordinate position, commercially subordinate to entrepreneurs who were not actors and artistically subordinate to the director, who controlled his performance. Acting style too changed, from the full-blooded and rhetorical to a quiet, muted conversational naturalism fitted for the drawing-room play. If the actor seemed to be more limited by these changes, he certainly became better prepared for his task in the interwar years. Drama education, already firmly established before 1914, continued to flourish, with an expansion of schools and students. Most importantly, the involvement of the University of London in creating a

179

Diploma in conjunction with RADA and the Central School sought to place drama training on a higher, more academic, professional basis. Finally, actors continued to enjoy their rewards of success in a flourishing social life carried on in a plethora of restaurants, night-clubs and private houses that gave a distinctive tone to the smart society of the twenties and thirties.

I

Following the sharp rise in entrants to the profession in the generation before 1914, the position stabilized in the interwar years. In 1921 there were 8166 actors and 9433 actresses recorded in the census for England and Wales, and in 1931 8210 actors and 9620 actresses. There was no census in 1941, but the stability of the 1920s continued in the 1930s. This is suggested by the constancy of Equity membership, which was around three or four thousand from the mid-1930s. Equity's operation of the closed shop in London, and its keeping of the amateur off the stage in the 1930s, prevented the surge in numbers that had characterized the 1890s and 1900s.

There was also a fair continuity in the social origins of actors. We saw in Chapter 1 the considerable change in family backgrounds from which recruits to the profession came before 1914. They came less from theatrical, and more from a respectable professional and commercial, milieu. The pattern established by 1914 was largely retained through the 1914–45 period.[1] The predominant back-ground from which players came was still professional, just under half of actors' fathers and just over half of actresses' fathers being of this social class. There was also an increase in players coming from higher commercial and industrial backgrounds and a slight decrease overall of those coming from the artistic, literary and theatrical occupations. 18.9 per cent of actors and 18.5 per cent of actresses of this 1914–45 generation had fathers who were also actors. This compares with respective percentage figures of 15.9 per cent and 17.7 per cent for the 1890–1913 generation. The overall picture that emerges is much the same as that of 1890–1913, without the sharp changes that characterized the increasing respectability of late Victorian and Edwardian times. Above all this 'respectability' of comfortable social origins was maintained in the interwar years. It

180

1   Sir Henry Irving, *c*. 1900

2   Sir Herbert Beerbohm Tree, 1907

3   Sir Johnston Forbes Robertson in the film of *Hamlet*, 1913

4   Sir Godfrey Tearle
the first president of Equity

5   Elsie Fogerty, *c*. 1935

6 Sir Kenneth
Barnes and RADA
students, 1935

7   Ralph Richardson and Laurence Olivier
with the Old Vic tour in Hamburg, 1945

8   An Equity
meeting on the film
industry, 1951

was still a profession that children from a working-class background found very difficult to enter, even if it occurred to them to try. Accordingly there was a certain social homogeneity about it.

The social origins of the legitimate actors and actresses with whom we are concerned were also reflected in their educational background. Using the classifications explained in Chapter 1 the educational experience of actors and actresses starting work in the 1914–45 period was as follows, with the 1890–1913 figures for comparison:

	Actors from 'public schools'		Actors who had attended university
	'The Nine'	Honey/Gathorne-Hardy	
Starting 1890–1913	$\frac{44}{260}$ 16.9%	$\frac{143}{260}$ 55.0%	$\frac{69}{260}$ 26.5%
Starting 1914–1945	$\frac{40}{335}$ 11.9%	$\frac{158}{335}$ 47.2%	$\frac{81}{335}$ 24.2%

	Actresses from 'notable schools'	Actresses who had attended university
Starting 1890–1913	$\frac{10}{95}$ 10.5%	$\frac{3}{97}$ 3.1%
Starting 1914–1945	$\frac{15}{211}$ 7.1%	$\frac{15}{211}$ 7.1%

There was little change over the two periods, other than a slight fall in the public-school element in the actors. The striking new feature, however, is the increase in actresses who had been to university. In fact, as many had been to university as had been to 'notable schools'. This was a sharp change from the 1890–1913 group and suggests that among the 1914–45 generation of actresses 'brains' was becoming as important an element as 'breeding'. By and large, the social and educational backgrounds of actors and actresses displayed more characteristics of continuity and similarity with the immediate pre-1914 years than serious change. Changes were to be more marked in the post-1945 years.

II

If we turn from the actors to the context of the theatre in which they worked, changes become much more apparent. A major change affecting the actor in the immediate post-war years was the control of the theatres themselves. The old actor–managers, as a generation, were disappearing. Lewis Waller died in 1915, Sir Herbert Tree in 1917, Sir George Alexander in 1918, Sir Charles Wyndham in 1919. Hare and Bancroft were retired. Hawtrey and Maude still acted, but not as actor–managers, while Matheson Lang, Martin Harvey, Fred Terry and Sir Frank Benson were largely provincial tourers rather than London actors. The actor–manager in London was now much more of a rarity. Gerald du Maurier and Gladys Cooper both worked as actor–managers but significantly both in conjunction with a businessman, Frank Curzon. The leading managerial figures of the twenties – Sir Alfred Butt, Frank Curzon, André Charlot, the Gattis, Frederick Harrison, Lady Wyndham and Bronson Albery, Sir Oswald Stoll and George Dance – were no longer, or (mostly) never had been, actors. They at least were ladies and gentlemen of the theatre of some standing. But to them was added another element.

They were being joined (and the actors replaced) by commercial businessmen, often having little artistic contact with the theatre:

> Businessmen who had suddenly grown rich by supplying War material to the Government, and owners of shipping whose shares showed fantastic appreciation, began to dabble in theatres . . . theatrical syndicates had been formed to buy up every theatre as it came on the market.[2]

For instance, Tree's lease of His Majesty's Theatre was bought up by Joseph Benson, the Liverpool nitrate king.[3] Part of the problem was the sharp rise in the cost of renting a theatre. On one estimate, theatres that had cost £75 a week to rent before 1914 now fetched £450–£500,[4] and these high costs often drove those actors who may have preferred to operate as old-style independent actor–managers into partnership with syndicates and businessmen. Owen Nares noted that 'the deadly list of expenses . . . forces an actor to secure the support financially and otherwise of a syndicate.'[5] Sometimes these arrangements could be quite satisfactory. Frank Curzon, for

182

example, was a financial commercial partner in management with du Maurier, Gladys Cooper, Hawtrey and Marie Tempest at various times. Nares was happy in his similar commercial–artistic relationship with Sir Alfred Butt, though he had less satisfactory experiences with others as did Godfrey Tearle, who severed connections with a syndicate which had been supporting his efforts as an actor–manager in the 1920s.

The new dominance of commercial interest aroused fierce opposition from within the theatre. Oscar Asche attacked the syndicates for their lack of artistic ideals or genuine interest in actors or the theatre.[6] Others deplored the fact that the replacing of actor-managers by syndicates had resulted in the abandoning of fixed policy styles by theatres.[7] Thirdly, the syndicates replaced the artistic judgement and control of the individual with an impersonal board whose only aim was moneymaking.[8] There were some beneficial new entrepreneurs, notably Stewart Cruikshank, a former builder and contractor, who built up Howard and Wyndham Ltd, with its excellent chain of provincial theatres. In London the period saw the rise of H. M. Tennent Ltd and Harry Tennent's manager, Hugh Beaumont. Yet many actors regretted that the new control of the theatre had largely passed from actors to businessmen from outside the profession.

This was reflected in the incidence of public honours. Before 1914, knighthoods tended to be awarded to actor–managers. After 1918 they continued to be given to actor–managers – Martin Harvey (1921), Gerald du Maurier (1922), Charles Hawtrey (1922), Nigel Playfair (1928), Ben Greet (1929) and Seymour Hicks (1935); but also to impresarios who were not actors – Oswald Stoll (1919), George Dance (1923), Alfred Butt (1918), Barry Jackson (1925) and John Gatti (1928). The logic of the situation suggested that eventually a knighthood would be given to an actor who was not an actor–manager. Such was Sir Cedric Hardwicke's accolade in 1934, the first to an actor, *pur sang*. It was a small watershed recognizing the changed conditions of the theatre over the previous decade.

One of the major changes in relationships affecting the actor in the 1920s was the rise of the producer or director. In the old stock companies an actor, especially playing in classics, was expected to 'know his business', as the phrase was. That is to say, he would

183

know the traditional moves, ways of speaking or gestures of a Polonius or Anthony Absolute, picked up apprentice fashion from watching others doing it over the years. Any advice from outside would be resented as a slur on his professional competence, as if he did not know his lines. Stage 'business' was part of the actor's stock of craft knowledge.[9] Under the actor–manager system the actor had to take direction whether he liked it or not. The actor-manager himself directed, or in the word of the time 'produced', the plays of his company, usually with a 'stage manager' as an assistant. Others elicited the advice of the author, which in itself was a step towards the emergence of the outside director. Cyril Maude noted: 'We actor-managers all stage-managed our own plays. We were nearly always aided in our work of production by the author of the play and by our stage managers.'[10] Pinero, Barrie and Shaw were especially keen to direct their own plays in conjunction with the actor–manager.

After the War the producer or director emerged much more clearly as an independent force. There were two main reasons for this. First, the actor–managers had largely disappeared and, since they had done their own direction, this left a serious gap. Moreover his entrepreneurial functions had been assumed by syndicates or financial backers. They often had little artistic expertise and so needed an intermediary between themselves and the cast, and someone to take the rehearsals and the overall responsibility for the production. Second, the technical aspects of production were becoming more complicated especially in the electrical and lighting systems in the 1920s. An actor could not be expected to master all these technicalities as well as playing his part. It was no coincidence that Basil Dean, one of the leaders of this new breed of directors in the 1920s, was an expert and innovator in lighting systems. Third, Ben Iden Payne thought that the need for a director arose with the advent of Ibsen and Shaw. In the new psychological drama, 'motives for action were less obvious than they had been, they were frequently veiled and so required explanation and guidance for the actors.'[11] They also needed someone to control the 'atmosphere' hence the advent of the director. The tradition was already well established in Broadway, with David Belasco best-known as the doyen of directors, quite as famous as his stars. In Europe the great

184

directors had emerged – Stanislavsky, Meyerhold, Max Reinhardt, Copeau – and London audiences too came to accept in the 1920s that the 'production' they saw had been shaped by a 'director' whom they would never see on the stage.[12] In both these ways – in his commercial subordination to the businessman theatre-owner, or in his artistic subordination to the non-actor director – the actor had, in the 1920s, reason to feel a certain loss of control.

Many characteristics of the agent's business in the interwar years remained much the same as before. There was still, for the actor, the endless grinding round of climbing staircases to dingy outer offices, keeping up sartorial appearances, waiting for an interview. With the wider use of the telephone it was the less successful actors who had to continue tramping; those able to afford a domestic telephone waited at home until being rung there.[13] The less favoured hung around agents in York Street near Waterloo Station or, further up the scale, around the Charing Cross Road, where several new agencies had opened during the War, making it 'the habitat of Agency-land'.[14] Here one found Blackerman and Day or Akerman May off Leicester Square, Denton and Warner in Cambridge Circus, Linnit and Dunfee in St Martin's Lane. As well as the commercial agents the trade union, the Actors' Association, also ran an agency.

Within the arrangements largely handed on from before the War there were three areas of change in the interwar years. First there was a concern to regulate the agency profession. There were nearly 200 theatrical agencies in London, regulated by the LCC General Powers Act of 1921. Agencies had to obtain a licence from the LCC, renewable annually, and any intending agent had to advertise his intention in the theatrical press to allow for any objections. There were some 100 agencies in the provinces, licensed by local authorities.[15] The agents joined together to defend their interests by forming the Agents' Association in 1927, which by 1929 was 'now firmly established with no agents of note outside its range'.[16]

A second new characteristic of the interwar years was a change in the relation of agents to actors, with the former taking on more the role of personal manager and adviser helping to shape a career. In the twenties Golding Bright, also a play agent, 'looked after the interests of certain prominent actors and actresses, more as a personal favour than as a matter of business. Thus began a system of

185

personal management that is now a commonplace of the entertain
ment world.'[17] An interesting example survives of Golding Brigh
advising Olga Lindo in her relations with Basil Dean, who made th
foregoing comment. Dean seemed to deal direct with Miss Lind
over her salary, about which she was not entirely happy. Then sh
seems to have enlisted the services of Golding Bright, who secured
rise, dismissed the wily Dean's attempt to hold down the salary unti
production costs were covered, and bluntly argued that in any cas
Miss Lindo was cheaper than Tallulah Bankhead.[18] In dealing with
the sometimes intimidating Basil Dean, a young actress like Mis
Lindo did well to have a 'personal adviser' type of agent like Bright
In the 1930s several agents envisaged their relationship to their acto
clients as passing considerably beyond merely sending them fo
interviews for jobs. For example Eric Barker, on leaving Birmin
gham Rep in the early 1930s, went to the agent Madame Arcana
who began reshaping his wardrobe and eventually moved his caree
out of legitimate theatre into variety.[19] In 1934 Margaret Lockwoo
was taken on by agent Herbert de Leon, 'who was to shape the whol
of my career for me. He has been my agent, manager, counsellor
friend and guide ever since.'[20] The agent John Glidden's care ove
Vivien Leigh,[21] and Miriam Warner's over the young Kennetl
More,[22] also suggest that the agent had assumed a far mor
supportive and directing role in relation to his clients than wa
evident prior to 1914.

A third change in agency business was the emergence of Spotlight
the photographic casting directory. Theatrical papers like *Era* an
The Stage carried much space devoted to personal advertising
usually as brief 'theatrical cards'. What was needed, however, was
more permanent record of the main corpus of the profession
classified by type – leading man, juvenile, character, etc. – with
photographs and agents to contact. This was provided by th
creation of Spotlight in 1927, run by Rodney Millington from 1931
Millington had been an actor with OUDS at Oxford and the
professionally. Ever since, Spotlight's thick volumes, like illustrate
telephone directories, have been an essential reference tool for agent
and casting directors. This new form of agency service placed
greater importance on photographs. Accordingly, the specialis
theatrical photographer became part of the business. Most notable i

the 1930s was Angus McBean, in his studio behind Victoria Station.[23]

Overall, the agent became more important in the interwar years. In 1936 it was noted that:

> the player who secures a part in London or the provinces without going through an agent is a fortunate exception. Managers cannot afford to be easy of access and between the aspirant and the audition yawns a gulf which can seldom be bridged without an intermediary.[24]

There were perhaps two main reasons for this. The first stemmed from the changed control of the theatre indicated at the beginning of the chapter. As control and ownership came more into the hands of businessmen with profit-making motives and less in to the hands of artists, so it paid actors to employ a hard-headed business intermediary who could find work and arrange terms. They could negotiate as businessmen in a context in which most actors may have felt themselves disadvantaged by their artistic will to work at any price. For the better established actor his resort to an agent was impelled by the same kind of motive that pushed the economically weaker actor into trade unionism. For the employers also, the agents were more useful. Unlike the old actor–managers, they were less likely to have at their fingertips a knowledge of a wide range of actors and their capabilities. The agents, whose business it was to know this, could (like the new producer/directors) fill in this gap of expertise between the syndicate businessman and the hired actor.

The second reason was the increasing importance of film work. Maud Gill noted, 'all film work is obtained through agents'. Although she used an agent only once to secure a stage part yet 'all my film work is done through agents naturally'.[25] This was not uncommon. Athene Seyler had no need of an agent in her stage career until she started acting in films, when she required one to deal with the more complicated contractual arrangements of such work. Fabia Drake, who also had a consistently successful stage career and did not undertake film work, did not employ an agent at all.[26] It was accordingly possible for established players with a sound reputation to pursue a stage career without an agent, especially if they had gained their first foothold without one. But even the most experienced and independent found it prudent to acquire an agent when making the transition to film work.

III

The interwar years saw a marked change in the style of acting to a more restrained form of naturalism. In broad terms, it was a decline of acting depending on rhetoric, fine ringing voice, broad sweeping gestures, larger-than-life powerful central characters and impersonation. In its place came new virtues, actors appearing to behave on stage exactly as they did in real life, quiet conversational voices, a minimum of gesture and an eschewing of the theatrical. To some degree this transition had started before the War with the Bancrofts and Society dramas. Yet in the interwar years, perhaps specifically in the 1920s, this change became more marked. Raymond Massey, who acted in London through the decade recalled that:

> all through the twenties the theatre in England was undergoing an important change, stylized, mannered plays were giving way to realistic dramas and comedies, and actors had to make some adjustments in their acting style.[27]

Some, who had doubts about the new quiet naturalism, attributed it to the decline of actor-managership. The removal of the central actor with his own company had led also to the lack of great authority, of 'personal domination' of leading actors in stage roles. While the general level of competence had risen there were no 'great' actors, the leading figures – du Maurier, Hicks, Hawtrey – playing naturalistic representations of their off-stage personas.[28] Others saw 'the school of restrained acting' as resulting from the revival of serious drama with Ibsen, Shaw and Galsworthy, and deplored that the kind of realism they required had been unfavourable for histrionic art.[29]

If any one actor was central to this change it was Gerald du Maurier. If he did not create the new style, no one had more influence on other imitative actors who diffused and even debased it. Raymond Massey, who knew him well, considered that du Maurier 'almost alone and unwittingly inspired the revolution in English acting which took place in the 1920s' with his low-keyed – 'relaxed', 'casual', 'natural', 'realistic', 'easy' – style of acting, which he had been evolving from before the War. Although it was thought that he made acting look easy – merely playing oneself and reproducing one's trivial drawing-room behaviour – for du Maurier it was art disguising art. He worked hard at it – 'the smooth naturalness of his performances came from laborious preparation' – practising 'business' with drinks and cigarettes in front of a mirror for hours at a time. 'Little things like that don't come easily to me', he told Massey.[30]

The new style did not meet with universal approval, and its debasement especially came in for criticism. Sydney Carroll thought that although acting had gained greatly in polish in the 1920s, it had 'lost in rhetorical power, something too of the faculty of magnetizing, of electrifying'.[31] He also deplored the loss of the mimic gift, and the concern to reproduce the characteristics of someone else, that had been sacrificed by actors playing their own personalities.[32] St John Ervine feared that 'acting seemed as if it might disappear altogether and be replaced by behaving.'[33] In practice, of course, a synthesis was effected. Devlin claimed in 1939 that 'in the heat of the conflict the two styles have been welded together, each cancelling out the worst faults in the other.'[34]

IV

In the 1920s there was a vigorous growth of schools and academies purporting to teach drama, many obscure, probably ephemeral and of slight account. There were various reasons for this. The commercially thriving state of the theatre in the mid-1920s – not yet sapped by the Depression and competition from the sound film – continued to attract entrants. Secondly, there was a large market of well-to-do young girls who needed some 'finishing' and who had no intention of going on the stage.[35] The War had made it impossible for girls to go to finishing schools on the Continent, and parents became used to looking for alternatives in London. Accordingly even major drama schools provided lessons in elocution and deportment, and there were plenty of potential pupils left over to feed the growth of a marginal commercial sector catering to the same need. Thirdly, there was the 1920s craze for ballroom dancing. Schools grew to teach the dances, and many of these taught elocution as part of the rounded social skills necessary on and off the floor.[36] For one reason or another there was a great deal of new drama training available at different levels in the 1920s.

At the apex of the system the two leading drama schools, the Academy and the Central School, continued to thrive and expand. The official status of the Academy was consolidated.[37] In 1913 it was accorded corporate status, which enabled it to raise money by issuing debentures, and in 1920, by Royal Charter, it became the Royal Academy of Dramatic Art. Increasing status and recognition entailed financial advantage. From 1924 Parliament made a £500 grant, putting RADA on the same footing as the Royal Academy and the Royal College of Music. Then, in 1930, after ten years of legal battling, it was accepted by the LCC that acting was a 'fine art', which enabled RADA to claim exemption from rates under the Scientific Societies Act of 1843.[38] Their rebuilt premises in Gower Street were opened in 1931, helped by £5000 from Shaw. Royal patronage followed the Charter, the Prince of Wales becoming patron in 1921, retaining his position when he became Edward VIII and handing it on to George VI and Queen Elizabeth. The Queen became a genuinely interested visitor to the Academy and in 1938 the principal, Kenneth Barnes, was knighted. All this reflected credit on the Academy itself. Also, the developments indicated the increasing seriousness with which drama education was regarded, which further enhanced the standing and professionalism of the actor.

The Academy continued to accord a central importance to voice production and elocution. For the principal, Kenneth Barnes, 'speech and class are very intimately connected'[39] and the inculcation of a received standard southern speech became a salient aim. This was in accord with the predominantly middle-/upper-middle-class character of entrants to the profession in the interwar years. There was also Delsarte expression and gesture, dancing and deportment, fencing, French and lectures in poetics, history of drama and theatrical representation.

The heart of the training, however, was the rehearsal of plays.[40] This seems to have been excellent, providing a rich diet both educationally widening and commercially useful. As well as working on plenty of Shakespeare, Shaw and pre-1914 classics, they struck out in new directions. The first Ibsen (*Pillars of the Community*) was

190

tried in 1921, Greek plays regularly from the same year, the first
Noel Coward (*The Young Idea*) in 1924 and the first Chekhov (*The
Cherry Orchard* with Laughton) in 1926. The Russian and Scandina-
vian classics were mixed with ancient Greek plays, 'Lancashire
School' comedy and solid West End fare like *The Barretts of Wimpole
Street* and *A Rose Without a Thorn*. In the early 1920s Flora Robson
recalled that a student attended two acting classes per week, one
studying a modern play and the other Shakespeare or Restoration
drama.[41] A student would have gained a very varied experience. For
example, John Gielgud during his year there in 1923 played
seventeen parts (including two Hamlets).[42] It was also one of the
strengths of the Academy that distinguished actors and producers
came from outside to rehearse plays – Sybil Thorndike for *The
Trojan Women*, Shaw for *Pygmalion* – these were golden privileges
enjoyed by the students of the Academy. Sir Kenneth Barnes greatly
appreciated them; he noted that 'these rehearsals by Mr Shaw at the
RADA remain in my mind as the most significant episode in our
working days.'[43]

The students increased over the period.[44]

1921	134	1927	172	1936	254
1923	146	1929	178	1937	267
1925	173	1931	181	1939	246

and the Academy began to produce some very notable students:
Flora Robson, John Gielgud, Charles Laughton, Robert Morley,
Kathleen Harrison and Celia Johnson in the 1920s and Anthony
Quayle, Stephen Murray, Margaret Lockwood, Nigel Stock, Joan
Greenwood and Ian Carmichael in the 1930s, to mention but a few of
the best-known. By 1936 some 39 per cent of leading actors and 46
per cent of leading actresses on the British stage had been students at
RADA.[45]

The Central School also continued to thrive in the interwar years,
the number of its students rising from thirty in 1919 to sixty in the
1920s and to just under 200 by 1938.[46] Elsie Fogerty continued to be
an active and stimulating teacher, especially of poetry speech. The
rest of the curriculum was rich and varied.[47] Dr Aikin continued
teaching voice production. Being a wealthy man he gave his services
free of charge to the School, even subsidising it by paying his own

191

part of the rent. Fencing was well-taught, deportment by 'a high society lady', Ethel Radmar, and the history of costume was introduced in 1920 by Herbert Norris, who was the costume adviser to Madame Tussaud's. Also distinctive was Fogerty's liking for Greek theatre dancing and mime. Ruby Ginner and Irene Mawer, both pupils of Fogerty, taught this at the Central and then established their own Ginner–Mawer School, which played an important part in the revival of mime studies in Britain in the interwar years. West End actors came in to direct and rehearse the students in plays which accordingly reflected the commercial theatre outside as well as the classics, though rather neglecting Restoration comedy and Ibsen and Chekhov. The firmly established character of the School was confirmed by its incorporation in 1925. More important, the prestige of the School was vastly enhanced by the fame of some of its notable students of these years – Laurence Olivier, Peggy Ashcroft, John Laurie (then a leading Stratford and Old Vic star of the 1930s) and Ann Todd, the film actress, especially caught the public attention. Equally important, Miss Fogerty herself was consulted as a voice teacher and therapist by major classical stars who had not been pupils at the School, notably John Gielgud, Edith Evans and Sybil Thorndike. The pioneering distinction of Miss Fogerty's work was recognized by the award to her of the CBE in 1934. On the outbreak of war the School moved to Exeter University. Miss Fogerty retired and died in 1945.

Three new schools were founded or reshaped by notable actresses in the 1920s. In 1919 Lady Constance Benson started her Dramatic School at Pembroke Hall in Pembroke Gardens in Kensington, which taught the normal curriculum of elocution, voice production, dancing, fencing, Shakespearian verse speaking and rehearsals.[48] Her most noted pupil was John Gielgud, who was there for three terms before going to RADA. In 1921 another distinguished actress, Dame May Whitty, took over the Etlinger Dramatic School[49] and in 1927 Fay Compton opened her Studio, perhaps chiefly remembered for Sir Alec Guinness, who was a pupil there in the early 1930s. Some further significant schools were started in the 1930s. In 1933 Ronald Adam and Eileen Thorndike formed the Embassy School, attached to the Embassy Theatre,[50] and in 1936 Michael Chekhov (the nephew of Anton) opened his Theatre Studio at Dartington Hall

192

in Devon.[51] Finally, in the late 1930s, the Webber–Douglas School, which was still predominantly a singing and opera academy, was turning increasingly to drama teaching.[52] In the 1930s the Webber–Douglas produced some attractive players – Michael Denison and Dulcie Gray, Stewart Granger, Renée Asherson – all from rather upper-class backgrounds, and valuable British film actors in the 1940s and 1950s.

Theatre companies also developed schools. The Liverpool Rep had ten students who watched rehearsals and walked on, but did not otherwise seem to receive much organized tuition.[53] Quite the most important was that attached to the Old Vic. The Old Vic took trainees in the 1920s who, unlike those at Liverpool, paid premiums of £40 a season. There was a little instruction. Dr Aikin from the Central School taught the voice and Ninette de Valois dancing and movement, but most of the tuition entailed walking on and playing small parts.[54] Esmond Knight and Margaret Rutherford were successful students from the mid-1920s, but most did not survive on the stage. In the 1930s the School became more organized under the direction of Esme Church, with much more tuition.[55] There was a great deal of strenuous physical activity in the mornings – acrobatics, fencing, movement and ballet – with diction, mime, voice production and makeup in the afternoon, with rehearsals taken by Miss Church. There seemed to be no 'finishing school' debutante element in this rather hard-working atmosphere.

Perhaps the most serious, even 'quasi-religious',[56] initiative in drama education in the 1930s was the London Theatre Studio, founded by Michel St Denis in 1936. St Denis had begun his career working with his uncle Jacques Copeau at the Théâtre du Vieux-Colombier in the 1920s. He founded his *avant-garde* Compagnie des Quinze in 1930, and settled in England to establish a company and school in 1936. The Studio was based in an old chapel in Islington, with George Devine and Marius Goring helping with the teaching. The classes consisted of improvisation, mime, acrobatics, relaxation, dancing, voice production and singing.[57] Great emphasis was laid on improvisation and mime, including the simulation of animals (Ustinov chose an inert salamander) and physically taxing gymnastics. The aim was 'suppleness', both physical and emotional, to break down the stiffness of bodies and the inhibitions of reserved upbring-

193

ings. Also distinctive, to this latter end, was considerable work with masks, directed by Devine. Most important were the ideas behind the Studio. St Denis was not interested in training actors for the West End, he wanted talents of the second rank who would accept the control of the producer. Above all he wanted to produce an ensemble troupe, with all the vocal and physical skills. Accordingly even their most successful pupils did not feel they were being trained for the existing theatre of the 1930s. The LTS produced few star names, Peter Ustinov and Yvonne Mitchell being perhaps the best-known, the former as a brilliant individualist fitting oddly and critically into the set-up. It was 'a tiny heroic enterprise'[58] and ceased with the War, only to be reborn again as the Old Vic School in 1946.

One important new development of the interwar years was the involvement of some of the leading drama schools with the University of London. There were early calls for this in the aftermath of the War as part of a concern to establish a high-level common academic standard for the nascent subject. A conference of the Drama League at Stratford in 1919 called for a University of Drama, and Elsie Fogerty of the Central School was strongly in favour of this.[59] Less ambitiously, the influential Board of Education's Departmental Committee on the Teaching of English encouraged the University of London to consider granting a Diploma in Dramatic Art. Fogerty had given evidence to them, expressing her hopes that the Central School could be affiliated to London University. The Committee had no view on this, 'but we hope that the University will seriously consider the possibility of granting a Diploma in Dramatic Art.'[60] On the strength of this Elsie Fogerty applied to the University, asking the latter to grant a diploma which could be taken by students of the School.[61]

In June a number of distinguished theatre people met to discuss the structure and content of a possible Diploma. It was evident from the range of views that an initial dilemma was raised that was to persist throughout the life of the Diploma and to become especially acute in the 1950s. How far should it concentrate on vocational technical training and how far, as a University Diploma, should it stress academic, theoretical matters? How far would immediate usefulness be sacrificed to notions of intellectual respectability?

194

Kenneth Barnes of RADA wanted to include French and even English social history, though he had little enthusiasm for psychology and physiology as part of the course. Sir Johnston Forbes Robertson, the most distinguished actor consulted, stressed that 'articulation is the main thing', reflecting his own concern for conspicuously beautiful and precise speech. Lena Ashwell, the most noted actress on the committee, broadly agreed with Forbes Robertson, while Dr W. A. Aikin also stressed the importance of voice training but unusually, as a medical man, wanted students to understand the physiology of the voice.[62] The most forthright views were expressed by George Bernard Shaw.[63] He dismissed the value of physiology and psychology, did not believe that acting could be taught, but wanted the chief emphasis on rhetoric. Most important of all, the Diploma must include lengthy practical experience: 'unless a period of training in a real theatre playing real plays to real audiences – be made part of the qualification for the proposed degree [sic], it will gain no credit in the profession.'

On the basis of these discussions a syllabus was worked out embodying most consultants' views. It was to be a two-year course at training institutions approved by the University of London through its Extra-Mural Board. The first year was to include the use of voice, phonetics, diction, movement and dance, and acting. The second year included poetry, history of drama, a modern language and one special study chosen from the history of theatrical art, social life and costume, music and physics for stagecraft, including lighting. For teachers the course could be extended to a third year including psychology and physiology, speech training and remedial speech. The central emphasis on speech and voice was rightly maintained, while advocates of a foreign language and aspects of history were satisfied. The medical aspects of physiology and psychology of the voice were postponed to the third, specialized year.[64]

The Committee was determined to establish and maintain a high standard for the diploma. Prestigious panels of examiners were formed including actors Sir Johnston Forbes Robertson and Henry Ainley for the oral tests, and actresses Lena Ashwell and Hilda Trevelyan for drama. Patiently the oral examiners sat behind screens (to avoid being influenced by a pretty candidate) listening to voices with recurrent faults and, Forbes Robertson noted resignedly, 'a tendency to stick too much on one note; and that for the most part a sad one'.[65] However, they had their reward in 1926 when at the Central they found 'one or two of outstanding merit',[66] one of whom would certainly have been Peggy Ashcroft, the most distinguished recipient of the diploma of the interwar years.

The content of the diploma changed scarcely at all over these years. The 1939 Regulations stipulated voice training, poetics, history of drama, a foreign language, music, physics for stagecraft, phonetics, anatomy and psychology of movement and the voice.[67] The heavy academic content was an inevitable aspect of the London University link which justified the seeking of university recognition. It clearly seemed as if, to make Drama an acceptable academic subject, it was necessary to incorporate some undoubtedly respect-able – if in this case marginally relevant – studies, like the physics, anatomy and foreign language. Inevitably some of this must have been superficial, while some subjects were criticized as being unnecessarily academic for actors.[68] These were strains within the dilemma of providing an academic university course of scholarly intellectual content for what was perhaps more truly a craft skill. It was important to the profession – to people like Fogerty and Forbes Robertson – further to increase the respectability of the calling and its educational claims at that time. Accordingly, they welcomed and accepted the academic content and the cachet of the London University link. The real strains that were to break up the Diploma did not arise until the 1960s, when the issue of learned profession versus craft skill were faced more head-on.

In perspective between 1923 and 1939 nearly 500 students were candidates for the Diploma, predominantly girls from the Central (408) and RADA (71). Their future careers were equally divided between the theatre and teaching, with some ancillary careers making up the balance.

	men	women	% of total
actor	3	19	37.3
producer	2	1	5.1
stage manager		1	1.7
teacher		26	44.1
therapist		2	3.4

196

	men	women	% of total
BBC		2	3.4
youth work	1		1.7
costume design		1	1.7
secretary		1	1.7

V

The interwar years marked a peak in the richness, variety and glamour of the actor's social life. The successful and would-be successful actor was advised that he 'must meet people – actors, producers, managers. He never knows who may be of use to him.'[69] As these were the thriving years of the smart restaurants, night-clubs and country house parties so they became a milieu for a profession, success in which was so often underpinned by sociability and a network of personal contacts.

Certain restaurants found favour. The Savoy Grill was perhaps the most usual place for first-night celebrations. Henry Kendall recalled, 'it was not uncommon for a star who had just made a big success to enter the Savoy Grill when the whole restaurant rose to applaud – waiters included.'[70] Yet if any restaurant was specifically associated with the theatre in the interwar years it was the Ivy. The Ivy had been built before the First World War by Bertie Meyer, the theatrical manager who had also built St Martin's Theatre across the road in West Street. After the War it came under the management of the remarkable Mario Gallati.[71] The Ambassador's and St Martin's Theatres were just across the street and eight more a few yards away. It quickly gained a reputation amongst actors, and a recognizable body of regulars soon emerged including Noel Coward, Ivor Novello, Marie Tempest, Gertrude Lawrence, Charles Laughton and Lilian Braithwaite. An observer in the 1930s noted: 'Those actors and actresses who stand for prosperity in the theatre have a pet restaurant, the Ivy . . . a salon in which the stars may meet and shine.'[72] So much was this the case that merely being seen around at the Ivy was considered beneficial to the actor's career. In 1947 Gallati left the Ivy to start the Caprice, which in turn became a leading theatrical restaurant of the 1940s and 1950s.

197

Some social life was focused in the homes of theatrical personalities and their patrons and friends. Out of town Frederick Lonsdale's house at Birchington, on the north Kent coast near Margate, was a centre of entertaining in the 1920s. Ivor Novello, Fay Compton and Gladys Cooper all had houses in the neighbourhood and Miss Cooper and the du Mauriers were frequent guests at Birchington, whence the house party would go on to Sandwich for golf.[73] So popular was this area as a favourite resort of theatricals that a midnight train was laid on, complete with supper car, to take actors and audience home there after the play.[74] Perhaps the best-known centre of theatrical entertaining in the twenties and thirties was Ivor Novello's house Redroofs, at Littlewick Green near Maidenhead. Novello bought the house in 1927, and from then until his death his new country home was the scene of a lively social life in the summer months. He entertained the cast of his current productions there, and a wide cross-section of the theatrical scene, with tennis, croquet on the lawn, a swimming pool and usually an afternoon cricket match for the men.[75] On Novello's death in 1951 Redroofs was taken over by the Actors' Benevolent Fund.

In London one of the leading hostesses to the profession was Lady Sybil Colefax at her home, Argyll House, in Chelsea. Max Beerbohm and Shaw were among her friends. She was a keen play-goer herself and 'her dining room sometimes resembled a stage set, the leading actors and actresses of the West End theatre playing their off-stage roles.'[76] She did not snobbishly concentrate on established stars but had the discrimination to encourage Noel Coward, Gielgud and Ivor Novello and bring them into the social swim early in their careers. It was at a Sybil Colefax party in the 1930s that Oliver Lyttelton took Olivier aside and stressed the need for a new big National Theatre other than the Old Vic.[77] Lord Ned Lathom's Mayfair flat was also a centre for exclusive and high-level theatrical entertaining. Lathom was a generous financial backer of Noel Coward and his luncheon guests often included Marie Tempest, Gladys Cooper, Mrs Patrick Campbell and the young, not yet famous, John Gielgud, who was bowled over by 'the elegance of his flat . . . the exquisite food and fascinating company'.[78]

Actors also became part of the new night-club scene of the interwar years. Night-clubs had grown up as a result of the DORA

198

licensing regulations during the First World War. The smartest, most exclusive and expensive was the Embassy Club in Old Bond Street.[79] The Prince of Wales frequented the Embassy and the Café de Paris in Coventry Street and helped to set the tone – smart, sophisticated, slightly daring. Henry Kendall recalled, 'there were parties after the show every night, dances, receptions. The profession was much smaller, and everyone knew everyone else.'[80] Among the other night-spots favoured by actors was Ciro's, Monseigneur (now a cinema in Piccadilly) and possibly, at the more Bohemian end, the Ham Bone or Kate Meyrick's Forty Three Club.

The more fashionable night-clubs were too expensive for lower-paid actors and, recognizing this need, the Fifty Fifty Club was founded in 1925 as, in the words of its founder, 'a place where actors and actresses in the lower income groups could eat reasonably well and cheaply after the show, and dance too if they felt like it.'[81] Ivor Novello and Henry Kendall jointly founded it in premises in Wardour Street next door to Clarkson's wig shop, decorated with caricatures of leading actors painted around the walls. They opened on Armistice Night, 1925. Thereafter it settled down to become 'the most popular Bohemian club in London'. While it lasted it was good fun. Constance Collier, one of the directors, remembered that 'they had a very good orchestra and with delicious eggs and bacon and coffee.'[82] Actors appreciated being able to come along after the show 'in sweaters and old clothes, without being stared at',[83] to enjoy an inexpensive dinner or after-theatre supper. But things began to go wrong. The club became too successful and was taken up and taken over by the 'smart set'. The club ended sadly. Novello and Kendall had to leave it to tour, mismanagement was followed by a police raid, closure, fines and bankruptcy. But in its heyday in the twenties it had been a lively and useful part of the social life of the London actor.

The Fifty Fifty was an attempt to marry the idea of the smartly fashionable night-club with a functional resort for working actors. As it failed through inclining too much in the former direction, so other clubs retained a more workaday purpose. The Gargoyle, next to the Royalty Theatre, was an informal haunt where the actor could enjoy 'sausages and bacon and a small dance band consisting of a pianist and a tap drummer'.[84] A similar egg-and-bacon-cum-cabaret establishment for actors was the Kind Dragon Club. This was run in Chippendale's former studio, the attic of an old oak-beamed barn off St Martins Lane. 'Here tucked away from the rest of the world, eating eggs and bacon after the show at night, we felt we were seeing life indeed!'[85] The premises were taken over by Motleys, the theatrical designers, and though ceasing to be a night-club it continued as 'an unofficial club for the acting profession', with John Gielgud, Alec Guinness, Peggy Ashcroft, Tyrone Guthrie and George Devine among regular callers, often adjourning to dine at a long theatrical table at Patmacks across the road.[86]

At the purely functional end of the spectrum were a wide range of institutions of more homely comfort than glamour, but of great value to the actor of modest means. One of the first of these was the Theatre Girls' Club, founded in 1915 by Mrs Edward Compton, the wife of actor-manager Edward Compton and mother of Sir Compton Mackenzie.[87] The idea was to provide residential accommodation for unemployed or low-paid actresses. There were twenty-five beds in cubicles, reading and recreation rooms, and the Hand-in-Hand Society provided meals at low cost. Mrs Compton was supported by Lilian Braithwaite, May Whitty, Madge Kendal and the wives and widows of Tree, Wyndham, Martin Harvey and Forbes Robertson. In 1917 they moved from their original premises in Little Portland Street to larger ones in Greek Street, Soho, which could take forty girls. The Club tried to find stage work for the girls and, failing that, obliged them to train for the secretarial, cooking and dressmaking trades as a stop-gap.[88] The ethos of the Club was firmly religious and Anglican, like Mrs Compton herself. Mrs Kendal told the girls not to neglect their religion[89] and Father Andrew (Lilian Baylis's confidant at the Old Vic) was the Club's chaplain.

Somewhat larger and more expensive, though serving the same purpose, was the Three Arts Club in Marylebone Road, opposite Madame Tussaud's. This had been founded by Lena Ashwell just before the First World War to provide accommodation for women working in music, painting and the theatre.[90] It was a five-story house with eighty bedrooms and cubicles (at 17/6d a week), dining room and common rooms with good oak furniture from Heals. It had a more middle-class, or at least genteel, ambience than the Girls' Theatre Club.[91] Binnie Hale, Gwen Ffrangçon Davies and Dodie

Smith had been noted theatrical members, though by 1932 a resident noted that 'the great days of the Club were over.'[92] Its members were by then largely elderly, and Noel Coward employed many of them for crowd scenes in *Cavalcade* in 1932.

The Actors' Association also ran a club. Since it had become a trade union its social amenities had rather been neglected, but in 1921 they revived their club as a registered company open to actors and authors, 'a bright Bohemian club at a nominal subscription'.[93] In 1927 the Interval Club was started by Mary Hewitt in Old Compton Street. Mary Hewitt and her daughter Molly, who took over its running in 1936, were stalwarts of the Catholic Stage Guild and the Club was primarily for Catholic actors. It served meals, had a residential house in Soho Square and acted as an agency. In 1928 the Interval Club moved to 22–23 Dean Street. Further along at number 77, in the same year, yet another actors' club opened for stage and film people. It provided cheap meals and a rest, and served as a casting pool where film producers in a hurry could round up a small crowd.[94]

Gadding about in Society was not approved of by the older generation of actors, but for others Society was something they liked to enjoy and which they felt could be useful to them. Gladys Cooper usually went home after the theatre:

> but if I want to go to the Embassy, Ciro's or the Savoy, I most certainly do go. No one can tell me that for an actress to be seen dancing or taking supper by a handful of people in the West End is going to do her any harm. On the contrary to be seen out now and then is probably an advantage.[95]

Others revelled in it and saw its significance. Denys Blakelock noted of his friend Laurence Olivier that 'he liked in those days [the 1920s and 1930s] the social life of the stage so necessary to a really successful career.'[96]

This rapid growth of clubs was a very characteristic feature of the 1920s and 1930s. They ranged from those where you could Charleston with the Prince of Wales to those with modest rooms where a tired actress could rest and drink a cup of tea. It was a different world from the gentlemen's club of Edwardian days, and there is nothing quite like it now.

NOTES

1 See Appendix I.
2 Philip Godfrey, *Backstage* (London, 1933), p.118.
3 *Era*, 16 January 1918.
4 *Era*, 11 January 1922.
5 Owen Nares, *Myself When Young* (London, 1925), p.193.
6 *Era*, 2 June 1920.
7 W. H. Leverton, *Through the Box Office Window* (London, 1932), p.123.
8 Sidney Blow, *The Ghost Walks on Fridays* (London, 1935), p.207.
9 Ben Iden Payne, *Life in a Wooden O* (Yale, 1977), p.140.
10 Cyril Maude, *Behind the Scenes* (London, 1927), pp.88–9.
11 Ben Iden Payne, *op.cit.*, p.58.
12 Norman MacDermott, *Everymania* (London, 1975), pp.89–90.
13 Philip Godfrey, *Backstage* (London, 1933), p.136.
14 *Era*, 13 October 1915.
15 'The Finding of Employment for Artistes', *International Labour Review*, vol. 18, Oct.–Nov. 1928, p.621.
16 *Era*, 6 March 1929.
17 Basil Dean, *Seven Ages* (London, 1970), p.174.
18 Letter, R. Golding Bright to Olga Lindo, 10 July 1925. Also letters April and June 1925 between Basil Dean and Olga Lindo. Olga Lindo's papers, British Theatre Museum.
19 Eric Barker, *Steady Barker* (London, 1956), p.114.
20 Margaret Lockwood, *Lucky Star* (London, 1955), p.35.
21 Anne Edwards, *Vivien Leigh* (London, 1977), p.50.
22 Kenneth More, *Happy Go Lucky* (London, 1959), p.64.
23 Patricia Don Young, *Dramatic School* (London, 1954), p.195.
24 *The Times*, 22 June 1936.
25 Maud Gill, *See the Players* (London, 1938), pp.227, 111.
26 Interviews with Miss Seyler, Miss Drake.
27 Raymond Massey, *A Hundred Different Lives* (London, 1979), p.69.
28 A. B. Walkley, 'The English Actor of Today' *The Yale Review*, April 1920.
29 E. V. Odle, 'Histrionic Art in the Modern Theatre', *The Contemporary Review*, September 1921.

30 Raymond Massey, *op.cit.*, pp.69–70.
31 Sydney Carroll, *Daily Telegraph*, 12 June 1930.
32 Sydney Carroll, 'The Art of Acting', *British Equity*, Feb. 1934.
33 St John Ervine, *The Theatre in My Time* (London, 1933), p.213.
34 William Devlin, 'English Acting Today' in R. D. Charques, *Footnotes to the Theatre* (London, 1938), p.229.
35 Interview with Mrs Nessa Hughes Smith, 17 February 1978. Mrs Smith, a stockbroker's daughter, in the 1920s studied singing in Paris and went to a finishing school. She then went to the Guildhall School for speech training with Basset Rowe, though with no intention of becoming an actress.
36 In the issues of *Theatre World*, Oct. 1926–April 1927, we find advertisements for the following new schools teaching drama and elocution: Claire Tufnell School of Dancing, Shaftesbury School of Dancing and Dramatic Art, West End School of Dancing and Dramatic Art, Alston Yates Academy, Westminster School of Music, Rudolphe Gaillard, London Repertory School.
37 The RADA Prospectuses for 1931 and 1944/5 contain surveys of these developments.
38 *The Times*, 7 December 1920, 'Is Acting a Fine Art?' for the issue. Irene Vanbrugh, *To Tell my Story* (London, 1948), p.89 for the deputation to the House of Commons, 1930, that led to the decision.
39 *Proceedings of the International Conference on Speech Training*, 1927. Kenneth Barnes, p.75.
40 Administrator's Diaries, 1919–39 notes on cast lists, plays, visiting producers.
41 Flora Robson in M. McCall (ed.), *My Drama School*, p.18.
42 Administrator's Diary 1923. John Gielgud, *Early Stages* (London, 1939), pp.61–3 for Gielgud's account and appreciation of Claude Rains, later a Hollywood film-star, who was an excellent teacher at RADA in the 1920s.
43 Sir Kenneth Barnes, 'G.B.S. and the RADA,' in *GBS at 90*, p.178.
44 These have been calculated from class lists in the Administrator's Diaries. The 1939 figure is cited in the 1944/5 Prospectus.
45 Calculated from *Who's Who in Theatre*, 1936. Names A–M inclusive of those starting careers after 1913. 35 – 101 actors, 45 – 113 actresses.

46 Interview with Miss Gwynneth Thurburn, OBE. Miss Thurburn was a student and teacher at the School from 1919 and succeeded Elsie Fogerty as Principal in 1942.

47 Interview with Mr John Laurie, 1 August 1977. *Viva Voce, passim*, 1919–1939. Marion Cole, *Fogie, the Life of Elsie Fogerty CBE* (London, 1967).

48 *Daily Graphic*, 4 January 1921; *Era*, 25 July 1923. Interview with Miss Oonah Todd Naylor, 1 August 1977.

49 Margaret Webster, *The Same only Different* (London, 1969), pp.290–2.

50 Ronald Adam, *Overture and Beginners* (London, 1938), pp.254–7.

51 *Chekhov Theatre Studio* 1936 (Syllabus in TUC Collection, Pamphlet Box P).

52 Michael Denison, *Overture and Beginners*, (London, 1973), pp.85–9. Dulcie Gray, 'The Webber–Douglas School', in *My Drama School*, ed. M. McCall (London, 1978), pp.57–68.

53 Grace Wyndham Goldie, *The Liverpool Repertory Theatre 1911–1934* (Liverpool, 1935), p.190.

54 Interview with Mr Esmond Knight, 23 August 1978.

55 Patricia Don Young, *Dramatic School* (London, 1954), pp.18–28.

56 Peter Ustinov, *Dear Me* (London, 1977), p.83 See pp.65–83 for Ustinov's account of the LTS.

57 Yvonne Mitchell, *Actress* (London, 1957), pp.6–9 and 'The London Theatre Studio' in *My Drama School*.

58 Irving Wardle, *The Theatres of George Devine* (London, 1978), Chapter 4, 'The London Theatre Studio'.

59 *Era*, 27 August 1919. 'Proposal for a University College of Speech Training and Dramatic Art', *Viva Voce*, April 1920.

60 *The Teaching of English in England, Report of the Departmental Committee* (Sir Henry Newbolt), HMSO, London, 1921, pp.322–3.

61 Minutes of the University of London Diploma in Dramatic Art, 22 March 1922, to consider Memorandum of Application.

62 Report on Discussion, 28 June 1922.

63 Letter G. B. Shaw, 25 June 1922.

64 Regulations for the Diploma in Dramatic Art, March 1923.

65 Minute, 5 June 1925.

66 Minute, 22 June 1926.

67 Regulations for the Diploma in Dramatic Art, 1939.

68 Minute, 23 May 1939, for the discussion on the History of Theatrical Art.
69 Donovan Maule, *The Stage as a Career* (London, 1932), p.104.
70 Henry Kendall, *I Remember Romano's* (London, 1960), p.59.
71 Mario Gallati, *Mario of the Caprice* (London, 1960).
72 Hector Bolitho, *Marie Tempest* (London, 1936), pp.230–1.
73 Gladys Cooper, *Gladys Cooper* (London, 1931), p.199.
74 Henry Kendall, *op.cit.*, pp.70–1.
75 MacQueen Pope, *Ivor* (London, 1951), pp.232–3.
76 Stella Margetson, *The Long Party* (London, 1974), pp.96, 122.
77 Nicholas Tomalin and John Elsom, *The History of the National Theatre* (London, 1978), pp.73–4.
78 John Gielgud, *Early Stages* (London, 1939), pp.111–12.
79 Basil Dean, *Seven Ages* (London, 1970), pp.195–6. Barbara Cartland, *We Danced All Night* (London, 1970), Chapter 9.
80 Henry Kendall, *op.cit.*, (London, 1960), p.59.
81 *Ibid.*, pp.86–90 on the Fifty Fifty Club.
82 Constance Collier, *Harlequinade* (London, 1929), p.281.
83 Noel Coward, *Present Indicative* (London, 1937), p.237.
84 *Ibid.*, p.236.
85 Esmond Knight, *Seek the Bubble* (London, 1943), p.57.
86 Irving Wardle, *The Theatres of George Devine* (London, 1978), p.32.
87 *Era*, 27 January 1915.
88 Lou Warwick, *The Mackenzies called Compton* (Northampton, 1977), pp.203, 220–3, gives a good account.
89 *Era*, 21 February 1917.
90 Lena Ashwell, *Myself a Player* (London, 1936), p.176.
91 Dodie Smith, *Look Back with Mixed Feelings* (London, 1978), p.72. Chapter V contains a vivid account of Dodie Smith's life at the club.
92 Jean Batters, *Edith Evans* (London, 1977), pp.8–9. Miss Batters had been there in 1932.
93 *Era*, 3 August 1921.
94 *Era*, 22 August 1928.
95 Gladys Cooper, *op.cit.*, pp.239–40.
96 Denys Blakelock, *Round the Next Corner* (London, 1967), p.58.

10 The New Media 1896–1939

In the interwar years the work of the actor was transformed with the advent of the new media. No longer was acting confined to a live stage performance before a few hundred patrons. The new forms of cinema, broadcasting and television brought the enjoyment of drama to a vastly extended audience. They presented to the actor both the new opportunities and problems of becoming a multi-media performer.

Film-making began in Britain in the 1890s, with stage actors gradually taking up the work over the next decade. In the three or four years before the First World War even leading stage stars and actor–managers were prepared to appear in the films. After a slump in the 1920s the film industry was stimulated by the Films Act of 1927 and most particularly by the advent of sound pictures in Britain from 1929. This gave an overwhelming advantage to the stage-trained and well-spoken player. In the 1930s the soundtrack displaced actors, especially women, who had specialized in films where their visual appeal in silent films could mask deficiencies of voice, and by the 1930s most leading British film actors were also stage actors, combining both types of work. This combination was made attractive by the very high earnings of film work, which were able to subsidize a stage income. Less lucrative, but also an expanding field of employment for the actor, was the starting of broadcasting and radio drama from 1922, followed by television from 1936. The technical difficulties of this work were offset by the quality of the drama, which could be cheaply produced. Through films and forms of broadcasting the actor was able to extend his name and work to vastly increased audiences at a time when live provincial theatre was shrinking.

I

The cinema industry began in England in the mid-1890s. The first 'Kinetoscope parlour' was opened in Oxford Street in 1894 and the pioneer films of Birt Acres and R. W. Paul produced in the following two years.[1] Most of the successful early films dealt with the direct reporting of events. However, the camera soon began to be turned not only on actualities but on crudely devised fictitious dramas played out by film actors. Birt Acres's *Arrest of a Pickpocket*, 1896, with unknown actors, was probably the first drama photoplay in England, and by the end of 1896 the cinema had established a temporary home in every major music hall in England. This rapid growth of the British cinema between 1894 and 1896 in turn changed and widened the audience beyond the carriage trade of Leicester Square. It created a demand not only for newsreels but for simple acted stories. But who was to play in them?

The earliest film producers did not initially think of using well-known stage actors, or indeed actors at all. J. Williamson of Hove, who made films between 1896 and 1914, used his friends and family in story sketches[2] and the best-known early producer, Cecil Hepworth, shooting at Walton, recalled, 'no thought of professional actors had ever entered our heads. The mere idea of films was abhorred by all stage people . . . So we played all the parts ourselves.'[3] In the 1900s it became more common to start using professional actors. George Albert Smith of Hove employed members of passing touring companies for simple films shown at fairs.[4] Hepworth first used professionals in 1905 and by 1912 had his own company, none well-known in stage terms but including Alma Taylor, one of the leading early film stars.[5]

Alma Taylor's entry into films well illustrates this early use of actors without stage experience. As a girl of twelve she delivered a note to the Hepworth studios in 1908. The producer took an interest in her and started giving her small parts, so that she became the most popular screen actress in England before and during the First World War.[6] It was more important to find non-stage girls like Miss Taylor for film work because film actresses and stage actresses at that time had quite different characteristics. Film actresses were then much shorter than those on stage, who tended to be older, altogether more

207

stately and of physically more impressive presence.[7] Film actresses like Alma Taylor and Chrissie White stuck to film work. Film actors were more likely to move between film studio and stage.

The use of unknowns without stage names or experience also had other consequences: the use of pseudonyms and the power of the producer. Since the public would never have heard of these actors, much care and money had to be expended on advertising and promoting them. If the actor then moved to another studio he took all this artificially added value with him, to the loss of the company that had given him his start. Hence the use of invented pseudonyms for film actors. These arose not to save any embarrassment to families, as with some stage actors, but to protect the investment of the producer. The new names were the property of the studio, advertised by the studio and ceasing to exist if the actor left, so that no subsequent employer could cash in on the goodwill of the name.[8] This began a tradition, much more prevalent on the screen than on the stage, of actors assuming false names. Their lack of prior experience gave the producer power over not only their names but also their performances. Hepworth has stressed the great care he took over pre-planning: 'When I went on the floor I knew exactly what I wanted, where every actor was to stand at the beginning of the scene, where and at what cue he was to move and of course what he was to portray',[9] though he allowed an interpretative scope to the actor. Hepworth was so sure of the result that he never troubled to see the rushes. In these ways the use of fresh inexperienced actors in the early years of the film industry was the root of these two characteristics, the pseudonym and the power of the producer-director.

Hepworth ran a film stock company of specialist film actors who began as unknowns. Other companies began to emerge who used actors with stage experience and even stage reputations. Gaumont were pioneers in this. In 1908 Godfrey Tearle made a film of *Romeo and Juliet* using Lyceum sets, costumes and cast. It was shot on an open platform in a field in Dulwich as a filmed play, and was 'the first English picture which exploited stage personalities'.[10] Sir Godfrey, the first noted English stage actor to become a film-star, enjoyed a film career through to the 1950s.

Another company which attracted notable stage actors was the

208

In the Cinema (*Punch*, 7 August 1912)

British Actors' Film Company. The antecedent of this was a film studio run by the wealthy portrait-painter Sir Hubert von Herkomer PRA at his mansion near Bushey Heath. In 1913 he engaged A. E. Matthews to star in his first major production, *Dick Turpin*,[11] while Owen Nares also acted for him.[12] Von Herkomer died in 1914 and Matthews bought up his Bushey studio and formed the British Actors' Film Company. Matthews induced Sir James Barrie to write a screenplay, and this trivial piece attracted the most distinguished cast of stage actors to appear in a British film to that date, including Irene Vanbrugh, Godfrey Tearle, Gladys Cooper and Owen Nares, among others. It was shown at a Royal Command Performance in 1916.

Film work became increasingly acceptable and attractive to film actors. It was noted that 'five years ago [c.1911] players of any repute were notoriously reluctant to act for the screen',[13] but this attitude changed markedly thereafter. A number of factors helped to bring this about. Firstly, there was apprehension among stage actors that their participation in films would incur the displeasure of the controllers of theatres, who feared the cinema's competition with the live drama. This fear seems to have been removed. Nobody before 1914 seriously thought that the cinema would replace the theatre, indeed the public might be even more interested to see a stage actor if they had seen him first in the new medium. Secondly, the beginning of film censorship in 1912 raised and guaranteed the tone of the industry. It was started within the industry by the Kinematograph Manufacturers' Association at the instigation of two leading producers, W. G. Barker and Hepworth.[14] They looked with alarm at the emergence of early pornographic moving films and feared that the whole industry would be damaged by them. Accordingly the trade set up the British Board of Film Censors, and the keeping of undesirable elements out of the trade further encouraged actors with reputations to guard to enter it. Thirdly, compared to the stage, filming was relatively lucrative and pleasant work. Tree established a precedent by demanding £1000 for *Henry VIII*.

The acceptability of film work for the stage actor was, however, most of all enhanced by the willingness of the leaders of the profession to appear on the screen. Much of the credit for the new development in England rests with W. G. Barker (the instigator of

210

film censorship). His Barker Motion Photography Company, with studios at Ealing, had made the first British film of *Hamlet* in 1910, and he induced Tree to allow his famous production of *Henry VIII* to be filmed in 1911. The cast included Tree, Arthur Bourchier and Violet Vanbrugh, and the whole performance was shot at Ealing in one day.[15] In the same year the Co-operative Cinematograph Company, in which Barker was also active, filmed Frank Benson and his company in *Richard III* and three other Shakespearian plays on the stage of the Memorial Theatre, Stratford. Other noted actors now followed Tree and Benson on to the screen. In 1913 Arthur Bourchier and Violet Vanbrugh made a film of *Macbeth*. The same year also saw one of the most successful of these early silents, Sir Johnston Forbes Robertson's *Hamlet*, produced by Hepworth for Gaumont and shot at Lulworth Cove.[16] The success of this still fine film made it clear that Sir Johnston's high nobility and dignity were projected and preserved rather than diminished by the cinematic medium. Doubts rapidly vanished. Sir Charles Wyndham came to Hepworth to have his *David Garrick* filmed; Sir John Martin Harvey to make *The Cigarette Maker's Romance*, both in 1913. Sir John Hare had his noted roles in *Caste* and *A Pair of Spectacles* recorded, and Sir George Alexander his production of *The Second Mrs Tanqueray*. Ellen Terry made her first film in 1916, the same year as Eleanora Duse.[17] The willingness of the great stage actors of the day to appear on film, especially from 1911 to 1913, was the most important element of the new dramatic medium.

By this time the industry was surprisingly large. There were forty-three principal film-producing companies in England, all (except one in Holmfirth and one in Bradford) in London and its environs.[18] In the British Isles in 1916 1000 million cinema seats were sold in 4500 cinemas.[19] The scale of this activity was putting pressure on the supply of film actors, which manifested itself in various ways. Firstly, there were gigantic competitions to find film actors. The International Cinematograph Exhibition at Olympia in 1913 ran a contest which attracted 3176 applicants, including many servants. The competitors had to express various emotions before a panel of judges including Cecil Hepworth, and as a result thirty-two of the successful ones were given jobs with film companies at £3–£7 a week.[20] Secondly, and more systematically, an embryo form of

211

cinema training began to emerge. The Victoria Cinema College and Studios run by Edward Godal in Rathbone Place, Oxford Street, had a good reputation in this specialized field. They trained for cinema acting under studio conditions and supplied a large part of the casts for Sir George Alexander's film of *The Second Mrs Tanqueray* and Cricks and Martin's *The Winner*, which suggests that they were taken seriously by the industry. They could supply up to 200 film actors on request for film companies.[21] Thirdly, a literature of advice began to develop. W. J. Elliott's *How to Become a Film Actor* of 1917 contained useful practical suggestions about such matters as approaching studios, photographs for casting, and so forth. It suggests that a sizeable number of people were eager to try their luck on the films, and these forty or fifty studios were equally anxious to find new faces and talent to retain the interest of the public.

The post-war silent decade of the 1920s was not auspicious from the standpoint of the British actor.[22] New studios started. Shepherds Bush, set up by Gaumont in 1913, was developed by the Ostrer brothers. Leslie Howard set up his own Minerva Films at Bushey in 1920 with fellow-actors Aubrey Smith and Nigel Playfair. Gainsborough Pictures began at Islington in 1920, Michael Balcon starting there in 1922, while the Elstree studio of British International Pictures began in 1926. Even so, it was the American film industry which dominated the British silent screen. Their own home market was so large that they could recoup the costs of production even before exporting. The British film industry could not compete with the better-financed and produced and relatively cheap Hollywood films. The undercapitalized Hepworth company collapsed in bankruptcy in the early 1920s, by the end of 1924 there was no British film production anywhere and by 1926 less than 5 per cent of British screen time was occupied by British film material.

Various characteristics of the body of film actors in the 1920s were not satisfactory. Firstly, many of the potential young male stars had been killed in the War, leaving a generation missing in the early 1920s. There were rather too many elderly stage stars like Martin Harvey, Hicks and Benson repeating stage roles for the camera. Secondly, the greater opportunities in Hollywood drew away some of the younger survivors of the War like Basil Rathbone and Ronald Colman, who were to achieve stardom in the American rather than

212

he British industry. Thirdly, German and American actors were mported to take leading roles in British films.

Film actors in the 1920s were more clearly divided into distinct roups, according to experience, than those of the 1930s. Male stars ended to have had stage experience rather than being exclusively lm actors. Among film actresses, however, there was a distinct roup who devoted their careers to specialist film work and who vere not stage actresses. Betty Balfour (of the *Squibs* series) was erhaps the first significant native British film star of this type. Alongside them, however, emerged young actresses of intelligence, raining and stage experience who combined stage and film careers in he 1920s. These included Edna Best, Madeleine Carroll and Nora winburne. Miss Swinburne enjoyed a varied career in films both in ngland and in Germany, as well as on the West End and Broadway tages, in this decade.[23] This was a new type of career pattern, lifferent from that of earlier specialist silent film actresses, which vould become more common in the 1930s.

In order to vitalize the dormant industry the Cinematograph ilms Act of 1927 introduced the quota. This stipulated that at least per cent of screen time had to be filled by British films, rising to 20 er cent by 1935. This did lead to an increase in production, notably f 'quota quickies'. These were rather poor short films of minimal uality rushed through production for little reason other than that heir screening would allow exhibitors to meet the obligations under he 1927 Act. Only then could they show Hollywood footage. The Act stimulated the formation of new film companies, twenty-six eing created in 1927, thirty-seven in 1928 and fifty-nine in 1929. These included major firms such as British Lion in 1927, British and Dominion in 1928 and Associated Talking Pictures in 1929.[24] Vithin a year of the Act, however, other more important developnents supervened. In September 1928 *The Jazz Singer* was the first ound film to be shown in Britain, and ushered in a new age.

The coming of sound was the most important change in the film ndustry and in the relation of the actor to it. Basil Dean, who set up he first film studios in Britain built expressly for sound, saw a Varner Brothers showing of their Vitaphone System in New York in 927 or early 1928. His reaction was elation: 'this is going to evolutionize films . . . it'll hand screen acting back to real actors.'[25]

213

The inevitable happened – silent actors unused to stage work and with inadequate voices left the industry. Film producers turned increasingly to vocally accomplished stage actors. It was noted that:

> the most vitally important matter of screen success today is a good voice, and it is fairly obvious that the majority of stage actors have by virtue of years of stage training, a decided advantage over those drawn from other ranks . . . the majority of British films of recent years that have competed at all favourably with American pictures have been represented by the cream of our actors.[26]

This was so from the beginning of sound films in Britain in 1929. Alfred Hitchcock's *Blackmail* in 1929 was originally intended as a silent film, but had to be reworked with a soundtrack to become the first British sound film. It was symbolic that the star, Anny Ondra, being Czech, spoke no English and accordingly had to be dubbed by an English actress. In future all films were to need actors with good English speaking voices and, almost always, stage experience. This was facilitated by the proximity of the film studios to the West End, enabling actors to work on films during the day before driving to their theatres in the early evening. 'London with its first-class theatres has its studios grouped within motoring distance and as a result it is from the London stage that the English film industry draws all but a very small percentage of its acting material.'[27]

Change and development took place in the studios in the early 1930s in response to sound. Associated Talking Pictures set up Ealing Studios in 1929 under Sir Gerald du Maurier and Basil Dean, the celebrated theatre director, while Michael Balcon took over Shepherds Bush in 1932 as the major studio of the Gaumont-British organization. The Elstree studios in Hertfordshire had been built in 1925 and then became part of G-B's rival, the Associated British Picture Corporation, in 1931. Herbert Wilcox's British and Dominions Film Company was also at Elstree. Wilcox claimed that it was the first sound studio in Europe;[28] it was in fact the first to have Western Electric sound equipment. Alexander Korda created London Film Productions in 1932 and built Denham Studios in 1936,[29] while Joseph Rank started production in 1934 and built Pinewood Studios near Denham in Buckinghamshire.[30] By 1938 there were twenty-two studios with sixty-five sound stages in

214

England, the largest being Elstree, Denham and Pinewood. All these studios were in the suburbs or immediate environs of London or in adjacent counties. Their location fused the close connection of the new sound film industry and the London theatre. In this England was in contrast with the American dichotomy of the theatreland of Broadway and the more specialist film actors of Hollywood, some 2400 miles apart.

Accordingly some of the very earliest British films, following *Blackmail*, relied on players of proven stage experience. Perhaps the first prestige production was Basil Dean's film of Galsworthy's *Escape* for Associated Talking Pictures in 1930. It was designed as the first British talkie (as opposed to the adding of sound to a silent) using the English countryside. Dean, as a theatre man, gathered a remarkable galaxy of West End players – Edna Best, Marie Ney, Austin Trevor, Lewis Casson, Felix Aylmer, Ian Hunter, Madeleine Carroll – headed by Sir Gerald du Maurier, who was chairman of ATP. Although not a commercial success, the seriousness of its intention and the gathering of so many luminaries of the West End stressed not only the need of the film industry for actors and voices of quality but also the respectability of being involved in such projects. Stage actors now flooded into film work. If we take a sample of the leading stage actors of 1936 we find the following incidence of starting in films:[31]

Before	1918	15	1924	3	1930	29
	1919	2	1925	nil	1931	33
	1920	7	1926	2	1932	24
	1921	2	1927	6	1933	11
	1922	2	1928	6	1934	19
	1923	1	1929	13	1935	4

The sharp increase over the years 1929–32 is evident, for the reasons we have indicated. By 1936 63.3 per cent of leading stage actors had worked in film studios and 36.7 per cent had not.[32] Clearly, by the later 1930s, most actors were prepared and able to encompass both media.

Some distinguished, and soon to be distinguished, actors began film work and appeared in notable productions with little delay.

215

Cedric Hardwicke appeared in *Rome Express*, Gaumont-British's first film at Lime Grove, in 1932, John Gielgud made *The Good Companions*, his second film, in the same year. Olivier had already been filming in Hollywood in 1931 and made his first British film, *Potiphar's Wife* with Nora Swinburne, in 1931. The most important film of these early years was Korda's *Private Life of Henry VIII* in 1933, starring Charles Laughton and Robert Donat, the first British film to achieve international success. Between 1930 and 1935 395 new production companies were created and between 1930 and 1936 British feature-film production rose from ninety-six a year to 215.[33] By 1934 eight British-made films were being shown in the West End. All this entailed a vast expansion of opportunities for actors wishing to take up film work.

A brief recession ensued in 1937, but between then and the outbreak of war the British film industry produced a spate of excellent films, including *The Lady Vanishes* (Michael Redgrave, Margaret Lockwood, May Whitty), *The Four Feathers* (Ralph Richardson, John Clements), *Fire over England* (Laurence Olivier, Flora Robson, Raymond Massey), among others. Various factors lay behind the vitality of this group of films from the last years of the 1930s. A new Quota Act came into operation in 1938. Now to qualify for the quota a British film must have cost £7500, or £1 per foot. This had the intended effect of stopping the production of the 'quota quickies' that had resulted from the 1927 Act and raising the artistic level of British production. Secondly, American companies, notably MGM, began to produce in Britain. *A Yank at Oxford*, *The Citadel* and *Goodbye Mr Chips* were MGM productions which helped to internationalize the stardom of British actors Vivien Leigh, Robert Donat and Greer Garson. Thirdly, the strength of the new sound-film industry in Britain, in contrast with its weak state in the 1920s, rested on the very high quality and range of leading acting talent on which it could call. Almost all leading British film players of the late 1930s combined screen success with distinguished stage careers. The exception was Margaret Lockwood who, although RADA trained and having appeared in the West End, was more exclusively a film actress than any of the others.

Legitimate stage actors did not always enjoy working in films, nor regard them highly. There was fair agreement on what stage actors

216

disliked about filming – the early rising, often after a previous night's work in the theatre; the ghastly yellow makeup; the hanging around on the set with spasmodic spurts of work and a lack of continuity during the day; the mechanical interferences for the placing of camera and microphone and the chopping of flowing narrative scenes into short, often meaningless, momentary shots out of context and out of sequence.[34] Others resented the power of the producer, which left no more artistic discretion to the actor than that of a schoolboy writing dictation.[35]

Whatever dislikes some actors may have harboured about work in the film studios, these could be readily set aside for the high financial rewards such work provided.[36] Film work was considerably more lucrative than stage acting, even five, six or seven times more. The situation was not a creation of the sound era but had been already apparent in the 1920s. Very high earnings per picture of £3–5000 for a star were also possible, due to the new economics of mechanized entertainment. A film costing £50,000 to make (and allowing a tenth of that cost for a leading actor's fee) would be more likely to cover its costs than a stage show costing £2000 to produce. There were 3600 cinemas in England in 1928 which would pay a rental of £50–100 for a film, thus giving a return of at least £90,000 if, say, only half the cinemas took the film at the lowest rental.[37] In the sound era five-figure sums became possible for major stars like Gracie Fields and Robert Donat. This had a beneficial effect on the stage in enabling actors whose chief loyalty was to the live theatre to subsidize their stage acting from their film work. It was noted in 1937 that 'play production . . . is in fact financed to an increasing extent by the film industry and the film studio contributes more than the stage to the salary of the stage actor.'[38] It was important to Olivier, Gielgud and Redgrave, and thereby helped to subsidize the Old Vic, where star wages of £20 a week were notoriously low.

The rise of the cinema reacted back on the theatre itself. Cedric Hardwicke found that the cinema was 'deadly to the reproductive theatre typified by touring companies which gave imitations of West End productions'.[39] It also had an astringent effect on the more banal plays of London and the provinces. An observer of the later 1930s thought that 'the cinema has swept the "mezzo-brow" theatre pretty well clean' of 'crook plays, adventure plays, farces, nice little

217

drawing-room comedies'.[40] There was no doubt of the attractions of the cinemas. They were relatively cheaper than the theatres. In 1930 a night at the theatre for two might cost 29/- for two stalls, compared with 5/- for an evening's cinema entertainment.[41] The cinemas were comfortable, even luxuriously so, there were a lot of them and they were easily accessible. In 1937, for example, there were 431 ABC, 345 Gaumont-British and 200 Odeon cinemas.

Not only did new cinemas compete with the theatres for audiences, but employment for actors in the live theatres was diminished by their conversion into cinemas. For example, the Margate Hippodrome in the 1920s showed London plays with visiting West End actors – Tearle, Nares, Lang and Fay Compton. In 1929 and 1930 it alternated between being a cinema and a theatre, and then from 1931 turned over entirely to film projection.[42] In Liverpool by 1934 the ordinary theatres which had received touring companies 'have been crushed out of existence' by 'the relentless efficiency of the cinema', leaving the Rep as the centre of live drama.[43] Overall, theatres presenting live drama declined from about 500 in 1928 down to 250 by 1933, by which time there were some 4000 cinemas.[44]

The impact of the rise of the talking cinema upon the provincial touring theatre may be seen quite sharply from the lodgings list published by the Actors' Church Union. The contraction of their availability reflects the contraction of the market among a diminished body of provincial touring actor clients needing temporary accommodation. From over 2000 theatrical lodging-houses in more than sixty towns in the heyday of the mid-1920s, accommodation had fallen to just over 300 in over fifty towns by the end of the 1930s.[45] That the fall in the number of towns was nothing like so great as the fall in the number of lodging-houses reflects the fact that live entertainment did not, of course, totally cease in most towns, but that there was much less of it. The live stage show competed now with three or four cinemas, and the landladies who would have lodged the visiting actors who might have formerly played in several other theatres in a town went out of business.

The rise of the British film actor in the 1930s produced an interesting paradox. Because of the close connection of the West End stage and the film studios, film actors and stage actors tended to be the same people. We have seen that they tended also to be men and

218

women of comfortable professional and commercial social background and of good education. In this they came from much the
same milieu as the people in the stalls and circles of their West End
theatre audiences. And yet the vastly larger cinema audiences
comprised the common mass of ordinary working- and lower-
middle-class folk, who were of much humbler social origins and
educational experience than the film actors they weekly, or twice
weekly, assembled to admire. It had been one of the great strengths
of the live theatre from the 1890s that there had been an identity of
social class between actor and audience. Actors of good breeding
drew in audiences of a new respectability, which in turn cast new
prestige on the actors' work. With the cinema there was no such
identity of actor and audience. Here the audience was called upon to
admire and empathize with players from whom they were socially
and educationally quite distant. The cinema audiences did not
demand a completely different set of film actors who had risen from
their own ranks, as was to be the case after the 1950s. Specifically
working-class film stars like George Formby and Gracie Fields were
enormously popular in comedy character films in the 1930s, especially in the North of England. But the backbone of the film industry
ran on producing straight drama acted by West End stage actors of
high standing and cultured accents for audiences quite unlike
themselves.

The leading British film actors of the 1930s were solidly men of
professional social origins and public school and/or university background.

	Father	*Public School*	*University*
Leslie Banks	Merchant	Glenalmond	Oxford
John Clements	Barrister	St Paul's	Cambridge
Robert Donat	Civil engineer	—	—
Rex Harrison	Private means	Liverpool Institute	—
Charles Laughton	Hotel proprietor	Stonyhurst	—
James Mason	Textile manufacturer	Marlborough	Cambridge

219

	Father	Public School	University
Raymond Massey	President of Massey-Harris	Appleby School, Ontario	Oxford
Laurence Olivier	Clergyman/ headmaster	St Edward's, Oxford	—
Michael Redgrave	Tea planter*	Clifton College	Cambridge
Ralph Richardson	Public School master	Xavierian College, Brighton	—
Emlyn Williams	Stoker/'General labourer'	—	Oxford

* guardian

Emlyn Williams, coming from a humble working-class family in North Wales, is the well-known exception to the general pattern of comfortable background and public school. Yet it is significant that he was enabled to enter the theatre by using his abilities to get to Oxford first.

The pattern is the same for women film-stars. The four leading film actresses in Britain in the 1930s were Madeleine Carroll, Greer Garson, Vivien Leigh and Margaret Lockwood. Miss Carroll and Miss Garson were both university graduates at a time when very few middle-class, and a minute proportion of working-class girls ever achieved such distinction. Miss Leigh was the daughter of a stockbroker, educated at a fashionable convent and at finishing schools on the Continent. Miss Lockwood's father was a chief railway manager in India and she was educated at Sydenham Girls' Public Day School Trust High School.

It is quite clear that British film-stars of the 1930s, both men and women, came from much higher social backgrounds and were much better-educated than the average population. They did not become an elite by becoming film-stars, they already belonged to a stratum of society that was privileged and well-to-do. They already possessed, through their youthful nurturing, the physique, good looks, accent and social poise that would make them admired by audiences lacking these attributes. Accordingly, becoming a
220

film-star was not a realistic route by which humble people could escape from the poverty of economic depression, as was professional sport. The ease of a Rex Harrison, the slightly haughty beauty of Vivien Leigh or a Margaret Lockwood, the aware intelligence of a Greer Garson, could not be acquired or learned. They were qualities nurtured by youthful experience of a lifestyle and background as far from most of the audience as the silver screen across which the actors' images moved.[46]

II

Even more pervasive in bringing the actor and drama to a mass audience was broadcasting. Early in its history the BBC became involved in the broadcasting of drama. Its first transmissions were scenes from Shakespeare in September 1922, with actors Robert Atkins and Arthur Bourchier.[47] At the same time excerpts from the live performances of stage plays were broadcast with microphones concealed in footlights and the scenery. They broadcast plays from the Old Vic, Lilian Baylis welcoming the ten guineas per play fee.[48] However, it became clear from the unsatisfactory nature of outside broadcast drama that 'if plays were to be broadcast at all they must be broadcast from studios' and 'they must develop a technique of acting and production peculiar to themselves.'[49] This healthy attitude was in any case forced on the BBC by the refusal of West End theatres to continue to allow the broadcasting of live performances.

The moving of such broadcasting out of the theatre and into the studio had fruitful effect. Cathleen Nesbitt adapted and produced several Shakespeare plays, and Lewis Casson both produced and appeared in broadcast plays with Sybil Thorndike.[50] The early stress on Shakespeare and the use of prominent stage actors was still somewhat derivative, almost seeking a reflected respectability from the prestige of the high culture of the live stage. In 1924–5 a greater independence became evident. In 1924 Richard Hughes's *Danger*, set in a coal mine, was the first play actually written for broadcasting. In July its producer, R. E. Jeffrey, established the dramatic department for the regular production of plays. In the following year the first BBC Repertory Company was formed and Reginald Berkeley's *White Château* was produced. This was regarded by some as

221

the effective beginning of a genuine radio drama.[51] The regular use of Lance Sieveking's 'dramatic control panel', enabling the mixing of voices, music, sound effects and crowds, further helped the development of radio drama as a medium in its own right.

The attitude of actors to the new medium was mixed or ambivalent. Val Gielgud, who was to become director of drama from 1929 until 1964, deplored that in those early years there was a 'contemporary view of the members of the theatrical profession that there was nothing in broadcasting but script reading and the equivalent of cigarette money' and that 'as far as the acting profession was concerned, Savoy Hill had failed to establish prestige'.[52] Some noted stage players – Dame Madge Kendal, Sybil Thorndike and Lewis Casson, and Henry Ainley – appeared in straight plays in the mid-twenties.[53] But it was the transfer in 1932 from Savoy Hill to Broadcasting House, with its proper studios for the drama department, that enabled the growth of professionalism in radio acting.[54] Through the BBC Drama Repertory Company, founded in 1925 and refounded in 1939, radio drama began to create its own specialist star actors. Carleton Hobbs, Gladys Young and Norman Shelley, to name but three, were already noted radio actors in the 1930s. The first two were former RADA prize-winners and were later distinguished by the award of the OBE for their radio acting. The drama schools too began to take radio acting seriously. RADA had a microphone and broadcasting equipment installed by the BBC in 1926, and the Central School did some broadcasting tuition in the 1930s.

Radio acting had its own special conditions of work, often marked by great precision. A play was preceded by eight intensive rehearsals, each lasting exactly three hours. Each actor had his script which he covered with notes:

> referring to which studio he has to be in for a certain speech, what his volume of voice, his position in relation to the microphone, the mood, stress, inflexion, at what point he has to wait to be cued in by a flick on a coloured light.[55]

The play was performed live as one continuous sequence, but the actors retained their annotated scripts. The problem was then to avoid the performance sounding like a reading to a microphone

222

There were physical difficulties also when a large cast had to work to one or two microphones, with 'bumping, boring, crowding and heading-off' like 'a flock of sheep going through a very narrow gateway'. By the mid-1930s the microphones for drama were hung over the heads of the cast, almost out of the line of sight. Accordingly, the actors could feel freer to move about and by forgetting the microphone could, it was hoped, give a more realistic performance.

Acting in the new medium, which made especial demands on the voice, was valued by some actors for its stringent discipline. Marie Ney described the approach of the radio actor:

> he spends an hour or two concentrating on purity of diction, using and practising every shade of speech he has within his range, to make his voice only convey the character. This is surely a very useful work for vocal tone and colour and his theatre work must benefit.[56]

Radio acting was also made attractive by the range of work available. In 1934 five Shakespeare plays were broadcast, two by Chekhov and two by Ibsen, as well as adaptations of five classic novels. The repertoire had to follow a fairly middle course. Following the relative failure of audience response to a series of Twelve Great Plays in 1928, there was a certain reluctance about broadcasting the less popular classics other than Shakespeare.[57] Even so there was enough in the diet, as that of 1934 showed, to provide rewarding and challenging work for the serious player. Moreover, radio proved an ideal medium for plays of ideas and verbal wit, notably by Shaw and Wilde. There was an attractive range of work, innovative excitement and occasional meaty roles for the serious player, all of which made radio acting a new form of satisfying career. The potential audience was now huge, rising from two million licensees in 1927 to nine million by 1939. Radio drama was only about three or four per cent of the total hours of output, but it was enough to establish a new distinctive dimension to the actor's art.

III

Broadcasting before the War involved not only sound radio but also the early stages of television. This too presented fresh challenges and

223

opportunities to the actor. On 30 March 1930 the first transmission was made of television with sound. It was inevitable that an attempt would soon be made to experiment with the new medium to explore its possibilities for drama. In July 1930 Val Gielgud, Lance Sieveking and Sydney Moseley produced Pirandello's *The Man with the Flower in His Mouth*, the first television play transmitted by the BBC. It had its inevitable limitations: 'only one figure could be projected at a time and that figure could scarcely move. The focus was still uncertain and variable.'[58] Regular BBC television broadcasts began on 2 November 1936, and by 1939 there were some 20–25,000 television sets in use.

Some plays were televised direct from theatres during their actual performance. J. B. Priestley's *When We Are Married* was the first so transmitted, on 20 November 1938. However, television drama proper was produced from Alexandra Palace near Mill Hill. Stage actors became aware of the need for quite new techniques and disciplines involving the minimum of movement, especially difficult when stage successes were adapted for the small screen. Esmond Knight remembered televising a play about Van Gogh after playing it on the stage:[59]

> An entirely new technique had to be developed, for the screen, on which an audience of not more than eight or ten might 'view', was very small, and plays were, therefore, acted in a series of large close-ups and very 'tight' groups.

Marie Ney, the distinguished Shakespearian actress, also acquired much experience of television drama before the War, starring in *Viceroy Sarah*, *Charles and Mary Lamb*, and televising her celebrated performance of Mrs Alving in *Ghosts*. She recalled shortly afterwards:[60]

> . . . the entire cast working in a limited space of an average drawing room mat, near the microphone, and having to think of camera, characterization and voice all at once . . . In *Viceroy Sarah* there was one close up that lasted for about six minutes. There were several of us in this scene, and we had to keep our noses level as we spoke so that everybody would be in focus. It was frightfully

difficult, but we finally managed it by imagining that we all had our noses stuck against a window pane.

As well as problems of technique, actors had to adjust to cramped conditions, extraordinary makeup, short rehearsal and performance runs. Wilfred Brambell (gaining belated fame as Steptoe) was already an experienced television actor in the 1930s. He gives a lively recollection of Alexandra Palace of these days:[61]

There was a long corridor which separated the two studios, up and down which the actors stampeded during the action of those live productions for their change of scene. In the light of present-day knowledge the studio lighting then was primitive, and the make-up grotesque. Character actors' faces were plastered in two tones: a base of putty grey with highlighting streaks of dusty yellow across the cheekbones and down the nose. The pretty 'juves' wore a coat of Jaffa orange which seemed utterly to obliterate all their features and cause their faces to vanish, vanquished. Nevertheless these extraordinary phenomena appeared natural, and were accepted by the wealthy and fortunate television owners of the day. Productions were rehearsed in 'Alley Palley' as it was affectionately called, for three weeks – (find your own fare), and the live performance took place on Thursdays and on the following Sundays each week. For which month's work we were presented with (and gladly accepted) the princely sum of eighteen guineas, as compared with my, at that time, current theatre salary of eighteen pounds a week.

The difficulties of the art were compounded by the fact that rehearsal was so divorced from final performance. It was only on the actual day of the show that producer and cast saw the set and cameras for the first time, and it was unusual to be able to run through a play with cameras more than once before transmission.[62] Bruce Belfrage thought, under these conditions, that 'for the actor it [television] is undoubtedly by far the hardest form of his art.'

Through the new means of cinema, broadcasting and television, the faces and voices of actors were brought to a vastly wider audience. Many of the leading actors themselves, hitherto largely confined to the West End or Number 1 tours, became nationally

225

known figures. This further increased the commercial value of the player and intensified the business context in which he sold the 'property' of his performance and personality. Both in this general way, and in some of the specific problems that the new media created, they contributed to the need for the protection of the actor through an efficient form of unionism. This was the other major change affecting the profession in the interwar years, to which we now turn.

NOTES

1 John Barnes, *The Beginnings of the Cinema in England* (London, 1976).
2 BBC 2, 'Bioscope Days', 18 May 1978.
3 Cecil Hepworth, *Came the Dawn* (London, 1951), p.52.
4 BBC 2, 'Bioscope Days', 10 May 1978.
5 Cecil Hepworth, *op.cit.*, pp.66–7.
6 *Era*, 17 January 1917.
7 *Era*, 21 February 1917.
8 Cecil Hepworth, *op.cit.*, p.81.
9 *Ibid.*, p.137.
10 R. H. Ball, *Shakespeare on Silent Film* (London, 1968), pp.75–6.
11 A. E. Matthews, *Matty* (London, 1952), pp.153–4.
12 Owen Nares, *Myself and Some others* (London, 1925) pp.195–6.
13 *Era*, 5 April 1916, 'The Actor in Film Plays'.
14 Cecil Hepworth, *op.cit.*, pp.108–9.
15 R. H. Ball, *op.cit.*, pp.78–82.
16 *Ibid.*, pp.83–7. J. C. Trewin, *Benson and the Bensonian* (London, 1960), pp.176–7.
17 Roger Manvell, *Ellen Terry* (London, 1968), pp.319–20.
18 William J. Elliott, *How to become a Film Actor* (London, The Picture Palace News Co. Ltd, 1917), Appendix.
19 *Era*, 3 April 1918. This suggests that about 600 people attended each cinema every night of the year.
20 *Era*, 5 April 1913.
21 *Era*, 14 February 1917.
22 The definitive study is Rachel Low, *The History of the British Film* 1918–1929 (London, 1971). See also Ernest Betts, *The Film*

Business, A History of the British Cinema 1896–1972 (London, 1973); George Perry, *The Great British Picture Show* (London, 1975), for the period generally.

23 Interview with Miss Swinburne. Also *Era*, 2 July 1924.

24 P.E.P., *The British Film Industry* (London, 1952), p.50.

25 Basil Dean, *Mind's Eye* (London, 1973), p.82.

26 *The Stage*, 9 November 1933.

27 J. P. F. Turner, 'The British Film Studio Notes', *British Equity*, February 1934.

28 Herbert Wilcox, *Twenty-Five Thousand Sunsets* (London, 1967), p.85.

29 Karol Kulik, *Alexander Korda* (London, 1975).

30 Alan Wood, *Mr Rank* (London, 1952).

31 Analysed from *Who's Who in the Theatre*, 1936, names A–K.

32 *Ibid.*, 1936, names A–C.

33 P.E.P., *op.cit.*, p.60.

34 John Gielgud, *Early Stages* (London, 1939), p.283; Basil Dean, *op.cit.*, p.189.

35 Ernest Thesiger, *Practically True* (London, 1927), p.138.

36 See Appendix 3.

37 *Era*, 14 March 1928.

38 R. D. Charques, 'What's Wrong with the Theatre Today?', *Footnotes to the Theatre*, ed. R. D. Charques (London, 1938), p.18.

39 Cedric Hardwicke, *Let's Pretend* (London, 1932), p.243.

40 Reginald Denham, 'Stage and Screen' in R. D. Charques, *op.cit.*, p.44.

41 Oscar Asche, *His Life* (London, 1929), pp.139–41.

42 Malcolm Morley, *The Theatre* (London, 1935), pp.139–41.

43 Grace Wyndham Goldie, *The Liverpool Repertory Theatre 1911–34* (London, 1935), p.212.

44 St John Ervine, *The Theatre in My Time* (London, 1933), p.189.

45 Actors' Church Union Lodgings Lists for the dates cited.

46 It is worth noting that this was also the case in Hollywood. The vast majority of American male film-stars established or emerging in the 1930s and 1940s were university men. These included Humphrey Bogart, James Cagney, Spencer Tracy, Gary Cooper, Bing Crosby, Edward G. Robinson, Fredric March, Clark Gable,

Gregory Peck, Van Heflin, John Wayne, Henry Fonda, James Stewart, Franchot Tone. Tyrone Power was perhaps the chief native-born American film-star who had not been to university. Cary Grant, Ronald Colman and Errol Flynn were migrants from England.

47 Val Gielgud, *British Radio Drama 1922–1956* (London, 1957; Asa Briggs, *The Birth of Broadcasting* (Oxford, 1961), p.280.

48 Richard Findlater, *Lilian Baylis* (London, 1975), p.166.

49 Val Gielgud, *op.cit.*, p.33.

50 Asa Briggs, *op.cit.*, pp.280–1.

51 Sydney Moseley, *Broadcasting in My Time* (London, 1935), p.94.

52 Val Gielgud, *op.cit.*, pp.25, 53–4.

53 Asa Briggs, *op.cit.*, p.282.

54 Val Gielgud, *op.cit.*, p.54.

55 Lance Sieveking, *The Stuff of Radio* (London, 1934), pp.44–7, depicts radio acting in the mid-1930s.

56 Marie Ney in the *Daily Telegraph*, 9 June 1930.

57 Asa Briggs, *The Golden Age of Wireless* (Oxford, 1965), p.161.

58 Asa Briggs (1965), p.550.

59 Esmond Knight, *Seeking the Bubble* (London, 1943), p.117.

60 *Barrier Truth Broken Hill*, 12 June 1941, article by Marie Ney in Miss Ney's scrapbooks. British Theatre Museum.

61 Wilfred Brambell, *All Above Board* (London, 1976), p.44.

62 Bruce Belfrage, *One Man in His Time* (London, 1951), p.195.

11 Association, Guild and the Rise of Equity 1919–40

A major change in the acting profession in the interwar years was the creation of an effective trade-union movement with the formation of Equity. The Actors' Association had been handed on from the years before the First World War, as we have seen. Yet, as it had been weakened and rifted by the splitting off of the left-wing Actors' Union in the 1900s, so similar schisms were to plague it in the 1920s. The Actors' Association initially flourished in the immediate aftermath of the War, but soon began to disintegrate under the impact of economic recession affecting the theatre. The AA shifted further to the Left in political terms, aiming to be a militant trade union with a diminishing clientele. In these circumstances it was severely damaged by the breaking away of non-political (or Conservative) members to form the Stage Guild. With its trade-union effort totally divided into two hostile groups, one of which had no intention of acting as a trade union, the profession was seriously weakened. The only resolution was a re-merger of the Association and the Guild in 1929, with the creation of Equity. In the 1930s Equity totally revived actors' trade unionism with its enforcement of the closed shop, suppression of the amateur and increasing influence in the provinces and the film studios. It was a remarkable renaissance and an important safeguard to the actors' profession after the vulnerable weakness and disorganization of the 1920s.

During the First World War actors' trade unionism had developed relatively little. Most actors were in any case away fighting, and actresses focused their attention on the activities of the Actresses'

Franchise League. Accordingly the Actors' Association was left very much in the hands of the ageing actor–managers. As the War drew to a close the AA began to resume trade-union characteristics under the leadership of Sydney Valentine. It was spurred by American Actors' Equity's securing of a standard contract in 1917 (followed by a strike in 1919) and the new situation at home, where control of the theatre was passing from actor–managers to commercial interests and syndicates. Accordingly, in November 1918, the AA formally became a trade union and its membership soared from 800 in 1918 to 5–6000 by the middle of 1919.

In April 1919 the Association agreed the Standard Contract with the West End managers which provided for a minimum salary of £3 for a week of eight performances with £2 a week for rehearsals. A similar Standard Touring Contract was eventually secured in 1920. The Association had flourished in the context of an immediate post-war boom both in the economy and the theatre, but two watersheds were marked by the death of Sydney Valentine in December 1919 and the severe recession that was evident in the theatre by 1921.

The removal of the moderate Valentine as chairman gave a prominence to the Secretary of the AA, Alfred Lugg, a Socialist who wanted to move the Association to the Left in solidarity with working-class trade-union groups. Lugg and his supporters favoured a closed shop, union-controlled entry into the profession and joint action with different types of non-professional theatre workers. This new 'working-class' Socialist tone of the AA led to the removal of interest and support of an increasingly suspicious West End elite. The Association was thus weakened internally. The recession exacerbated the situation. The West End managers who had accepted the Standard Contract in the 1919 boom now began to feel, in the slump, that it was not in their best interest and determined to reopen the discussion. The actors' position was accordingly weakened and the AA's relations with some of the employing groups was breaking down. The Theatre Managers' Association were resisting the Standard Contract and the Touring Managers gave notice in July 1922 that they were terminating their observation of the Touring Contract. Membership of the AA fell steadily and sharply to 600 by 1925.

230

II

In 1924 the actors' trade-union movement was split by the creation of the breakaway Stage Guild. The immediate occasion had been the closed shop boycott at Barrow-in-Furness in April. There the local trades council had been trying to insist that every performer coming to Barrow should be a member of a trade union. This had precipitated resolutions in trade and labour councils throughout the country in support of the complete unionizing of all places of entertainment and urging members to boycott any non-unionized theatres. This was too much for the more 'professional' and non-union-minded actors, already exasperated by the Leftist tendencies of the AA. On 6 June 1924, they met at the Criterion Restaurant to inaugurate the Stage Guild.[1] Sir Frank Benson presided, with Fred Terry, Lady Wyndham, Sir John Martin Harvey and Eva Moore. Their aim was to set up an organization to represent the whole of the dramatic profession, managers as well as actors. They made it clear that the Guild, unlike the Association, was not interested in trade unionism, 'direct action', or actors regarding themselves as industrial workers on a par with backstage technicians and pit musicians.

The Guild pursued a variety of activities. It drew up Standard Contracts, for London and for Touring, providing for a £3 minimum wage and obliging managers to supply costumes.[2] It ran an agency for finding employment and in 1928 started its own benefit fund.[3] In keeping with the lifestyles of many of its leading members, the Guild ran an active and rather smart social life. It held an annual ball, starting in 1925 at Covent Garden, supper parties at Claridges and the 1927 ball aboard the luxury liner *Berengaria*. These posh junketings, remote from the ethos of the Actors' Association, reinforced the distance that the Guild wished to maintain between itself and traditional working-class trade unionism. This posture was equally evident during the General Strike, when the Guild gained prestige for its activities not in contributing to the stoppage but in enabling the show to carry on by co-operating with the Theatrical Managers' Association. The AA, by contrast, was too weak to support the Strike.

From 1924 to 1928 the Guild thrived. It benefited from the booming prosperity of the theatre in 1925. Most important, some

231

managers offered actors working for them a free gift of several months' subscription to the Guild and made it clear that all future engagements would be made through the Guild.[4] This was a powerful element in the Guild's success. Accordingly, numbers rose from 1200 in February 1925 to 3000 by July 1928. This was perhaps the peak, but even so was only half of the peak membership of the Actors' Association before the advent of the Guild.

From the summer of 1928, however, the Guild began to fall apart as the bulk of the managers withdrew.[5] These were the provincial touring managers rather than *actor*–managers like Martin Harvey and Nares, who wanted to remain members. The defectors had originally been absorbed into the Guild from the old Association of Touring Managers. They had been as uneasy within it as union-minded actors were. For four years the touring managers had resisted progressive moves by the Guild on behalf of equitable conditions for actors, and now quit altogether.

In this later phase Godfrey Tearle emerged as a leading articulator of views. His position was that, with the removal of the touring managers, Guild members could agree with everything the AA stood for except the right to strike.[6] Of Guild actors, 75 per cent were former AA members. Tearle now wanted an effective re-merger of the Guild and Association. By 1929 the Actors' Association was in a moribund condition and the Stage Guild had lost its manager members. The future clearly lay in a union of the two organizations if the AA could relinquish its political aspirations and if the Guild could give up its hostility to trade unionism and its desire to keep links with the managers. The very weakness of the AA had already robbed it of any realistic political aims, and the separation of the managers from the Guild had already freed the path of the latter. A synthesis was to come about in 1929 with the creation of Equity.

III

Apart from the decayed state of the Actors' Association and the Stage Guild, various factors lay immediately behind the creation of Equity. These were firstly an awareness of analogous events abroad and secondly a specific crisis of bad faith at home. The knowledge of foreign developments encouraged the creation of a strong actors'
232

union in England, for in the late 1920s the entertainment industries organized on an international scale.[7] 1926 saw the creation of the International Institute of Musicians, the Universal Theatrical Society, based in Paris, and the International Union of Artistes, claiming to have 35,000 members in twenty-one countries. In France the French actors' union, the Union des Artistes, secured from 1929 a system of obligatory licensing of actors.[8] Even more sharply relevant was the awareness of the tough position of American Equity. Following the barring of an American actress (Alden Gay) by the Ministry of Labour, and her return to the USA, American Equity made restrictive regulations against British actors coming to America.[9] In this atmosphere, both rich with international co-operation and threatening with international retaliation, it was necessary for the English stage to resolve its divisions and create one strong union to represent its interests.

In the autumn of 1929 a crisis arose which drove the AA and the Guild closer together. The *Open Your Eyes* Company was left stranded on tour, and unpaid, by a bogus manager. What made this case somewhat unusual was the standing of some of the artists, including Marie Burke, who were all too eager to voice their grievances. A meeting was held at the New Theatre to discuss the fiasco. Not only did the Guild and the AA co-operate in this, but John Emerson of American Equity spoke and expressed the hope that the incident would lead to the creation of a 'British Equity' – perhaps the first time that the term was used.[10] A sequel meeting at the Duke of York's Theatre discussed the formation of such a British Equity and was addressed by Alfred Wall of the London Trades Council and representatives of German and French acting unions. The way forward could be achieved only by the merger of the AA and the Guild, the former forgoing its Left political bias and the latter its hostility to unionism as such.[11]

Equity was formed as an organization on 1 December, basing its aims and objects on those of American Equity, 'which means strict trade unionism'.[12] The leading spirits were Dame May Whitty and her husband Ben Webster, Godfrey Tearle, Brian Aherne, J. Fisher White, Lewin Mannering and Bromley Davenport, who all formed a provisional committee. Often they met in May Whitty's flat in Bedford Street. Her daughter remembered that 'the dining room

233

became more difficult to eat in . . . it was generally occupied by anything from four to forty actors.'[13] It was fitting that Dame May's big mahogany dining table is still used for committee meetings in the Equity Council Room. That Equity should have started around the fine dining table of a Dame of the British Empire was symbolic of a very important characteristic of the union. It was a trade union created from above by the elite of the profession. Alfred Wall noted how unusual this was: 'usually you know the demand for organization comes from below. In this case the activities and enthusiasm have come from the leaders of the profession.'[14]

The leaders sold the idea to the rank and file at a series of meetings, notably one in May 1930 at the New Theatre amidst 'fighting talk and emotional uproar . . . cheques for a hundred pounds fluttering down on to the stage from the crowded boxes', as Edith Evans recalled.[15] A subsequent meeting in July at the same theatre heard Ethel Barrymore talk of American Equity and their strike of 1919. After this period of publicity, the first council was elected in September 1931. It consisted of forty people, including Tearle, May Whitty, Edith Evans, Leslie Henson, Sybil Thorndike, Raymond Massey, Austin Trevor, Ben Webster, Sebastian Shaw and Evelyn Laye. The 1932 election added du Maurier, Gielgud, Hardwicke and Gertrude Lawrence. These were prestige names that were to guarantee the strength and success of the union in the coming decade.

Tearle, claiming to speak for his Council, stressed the non-political and even Conservative stance of his fellow-Equity leaders:

> Neither I nor any other Council member of British Equity is politically minded. If we vote at all we vote Conservative simply because ours is a luxury business that caters for the leisured classes. The theatre itself is innately Conservative, but frankly we have no time for politics.[16]

Shortly afterwards he reiterated that 'Equity is to be regarded not as a militant trade union, but as a professional organization.'[17] It was hoped that the fears of many actors about the old AA and its trade-union Leftism in the early 1920s had been scotched.

IV

It was evident that the new union would have to be distinctive in aiming for a closed shop. The old Actors' Association had failed because it could not enforce the acceptance of Standard Contracts. This in turn was so because it lacked the sanctions, backed if necessary by a strike, that only a closed shop would provide. If the failure of the AA was one influence, another was the success of American Equity, with its frank espousal of strike and closed-shop strategies in a tough commercial context.

One major problem that the union sought to eradicate by the closed shop was that of the bogus manager. It will be recalled that it was the ditching of Marie Burke by such a manager that was the immediate occasion behind its creation. It was a long-standing problem that plagued actors' unions back to the old AA in the nineteenth century, and actors long before that. Godfrey Tearle's father Osmond had himself once been the victim of a bogus manager and had sustained a cruel financial loss as a result. This must often have been in his son's mind. 'Managers' could recruit a body of actors, rehearse them without payment, open for a week or two on tour and then decamp with the takings, leaving the actors unpaid, and with no money to return to London. This was a not uncommon occurrence, in spite of the Theatrical Employers' Registration Acts of 1925 and 1928. Equity stressed the problem in 1932, holding meetings to complain of, and publicize, managers who were unable to meet their liabilities.[18] It was clear that the irresponsible manager could be eliminated from the system only by a strict closed shop. In that way Equity could enforce that actors should not sign contracts with managers without consulting with the union. Equity could starve the bogus entrepreneur out of business by depriving him of actors.[19]

The union also appreciated that gaining control of the manager through securing closed-shop control of the actor was the only way of securing the enforcement of any Standard Contract. The experience of the 1920s, the failure of the Valentine contract and the unions' difficulties with different organizations of managers had shown that tougher measures were necessary. In their first Report Equity observed:

235

With a 100 per cent membership we shall not hesitate to use every possible weapon to enforce the terms of our contract. We confidently look forward to the day when we shall have a closed Equity shop in every theatre, and shall refuse to allow any actor or actress to work for any manager for less than the standard minimum contract.[20]

Another problem that the closed shop was intended to eradicate was the employment of unpaid (or even paying) amateurs on the stage. The unqualified and inexperienced players who were merely doing it for fun undercut and crowded out the true unemployed professionals and filched their livelihood. The problem threatened to become acute in 1932, since thousands of unemployed people were turning to amateur acting. In such a situation, where amateurs could too easily sidle on to the boards abetted by penurious managers, it was urgent in 1932 for Equity to assert the principle of a totally professional acting body, at least in the West End.

Accordingly an Equity meeting on 4 November 1932 voted in favour of enforcing the closed shop by 1140 to 12.[21] At that time, of 881 actors working in London, 736 were already members of Equity and thirteen belonged to the Guild, while 142 belonged to no union.[22] In this situation the decision to declare the closed shop from 1 January 1933 seemed realistic. Within the profession Ivor Novello and Owen Nares expressed unease, though Nares became a very keen supporter of Equity. Most actors outside the union probably had no strong views one way or the other, but 'immediately the result became known there was a great influx of new members. A keen anxiety to get inside Equity before 1 January was shown and recruits poured in during a short period at the rate of one hundred a week.'[23]

Scarcely had the policy of the closed shop been declared than Equity was faced with two crises. The first was over *The Beggar's Bowl* at the Duke of York's Theatre. The play was stopped by the union because the management had paid nothing for rehearsals nor for a week's performances. Furthermore, it was evident that the management could not pay. In some quarters the withdrawal of labour by the actors was interpreted as a strike; more correctly it was a breach of contract by the management.[24] The cast was withdrawn

236

and compensated from Equity's Benevolent Fund. The whole incident created a sensation and was widely reported as clear proof that Equity would act toughly in defence of its members' interests.

This was just as well, since the next crisis was a direct threat to the closed shop. George Robey and his *Jolly Roger* Company were touring in the provinces prior to opening at the Savoy. Robey had strong prejudices against trade unions, which he associated with 'Moscow'. He refused to join Equity, realizing that his refusal would be a clear breach of the closed shop if he attempted to open in London. The situation worsened as a real threat arose that Robey's cast, who were members of Equity, might resign from the union. The Council held a full meeting of members at Drury Lane on 26 February 1933 to decide on a course of action. It was one of the most important meetings in the history of the union.[25] For the first time they were displaying a great sense of unity and determination. They had to resolve whether to act in a conciliatory fashion or to defend the closed shop with an all-out strike if Robey tried to open at the Savoy without joining. Following a powerful speech by Llewellyn Rees, a future general secretary of the union, the meeting determined to stand firm on strike action. In the end Robey took a financial interest in the show, thereby turning himself into a manager without the obligation to be a member of Equity, duly opened, and the closed shop remained unbreached.

It is difficult to exaggerate the importance of this incident for the union. Its adversary was in many ways a man of eccentric views, but behind and alongside him were many other theatre people like the Littlers, C. B. Cochran, A. P. Herbert and perhaps most of the Society of West End Theatre Managers, who viewed Equity with suspicion and hostility as an interfering and possibly malign political force. The whole event took place in a blaze of popular publicity. To have failed would have set back the union for years and destroyed its credibility; its firmness and success brought further benefits in its wake. The SWETM decided to recognize it and negotiate a Standard Contract; 'contrary to its intention, George Robey played a leading role in setting Equity on its feet.'[26] By May 1933, of twenty-four West End theatres employing 610 artistes, twenty were already closed-shop. In the touring theatres (which were not closed-shop) there were only nine actors who were not in the union.[27]

237

V

The strength that Equity had been able to show over the closed shop in 1933 had a decisive effect on the surviving rump of the Stage Guild. After the formation of Equity the Stage Guild continued its independent existence, suspicious of any connection with trade unionism or the Labour Party. It was still fairly thriving, with 2697 actors, under Sir Johnston Forbes Robertson as its President. It was active in pressing for a Bill to regulate agencies and espoused the cause of a National Theatre, dear to Sir Johnston's heart. The leading actors in the Guild, apart from Forbes Robertson, were Nicholas Hannen, O. B. Clarence and Ernest Thesiger. It was indicative of the rather patrician tone of the Guild that the last three gentlemen were all the sons of judges. It also explains much of the psychological resistance to accepting membership of a trade union. A further division between the Guild and Equity arose over the question of the Sunday opening of theatres. Many Equity members were in favour of opening but the Guild remained consistently opposed.[28]

However, the enforcing of the closed shop in London by Equity from 1 January 1933 precipitated the final phase of the Guild's decline as actors increasingly transferred from the Guild to the union. By the end of 1933, and a year of the closed shop, the strength of Equity was such that the independent existence of the Guild ceased to make sense. Nicholas Hannen, who had taken over as president from Forbes Robertson and who had strongly resisted any merger in 1930, changed his mind. The Guild held a referendum and decided to join Equity by 236 votes to 31,[29] the voting figures showing how low its membership had sunk. The merger was effected on 16 December 1933 merely by Equity accepting all the Guild actors into its own membership.[30] It was, observed a reluctant Guild member, 'much like the incorporation of Jonah with the Whale'.[31]

VI

Equity maintained the closed-shop policy throughout 1933 and 1934 and by the end of the latter year, having absorbed the Stage Guild,

238

felt sufficiently strong to insist on this policy being included in all contracts whether managers liked it or not. It had been trying for some months to negotiate the standard contract with SWETM the union insisting on a closed-shop clause and the managers resisting it. Negotiations had been broken off and the threat of a strike was in the air.[32] Felix Aylmer and Lewis Casson strongly advocated the firm line that members should decline to enter into any contract with managers where the terms of employment were less favourable than those in the basic contract approved by Equity. It was stressed that there was no effective means of enforcing the contract other than through the Equity closed shop.[33]

At this point, Dame Marie Tempest, not hitherto seemingly much interested in union matters, pulled off a fine theatrical coup.

> Suddenly she commanded all the elite of the London stage to a luncheon at the Savoy Hotel. They came one and all, much flattered. They consumed impeccable food and drink. She then arose, exquisite and imperious, and issued her instructions. A Roll of Honour had been prepared and was laid out on a table beside the exit door. It pledged those whose names appeared on it to sign only one-hundred-per-cent-Equity contracts . . . They laughed, applauded and signed.[34]

Now the signatories agreed not to sign contracts without a clause allowing their right to refuse to act with non-Equity members. The scroll is still proudly kept on the staircase of the present Equity offices in Harley Street. A subsequent meeting at the Criterion Restaurant at the beginning of December decided to enforce the closed shop with relation to contracts from 1 January 1935.[35]

As the closed shop of 1 January 1933 was followed by the *Jolly Roger* crisis, so that of 1 January 1935 led to the Drury Lane crisis and the dispute with H. M. Tennent's, Ivor Novello and the *Glamorous Night* production. Tennent's were refusing to insert a clause in the contracts which would uphold the Equity shop.[36] Novello threatened to resign from Equity but his leading lady, Mary Ellis, accepted her union's instructions and refused to sign her contract, as did all the cast, with one exception. The dispute threatened to spread as thirty-seven managers met to discuss the incident and thirty-six voted to back the Drury Lane's action. André

Charlot, who had already supported Equity over the Robey affair, was the sole abstainer.

The Drury Lane dispute resulted in one highly beneficial outcome, the London Theatre Council. The management of Drury Lane had approached the Ministry of Labour, which appointed F. W. Leggett, a principal assistant secretary, to assist the parties.[37] Leggett held a meeting of Equity and SWETM at the Ministry of Labour on 31 January 1935. He suggested a broad scheme for a joint board consisting of actors and managers, with both sides having the right of appeal to it in the case of differences over the engagement of artists. Aylmer, Tearle and Wall represented Equity at these early meetings in February, which culminated in a full meeting on 15 February of twenty-one London managers and twenty-two leading actors.

> At this meeting Mr Leggett made a very strong appeal for co-operation between the two sides and suggested that the London Theatre Council would form a body which would enable managers and artistes to work together for the development of the theatre as a part of the national life.[38]

Both sides agreed and created the LTC with twenty members, half managers and half actors, under the chairmanship of Lord Esher. Its purpose was to enforce the Esher Standard Contract by issuing certificates to managers producing plays and actors accepting engagements and 'to devise ways and means of settling any differences that may arise'.[39] The actors who participated in the first Council, and subsequent Councils of the thirties, included Aylmer, Tearle, Casson and Leslie Henson, among others. Tearle explained its purpose: it would safeguard the development of the theatre, be a means of settling differences, and secure the recognition of the Standard Contract.[40]

Much of the activity of the LTC, and of Equity within it, consisted of fine-tuning certain issues within the broad context of the Esher Contract. For example, they insisted that the ever-troublesome C. B. Cochran (who was not a member of the Council) should take up options on artists' services not less than two weeks before the end of a run rather than at any point he thought fit.[41] They decided that an actor already acting with a company could not claim rehearsal

240

payments while at the same time preparing for the next production[42] and took fine decisions about whether certain parts were actors' (subject to the Esher contract) or supers' and walk-ons' (not so subject).[43] Most of the work of the LTC was of a detailed nature trimming a ship already, since 1935, sailing strongly and fairly steadily. No profound issues of principle seemed to arise, and no great disputes. The decisions on issues seem very even-handed and pragmatically sensible – as indeed we would expect from its balanced composition.

The Council was important. It stabilized theatrical relations – 'it has brought more order and regularity into the economic questions inseparable from many West End productions.'[44] Both Equity and SWETM were thought to have gained in strength and influence following the formation of the LTC. The Minister of Labour stressed that the Council had come about not so much through his activities or imposition of control, as from the goodwill of both sides within the industry.[45] The LTC, quite fairly, praised itself as 'the highest form of voluntary self government yet achieved in any profession or industry'.[46]

VII

Having established some control in the West End, Equity's chief problem in the second half of the thirties was to extend itself into the provinces and the film studios. The 1935 AGM considered that the unionization of the provinces should take precedence.[47] A number of factors suggested the wisdom of this. Firstly, touring members in the provinces had already been joining Equity and it was time to provide them with the benefits of a Standard Touring Contract.[48] This was connected with the fact that 50 per cent of the profession was in London, and after working in the provinces returned to London.[49] The implication was that a sizeable number of actors in the provinces had had London experience and hence knew of Equity's activities and would be amenable to its spread beyond the capital. Secondly, conditions in the provinces were prosperous and hence suitable for unionization in 1935, which was regarded as the best year for British theatres since the War. Equity was urged to unionize the provinces, to stop premium players and the racket of 'student' free labour, and to secure rehearsal pay for provincial actors.

Meetings with the Theatrical Managers' Association and the Association of Touring and Producing Managers were held, with the aim of creating a Provincial Theatre Council on the lines of the LTC[50] and securing a provincial Standard Contract. Godfrey Tearle himself toured the provinces in order to renew his experience of the provincial stage and claimed: 'we are hammering away to get the standard contract in the provinces and the closed shop will be an essential part of it.'[51] In the spring of 1939 the draft Standard Provincial Contract was drawn up with a minimum salary of £2.10s, rehearsal payment (new to the provinces), the limitation of students to 20 per cent of the company, the abolition of premium payment and the acceptance of the closed shop. In May Equity approved the Provincial Contract and the formation of the Provincial Theatre Council.[52] Since the outbreak of war intervened, both matters were finalized on 1 January 1942.

VIII

The rise of the film industry likewise posed problems for the actor and the unions. These arose from what, in its early days, were relatively free and chaotic modes of working. In the first place there were no regular hours and more care was taken to fit in with the convenience of the technical craftsmen than the actors. Secondly, the genuine actor had to compete with hordes of amateurs, who made a hobby of playing small parts in films simply for the 'fun' and curiosity of being in a film studio.[53] In an attempt to regulate the situation Coulson Gilmer, a former businessman and film actor, formed the Film Artists' Guild in 1929.[54] By 1930 it had several hundred members and Ronald Colman became a vice-president, which gave it some status. Equity, too young and weak as yet to get involved in the film industry, hoped that producers would employ members of the FAG.

In 1934, following the initiation of the closed shop, suggestions were made that Equity should unionize the film studios.[55] The leading British film actors were in any case members of Equity through their stage work, and it was argued that this would give

242

them influence in unionizing the less important actors. Yet the chief problem holding back unionization was the difficulty of defining what a film 'actor' was, with its amateur crowd players, 'foreign types' from Soho, Chinese waiters and British Legion extras on 12s 6d a day.[56] George Arliss, the distinguished film actor and a keen trade unionist, used his star influence to ensure that small-part players in British productions in which he appeared were genuine actors with stage experience.[57] Elsewhere amateurs, ranging from the Mayfair smart set to chars and crooks, turned up to play themselves, taking their small fees away from actors, whose livelihood it was. In 1935 a further effort was made to control the situation with the formation of the Theatrical Artists' Film Society to protect the interests of small-part players.[58] The Society compiled lists of members with qualifications and experience for sending to casting directors. But less than 40 per cent of British crowds consisted of bona fide performers, and the TAFS had no hope of enforcing the kind of closed shop with bit-part and crowd players such as Equity had secured in the legitimate stage.

Shortly after the formation of the TAFS and in the same year, 1935, Equity felt the time was ripe to tackle the problem of the film studios. It decided to make overtures to the studios to make a Standard Contract[59] and early in 1936 it noted that 'consultations have taken place between Equity officials and the managements of important film studios with a view to facilitating negotiation of a standard contract for film productions.'[60] A draft contract was devised by Felix Aylmer allowing for a working day of 9 a.m. to 6.30 p.m. with 1½ hours' rest, overtime rates and 12 hours' complete rest away from the studios between working days,[61] and in April 1937 a Film Producers' Group was formed to enforce standard conditions in film studios in conjunction with Equity.[62] The union noted that 'Equity is confident that the methods which have proved invaluable in the theatre will be equally successful when applied to motion picture production.'[63] At the end of the year it appointed an officer to organize the film studios.[64]

A second problem created by the film industry was that of actors working all day in the studios and returning to act on the West End stage in the evening. In contrast to the American scene, the proximity of the film studios to London and the fact that leading

British film-stars were also West End actors imposed severe strains on the actor engaged both in film-making and in a long stage run. In the 1930s this began to arouse opposition from managers. It was not Equity's business to prevent its members from earning as much as they could, nor to impose a ban in the interests of managers. But Tearle agreed with the managers' position[65] and there was no opposition to managers making this stipulation in contracts. Most notably, H. M. Tennent Ltd brought the issue to a head in 1938 by forbidding its artists to work in films during the day. Equity raised no objection to this.[66]

IX

A major long-standing problem which Equity had to deal with was the relationship with the United States; both the British actor in America and the American in Britain. As American actors' unionism had been influenced by the old AA, so it in turn influenced the formation of British Equity. The British organization took its 'Equity' name from the American and the American experience lay directly behind Equity's closed-shop policy. The Americans had also provided the example of an actors' strike, that of 1919. Accordingly in its first year Equity stressed its amicable relations with its American counterpart. They had arranged reciprocal agreements for British and American actors working in each other's countries and joined each other's unions.[67] At home the Ministry of Labour agreed to consult with Equity over the regulation of foreign artists.

By the end of 1931, with depression hitting the theatre, relations between the two stages became more edgy. After Britain left the gold standard in September 1931 American Equity insisted that British actors in the United States should have their salaries specified in dollars so that they could not undercut American actors by the devaluation of the pound.[68] The anxiety and resentment of the Americans was exacerbated by the strong presence of British actors in New York at the end of 1931. The British contingent, including Celia Johnson, Edith Evans and Leslie Banks, were reputed to be making £25,000 a week in America and there were eight plays with

British casts on Broadway at the time.[69] In this context American Equity began to operate a tougher line against the British, levying 10 per cent on their salaries. Britain began to feel aggrieved, since while British actors went to America so we in turn accepted alien, chiefly American, actors in Britain and the British attitude to Americans was felt to be more generous.[70] The Ministry of Labour had received 135 applications from Americans and, on Equity's advice, had refused only seven of them, 5 per cent.[71] This generous policy which Equity followed was in their interests, since four British actors were appearing in America for every one American in England.[72] Any tough line adopted by British Equity could be met by even greater retaliation from the Americans.

Most serious was the Dickstein Bill. The Americans were, not unreasonably, concerned that in the depression their own actors had to compete with British actors for places on the stage. They did not object to stars who generated work for others but, as Frank Gillmore, President of American Equity, observed, 'in times like these it stirs us deeply to see alien actors from the lower classifications being cast for parts we could play just as well ourselves.'[73] Accordingly the Bill proposed to exclude British actors from the United States unless 'they are of distinguished merit and ability as actors and their professional engagements within the United States are of a character requiring superior talent.'[74] Gillmore assured British Equity that leading actors and whole unit companies would not be affected; it would merely make things more difficult for the younger, unimportant British actor trying to establish himself in America before having done so in England. Hoover signed the Bill in 1932 and it was feared that 1500 British actors might lose their jobs in the United States.[75] We need have less sympathy for them than for the plight of the American actor and theatre in a recession considerably more severe than that experienced in England; in New York forty of the city's seventy theatres were unoccupied and salaries were slashed.[76] In this context British Equity could appreciate its counterpart's concern and restrictions, disadvantageous as they were to British interests.

Later in the thirties Equity established relations with the Hollywood film studios. They had become highly unionized in 1933 when the NRA obliged Hollywood to reduce film-stars' salaries. This

245

prompted a flood of screen actors – including Cagney, Cooper, and the British actor Aubrey Smith – into joining the Screen Actors' Guild. In turn the SAG merged with American Equity. In 1936 British Equity came to an agreement with SAG to enforce standard conditions in both countries. Members of British Equity automatically became members of SAG when in the USA, and vice versa. It is notable that this agreement had been negotiated by Boris Karloff (William Pratt) and George Arliss, two celebrated British actors who had become Hollywood film-stars and who had advised Equity on its own British film contract. Equity concluded: 'this agreement is very satisfactory in view of the fact that the motion picture industry, so far as English-speaking films are concerned, is becoming more and more dependent upon the joint efforts of American and British artists.'[77]

X

Back home, Equity faced the serious problem of unemployment among actors in the depression years. In 1934 St John Ervine calculated that there was at any given time professional work for only 2000 actors and actresses.[78] Another observer agreed with this, suggesting that 1000 actors and actresses were fairly regularly employed in London and 1000 in the provinces. Yet there were 6000 actors and actresses 'whose training at least justifies the name'. This left 4000 who were unemployed, or so occasionally employed as to be unable to earn a living.[79] This suggested a virtually inevitable unemployment level of two-thirds. But this overall problem of inevitable unemployment was exacerbated by great imbalances in opportunities between the sexes. Two-thirds of parts were normally for men (in Shakespeare four out of five), whereas three-fifths of players were women.[80] This would give men a one in six and women a one in fourteen chance of work. The rising incidence of unemployment and financial difficulty among actors can be seen from Equity's figures. An increasing disparity began to arise between members fully paid up, those in arrears and those in a separate category of unemployed members contributing at a reduced rate.[81]

	Fully Paid Up	In Arrears	Arrears % of Total	Unemployed members at reduced rates
1931	241	162	40.1%	
1932	997	702	41.3%	123
1933	990	2558	72.1%	629
1934	1011	3559	77.9%	695

The unemployment was exacerbated by two factors. Firstly, in the West End, in spite of lower stars' salaries and seat prices,[82] there was a marked increase in failing productions and short runs. New plays produced and running for fewer than forty performances rose sharply:[83]

1930 . . . 34   1931 . . . 56   1932 . . . 50   1933 . . . 73

More stringent times may have been making audiences more selective and unwilling to support the mediocre. This led to a more rapid turnover of plays and hence of actors, throwing individuals back into unemployment more quickly without perhaps greatly diminishing the total stock of employment.

Secondly, in the provinces the situation was worse, with a positive reduction in the overall level of employment. From 1929 to 1934 over 200 theatres had turned over to being cinemas, causing a state of unemployment 'never before experienced in theatrical history'.[84] This was further reflected in the decline of touring companies as venues diminished. It is interesting to note that attendance at dog-racing tracks increased from five million to seventeen million between 1931 and 1934,[85] suggesting some possible diversion of working-class interest away from the theatre to the cheaper forms of entertainment.

There was probably not much that Equity could do about unemployment except to banish the amateur actor from the stage. The union could, however, ease the relations of unemployed actors and the official bodies designed to help them. In July 1933 it suggested to the Ministry of Labour that there should be a specialized labour exchange for the theatre.[86] The minister was sympathetic to the idea and asked Equity to appoint a representative on the Great Marlborough Street Employment Committee. Equity was an approved association under the Unemployment Insurance Acts, and

247

so could represent members before such tribunals. On the employment side the Equity representatives were successful in stopping the Exchange sending actors to unsuitable non-theatrical work. On the benefit side they eased the reinstatement of benefit for members of companies whose runs ended abruptly.[87] So began the continuing special relationship between the unemployed actor and Great Marlborough Street.

XI

Equity assumed a valuable role in the thirties as an arbitrator in theatrical disputes. There had been a long tradition of this. When Sir Squire Bancroft was alive he was frequently appealed to as an arbitrator since he was experienced, respected and his great wealth and early retirement from the stage placed him in a personally disinterested position. In the 1930s, however, there was no comparable figure. The divergence of interests between actors and managers, highlighted by the experience of actors' trade unionism since the War, now meant that such arbitration would have to be by a panel of representatives of these balanced interests. From 1933 Equity provided this service with some of its elder statesmen, like Lewis Casson and Ben Webster, meeting with prominent managers like Bronson Albery or H. M. Tennent to decide cases referred to them.[88] Sixteen actors and managers, working in pairs, dealt with sixteen cases between 1933 and 1939. Contracts were firmly upheld and actors who tried to evade touring responsibilities, who had relied upon purely verbal agreements or claimed unwarranted transatlantic fares received short shrift. Equity would also act very toughly against its own members whom it regarded as behaving unprofessionally towards their managers. An actor of great future popularity was disciplined for refusing to act because of his dissatisfaction with his dressing room. Casson adjudicated that he should pay £150 to compensate his manager.[89] It is noteworthy that Casson, who did a lot of adjudicating, was originally regarded with suspicion by the managers for his evangelical Socialism. They came, however, to respect his 'unequivocal honesty of purpose,'[90] of which the dressing-room case was an example. These events were of great value both in asserting the power of the union over its members and, more

248

strikingly, in establishing the union's credibility with the managers. It was clear that Equity really was striving for professionalism and even-handed fairness. This enhanced the respect and trust with which the union was regarded within the industry, strengthened its hand and kept the wheels of the West End lubricated and running smoothly.

XII

Equity had its failures, notably in its attempts to secure concessions over the double taxing of American earnings and over Entertainments Tax, yet in the main its record in the 1930s was a creditable and successful one. Its enforcing of the closed shop, negotiation of Standard Contracts, banishing of the amateur actor and hounding of the bogus manager, its regularizing of relations with the American stage and its power to arbitrate on disputes at home, as well as its unemployment work, all made it worthy of support. Accordingly, its membership rose.[91]

1931	446
1932	2190
1933	3686
1934	4795
1935	4055
1936	4078
1937	4599
1938	3469

The union's peculiar strength lay in its combination of professional association and trade union. Unlike the old Actors' Association and the Stage Guild, it was not compromised by the membership of the employers. It could negotiate firmly with the managerial associations like SWETM and ATM clear in its mind that its clients were employed actors. Yet, also unlike the Actors' Union and the Actors' Association in Lugg's day, Equity was free of any particular connection with Socialism or the Labour Party which would have driven away most members of the profession. Also unlike its predecessors, its willingness and capacity to discipline its own members gave it a credibility

249

as a professional association more analogous to those in law and medicine. Bernard Shaw stressed the connection between strong union organization and professionalism. He told RADA students, 'only by strong professional organization can the profession attain the social consideration and official recognition accorded without question to the "learned professions"'.[92] Most important, it was an unusual case of unionization from above, by the elite of the profession on behalf of the rank and file. Certainly players like May Whitty, Godfrey Tearle, Felix Aylmer, Marie Tempest, George Arliss, Lewis Casson and the other leaders had no need whatever of a trade union to advance their own personal careers. They gave their efforts selflessly for the good of the profession as a whole and for the benefit of actors far less successful than themselves who needed the union's protection. It was the power of the Equity stars in being able to refuse to play with non-Equity casts that gave such strength to the closed-shop policy. An obscure bit-part player's refusal to play with a non-union star would have caused no effect whatever, except his own non-engagement or dismissal. Sir Gerald du Maurier or Dame Marie Tempest refusing to play with any bit-part player who was not a member of Equity caused the immediate unionization of all actors. This was the strength of unionization from above.

This phase finished not with the outbreak of war but in 1940, when Equity resolved to join the TUC. Its motives were plain and had arisen out of the new power of trade unions in the War. It explained:

> owing to the increasing authority of the Trades Union Congress in National affairs consequent upon certain of its leading representatives accepting office in the Government, the Council of Equity unanimously decided that it would be detrimental to the interest of the Association to remain outside Congress and decided to apply for affiliation forthwith.[93]

This proved a symbolic parting of the ways. Godfrey Tearle, whose personal views were somewhat Conservative, had always insisted on the non-political character of Equity. Accordingly he felt obliged to resign as its president over this issue. He was replaced by Lewis Casson, who had a long record of Socialist sympathies and of Leftist activity in the interwar years. Casson was perhaps a more appropriate leader for a body now so committed to trade unionism and to allying itself with an organization which was integrally a part of the politics of the Left. Yet Tearle had been a fine and necessary president for the 1930s. He was possessed of handsome good looks and great charm, and a persona which was every inch that of the respectable 'professional man' and gentleman. These both won over the West End elite of which he was a part and presented the very best public face of the new union to the managers, the press and the nation at large. He was belatedly rewarded in 1951 with a knighthood, which he briefly enjoyed until his death two years later.

NOTES

1 *Era*, 11 June 1924.
2 *Era*, 10 December 1924.
3 *Era*, 25 January 1928.
4 Philip Godfrey, *Backstage* (London, 1933), p.58, made this claim.
5 *Era*, 1 August 1928; 8 August 1928.
6 *Era*, 10 October 1928 Godfrey Tearle's explanation.
7 'Organisation among Intellectual Workers', *International Labour Review*, Oct.–Nov. 1928.
8 *Era*, 24 July 1929.
9 St John Ervine, 'Protecting the Actor', *The Nation and Athenaeum*, 21 July 1928.
10 *Era*, 16 October 1929.
11 *Era*, 4 December 1929.
12 British Actors' Equity Association First Annual Report, 1931.
13 Margaret Webster, *The Same Only Different* (London, 1969), pp.359–60.
14 *The Stage*, 10 July 1930.
15 Bryan Forbes, *Ned's Girl* (London, 1977), p.141.
16 *Era*, 8 March 1933.
17 Tearle's Presidential Address, 24 February 1935, Minutes of Equity AGM, 1935.
18 *The Times*, 25 October 1932. *The Stage*, 8 December 1932.
19 Minutes of Equity AGM, 24 October 1932.
20 British Actors' Equity Association First Annual Report, 1931.
21 Minutes of Equity AGM, 4 November 1932.

22 *Ibid.*
23 British Actors' Equity Association, Second Annual Report, 1933.
24 *The Stage*, 2 February 1933.
25 Margaret Webster, *op.cit.*, p.362.
26 Peter Cotes, *George Robey* (London, 1972), pp.97–9.
27 PRO Lab 10/20 Ministry of Labour Industrial Relations Division. Memorandum 12 May 1933.
28 *The Times*, 23 February 1931.
29 *The Stage*, 30 November 1933.
30 British Actors' Equity Association, Third Annual Report, 1933–4.
31 Margaret Webster, *op.cit.*, p.360.
32 *Daily Telegraph*, 3 November 1934.
33 Minutes of Equity AGM, 4 December 1934. 'Memorandum on the Enforcement of Contracts', 13 November 1934.
34 Margaret Webster, *op.cit.*, p.364.
35 *The Stage*, 6 December 1934.
36 *The Times*, 21 January 1935.
37 Sir Frederick Leggett was later one of Ernest Bevin's right-hand men at the Ministry of Labour during the War.
38 PRO Lab 10/19 Memorandum on the London Theatre Dispute, 15 February 1935.
39 London Theatre Council Constitution 1935.
40 Minutes of Equity AGM, 24 February 1935.
41 Minutes of Executive Committee of the London Theatre Council, 10 April 1935.
42 *Ibid.*, 25 June, 12 October 1936.
43 London Theatre Council Executive Committee, 18 January 1937.
44 London Theatre Council Third Annual Report, 1938.
45 PRO Lab 10/19 'Note for Minister'. Memorandum or speech typescript, 31 March 1936.
46 London Theatre Council Fourth Annual Report, 1939.
47 Minutes of Equity AGM, 18 June 1935.
48 'And Now the Provinces', *British Equity*, July 1935.
49 Minutes of Equity AGM, 28 June 1938.
50 Minutes of Equity Executive Council, 13 October 1936.

51 Minutes of Equity AGM, 28 June 1938.
50 Minutes of Equity Executive Council, 13 October 1936.
51 Minutes of Equity AGM, 28 June 1938.
52 *The Times*, 16 May 1939.
53 *The Stage*, 5 October 1933.
54 *Era*, 25 March 1931.
55 Ben Williams, 'British Actors Film Equity' *British Equity*, July 1934; *Daily Telegraph*, 20 June 1934.
56 P. L. Mannock, 'What is a Film Actor?', *Kinematograph*, 28 June 1934.
57 *Daily Herald*, 19 June 1935.
58 *The Stage*, 6 July 1935.
59 Minutes of Equity Executive Council, 27 August 1935, 8 October 1935.
60 British Actors' Equity Association Fifth Annual Report, 1935–6.
61 Minutes of Equity Executive Council, 17 July 1936.
62 *Ibid.*, 13 April 1937.
63 British Actors' Equity Association Sixth Annual Report, 1936–7.
64 Minutes of Equity Executive Council, 14 December 1937.
65 Minutes of Equity AGM, 16 June 1936.
66 *Daily Telegraph*, 26 January 1938.
67 British Actors' Equity Association First Annual Report, 1931.
68 *Daily Dispatch*, 23 October 1931.
69 *Sunday Express*, 22 November 1931.
70 *The Stage*, 19 November 1931. 'Stage Economics'.
71 *Manchester Guardian*, 30 March 1932.
72 *Manchester Guardian*, 29 February 1932.
73 *Ibid.*
74 British Actors' Equity Association Third Annual Report, 1933–4.
75 *Daily Telegraph*, 19 March 1932.
76 *Glasgow Evening Times*, 15 April 1933.
77 British Actors' Equity Association Fifth Annual Report, 1935–6.
78 *Birmingham Gazette*, 17 January 1934.
79 *Manchester Guardian*, 8 August 1935.
80 *The Observer*, 30 September 1934.
81 Minutes of Equity AGM, 29 October 1935.
82 *Evening News*, 27 August 1932 noted that stall prices fell from

14/6 to 12/-, dress circle from 8/6 to 6/- and gallery from 1/3 to 1/-.

83 *The Stage*, 3 May 1934.

84 *The Stage*, 18 January 1934.

85 *The Stage*, 22 March 1934.

86 Minutes of Equity Executive Committee, 4 July 1933.

87 'Great Marlborough St. Employment Exchange', *British Equity*, July 1934.

88 Minutes of Equity Arbitration Proceedings, 1933–9.

89 *Ibid.*, 8 June 1937.

90 John Casson, *Lewis and Sybil* (London, 1972), p.201.

91 Figures as at 31 December of each year. These were reported in the Annual Reports. There was no report for 1939.

92 The RADA *Graduate's Keepsake and Counsellor* (London, 1941), p.20. Shaw paid for this booklet, to be given to all students leaving the academy. Among other things it stressed the importance of strong unionism in the profession.

93 British Actors' Equity Association Tenth Annual Report, 1940–1.

12 The Second World War 1939–45

During the War the theatres, and accordingly the fortunes of actors working in them, underwent severe fluctuations. There had already been a slump in theatre-going in the summer of 1939, as people preferred to frequent pubs and hotels to discuss the threatening situation.[1] The outbreak of war in September brought the immediate closure of theatres, on government orders. Indeed, the very radio bulletin in which Chamberlain announced the declaration of war continued with the announcement of the closure of theatres and cinemas. This seemed to many people an excessive reaction that took too little account of the need to sustain morale. Lord Wigram, the King's former secretary, used his influence to press this latter view and within a week the ban was lifted.[2] Outside cities theatres and cinemas were allowed to open freely, while from 14 September those in cities could open until 10.00 p.m. and in the West End a six o'clock closure was enforced for a time.[3] Theatres were open during the winter of 1939–40 and continued playing to large audiences through the dangerous summer of 1940. The opening of the Battle of Britain on 7 September 1940 led to the second period of theatrical crisis. After ten days of blitz only the Windmill remained open and the Shaftesbury, Little, Queens, Royalty and Kingsway theatres were destroyed or irreparably damaged, while Drury Lane and the Saville were badly damaged by the bombing.

With the closure of London theatres Hugh Beaumont of Tennent's sent most of his companies on tour for £10 a week and a share of earnings, with the condition that they did six weeks' work for

ENSA between each tour.[4] From the ending of the blitz on 10 May 1941 until February 1944 the London theatre revived and flourished. This lasted until the advent of the V-1 rockets, which reached central London in June 1944. Most theatres closed yet again, only ten staying open, audiences disappeared and the St James Theatre was badly damaged. From September 1944 to March 1945 the V-2s hit London, but the psychological mood had changed with the expected end of the War. By the end of 1944 'every available playhouse re-opened . . . throughout the winter [1944–5] capacity audiences were the rule rather than the exception.'[5] These severe fluctuations applied especially to the theatre in London, which was the prime target. Outside London the theatre prospered in wartime as 'never before in its history'.[6]

In spite of these vicissitudes the artistic quality of much wartime theatre was remarkably high, and in this the Second War was in sharp contrast to the First.[7] This rather serious cast of mind was reflected also in the attendance at the concerts at the National Gallery and the troops' discussion of the Beveridge Report. Most British dramatists of the first order were represented on the London stage in the War years. Indeed Congreve's *Love for Love* and Shaw's *Heartbreak House* both had their longest-ever runs in London during that time. Plays of fairly serious import that did well were *Thunder Rock*, on the theme of facing up to responsibility, *Dear Brutus* in 1940; *Life Line* and *Flare Path*, on military service themes, in 1942; *They Came to a City* in 1943. Russian plays also found favour, three in 1941 and *A Month in the Country* in 1943, while Athene Seyler led a noted tour of *The Cherry Orchard*. The last eight months of the War saw the major achievements of the Old Vic at the New Theatre, Olivier's *Richard III* and Richardson's *Peer Gynt*. Some remarkable long runs achieved commercial success – *Blithe Spirit* (1997 performances from 1941), *Arsenic and Old Lace* (1332 from 1942), *Quiet Week-End* (1059 from 1941 and the longest run achieved by a British woman dramatist), *The Man Who Came to Dinner* (709 from 1941). It says much for the taste of the time that all these long runs were comedies of considerable wit and style, good fun and durability. One finds in the Second World War much less of the craving for inane distraction of almost any kind that characterized, and was criticized in, the First. The actor was seen to be doing a worthwhile job of

256

national value in work of good quality; Margaret Rutherford as Madame Arcati and Robert Morley as Sheridan Whiteside, no less than the Shakespearians of the Old Vic.

II

In the early stages of the War the problem of the call-up and deferment of actors was bound to arise. In April 1940 Walter Payne and Godfrey Tearle, acting on behalf of the London Theatre Council, contacted the Ministry of Labour. They were 'apprehensive of the difficulties which may arise at no distant date in conjunction with the calling up of some of those at present employed in management or acting or in the technical departments of theatres', and accordingly asked for a meeting of the two bodies.[8] At this meeting, attended by Tyrone Guthrie, Lewis Casson, H. M. Tennent and Walter Payne on behalf of the theatre, Casson admitted that there was no case for general exemption, though Tennent claimed that 'important' people should be reserved.[9] These commonsense views carried weight with the Ministry, which internally agreed that certain actors could be reserved to finish the runs of their productions to prevent premature closures.[10] There were several urgent cases cited as examples. Hugh Beaumont (aged 32) was virtually running Tennent's and a large section of the West End, while Rex Harrison (32), Roger Livesey (34), Jack Hawkins (30), Emlyn Williams (34), and Alec Guinness (26) were others cited to the Ministry as worthy of temporary deferment.[11]

Following a meeting on 17 May 1940, 'It was suggested that a small committee representing the industry should vet any applications for the deferment of calling up and present those about which they are quite satisfied to this Department', i.e. to the Ministry.[12] Payne had proposed an Entertainments National Service Committee, chaired by himself, to consider cases for deferment of actors and to recommend to the Ministry those whom it thought worthy. The Ministry of Labour itself considered various policies ranging from a stringent one of calling up everyone, including stars, to a generous one of wide deferment, and decided on the middle way of admitting special cases, deferring stars and key performers.[13] Payne's ENSC could now go ahead following this Ministry policy. Another, less

257

powerful, government body held a similar view of the actor's importance. The Home Morale Emergency Committee, on being formed in May 1940 (with Harold Nicolson and Kenneth Clark), suggested: 'tell actors that they are counted upon to keep people cheerful.'[14]

The first list of proposed deferments contained several key legitimate stage actors, Rex Harrison (*No Time for Comedy*), Roger Livesey (*The Millionairess*) and Marius Goring.[15] Basil Dean was confidentially shown the deferment list so that he could call on their services for ENSA. It was not a condition of the deferment that actors should do some work for ENSA. However, the Ministry of Labour made it clear that it would take into account how co-operative Dean had found certain actors when they came to consider extensions to deferments.[16] This seemed to clarify the matter, but for the actor not privy to these negotiations the situation seemed unduly mysterious. Rex Harrison was aware that, in the interests of maintaining an entertainment industry to help sustain morale, the government had 'issued an edict that key actors should remain at their posts as actors and entertainers, and be exempt from the Services.'[17] Yet the government refused to name the 'key actors' it had listed. Many actors, of course, joined the Forces whether they were on the list or not. Rex Harrison, for example, was told by the RAF Board that he was exempt from military service but, declining this exemption and pointing out that the 'key actors' had not been defined, he enlisted and became an RAF officer. Robert Morley likewise found that he was on 'a list of actors who it was felt were more use in the theatre than in the forces . . . I was told that provided I kept acting I was unlikely to be called up.[18] He continued with his theatre and film work.

By February 1941, when it summarized its work, ENSC had received 191 applications and approved 137 cases for deferment. These it passed to the Ministry, which accepted almost all the recommendations.[19] It was a tribute to the acting profession, and the theatre generally, that the Ministry placed such trust in its capacity to run its own affairs with fairness and good sense.

In February 1942 Lord Lytton took over the Entertainments National Service Committee from Payne, who had been injured in a bomb blast. Shortly afterwards, on 2 March 1942, a meeting was held at the Ministry of Labour attended by managers, agents, actors

258

and Ernest Bevin, the Minister. As a result it was agreed that all actors should offer six weeks' work a year to ENSA or other national service entertainment. Oddly enough Basil Dean, the Director of ENSA, was in the habit of meeting Ernest Bevin to discuss matters in a Turkish bath they both frequented on Saturday afternoons. Finally, at Bevin's suggestion, a bureau of information, the Theatre's War Service Council (TWSC), was established to collate offers of service from actors and to keep a record of those available. Some managements, notably Hugh Beaumont of H. M. Tennent Ltd and 'Bill' Linnit of Linnit and Dunfee, required actors working for them to work for ENSA at the end of their commercial engagement. In this way something like order was brought into the call-up of younger actors and the alternative ways of serving the theatrical war effort. Bevin himself attached great importance to recreation and entertainment, especially of factory workers,[20] though it must have been a very minor part of his preoccupations.

III

The main thrust of organized entertainment for the armed forces and war workers was provided by ENSA. In World War I, as we have seen, Basil Dean organized NAAFI entertainment and in 1938 he met with Godfrey Tearle, Owen Nares and Leslie Henson to discuss what role the theatre should play in the expected war.[21] Even before the outbreak, Equity prepared a register of actors unlikely to be fit for military service which could be used for casting wartime productions should the emergency arise. By June 1939, 500 actors and actresses had enrolled in a scheme for the entertainment of troops and evacuees.[22] Dean also wrote a pamphlet which he circulated to all MPs in 1939.[23] He foresaw an 'insatiable demand for entertainment in time of war which no modern government dare neglect for long', as necessary for 'upholding the morale of the nation' and he envisaged groups of actors formed to serve munitions centres, hospitals, evacuated populations and army camps. After consultation with entertainment bodies the Entertainments National Service Association (ENSA) was formed and paid for by NAAFI. Dean secured Drury Lane as a headquarters and installed Sir Seymour Hicks as controller. The value of Drury Lane lay in its vast facilities

259

for building equipment, and standardized stage designs were constructed there for sending overseas and for the network of fifty garrison theatres.

Drama was initially the Cinderella of the services provided by ENSA, which had more call for films and variety. However, Godfrey Tearle was the original chairman of the Drama Section, assisted by Henry Oscar, in Room 6 of Drury Lane. They started in 1939 by sending James Mason in two plays to France, where they established bases at Rheims, Arras, Le Havre and Rennes, but closed down the Section completely for five months after Dunkirk. Their revived activities concentrated on home activities, well described by a humble participant:[24]

> Since last December I have been on tour with an ENSA Company. We have now covered all parts of the country, entertaining all three branches of the Services. For the first seven months we were on what is known as Category A tour, playing in big garrison theatres up and down the country . . . Now we are on Category B, touring as a self-contained unit in a motor coach with a portable fit-up stage and curtains, lighting, furniture, props and costumes, and we play in every type of hall or hut imaginable in the most out of the way places . . . In these places we play to men who get little in the way of entertainment . . . In this way we feel the Stage is doing a little to cheer the leisure of those who are doing so much for their country.

Also at home Dame Sybil Thorndike and Dame Lilian Braithwaite played an important part in running the Hospital Concert Section of ENSA from September 1939, Dame Lilian taking over sole direction during Dame Sybil's absence on CEMA tours. Based on Drury Lane and with Naomi Jacob and Jean Webster Brough, Dame Lilian sent out ten hospital parties circulating among 300 hospitals, including small teams of young actresses.[25]

As the Allied forces won increasing military success, so ENSA was able to extend its activities abroad, into the Mediterranean, the Middle East and beyond. The difficulty of developing entertainment in the Middle East stemmed from the need to make a thirteen-week sea journey round the Cape. However, after Alamein in 1942 Hugh Beaumont sent a party, including Vivien Leigh, which was the first to visit the troops after the victory. It gave a Royal Command performance and began a much higher level of ENSA activity in the area. Nigel Patrick was in charge of ENSA , initially from Algiers, and 'applied himself with zest to tightening up our affairs'.[26] With the invasion of Italy he ended up with a base in Naples, administering ENSA from Austria and Greece to North Africa. In an equivalent, though more difficult position, Jack Hawkins took charge of ENSA in India and the Far East from 1944. He regretted that the best performers went to Italy and the Middle East, 'and finally the flotsam and jetsam no one else wanted would be forwarded to us.'[27]

After D-Day and with the approaching end of the War, a large amount of very high-quality entertainment could be sent to Europe. Ivor Novello, Diana Wynyard and Margaret Rutherford toured Normandy and Belgium for four months in 'barns, sheds and bombed buildings'.[28] Margaret Rutherford also toured with Gertrude Lawrence and Jessie Matthews. Deborah Kerr appeared in *Gaslight* in Belgium, Holland and France,[29] Cedric Hardwicke returned from America to tour in *Yellow Sands*, while Godfrey Tearle led a company in Italy and Austria. Most prestigiously, the Old Vic went to Europe, Olivier presenting *King Lear* at the Comédie Française and Olivier, Richardson and Thorndike appearing in Hamburg a fortnight after the peace. In all Dean had twenty-six companies at work for ENSA in the later stages of the War.

In the Middle East the Cairo Opera House became a lively centre of British drama under ENSA. Drama festivals began there from March 1944 with the highly popular wartime successes *Blithe Spirit*, *Night Must Fall* and *Flare Path*, with a strong group including Kathleen Harrison. Wolfit also appeared in his noted *Volpone*. Then most fortunately they secured John Gielgud, returning from a tour of the Far East. Indeed, the Cairo Opera House witnessed Gielgud's last *Hamlet*. Further East, Colonel Jack Hawkins was receiving a better deal than hitherto. Edith Evans and Dorothy Hyson went out to India in *The Late Christopher Bean*, to be followed by Roger Livesey and Ursula Jeans. Most arduous, John Gielgud did a five-month ENSA tour of *Hamlet* and *Blithe Spirit* through Madras, Ceylon, Singapore and Saigon from the autumn of 1945. There were about four repertory companies touring India and the Far East.[30]

261

IV

Another organization providing entertainment for the troops was the Central Pool of Artists, the so-called 'Stars in Battledress', established by the Director of Army Welfare. Unlike ENSA, which comprised civilian artists, the actors and entertainers of the Central Pool were serving soldiers remaining under military organization and in uniform. This was housed in No. 10 Upper Grosvenor Street and based on the premise that 'serving actors, properly administered, could and would provide entertainment of a suitable nature for the troops.' Many noted variety artists were getting a start there, but it also had its legitimate theatre activities, though under certain constraints. Officers could only produce plays, not appear in them, and all female roles had to be played by serving members of the ATS. According to Bryan Forbes, 'the legitimate actors spent abortive weeks rehearsing unsuitable plays' whose productions had to be approved – though most were not – by referees from the War Office before being sent to camps for performance.[31] After the ending of hostilities in 1945 Michael Denison joined the Pool, producing various reviews and plays, then most importantly started the Pool's 'School' at the instigation of Lieutenant-Colonel Lasbery (Jack Carleton), the CO.[32] The School was intended to compensate for the diminished professional experience of many late-War recruits to the Pool and combined ballet classes, acting, makeup, play-reading and much else. Although sometimes presented as a rather jokey institution by some of its affectionate participants, it served as a useful means of employing the talents of those whose abilities were decidedly more entertaining than military. With Denison's School it was also a valuable transition back to civilian show business.

As well as the Central Pool in London, individual corps in the field could also have their own pools, run by their welfare staff. General Sir Brian Horrocks placed great emphasis on this when after VE day the duties of his 30 Corps changed from fighting to occupation in Northern Europe. Entertainment became an important factor in morale. Accordingly the '30 Corps Theatrical Pool' was assembled by Major Richard Stone, MC, formerly of RADA and subsequently a leading London agent. He was assisted by Major Ian Carmichael.[33] Together they ran play companies – with actresses sent by ENSA –

variety, and innumerable touring German circuses. Carmichael took over when Stone set up the Combined Services Entertainment Unit in London in 1946 under the Welfare Department of the War Office. This became the post-war peacetime replacement of the wartime ENSA.

A new element influencing the theatre during the War was the Council for the Encouragement of Music and the Arts, CEMA, the later Arts Council. On the outbreak of war a pressure group called the Arts and Entertainment Emergency Council was formed, with Sir Charles Trevelyan. They called a meeting in the National Gallery, attended by Nicholas Hannen and some representatives of Equity. However, this was completely pre-empted in the same month by Lord de la Warr, President of the Board of Education, who contacted Thomas Jones and Lord Macmillan, respectively secretary and chairman of the Pilgrim Trust. De la Warr wanted the Pilgrim Trust, a wealthy American-financed endowment, to help support the arts in wartime. Lord Macmillan, who was also Minister of Information and hence concerned with civilian morale, concurred.[34] With Pilgrim Trust money, CEMA was formed in December 1939 and opened its offices on 1 January 1940. In April the government assisted it for the first time with a £50,000 grant, to general approval save that of the *Daily Express*, which held that 'there is no such thing as culture in wartime'.[35]

The war years were to prove quite the reverse. CEMA's drama effort seemed to have got off on the wrong foot, with too much encouragement of amateurs to the neglect of the professional stage. In response to criticism[36] Lewis Casson was brought in as drama adviser to start a proper programme of professional drama.[37] By the summer of 1940 important developments were under way. The Pilgrim Players of the Religious Drama Society were touring, starting in Dorset, and the Old Vic began tours in Lancashire and South Wales. In August the Old Vic, based on Burnley, began a tour of twelve Lancashire towns with a company including Alec Clunes and Renée Asherson, while Sybil Thorndike and Lewis Casson toured to towns in South Wales with *Macbeth*. Their son describes their activity:

Lewis got together a small company of enthusiastic, have-a-go-at-anything actors. They had a lorry for the bits of scenery, the props

263

and two hampers for the 'acting clothes'. The company travelled in a small bus. Each afternoon they would arrive at the new place, find their billets and then set up the very simple set and lighting in what was usually the scout or parish hall. The scenery consisted of a couple of screens, a bench, two 'throne' chairs and perhaps a drape or two at the side.[38]

In the autumn CEMA supported Donald Wolfit's scheme of lunchtime Shakespeare for City workers and the Old Vic's permanent shift of base to Burnley in November.

In 1941 CEMA took under its wing an increasing number of professional companies whose activities covered the country. The Cassons toured North Wales, the Market Theatre Company toured Buckinghamshire, Cambridgeshire and Yorkshire, Robert Atkins was in Southwark Park, the Pilgrim Players were ubiquitous, while Basil Langton produced drama in the Birmingham parks. In all there were nine professional companies touring under CEMA, including three Old Vic groups – the Cassons, the Northern Company and Athene Seyler's prestigious *Cherry Orchard* direct from the New Theatre. In the following year there were one or two new directions as well as the normal touring by the regulars. CEMA adopted an entrepreneurial role in starting to take over theatres. It leased the Theatre Royal, Bristol, in November 1942 to save it from destruction and reopened the Liverpool Playhouse. Although controversial at the time, its saving of the former, one of the finest eighteenth-century playhouses in the country, was surely justified by events. Also CEMA began to focus much attention on sending touring companies, including the Old Vic and Wolfit, to military camps and ordnance factory hostels.

In January 1943 a Drama Panel was formed with Athene Seyler, J. B. Priestley and Emlyn Williams. Tennent's provided a tour of Priestley's *They Came to a City* and ran a season of some of their successful West End productions as free Sunday performances for the troops. CEMA was also behind the formation of the Apollo Society in 1943. This began as an experimental poetry reading given in Cambridge by Peggy Ashcroft, John Laurie and Robert Harris and developed into the Society, with leading actors taking poetry to wartime audiences in camps, factories and schools. In these later

264

years of the War one of CEMA's most important activities was sending small touring companies into humble locales – factories and hostels. Walter Hudd had spent 1943 taking his CEMA troupe on a tour playing Shaw and Ibsen to munitions hostels in smaller provincial towns. The hostels were usually attached to Royal Ordnance Factories, where he found audiences 'drawn almost entirely from the working class . . . completely unsophisticated audiences unaffected by convention or theatrical prejudice . . . Many of them had never seen a play before in their lives.'[39] The actors stayed with the workers in their hostels. The extent of CEMA's activity in this area was very considerable. Between 1942 and the end of the War it sent out 300 actors in thirty-three touring companies, including nine specially formed for hostel visits. The record of individual performances for CEMA was held by Stanford Holme, with 481.[40] Here was real grinding work, often in depressing surroundings, taking theatre to humble audiences for whom, indeed, 'there was no such thing as culture in wartime'.

VI

The War created special problems for the British actor in America. Many of the 'British colony' in Hollywood had been regularly domiciled in the United States for some years. Several of them had already fought in the First World War, some with especial distinction and personal injury. Such were actors like Cedric Hardwicke, Charles Laughton, Basil Rathbone and Ronald Colman, who were too old to be of active service even if they had returned to England. Of an even older generation were Dame May Whitty, Ben Webster and C. Aubrey Smith. It clearly made no sense for them to cease working, taking up valuable transit space to return to a beleaguered England that could barely support them. Actors in their early thirties and younger were faced with dilemmas. A few who were of serviceable age and who had a moral obligation to return did not do so. They aroused considerable anger in Britain, where they were vilified as having 'Gone with the Wind Up', in Sir Seymour Hicks's phrase. Public attacks came not only from Hicks of ENSA and J. B. Priestley but most strongly from Michael Balcon, a Jew, who, having good cause to leave, had stayed. He condemned those actors

265

accumulating fortunes abroad when, in his view, they should have returned if not to fight then to build up ENSA or play at home for small salaries as Donat, Redgrave and Richardson were doing – 'keeping the tradition of the theatre going, keeping the people happy, putting the British viewpoint to the world. That is the one thing we want them for – not to fight, but to make propaganda.'[41]

Those who did not heed these appeals from Britain stayed in America with their consciences. At the other end of the scale David Niven, who had been an army officer before becoming an actor, declined the contrary advice even of his own ambassador and returned to the colours immediately. In the middle was a small group of highly patriotic actors (including some future knights and dames) who were faced with problems and dilemmas they did not relish. In the early stages of the War official government policy was that British actors of note should stay put and carry on working in America. The Los Angeles consul made this clear to the British Hollywood community. Sir Cedric Hardwicke went to see the Consul hoping to take up again his British Army Reserve captaincy but was told that, at forty-six, he was too old and should stay put. Duff Cooper, the Minister of Information, also reiterated this view to Olivier.[42] Many of the British community wishing to return to England in 1940 fretted under this restriction and sent a delegation consisting of Olivier, Hardwicke, Cary Grant and Herbert Wilcox to see Lord Lothian, the British ambassador.[43] Lothian re-stressed the need to stay because he believed in the propaganda value of good British actors portraying the best type of Englishmen on the screen.[44] As he put it,

> The maintenance of a powerful British nucleus of older actors in Hollywood is of great importance to our own interests, partly because they are continually championing the British cause in a very volatile community which would otherwise be left to the mercies of German propagandists, and because the production of films with a strong British tone is one of the best and subtlest forms of British propaganda.[45]

Lothian's policy was 'that all British actors of military age, that is, up to thirty-one should go home, and that older actors should remain.'[46] When Lord Halifax succeeded Lothian as ambassador in

Washington in 1940 he perpetuated the policy on the further, graceless, grounds that England could not cope with 'unnecessary people'.[47] It was early in 1941 before Olivier and Vivien Leigh could return to England, and August in the same year before Anna Neagle and Herbert Wilcox obtained permits to do so. Flora Robson, who was also ensnared in these policies, was not able to return until 1943, when Tyrone Guthrie obtained her a priority passage back for a CEMA tour.[48]

These delays would have been senseless and intolerable had not the leading actors involved been engaged in some valuable work in the States. Indeed, it was the celebrity and unquestioned patriotism of the few actors involved that made worthwhile their continued working in the American film industry rather than returning to an England where filming was likely to cease.[49] Some fine work with clear war propaganda overtones was undertaken by British actors in Hollywood. The Neagle–Wilcox film *Edith Cavell* was regarded by Lord Lothian as 'a first-rate propaganda film'; indeed almost too much so, since there were fears that it violated American neutrality.[50] After three light musicals they then made the overtly patriotic *Forever and a Day*, 'symbolizing England and the British Empire',[51] using many British artists including Aubrey Smith and Cedric Hardwicke, who appeared without fees. The project was Sir Cedric's idea as both 'a patriotic piece of wartime sentiment' and a gesture of thanks from Britain to the USA and Canada for their aid.[52] It merited a telegram of thanks from the King on its British première.

In Hollywood Flora Robson made *The Sea Hawk* (1940), repeating her noted role as Elizabeth I, ending with an impassioned speech about Britain's role in resisting the attempts of an aggressive power (Philip II's Spain/Hitler's Germany) at world domination. Olivier's famous Hollywood patriotic film was *Lady Hamilton*, made by Alexander Korda, with the star as Nelson to Vivien Leigh's Emma. The parallels with the war against Bonaparte were again made quite explicit in a rousing speech: 'You can't make peace with dictators. You have to destroy them – wipe them out!'[53] A great success on both sides of the Atlantic, it became one of Churchill's favourite films during the War. Perhaps the chief Hollywood film portraying Britain at war was *Mrs Miniver*, with British actresses Greer Garson

267

and Dame May Whitty depicting shades of upper-middle-class and aristocratic courage in the face of German aggression. It was exactly the kind of 'strong British tone' that Lord Lothian had hoped for from the British actors doing their bit in Hollywood.

As well as making films of patriotic content, British actors in America undertook various other activities in support of the War and morale. They were especially effective in appealing for Bundles for Britain and for the British Red Cross. Anna Neagle performed at the Lockheed aircraft factory, where the workers paid for an aircraft for Britain out of their own wages. She likewise attended the 'Anna Neagle Stakes' at San Francisco, the proceeds of the meeting being given to Bundles for Britain.[54] Flora Robson similarly made appeals for war charities, selling bonds and giving performances for troops, while octogenarian Sir Aubrey Smith, the only British actor to be knighted during the War, tirelessly raised money for Britain even to the extent of signing autographs after the show at 10 cents a time.[55] Dame May Whitty established a Hollywood Fund to help actors in distress in Britain, and this was administered by Athene Seyler here.[56] Dame May also organized a Hollywood committee of actors to look after the children evacuated from the British Actors' Orphanage. Noel Coward, as president of the Orphanage, went to the USA to arrange this evacuation and stayed to tour America speaking on behalf of Britain's war aims with the approval of Lord Lothian, the British ambassador.[57] Coward used £11,000 of his own money on this activity and ironically found himself prosecuted on his return to England for having spent and not declared his American assets.

VII

Back home, the film industry played an important part in sustaining morale by productions embodying high patriotic content. Cinema-going was a compulsive habit during the War. Some twenty-five or thirty million cinema seats were sold every week and three-quarters of the adult population were cinema-goers.[58] Most of the films would have been American, the British output being only forty-six in 1941–42 and seventy in 1943–44, but although the diversion of space and personnel from the industry had resulted in diminished quantity, the War years led to the production of many films of high quality and prestige.

Britain's most noted Hollywood film-stars played their part by making patriotic films in England: Robert Donat portrayed *Young Mr Pitt* in 1942, drawing the obvious parallel with the Napoleonic Wars and resistance to tyrants. Less successfully, he made *The Adventures of Tartu* for MGM about an agent sent to sabotage a gas factory in Czechoslovakia.[59] Scarcely any other actor threw himself more thoroughly into making films with a positive bearing on the War than Leslie Howard.[60] He produced and appeared in *Pimpernel Smith*, about an Oxford don outwitting the Gestapo in Germany, echoing his successful 1934 film of *The Scarlet Pimpernel*. In *49th Parallel*, about a German submarine crew escaping across Canada, he appeared as a liberal intellectual expressing civilized thoughts by a Canadian lakeside. In *From the Four Corners* he played himself, showing three Commonwealth soldiers around London, stressing London's heritage as the centre of the Empire. He produced and narrated *The Gentle Sex*, a somewhat plotless but interesting semi-documentary about the training of ATS girls. Most impressive was his *The First of the Few*, with David Niven, about R. J. Mitchell and the creation of the Spitfire, an exciting tribute to the plane of the Battle of Britain and its designer. Howard served on the 'Ideas Committee' of film producers for the Ministry of Information, along with Michael Powell. He was killed in 1943 when his plane was shot down as he was returning from a propaganda mission to Spain and Portugal, which he had undertaken at the request of Anthony Eden.

There was also an official involvement in films through the Army Kinematograph Service. Carol Reed, joined in 1942 by Peter Ustinov, was devising films for the army. After the success of Coward's *In Which We Serve* for the navy, the Army Council was concerned to match it with a military equivalent. Accordingly Reed expanded the idea of an earlier short film for recruits, *The New Lot*, into the full-scale *The Way Ahead*, starring David Niven, and created in the Ritz Hotel by Reed, Ustinov, Niven and Eric Ambler. This fine film, tracing the progress of a squad of recruits to their first experience of battle, fittingly began its showing on the morning of D-Day. Ustinov, at the request of the Air Ministry, went on to write and direct *The School for Secrets*, about the discovery of radar.[61]

Perhaps the most successful and famous war films were Noel Coward's *In Which We Serve* and Olivier's *Henry V*. The former arose from the close personal acquaintance of Coward and Lord Louis Mountbatten. Coward wrote his film loosely based on the incident of the sinking of Mountbatten's ship *HMS Kelly*, casting himself as 'Captain D'. Intended by Coward as a serious tribute to the navy, it was certainly taken seriously by them.[62] Mountbatten discussed the project; the Royal Family (the King in Naval uniform) visited the filming; Admiral Vian took Coward cruising in the North Atlantic for 'atmosphere'. The result, sometimes shown privately at Buckingham Palace to distinguished visitors, was the most celebrated naval film of the War. As *In Which We Serve* was a celebration of the Royal Navy, so each service received its cinematic tribute of considerable quality – *The Way Ahead* for the army, *The Way to the Stars* for the RAF, *San Demetrio London* for the merchant navy, *The Bells Go Down* for the fire service.

Olivier's *Henry V*, shot in Ireland during the time of the campaign in Europe, was an explicit tribute to the invasion forces of 1944 through the parallel of those of 1415. The Harfleur and 'St Crispin' speeches and the prayer 'O God of battles steel my soldiers' hearts' took on a directness of meaning and relevance to the current war situation that enhanced the film's artistic impact. The *Henry V* theme, in fact, resonated through the War, from Ivor Novello's post-Munich production at Drury Lane, radio broadcasts in 1939 and 1942, to Olivier's film. It enjoyed an interesting echo when Fabia Drake produced the play with American servicemen actors taking a course at RADA before demobilization. She was able to use the costumes from the film, with Renée Asherson repeating her role as Princess Katherine.[63]

The actor also contributed to the patriotic effort through the radio. Indeed, the audience for broadcast drama was thought to have doubled during the War[64] and it greatly increased in popularity. The BBC Repertory Company moved to Evesham then Manchester before returning to London in 1943. They soon began a drama output, with distinguished actors, much of which had a close bearing on the War.[65] In October 1939 the BBC broadcast their first wartime Shakespeare, including the Agincourt speeches from *Henry V*. In 1942 Olivier also broadcast the Henry V speeches in a radio programme *Into Battle*, 'unashamed flag-waving', which was the root of his idea for the film.[66] Among the noted radio drama series were *The Shadow of the Swastika*, tracing the rise of Nazi power, with Marius Goring as Hitler,[67] and an adaptation of *War and Peace* in 1943 with Celia Johnson, which drew the natural parallels of the 1812 and 1942 Anglo–Russian alliances against a European aggressor.[68] As a result of successive productions of high quality performed by actors of the first rank there was a sharp rise in the popularity of the radio play in 1942. This found expression in the beginning of 'Saturday Night Theatre' in 1943, both reflecting a rising popular appreciation of radio drama, and drama generally, and widening the range of work of the acting profession. Perhaps the most remarkable use of an actor on the radio in the War was Norman Shelley's standing in for Winston Churchill. Churchill was too busy to broadcast his 'We shall fight them on the beaches' speech, which he had given to Parliament. Shelley was called upon to deliver it, imitating the Prime Minister's voice. For long after it was not realized, until Mr Shelley revealed the secret just before his death, that the often-mimicked tones of the speech were not those of its originator but of an actor.

Actors also appeared in the pageants which were an important form of patriotic expression in wartime. There was the 'Battle for Freedom' pageant at the Albert Hall, including an oration by Olivier. He also took part in the 'Salute to Russia' pageant in July 1943 along with Ralph Richardson, Sybil Thorndike, John Gielgud, John Laurie and Marius Goring. In the 'Arts at War' pageant, also at the Albert Hall, Olivier delivered an oration of stunning vocal power, listing various warlike qualities and finishing with a trumpeting 'And may God prosper our Cause'[69]. It was almost identical, in form and style of delivery, to his famous Harfleur speech in *Henry V*. Equally vast in scale and prestige was Basil Dean's 'Cathedral Steps', produced on the steps of St Paul's with Sybil Thorndike, Edith Evans, Leslie Howard, Lewis Casson and others.[70] It was also produced at Coventry.

VIII

Many actors served with distinction in the War, reflecting credit on the profession. Jack Hawkins became a full colonel, while Nigel

Patrick, Robert Flemyng, Philip Ridgeway, Torin Thatcher and Leo Genn rose to the rank of Lieutenant-colonel. Dirk Bogarde, Derek Bond, Anthony Quayle, André Morell and Andrew Cruickshank became majors and Ralph Richardson, Michael Hordern and Peter Bull Lieutenant-commanders. Bond, Flemyng and Trevor Howard won the MC, Bull the DSC, Glenn the Croix de Guerre, Gerald Glaister the DFC and Hugh Goldie a DFC and bar. The tally of decorations won by actors in the War was thought to be two DSOs, three MCs, one DSC, four DFCs.[71] Robert Flemyng and Cyril Raymond were awarded the military OBE and MBE respectively. This development had two main effects. Certain actors who rose to the rank of major and above, or who were decorated, acquired a personal authority that lent greater weight to their acting. John Laurie put the point perceptively about some of his younger contemporaries: 'they'd all become officers, and no question about it that gave them an authority which no actor could get by playing leading parts.'[72] The habit of real military command acquired by some actors gave a new dimension to their portrayal of leading Shakespearian roles, while in the cinema it underlay the distinction brought by Jack Hawkins to a series of roles, notably from *The Cruel Sea* onwards. Secondly, the creditable performance of actors during the War further indicated that the profession of rogues and vagabonds could acquit itself with gentlemanly gallantry off-stage as well as on, though this needed proving less in 1939 than it had in 1914.

The actor was even more important in the Second World War than in the First. In both he had provided entertainment and distraction, but in the Second he performed other functions. His work became intimately connected with the maintenance of morale among fighting and civilian populations, both suffering danger in a People's War. Most important, the actor could present images of emotions and responses to War with which the British people could identify – from the proud rhetoric of Olivier or Flora Robson, the reflective idealism of Leslie Howard, the supportive wifely resourcefulness of Celia Johnson or Greer Garson, the stiff upper lip of Coward and Niven as officers and gentlemen doing their duty, through to the cheerful, cheeky defiance of a Tommy Trinder, George Formby or Will Hay. Equity induced the 1944 TUC at Blackpool to resolve that 'Congress notes with satisfaction that the

Government appreciates the value of entertainment in the maintenance of morale' and it 'believes that a virile British theatre and film industry portraying the true democratic ideals and character of British life is an indispensable factor in the post-war world.'[73] It was a fitting comment on the honourable role played by the actor in the War.

NOTES

1 Esmond Knight, *Seeking the Bubble* (London, 1943), p.122.

2 John Counsell, *Counsell's Opinion* (London, 1963), p.103.

3 Angus Calder, *The People's War* (London, 1969), p.64.

4 Cathleen Nesbitt, *A Little Love and Good Company* (London, 1975), p.199.

5 Edgar Ralph, 'Survey of the War Years', *The Stage*, 17 May 1945.

6 *Ibid.*

7 Edgar Ralph, 'Plays of the War Years', *The Stage*, 2 August 1945, for this paragraph.

8 Public Record Office, Ministry of Labour files, Lab 6/175, Letter, Walter Payne and Godfrey Tearle, 4 April 1940.

9 Lab 6/175, Notes of a Meeting, 18 April 1940.

10 Lab 6/175, Letter, F. N. Tribe to Sir Alan Barlow, 14 May 1940.

11 Lab 6/175, Letter, Walter Payne, 22 May 1940 and Notes of a Meeting, 17 May 1940.

12 Lab 6/175, Letter, J.S.L. of Min. Lab. to Payne, 6 June 1940.

13 Lab 6/175, Memorandum on the Reservation and Deferment of Call-Up of Persons Employed in the Entertainment Industry, 29 June 1940.

14 Ian McLaine, *Ministry of Morale* (London, 1979), p.69.

15 Lab 6/175, List of Deferments, 10 July 1940.

16 Lab 6/175, Memorandum, R. E. Gomme, 25 July 1940.

17 Rex Harrison, *Rex* (London, 1974), pp.67–8.

18 Robert Morley, *Responsible Gentleman* (London, 1966), p.122.

19 Lab 6/175, ENSC to Min. Lab. Summary of Workings, 7 Feb. 1941.

20 Alan Bullock, *The Life and Times of Ernest Bevin*, Vol II, *Minister of Labour 1939–1945* (London, 1967), p.83.

21 Basil Dean, *The Theatre at War* (London, 1956), for the whole section on ENSA.
22 *Daily Telegraph*, 24 June 1939.
23 'The Theatre in Emergency', Appendix 1 in Dean, *op.cit.*
24 *Actors' Church Union Call Board*. September 1941. Letter from an anonymous member in ENSA.
25 Basil Dean, *op.cit.*, pp.195–7.
26 *Ibid.*, p.458.
27 Jack Hawkins, *Anything for a Quiet Life* (London, 1973), p.69.
28 W. MacQueen Pope, *Ivor* (London, 1951), p.462.
29 E. Braun, *Deborah Kerr* (London, 1977), p.79.
30 Basil Dean, *op.cit.*, p.498.
31 Bryan Forbes, *Notes for a Life* (London, 1974), pp.120–1.
32 Michael Denison, *Overture and Beginners* (London, 1973), pp.200–2.
33 Ian Carmichael, *Will The Real Ian Carmichael* . . . (London, 1979), pp.180–3, 187, 191.
34 *CEMA Bulletin* May 1942 contains an account of its origins by Thomas Jones. See also R. Walford, 'The Arts in Wartime' (typescript in Arts Council Library).
35 *Daily Express*, 13 April 1940.
36 Lord Esher's letter, *The Times*, 3 February 1940.
37 The following account is based on the *CEMA Bulletins* from May 1940.
38 John Casson, *Lewis and Sybil* (London, 1972), p.216.
39 Walter Hudd, 'New Audiences for Old' *CEMA Bulletin*, January 1944.
40 Leonard Crainford, 'CEMA Play Tours', *CEMA Bulletin*, March 1945.
41 *Sunday Dispatch*, 25 August 1940.
42 Felix Barker, *The Oliviers* (London, 1953), pp.164, 178.
43 Herbert Wilcox, *Twenty-Five Thousand Sunsets* (London, 1967), pp.124–5.
44 Sir Cedric Hardwicke, *A Victorian in Orbit* (London, 1961), p.199.
45 *Ibid.*, citing a cable from Lothian to Halifax, p.200.
46 John Cottrell, *Laurence Olivier* (London, 1975), p.171.
47 Anna Neagle, *There's Always Tomorrow* (London, 1974), p.171.

48 Janet Dunbar, *Flora Robson* (London, 1960), p.221.
49 This was Lothian's argument to Herbert Wilcox.
50 Anna Neagle, *op.cit.*, p.123.
51 Herbert Wilcox, *op.cit.*, p.126.
52 Sir Cedric Hardwicke, *op.cit.*, p.206.
53 Felix Barker, *op.cit.*, p.183.
54 Anna Neagle, *op.cit.*, p.126.
55 Jean Webster Brough, *Prompt Copy* (London, 1952), pp.172–3.
56 British Actors' Equity Association (Withdrawn) Report, 1939–40.
57 Noel Coward, *Future Indefinite* (London, 1954), pp.155, 219.
58 Angus Calder, *The People's War* (London, 1969), p.367.
59 J. C. Trewin, *Robert Donat* (London, 1968), p.136.
60 L. R. Howard, *A Quite Remarkable Father* (London, 1960), pp.248–65.
61 Peter Ustinov, *Dear Me* (London, 1977), pp.119–47.
62 Noel Coward, *op.cit.*, pp.208–16, 225.
63 Fabia Drake, *Blind Fortune*, Chapter 12. Leonard Freyman, 'In Retrospect', *Royal Academy of Dramatic Art Magazine*, May 1946.
64 Asa Briggs, *The War of Words* (Oxford, 1970), p.46.
65 Val Gielgud, *British Radio Drama 1922–56* (London, 1957), Chapter 8.
66 Felix Barker, *op.cit.*, p.198.
67 *Picture Post*, 2 March 1940, has an interesting feature on the making of the programme. Mr Goring who was educated in Germany, worked for the BBC German Service as a supervisor of productions.
68 Val Gielgud, *op.cit.*, p.103.
69 Newsreel excerpt in 'ENSA', ITV, 29 June 1980.
70 Basil Dean, *op.cit.*, p.295.
71 *The Stage*, 30 May 1946.
72 John Laurie cited by John Cottrell, *Laurence Olivier*, p.196.
73 British Actors' Equity Association Fourteenth Annual Report, 1944–45.

13 The Changing Context of the Actor's Work 1945–83

Since the War the context within which the actor works has changed drastically. In the immediate post-war years provincial repertory and touring companies flourished, providing an undemanding entertainment for a mass audience. This was rapidly undermined by the rise of television from the 1950s, which drew away the traditional provincial audience from the emptying theatres. Films, which had already been competing with the theatres since the 1930s, in turn faced the competition of television. Film production contracted and cinemas were closed as ruthlessly as live theatres. Although the sheer quantity of available employment for actors diminished as a result of these changes, in many ways there was an improvement in the artistic quality and interest of the work. The new civic theatres and the new RSC and National Theatres in London provided work of considerably higher standard than the old reps, and tourers of the 1940s and 1950s, though for a much smaller body of actors and audience who could enjoy it. The rise of a more serious drama, both on stage from the 1950s and on television from the 1960s, also increased the artistic satisfaction of theatre work. Fewer jobs meant better jobs, more severe competition and rising standards, but for those actors who could survive the outlook was improving.

I

With the ending of the War in Europe in May 1945, actors gradually resumed their careers as best they could. Olivier and Richardson, after touring in Germany and Paris, reopened with the Old Vic Company at the New Theatre, John Clements took the St James,
276

Wolfit the Winter Garden for *Macbeth*. At the other end of the spectrum a group of actors pooled their savings and gratuities to take the Gateway Theatre for a six-weeks repertory season. Various forms of help were forthcoming. Equity ran a Demobilization Service Bureau to help actors back into jobs. Also, by an imaginative government concession, actors could obtain extra clothing coupons for buying clothes to be used on stage.[1]

After the War many ex-servicemen actors were helped to get started again by the Reunion Theatre Association formed by Major Torin Thatcher and Major William Fox.[2] They produced their most successful play, *Exercise Bowler*, first at the Arts and then at the Scala as a shop-window for their members, but after *Bowler*, instead of mounting any new productions, they decided to concentrate on providing a casting service.[3] By April 1947 they were able to look back on a period of creditable achievement. They had 1200 members and had secured 400 engagements for ex-servicemen. They held social gatherings at the Interval Club and their closely associated Services Sunday Society put on weekend plays. They also had a wider impact in political circles. Torin Thatcher and Reginald Tate (who had succeeded Fox as chairman) persuaded the Ministry of Labour to make a £50 per head grant to ex-service actors, to buy good civilian clothes that could be worn on stage.[4] In 1948 the Association was in existence, with Olivier as president, though with a declining membership of 800.[5] Its original purpose was losing its urgency, as any ex-service actor who was seriously intending to return to the stage must already have been reabsorbed. Recognizing this, it disbanded itself at a meeting on 22 December 1952.[6]

II

The post-war actor, once returned, soon found that he had to work in a context changing more in the 1950s than at almost any other time. Basically it was a decline in the provincial touring and repertory theatre under the impact, not so much of the cinema – as had been the case in the 1930s – as of television. In the late 1940s the touring and repertory theatres were fairly flourishing. In 1949 there were 150 resident repertory companies,[7] organized in their Conference of Repertory Theatres (CORT) since 1943. The Local Government Act of 1948 also empowered corporations and municipalities to engage in theatrical management with a 6d rate. This was to be a basis of later civic repertory theatres. In 1949 there were, for example, sixteen resident repertory companies in Lancashire and even seven in Norfolk and Suffolk. In addition there were some thirty touring drama companies.[8] John Osborne remembered with affection his time as a provincial touring actor around 1950: 'we progressed to a different town each week . . . cheap delicious food, northern beer, sleeping till noon, feather beds, free films . . .' playing 'Home Counties comedies and murder mysteries, plays with maids and middle-class girls compromised in their cami-knickers' for £6–£14 a week.[9] At the top end of the spectrum of touring companies was Donald Wolfit. Somewhat lower down were companies like that of Harry Hanson, who ran half a dozen troupes, 'a byword for tatty ill-paid, tyrannical, joyless work'.[10]

The provincial theatre's position was helped in various ways. Entertainment Tax was practically halved in 1948, and from 1951 provincial theatres were allowed to play London successes earlier than hitherto in a scheme organized through the Theatres National Committee. Also, the Esher Standard Contract for Repertory Theatres was revised in 1952, regulating the employment of students. Accordingly the reps were enormously fruitful experiences for young actors and there were enough of them to facilitate frequent changes, mobility and variety of experience. Yet from 1953 the impact of television began to have a sharply devastating effect on the provinces, compounded by the advent of commercial television on 22 September 1955. By 1956 the economics of the provincial theatres were becoming critical and they were thought to have lost up to 10 per cent of their audience to television in the last three years. Although more seats were being sold than in 1939 expenses had tripled, outstripping seat prices, which had only doubled.[11] Seat capacity could not be expanded and many managers dared not raise seat prices further for fear of driving audiences back home to their television sets. It was not surprising that even some notable theatres and companies began to close down. In January 1957 the Royalty Theatre, Morecambe, closed. This was highly symbolic, since it ended the longest run – thirty-one years – of continuous repertory in the country.[12]

278

This was but one of the fifty-nine theatres that closed in the few years before 1956.[13] Various forms of help tried to stay the decline. The BBC kept theatre managers informed of TV play productions well in advance so that reps could avoid ruinously producing a play which was also appearing on television in the same week. In 1956 changes in the law made it easier for coach parties to hire buses for theatre outings, both legalizing and increasing the important coach-party trade. In the same year Equity conceded the status of the probationer artist with under forty weeks' experience who could accept a lower minimum wage. This helped the hard-pressed reps, as did the abolition of Entertainment Tax in 1957. Yet the theatrical scene by the end of the decade was a contracted one. By 1962 there were 120 provincial theatres left in England, compared with 300 in 1939, with about 50–60 active reps.[14] Whatever contraction was experienced by the reps, the touring system was even worse hit and had largely collapsed. Many of their theatres had disappeared and most of their fare appeared now very second-rate compared with the cinema and television, while many of the Victorian and Edwardian theatres used by the touring companies were demolished by the real-estate development boom. Declining variety and touring legitimate drama was increasingly being infiltrated by nude shows, especially between 1954 and 1955, in a desperate search for some attraction to draw audiences away from their fireside television sets. All this betokened a diminishing sphere of activity both for the young actor trying to get started and for the actor not perhaps of the first rank in talent or ambition who had been happy to earn a modest living jobbing around the provinces.

III

The great engine of change has, of course, been television. Its impact has been crucial in reshaping and contracting the live theatre and in opening up opportunities for the 'working-class' or 'classless' actor. Television drama had ceased during the War and resumed in 1946. In the very early days West End plays were televised from theatres even while they were still running – *Frieda* and *George and Margaret* in 1946, *Reluctant Heroes* in 1952.[15] This was scarcely satisfactory, and suggests both the tiny audience for television and the theatre's

279

feeling of security from commercial competition. TV was, of course, developing its own drama, notably with a production of *St Joan* as early as 1946.

From the mid-1950s and into the 1960s important changes in television began to reshape the work of the actor. Firstly, there was a great deal of television drama. In 1956 the BBC TV drama department produced seventy studio plays of ninety minutes and above, forty-six shorter plays, eleven drama series or serials and eighty-four weekly episodes.[16] This was a powerful flow of theatrical experience for the viewer and work for the actor. To it was added the competition of Independent Television, which began in 1955. Secondly, the technical conditions of production made the actor's work more attractive. There was increasing use of film and videotape, getting away from the cramped, nerve-racking conditions of live studio transmission. This made for more polished performance and the use of genuine and varied backgrounds. However, it did lead to confusion over what *television* drama was in this curious transitional situation. For example in 1955 ATV had no drama studio, unlike BBC or A-R TV; accordingly their output was film, which was a costly way of producing drama. Abandoning this policy they swung to the other, almost 1940s, extreme of televising their drama from theatres with the actors on stage and the camera in the auditorium.[17] These were confusions of a changing technology and an emergent art form. Thirdly, the high output of drama and its improved technical quality had a devastating effect on variety, touring and small commercial rep in the 1950s, as we have seen. Many ex-rep actors turned to television as alternative employment, but often with strong feelings of resentment. Pat Phoenix recalled that in her pre-*Coronation Street* days, 'I was resentful of TV then. It had closed so many theatres and, as an extra in crowd scenes, I would meet so many old actors and actresses that I had known and respected in the theatres; all out of work like me.'[18]

Whereas up to the early 1950s television plays were mostly adapted from the stage, from the mid-1950s a more distinctive form of television drama began to emerge. This was often socially committed, dealing with working-class life and its problems, critical of existing institutions and its attitudes, emphasizing a certain 'kitchen sink' realism in style. To some extent this is dated from the 'drama documentary' plays of Colin Morris from 1955, 'filmed in true-life backgrounds against ordinary people'.[19] More particularly it became associated with Sydney Newman, a Canadian disciple of the documentary pioneer John Grierson. Newman became responsible for the ITV 'Armchair Theatre' from 1958 before becoming head of BBC drama in 1963, where he shaped 'The Wednesday Play' 1965 and 'Play for Today' 1966. He was committed to the production of the single play (as opposed to the series and serial) and to encouraging the type of 'anger and after' new playwriting of the period. He said, 'I am proud that I played some part in the recognition that the working man was a fit subject for drama.'[20] The implications for the actor were evident. The new television drama provided employment for, and indeed required, large numbers of actors close enough to working-class experience to be able to convey it credibly. They might not be very well-known in the West End, but ideally gave the viewer the impression that they were scarcely actors at all but brought in for the occasion off the street, the factory floor or football terrace. Conversely, now that the working classes were being presented in their own sitting rooms with a drama that depicted their own life and problems, the idea of taking up acting must have been planted in the minds of many youngsters from such a background. Such people would have regarded the middle-class West End of the 1950s and its television extension of the early 1950s as alien and remote from them. It was a factor drawing the working-class actor into the profession and effecting the change in its social origins in the post-war years.

Television had some reaction on the drama schools, most of which initially felt obliged to take account of the new medium in their training. A survey in 1962 found that only two major drama schools did not consider specific television training necessary.[21] The Central retained Norman Marshall, the A-R TV head of drama, as an honorary member of staff to introduce television acting to third-year students. RADA booked television studio space for training fourth-year students, while LAMDA and Webber Douglas employed similar systems. These intentions do not seem to have lasted. RADA abandoned television training because its very high cost – £300 a day for studio rent – outweighed any marginal gain in technique.[22] By the 1970s there had been a retreat from the hopes of the early 1960s. The

281

schools believed that, given thorough training in voice and movement, the actor could adjust to the special conditions of television and film studios as long as the basic acting craft was there.[23]

The coming of television created an increasing problem for Equity. When transmission was resumed after the War the BBC declined to accept that it was a separate medium requiring its own contract and fees, as Equity wished. By 1949 Equity became presciently concerned about the future, asking, 'is television a mere poor relation of sound or is it destined to absorb it altogether?' and noting, 'we are here faced with startling prospects which may revolutionize entertainment.'[24] In 1950 they secured a minimum performance rate of 5 guineas with 1 guinea per day of rehearsal. When minimum fees were raised in January 1953 the BBC merely economized by freezing fees above the minimum. It also showed old films in abundance, and Equity was unable to get any agreement with the BBC or the Joint Film Council about extra payments to actors appearing in such films on television.[25] The relatively weak position of the actor in television in the late 1940s and early 1950s is attributable to a number of factors. The BBC 'managed to persuade most of them to accept ridiculously inadequate fees by explaining that this was a new and experimental medium with little money behind it and that it would be to their ultimate advantage if they became pioneers in its early stages.'[26] Actors looked on television as a means of personal publicity, at nominal fees, for their more serious work elsewhere. The BBC did not like collective bargaining with Equity in the 1940s and Equity found the BBC a slow and cumbersome bureaucracy, using its monopoly power in a shabbily exploitive fashion. In 1953 a leading actor earned 55 guineas for three weeks' rehearsal and one transmission. Accordingly, he could entertain six million people for ninety minutes and earn *less* for each week's work than a leading actor in repertory. As Gordon Sandison of Equity observed, 'this is a situation of high fantasy.'[27]

The situation was bound to change from the mid-1950s. Firstly, television spread and its audience increased from 400,000 receivers in 1950 to five million by 1956 and to ten million by 1960. Secondly, independent commercial television began in 1955, with its advertising and overtly profit-making aims. Thirdly, the expansion of both forms of television caused a decline in the provincial theatre and in

282

film work, diminishing traditional employment opportunities. All these reasons made it more justifiable, possible and necessary for the actor to adopt a harder, more demanding stance *vis-à-vis* the television companies.

Equity welcomed the coming of independent television since it would increase employment and, hopefully, strengthen the actor's bargaining power with the BBC. Equity accordingly declared an Equity Shop in radio and TV from 1 March 1955. Remuneration remained low and had not remotely kept pace with audience size or licence income. Accordingly, the union came increasingly to claim that remuneration should relate to these factors. Television acting neither offered the financial benefits of a long run on the stage nor took into account large audiences, as did the cinema. This had to be rectified. Equity calculated that an actor working on television earned 4d per week per 1000 viewers compared with £12.10s.0d. per week per 1000 audience in the theatre. It regarded 1/- per 1000 as a fairer TV equivalent.[28]

In 1958 Equity made a modest agreement with the television companies, merely raising the basic minimum fee from 7 to 10 guineas, to last for two years. In the meantime it became clear that ITV was 'making profits on a staggering and increasing scale',[29] and as the 1958 agreement ran out Equity determined to gain a fairer share of the rewards. In 1961 the union proposed that there should be a minimum fee based on the single use of an actor's performance in one region. If a play were more widely networked the basic fee would be increased according to the number of receivers in the additional regions. In this way audience size could be made a determinant of pay. These proposals met with blank refusal and occasioned Equity's first strike from November 1961 to April 1962. After five months the strike was resolved and the multiplication of a basic fee according to more widespread networking was accepted. For example, an artist receiving 100 guineas for a performance in one region would now receive 175 guineas for its transmission over the whole network. Equity noted proudly that 'this was the first major industrial battle undertaken by the whole profession against a powerful group of employers.'[30] It was thus television that had brought the union into its first strike and perhaps given many actors a clearer and more militant perception of the commercial context within which they operated.

Television has also brought Equity into its most important dispute since 1961–2. This involves the payment of actors making television commercials for Channel 4 and the breakfast TV-am. Much smaller audiences were expected for both these channels than for normal commercial television. The Institute of Practitioners in Advertising accordingly claimed that actors in these commercials should be paid commensurately lower fees. Equity conceded that 50 per cent of the normal rate would be appropriate, but the IPA offered only 30 per cent. Equity, having already moved from an original 75 per cent claim, declined to compromise on a point lower than the 50 per cent or to accept the principle that fees should be directly related to audience size. The situation became acute as Channel 4 began on 2 November 1982 without its being resolved. As the dispute has dragged on more individual member firms of the IPA have agreed to Equity's terms. Fifty-six firms have come to such agreements, including thirteen of the twenty leading advertising agencies, and the union has approved of 725 commercials using actors.[31] This accounts for the curious feature of a limited number of actors appearing in only a few commercials in 1983 – notably the engaging Ian Carmichael with his Californian wines. The eventual settlement of this issue should give a refreshing variety.

IV

If television had such marked effects on the context of the actor's work from the 1950s, the position of the film industry was more problematic since, unlike the 1930s, when the cinema appeared as a threat to the stage, both film and stage shared a common vulnerability to the rise of television. The opportunities for work in films as a supplement or alternative to stage work were subject to considerable change during this time. From the beginning of 1948 the British Film Producers' Association and Equity entered into an agreement so that Equity 'is thoroughly and soundly established in the film industry.' In 1949 a Joint Film Council was established by the BFPA and Equity, and this approved a Standard Contract.[32] By 1950, due to the energy of the films organizer Eddie Lattimer, 'we can now claim that an effective union shop exists in the film studios with Equity's being the only card recognized for all performers.'[33]

284

This consolidation of the actor's position in film-making took place in the context of a troubled industry. Internally, film production was contracting in the late 1940s and cinema audiences fell from thirty-one million per week to twenty-six million between 1946 and 1951.[34] In the 1950s the cinema underwent a continued and more severe contraction under the impact of television and a crippling entertainments tax. Between 1950 and 1960 1500 cinemas closed, and tickets sold fell from 1396 million in 1950 to 515 million by 1960.[35] In 1982 cinema attendances were down to sixty million, about a quarter of those of 1950. Commensurately, British film production fell from 144 films in 1954 to 105 by 1961. The films of 1961 represented employment for 5000 actors but by the early 1970s the annual requirement for film actors was down to just over 2000.

The contraction of film employment had a number of effects on the actor. Firstly, Equity became protectively defensive, with the Film Casting Agreement of 1966, by which the employers agreed to consult with the union before a non-member could be offered an engagement. Film casting directors would interview only professional artists in the business, or people who had completed drama training, before using outsiders.[36] Secondly, film actors' fees have probably become more reasonable with the contracting market. In 1949 Sir George Gater's Committee on Film Production Costs was critical of the high salaries of stars as an element in the extravagant cost of films.[37] For example Jack Hawkins, one of the highest-paid British stars of the 1950s, earned £30,000 a picture. Reacting to the competition of television Hawkins accepted a cut in fees to £10,000 a film plus a share of profits.[38] Other leading actors also increasingly adopted this policy in the 1960s. Thirdly, the relative decline of cinema film-making has been paralleled by the rise of TV film-making. In 1953 films for television employed 505 actors, by 1958–9 they were employing 3901.[39] By the mid-1950s this work was increasing on such a scale that Equity recognized it with the TV Film Standard Contract, formalized from 1957. The competitive relations of the rising television and declining film media posed dilemmas for some actors. Dirk Bogarde tartly regarded television actors of the 1950s as rejects from the film industry and determined that he was not going to 'lower his sights' by moving into television when film work was undermined by it.[40]

By the late 1960s British television films were increasingly succeeding in capturing the international market. In turn, this is a root of one of the most pressing problems facing actors' unions now – the loss to the actor of remuneration for his work resulting from the private videotaping from television of his performances. In 1979 a Videogram Agreement was concluded between Equity and the ITV companies preventing the disposal of TV programmes in videotape form without royalties to the actors concerned. A similar agreement followed in 1981 with the British Film Producers' Association. In 1982 the public spent £51 million on video films,[41] and an estimated five million people watch video recordings every night.[42] The serious problems arising from this are the illegal home recording from television and the pirating of films on to videotape, both entailing losses to the actor. Equity calls for a tax on blank videotapes to meet the former problem, while the creation of the Video Copyright Protection Society expresses the common cause of actor and producer against the pirate.[43] Fourthly, the contraction of the cinema film industry, and indeed the pornographic and violent directions some of it has taken, had led to most of the ablest younger actors not being significant film-stars. While most of the leading stage actors from 1930 have also enjoyed notable film careers, this is no longer so. For the modern serious younger leading actor television has been more usually the preferred medium. In the last year or two there have been signs of revival in the British film industry, with Oscar-winning products like *Chariots of Fire* and *Gandhi* employing British stage actors of note. Television itself has given a boost to British film production of quality and intelligence with, for example, Goldcrest, Euston Films (a part of Thames Television) and the Channel Four 'Film on Four' slot, providing a venue for new specially made films of more artistic worth than commercial cinema-showing appeal.

V

Although the competition of television had such an adverse effect in contracting the mass provision of lightweight provincial theatre and consequent employment opportunities for the actor, this contraction has had certain beneficial effects on the theatre and the satisfaction of the actor's life. It has led to fewer theatres, but with a more serious artistic purpose. This has been evident in the new subsidized civic theatres, the new type of 'anger and after' drama, and the Fringe.

Following the decline of many old theatres and the touring companies that served them in the 1950s, a new dynamic element in the early sixties was the creation of several provincial civic playhouses using the 1948 rate.[44] The Belgrade Theatre Coventry, which opened in 1958, led the way. It was followed by new repertory theatres in Cheltenham (1960), Barrow (1961), Bromley, Croydon, Harrogate (the revived White Rose) (1962), Nottingham, Leicester, Newcastle (1963), Edinburgh and Watford (1965). All these were Non-Profit Distributing institutions and so qualified for Arts Council and municipal grants. These joined twenty-six surviving N-PD reps, half of which had been founded in the flourishing pre-TV days 1945–53.[45] The changes of the 1950s had resulted in a radical relocation of entertainment. Variety went into the pubs and working men's clubs.[46] Legitimate drama moved out of the collapsing touring theatres and second-rate provincial commercial resident companies into television and into far fewer, better, prestigious theatres of quality with audiences of a higher discernment than hitherto.[47]

The Shakespeare Memorial Theatre Company at Stratford opened its London base at the Aldwych in 1960, became the RSC in 1961, and with Scofield's *Lear* in 1962 and the *Wars of the Roses* in 1963 emerged as one of the major companies of the world. The new open thrust stage theatre at Chichester opened in 1962 and the National Theatre at the Old Vic in 1963. This shift from the widespread amplitude of mediocrity that characterized the provision of drama in the early 1950s to a more selective high quality in the early 1960s reduced the possibility of livelihoods for the large body of routine actors that the theatre had needed since the 1890s. But it enormously increased the artistic opportunities and attractiveness of the profession for the better-educated, more dedicated and serious-minded player.

A new seriousness of purpose is also thought to have marked the content of the theatre from the late 1950s, with a watershed focusing on the English Stage Company's production of *Look Back in Anger* in May 1956 and Joan Littlewood's Theatre Workshop production of *The Quare Fellow* in the same month. It would be easy to exaggerate

287

this since the early 1950s were full of many good things, betokening a lively theatrical culture. Yet the mid-1950s did, however, find a change in climate. In 1955 *Waiting for Godot* was produced and in 1956 Brecht's Berliner Ensemble visited London. In March 1956 Peter Hall, then Director of the Arts Theatre, spoke of 'the Dead Theatre' as too respectable and of the need for a new lusty drama to appeal to all walks of the population to save the theatre from 'rigid mortification'.[48] In the following May, *Look Back in Anger* was produced. *The Stage* noted, 'after the lean years new young playwrights of importance are at last beginning to appear'[49] – Osborne, Harold Pinter (*The Birthday Party*, 1958), Bernard Kops (*The Hamlet of Stepney Green*, 1956), John Arden (*Sergeant Musgrave's Dance* 1959), Arnold Wesker (*Roots*, 1959), Shelagh Delaney (*A Taste of Honey*, 1959). The close clustering of these developments created an impact and a sense of radical change. Managers perceived a change in the attitude of the audiences. They were getting younger, better-educated, less interested in stars and glamour than in the real values of the play; they now went to the theatre 'as much for enlightenment and culture as entertainment' in the belief that theatre had 'some contribution to make to modern thought'.[50] The effect of this on the actor was twofold. It increased the seriousness with which the theatre and the profession were regarded – 'the theatre will no longer be regarded as half wanted, half unnecessary, even half witted.'[51] Secondly, the new dramatists were of 'predominantly working-class origin,'[52] in contrast to the hitherto middle-class character of West End writers, actors and audiences since Edwardian times. Accordingly the new drama required, if not always the working-class actor, then certainly a more classless type of actor than had characterized so much drama since the 1890s. There was no advantage, for most of the cast in the plays referred to above, in possessing or acquiring an 'upper-class' accent or the graceful manipulation of cocktail glass or cigarette case. On the contrary, to have come from, or had first-hand experience of, rough working life and its speech and body language styles was a positive help to the credible portrayal of certain types of working-class character. It is no coincidence that the first 'Jimmy Porter', Kenneth Haigh, was a former builder's labourer. It is a piquant paradox that Mr Haigh is also a professor at Yale.

288

A major development of the 1970s, combining both a seriousness of purpose and a working-class context, has been the rise of the Fringe. Fringe theatres are small-scale touring companies, often with the avowed aim of bringing theatre to a mass working-class audience. Such were groups like Pip Simmons, 7/84, Belt and Braces and some 100 Fringe theatre companies, playing in small halls, university student unions and the like. Their growth in the 1970s was stimulated not only by finding receptive working-class audiences but by generous state finance through the Arts Council, rising from £7000 in 1971 to £1½ million by 1978.[53] Subsequent cuts have stunted this development. However, its rise has had a number of effects on the actor's life. These Fringe groups often provide the first step into employment for young actors from drama school, especially with the decline of provincial reps with their permanent companies. This in turn has led to a recent important change in Equity's regulations. Actors used to have to work for forty weeks outside London before being allowed to play in the West End. With the decline of rep and the lack of long contracts this has become so difficult that the Equity Council in 1983 changed this to thirty weeks, making it more possible for actors gaining their experience in the Fringe to break through to London.[54] Equity has also recognized the Fringe by the establishment of its Fringe Theatre Committee in 1977–8. Contracts were devised in 1978 with the Independent Theatre Council representing the managers, and by 1980 some 350–400 actors were engaged in this work.[55] The Fringe cannot remotely be regarded as replacing the old provincial rep system. It is only a marginal element in the broad pattern of change away from the copious supply of cheap, widely diffused, mediocre stage entertainment with many jobs for actors, towards a less available, more geographically concentrated, but much higher quality of theatre.

NOTES

1 *Equity Annual Report*, 1946–7.
2 *The Stage*, 6 June, 1 August 1946.
3 Brian Rix, *My Farce from My Elbow, an Autobiography* (London, 1975), p.55. Rix used the RTA-organized mass auditions, his sister had been in *Exercise Bowler*.

4 *The Stage*, 3 April 1947.

5 *The Stage*, 29 July 1948.

6 *The Stage*, 29 January 1953.

7 *The Stage Year Book*, 1949, p.46.

8 *The Stage*, 21 May 1953, lists thirty-three plays and sixty-three revues on tour.

9 John Osborne, *A Better Class of Person* (London, 1981, Penguin, 1982), pp.202, 215, 219.

10 *Ibid.*, p.245.

11 *Stage Year Book*, 1956.

12 *The Stage*, 20 December 1956.

13 *Stage Year Book*, 1956.

14 *Tatler*, 8 August 1962; *Stage Year Book*, 1960.

15 Henry Sherek, *Not in Front of the Children* (London, 1959), p.226. *The Stage*, 21 November 1946. Brian Rix, *op.cit.*, p.118.

16 *Stage Year Book*, 1957.

17 *The Stage*, 19 January, 1956.

18 Pat Phoenix, *All My Burning Bridges* (London, 1974), p.85.

19 Irene Shubik, *Play for Today* (London, 1975), p.37.

20 Edwin Eigner, 'British television drama and society in the 1970s', in *Drama and Society*, ed. James Redmond (Cambridge, 1979), p.212.

21 *Television Today*, 26 April 1962. The exceptions were the Birmingham School of Speech Training and Dramatic Art and the Bristol Old Vic School.

22 Michael Billington, *The Modern Actor* (London, 1973), p.10.

23 Interview with Miss Thurburn. The Central School under Miss Thurburn produced many successful film and television actors – Claire Bloom, Virginia McKenna, Heather Sears, Mary Peach, Vanessa Redgrave in films; Wendy Craig, Frank Windsor, Ian Hendry, James Bolam, Judi Dench in television, for example.

24 Equity Annual Report, 1948–9.

25 Equity Annual Report, 1953–4.

26 Bruce Belfrage, *One Man in His Time* (London, 1951), p.232.

27 *The Stage*, 21 May 1953.

28 'Fees in BBC Television', Appendix A in Equity Annual Report, 1956–7.

29 Equity Annual Report, 1960–1.

30 Equity Annual Report, 1961–2.
31 *The Stage*, 28 April 1983. Peter Plouviez at Equity AGM.
32 British Actors' Equity Nineteenth Annual Report, 1949–50.
33 British Actors' Equity Twentieth Annual Report, 1950–1.
34 P.E.P., *The British Film Industry* (London, 1952), p.186.
35 John Spraos, *The Decline of the Cinema* (London, 1962), pp.14, 165.
36 British Actors' Equity Thirty-Sixth Annual Report, 1966–7.
37 Ernest Betts, *The Film Business* (London, 1973), pp.218–19.
38 Jack Hawkins, *Anything for a Quiet Life* (London, 1973), pp.136–7.
39 British Actors' Equity Twenty-Third and Twenty-Eighth Annual Reports, 1953/4 and 1958/9.
40 Dirk Bogarde speaking in 'Omnibus', BBC 2, 27 March 1983.
41 'The Future of Radio', 16 January 1983, BBC Radio 4.
42 *Daily Telegraph*, 18 February 1983.
43 British Actors' Equity Reports 1980–1, 1981–2. Appendix D, 1981–2, 'Equity and the New Technology'.
44 John Elsom, *Theatre Outside London* (London, 1971).
45 *Who's Who in the Theatre* (1970), pp.1560–1.
46 The *Stage Year Books* of 1962 and 1963 first noted this as a strong trend.
47 Michael Codron and Charles Landstone thought this – *The Stage Year Book* 1961, as did Frank Hauser, 'Second House', BBC 2, 16 February 1974.
48 *The Stage*, 22 March 1956.
49 *The Stage*, 21 June 1956.
50 Michael Codron, Charles Landstone in *Stage Year Book*, 1961.
51 *Stage Year Book*, 1966.
52 J. R. Taylor, *Anger and After* (London, 1963), p.12.
53 'Is Jimmy Porter Dead?', Channel 4, 10 March 1983.
54 *The Stage*, 6 January 1983.
55 *Equity Annual Report*, 1979–80. Catherine Itzin, *Stages in the Revolution* (London, 1980), discusses some Fringe groups and the ITC.

14 A New Type of Actor

As there have been major changes in the theatrical context of the actor's work, so too the post-war years have seen the emergence of a new type of actor. The well-bred, public-school actor, often from a professional family background, was ceding the dominance that he had enjoyed in the profession since the 1890s. Alongside him was emerging the working-class actor who had hitherto had little chance of making his way in the profession. Yet if there was a decline in the social origins of the actor, the level of his education and training was raised. More post-war actors have been to university, and the universities themselves have engaged in drama education. Reciprocally, the drama schools have been able to shift their concentration away from the kind of cultural education represented by the old London University Diploma to vocational craft training. If the modern actor is better-educated, though more democratic, he has suffered an ever-increasing likelihood of remaining unemployed. This has carried its attendant penalties of low wages when in work and very low incomes over intermittent periods of work and 'resting'. This in turn has led to increasing demands for tougher forms of restricted entry into the profession. The working-class origins of many of the newer generation of actors has underlain political rifts within Equity itself and differing views about the degree of militancy and politicization appropriate to that body. The modern actor is less concerned about a glamorous social life than those of the 1890s–1930s generations, but the religious social sub-culture has continued to flourish. And whatever their problems and poverty, the leading actors have even more been able to break through into higher levels of social recognition and prestige.

I

The older generation of actors went back to work after the War, and they were joined by younger newcomers. Over the years it became clear that the post-war profession was taking its entrants from a somewhat different social spectrum than had the previous generations.[1] There was a great reduction in actors and actresses coming from professional families, traditionally one of the chief sources of the 'respectable' actor. Fewer actors also came from executive and entrepreneurial backgrounds, though more actresses did so. Slightly more players came from artistic, literary and theatrical families, though these were remarkably stable in line with the proportions of the interwar years. However, the really significant change was the rise in actors and actresses now coming from working-class artisan and manual backgrounds. In addition, they were coming from the new category of 'working-class shops' such as small barbers, newsagents and the like. This rise of the working-class actor and relative decline of the upper and middle classes has not led to a working-class replacing a middle-class predominance in the profession, but rather an acting body much more diversified in origins and type than hitherto. There were various causes and effects of this new working-class element in the profession. It was partly caused by the increase of local authority grants for drama schools in the 1960s and changes in attitudes, notably at RADA itself. It related also to the emergence of a working-class 'kitchen sink' naturalism in the theatre from the late 1950s and a television drama depicting characters with whom mass audiences could identify.

The changes in the social origins of actors were also matched by changes in their educational background. There was a relative decline in the proportion of actors having attended public schools and of actresses at our sample of 'notable' schools.

	Actors from public schools		*Actresses from 'notable' schools*
Starting career	'The Nine'	Honey/ Gathorne-Hardy	
1914–45	11.9%	47%	7.1%
Post-1945	7.98%	27.8%	5.8%

This reflects the decline also in actors coming from very comfortable backgrounds, though the single school producing most significant actors in the post-war years was actually Eton (9) followed by Alleyn's School, Dulwich (5), which was the launching-pad of the National Youth Theatre.

The most important school in the education of future actresses was the Elmhurst Ballet School, but most striking of all is the fact that nearly 24 per cent of the sample (41/173) had been convent-educated. It prompts speculation over how far some of the colour and ritualism, especially of a pre-Vatican II (1965) Catholic upbringing, had the effect of stimulating the dramatic instincts of young girls.

If fewer actors were coming from the most prestigious schools, more had been to university.

	Actors with university education	Actresses with university education
Starting 1914–45	24.2%	7.1%
Starting post-1945	27.8%	11.6%

Equity found that 25 per cent of entrants to the profession in 1971 and 1973 had been to university.[2] Even more had been to drama schools. Of actors starting careers after 1945, 54.4 per cent had been through drama training, and 86.1 per cent of actresses. RADA was the predominant academy, accounting for about half the actors in this sample and about a third of actresses. The Central, LAMDA, Webber –Douglas, Old Vic and Bristol Old Vic Theatre Schools were also leading suppliers, as we may expect. Some 70 per cent of new Equity members of 1971 and 1973 had been to drama schools,[3] and over 70 per cent of final year students from drama schools in the Conference of Drama Schools entered the profession in 1977.[4]

The increasing tendency for actors to have been to university is in itself scarcely surprising and is in line with the increasing experience of higher education, especially by the middle classes, whence most actors came. The increasing graduate element in the profession is undoubtedly desirable, for two main reasons. Firstly, it enables the drama schools to concentrate on craft training, often now post-graduate, in keeping with the other professions. It removes from
294

them the need to include some not always satisfactory wider cultural education. The shift in policy at RADA and the collapse of the old London University Diploma in the 1960s reflects this, as we shall see. It is undoubtedly of value to an actor to have acquired a good knowledge of English or foreign drama, literature and history prior to training, apart from the general virtues of intellectual and personal self-discipline that a good degree betokens. Secondly, university education has in practice been an unspoken qualification for higher theatrical administration since the War. The Old Vic was largely run by ex-Oxford OUDS men between the death of Lilian Baylis in 1937 and the advent of the National Theatre in 1963.[5] All the principals of RADA have been Oxford men,[6] while at the RSC it was a Cambridge elite that emerged from the 1960s.[7]

II

In the field of drama training which followed formal education there were important changes in the post-war years. At RADA Sir Kenneth Barnes was already sixty-seven when the War ended, but he soldiered on for another ten years. A major preoccupation of the principal and the Academy in the post-war years was the raising of money for rebuilding after the bomb damage which had demolished their theatre in 1941. Relations were further cemented with leading managements. The Old Vic sent advisers to discuss the work to be done by students likely to join the Company. Tennent's made an award of an annual contract to be judged by Hugh Beaumont, and Emile Littler and Alexander Korda also made awards.[8] This close connection with the wealthy grandees of the commercial theatre was lifeblood to RADA, and Barnes was adept at fostering them, as also the links with Royalty.

Yet for many pupils, and even teachers, who experienced the final years of Barnes's regime, things were not entirely satisfactory. Ronald Harwood, who was there in 1951, found that the Academy had declined to a 'genteel finishing school', with the teaching methods 'outdated, sterile and lifeless'.[9] This is rather harsh but even a teacher there, Denys Blakelock, admitted that Sir Kenneth, at over seventy, was too old and 'unable to get the measure of the new post-war world of the theatre'.[10] More specifically, a causal

295

linkage of problems weakened the institution. Barnes's preoccupation with money for the recovery of the Academy after the War had led him to yield to the great demand for places and pack it with fee-paying students, many of whom had minimal talent.[11] The student body and classes were too large. Moreover, since there was a close reliance on fee-payers, 'there was an abundance of upper-middle-class girls with minimum theatrical flair, who seemed to regard RADA as a rather amusing finishing school.'[12] Whatever the criticisms of these later years of Barnes's regime, we should bear in mind that he had successfully borne, since before the First World War, the responsibility of creating a major centre of drama training. At a time when it was far from clear what training for the stage should be or that it could be relevant to the real theatre, he had made RADA the premier prestigious academy, taken seriously by the commercial theatre, the University of London and Royalty alike. His knighthood in 1938 was an accolade for the whole idea of drama education and the career that had won it was of the greatest importance in the shaping of the modern acting profession.

However, a new view was needed and this came with his successor, John Fernald, whose innovative principalship spanned the decade 1955–65. New circumstances and policies came into play. First there was a drastic reduction of student numbers to cut away the kind of untalented all-comers who had diluted the student body in the late 1940s and early 1950s. In 1955 there were 320 students and by 1965 only 110 student actors, and twenty-five student stage managers.[13] Also students were obliged to take the whole course, and were no longer admitted part-time for parts of it. Fernald said frankly that 'quality and not quantity [was] now what is sought.'[14]

As the numbers declined, so the finances were balanced by a sharp raising of fees. In 1954 the fees were 30 guineas a term, by 1962 they were 80 guineas and by 1969, £140. This did not entail a further resort to the wealthy applicant, since there were changes in the grant system. In the mid-1940s there were only 'a negligible number of scholarships'[15] to drama schools. In the 1950 RADA prospectus students were first advised that some local authorities made awards, but in 1956 (Fernald's first prospectus) candidates were positively urged to secure such grants.[16] Indeed, from 1968 no student could be considered for a scholarship at RADA until he had explored the

296

possibility of an LEA grant. Accordingly in the late 1950s and 1960s the local authority grant student replaced the student supported by wealthy parents, and by 1966 80–90 per cent of RADA students received local authority grants.[17] The democratization of the intake was in keeping with trends elsewhere in higher education in the 1960s, and it lay behind the emergence of the actor from a working-class background that we noted earlier.

The academic activities of the students also changed. The Diction classes inculcating 'educated' English into students from different backgrounds were dropped and replaced with classes in audition technique.[18] The annual competitive Public Performance was abolished and replaced with regular and frequent full-scale performances in the new Vanbrugh Theatre. This gave students a more realistic taste of theatrical work than the once-a-year excerpts in a West End theatre. It also brought students before the public, managers and agents, who could judge a range of performances over a period of time. Also importantly, RADA students were sent on tours with their productions not only in Britain but to Norway, Switzerland and the United States. In response to modern conditions they undertook TV, Light Entertainment and revue technique. RADA also withdrew from the London University Diploma in Drama, since its academic emphasis diverted too much attention away from the professional training.

The emphasis on vocational craft training was the hallmark of Fernald's policy: 'it is Technique which is ever and again in emphasis . . . The search for a secure technique for all its students is the recurring theme of the RADA's two-year course.'[19] The policy was successful, and almost all RADA graduates gained employment on leaving: 76/81 in 1961, 58/63 in 1963 and 52/57 in 1964, reflecting partly the contraction in output. At the top end RADA produced some very able actors indeed in the Fernald years. It may not be too invidious to mention Albert Finney, Tom Courtney, Richard Briers, John Hurt, Siân Phillips, Susan Fleetwood, Glenda Jackson as but a few. In the 1978 list of Associates of RADA – all well-known former students who have achieved notability – and selecting those starting careers since 1945, we find nineteen from the decade of the last Barnes years and twenty-nine from the Fernald decade, with some nine not exactly dateable but almost certainly from the Fernald years

297

or later. This reflects the raised quality and the actual relevance of the Academy from the late 1950s and 1960s. In 1966 Fernald resigned and was succeeded as principal by Hugh Cruttwell, under whom the Academy has retained its distinguished position. Mr Cruttwell retired in 1983.

The Central School continued to flourish under its Principal, Gwynneth Thurburn OBE, who succeeded Elsie Fogerty in 1942 and remained until 1967. She described the course:

> In the three year Drama Course at the School, students spend the first two years studying movement, voice production, acting and its background. The plays they rehearse during that time are produced by members of the permanent staff. In the third year, in order to encourage variety of approach, they are directed by a number of different outside producers who are experienced theatre people. These plays are performed to outside audiences.[20]

This play performance was greatly facilitated by the Central's move in 1958 to the Embassy Theatre complex in Swiss Cottage, where it now resides.

The major schools founded before the Second World War were joined by new foundations. One of the first and most influential of the new schools was the Old Vic School, opened in 1947. Run by Michel Saint-Denis, George Devine and Glen Byam Shaw, it was in many ways a revival or continuation of the London Theatre Studio of the 1930s. Located initially at the Old Vic and then from 1949 in a girls' school in West Dulwich, it admitted about forty pupils a year. The curriculum consisted of dancing and movement, elocution and voice production and working with masks, which was Devine's speciality. Great stress was laid on improvisation in ways reminiscent of the LTS. A great advantage enjoyed by the Old Vic School, and not by the LTS, was the chance for successful pupils to move into the main company, 'thus supplying the parent stage with a regular flow of new talent'.[21] Many notable post-war actors were produced by the School – Derek Godfrey, Alan Dobie, Denis Quilley, Joan Plowright, Prunella Scales, among many. This was the more remarkable in that the life of the School was short, a mere five years. In 1951, following complicated reorganization at the Old Vic and the arrival of Sir Tyrone Guthrie, it was closed down. But in its short life it was

298

the most important development in drama training between the War and the creation of the university drama departments of the 1960s.

The *Stage Year Book* of 1950 listed drama schools from the venerable LAMDA, which could trace its origins to 1861, to the Week End Theatre School of East Dulwich, started in 1949.[22] Expansion continued. In 1950 Rose Bruford, who had trained with Fogerty, taught at RADA and been Director of Drama at the Royal Academy of Music in the 1940s, left to establish her own School in Kent. In the early 1960s the Actors' Studio, based on the Jeannetta Cochrane Theatre, was intended as a joint training ground for the Royal Court and the National Theatre, among others. George Devine taught at these, since the Royal Court never established its own school.[23] Between 1961 and 1972 fourteen leading drama schools were inspected by HMI and found 'efficient'. Then in 1969 twelve of these fourteen, with two others, formed the Conference of Drama Schools as a 'nucleus of established and reputable full-time vocational drama schools'.[24] In addition, seven more schools are regarded as 'principal drama schools' by the DES and seventeen others are well-known through advertisements in the trade literature and (like Italia Conti) historical repute.[25] There were thus about fourteen elite drama schools, and a further twenty-six of some repute, in the 1970s.

A new element in training was the National Youth Theatre. This was begun by Michael Croft, a schoolmaster at Alleyn's School, Dulwich.[26] He had established a high reputation as a producer of school plays, and on resigning to pursue a career as a writer in 1956 continued producing with boys from Alleyn's and other London schools. Following the success of their first production of *Henry V* in 1956 their activities expanded, so that by 1960 they were recruiting youngsters, including girls, from the whole of England, undertaking international tours, and receiving financial support from the Ministry of Education. Central School teachers helped with the training of the young players. Croft also stressed that they were a movement 'with one foot in the theatre and one in the Youth Service'; in particular they helped ten youth club theatre groups in London.[27] Less than 5 per cent of their members became professional actors, though they include some notable names – John Stride, Julian

299

Glover, Simon Ward, Derek Jacobi, Martin Jarvis, Hywel Bennett and Helen Mirren. The NYT is not a drama school in itself. Of the above names six went on to drama schools (five to RADA) and one to Cambridge, while Stride, Glover and Ward are all ex-Alleyn's pupils. In 1980 the NYT lost its Arts Council grant but in 1982 secured sponsorship from Texaco.

The continued pressure on available places is maintained by various factors. First, many secondary schools built since the War had stages incorporated, thirty LEAs had drama advisers and there was an HMI in Drama.[28] This stimulated many young people's practical interest in the amateur theatre and awakened ideas of professionalism. Second, the demographic pressures occasioned by the post-war birth bulge, which led to the general expansion of higher education of the 1960s, were felt also by the drama schools.[29] Third, the new wave of drama, Osborne-and-after, must have aroused the enthusiasm of a wider range of young people who would not have felt drawn to the West End of the 1940s and 1950s. The advent of television in the latter decade brought good quality drama – notably through its weekly Sunday evening plays – to the attention of many non-theatre-goers. Fourth was the very important change in the grant system. From the early 1960s LEAs began to make grants to pupils attending drama schools, on a par with other forms of higher education. This greatly widened the social catchment area from which drama students were drawn. Whereas in the 1940s and 1950s they were still mostly well-to-do, able to afford private fees and with parental backing for living expenses, from the 1960s they covered a much wider social spectrum.

This pressure on the Schools is made worse by the imbalance between men and women. Far more women want to go on the stage than men. Whereas in 1961 LAMDA took only a quarter of all applicants, it took only one in ten of girls applying. The same was evident when it came to looking for work. Of sixteen applicants to join the Bristol Old Vic in 1951, thirteen were girls.[30] None was of note or made a name, yet in terms of likely job opportunities in the real theatre outside there were twice as many roles for men as for women. All the plays produced in London in 1961 required 1019 men's parts and only 421 women's, a proportion of nearly two-and-a-half to one.[31]

300

III

Changes in drama education were reflected in the position of the London University Diploma, whose administrators had to face some central dilemmas over its purpose. Basically it was a question of how far the Diploma should be useful for the craft training of the actor and how far it should retain a large element of literary and historical culture for his wider education. This clash of interest had already been evident in 1939 when Sir Kenneth Barnes of RADA objected to some of the history papers as unnecessarily difficult for actors and was told by the examiners that the Diploma approximated to a university degree and ought to be 'more exacting or wider in scope'.[32] After the War the problem was faced head-on and a subcommittee of Barnes and Gwynneth Thurburn of the Central School considered whether the Diploma was still necessary. They suggested that it 'does not provide the key to a successful stage career' but that it provides evidence of a 'high standard of knowledge in such cultural subjects as are of special value for background purposes to the craft of the actor.'[33] They proposed dropping foreign languages, music and physics, making poetics optional and including a Shakespearian subject. These were incorporated into the 1949 Regulations. Problems still remained. Sir Lewis Casson, writing a visitational report on RADA in 1953, found the timetable so overloaded that 'it is difficult for students to follow the Diploma course without risk of stress and strain'.[34] Yet was more and more education really necessary to the craft training of the actor? Did they really need as much as potential producers and teachers, and could this be secured without sacrificing time better spent on technical stagecraft?

These considerations prompted something of a crisis in the running of the Diploma around 1959–60, which throws much light on the training of actors at the time. In 1956 John Fernald, who had succeeded Sir Kenneth Barnes as principal of RADA, regarded the Diploma with a certain cool scepticism. RADA withdrew from the Diploma in 1957 and Fernald made his position clear. The best RADA students could not afford the time for the Diploma. Its academic approach was more relevant for producers than actors and its practical work was of too low a standard (much below RADA's) to be

301

valuable to the actor's training.[35] The two-year RADA course had to be focused on the creative imagination and technique and these were more important than the cultural background provided by the Diploma and university link. In 1960 Fernald resigned from the Diploma committee, along with Michael MacOwen of LAMDA. Sir Lewis Casson agreed with Fernald, 'there seems no evidence that Theatre managements set any value on the Diploma'[36] and it was probably of more use to directors than to actors.

In the 1960s the Diploma came to be almost entirely for intending teachers rather than actors. The New College (the former Drama Department of the Royal Academy of Music) started taking the Diploma after the College's inception in 1962 and the principals saw the future of the qualification as geared to the needs of the teacher and providing a good general education.[37] The Central withdrew in 1974 to take the Cert. Ed. of the University of London and in 1976 the New became part of the Middlesex Polytechnic. The Diploma was clearly overtaken by events, but it had been a peculiarly sensitive indicator of broad changes elsewhere in drama education. It had been created in the 1920s by people eager to secure a professional status for the actor and perhaps too concerned with academic studies as a means to this end. It had also begun in a context in which relatively few actors had been to universities and there was need for a qualification that would entail some intellectual 'stretching' for those with such abilities and inclinations. With the much wider opportunities for university education becoming available since the War, and especially since 1960 with the general expansion and the rise of university drama departments, there was less need for this kind of university-substitute qualification. Drama schools, often now taking post-graduates, could concentrate on technical craft training for actors or on being teacher training colleges, and the Diploma was adjusted to serve the latter purpose. Both its creation in the 1920s and its demise in the 1960s were significant turning points in the training of the actor and in attitudes to it in this century.

One of the factors overtaking the old University of London Diploma has been the development of university drama departments since the War. In the United States there had been a long tradition of drama departments in major universities; at Harvard from Professor G. P. Baker's '47 Workshop' in 1912 and at Yale from the building

302

of the theatre there in 1925 by Edward Harkness and the establishment of the Department of Drama under Baker's headship.[38] Accordingly the idea of associating drama training with British universities gained ground. Alexander Korda gave £5000 to Oxford in the late 1940s to investigate American drama departments with a view to establishing one of their own, although nothing came of Korda's proposal.

Bristol was the first university to establish a drama department in 1947, with the first English professorship of drama from 1960. The city housed the Theatre Royal, the oldest theatre in Britain, with its resident Old Vic Company, and the West Region Studios of the BBC. The University concentrated 'on the academic aspects of drama – dramatic theory and literature, theatre history, criticism and so on . . . practical classes are given with the invaluable aid of the staff of the [Bristol] Old Vic Theatre Company and School.'[39] At first the department was barely distinguishable from a department of English Literature, but soon it began play production and in 1954 had a three-studio suite of radio equipment. By the early 1970s film production was a significant activity.[40] Bristol led the way and was followed by others, not immediately in the 1950s, but in the general expansion of the universities in the 1960s.

In 1961 Manchester University set up its drama department under Hugh Hunt, a former director of the Old Vic, with an endowment from Granada TV. Further departments followed at Hull (1963), Birmingham (1964), Bangor (1965), Glasgow (1966) and Exeter (1968), all except Bangor and Exeter having full chairs of drama.[41] Among the new universities Warwick, Sussex and East Anglia have established drama departments. It is too early to assess the long-term effect of such departments or whether they will come to rival OUDS, ADC or RADA as nurseries of the future elite of the profession. They represent a viable middle road between, on the one hand, the Oxbridge graduate devoting himself to amateur dramatics while coasting to an 'actor's third' in a degree that holds little interest for him, and on the other the relatively narrow non-liberal craft training of the drama schools.[42] Some 15 per cent of entrants to Equity in 1971 and 1973 came from university drama departments though only a small proportion of all such students went into the theatre.[43]

Following the Gulbenkian Report of 1975 the National Council

303

for Drama Training was set up, consisting of Conference of Drama Schools principals and representatives of Equity. The NCDT Accreditation Panel set to work to investigate and validate the courses of vocational drama schools. By 1980 they had approved eleven acting courses and rejected seven. Many people hoping to control the numbers of actors through tighter control of entry into the profession welcome these sieving activities of the NCDT Accreditation Panel (now Board) which is now turning its attention to drama in higher education.

These developments in drama education were among the most important changes in the actor's profession in the post-war years. The shift towards a greater concern for craft training evident at RADA and in the London Diploma, the expansion of drama schools, the changing social class of students, the involvement of the universities in the field, all shaped actors better-educated, more craft-trained and serious than hitherto. Unfortunately, these improved qualities did not safeguard the actor from the perennial problem of unemployment.

IV

The high levels of unemployment associated with the profession remained endemic and deteriorated throughout the post-war period. In the early 1950s 30 to 40 per cent of actors were unemployed.[44] Bad as these unemployment levels were in the early 1950s, they have risen since to around 60 per cent[45] and 70 per cent by the early 1970s[46] and 80 per cent by the later 1970s.[47] The unemployment levels, of course, represent those actors out of work at any point of time; accordingly they mask the underemployment characteristic of the work. For example, in the early 1950s an actor worked on average for thirty-three weeks in the year but by the early 1970s this had fallen to twenty weeks.[48] Olivier considers that only about 800 actors, or 2½ per cent of the profession, are in fairly constant work at the present time.[49] Both employment levels and weeks worked per year had deteriorated between the early 1950s and the 1970s. This is accounted for by the flood of applicants wishing to go on the stage, aided by the increase of drama schools and the greater availability of local authority grants. This increasing supply was faced with a

diminution of employment opportunities with the decline of provincial and touring theatre in the 1950s.

Such levels of unemployment and underemployment were also a
factor in depressing the low income levels of the rank-and-file actor.
This was evident both in the movement of basic rates over time and
in the spectrum of earnings. The minimum West End wage was £8 a
week in the early 1950s and £70 a week in 1979. The provincial rates
were lower *pari passu*, ranging from £4.10s in 1953 to £55 by 1979.
These are obviously extremely modest. If a West End actor on the
minimum worked for a whole year in 1979 he would earn £3640, and
a provincial actor £2860. Both would be considerably less than the
national annual average male wage of £6000.

Not all actors, obviously, remain on the minimum salary or expect
to do so. It is important to see something of the spectrum of incomes
through the profession as a whole. In 1953 this was:[50]

	Weekly Income £				
	Under £7	*£7–12*	*£12–20*	*£20–40*	*£40+*
Percentage of actors	14	47	23	11	5

Some 40 per cent of Equity members made 'a fair living', 26 per cent
a marginal living and 34 per cent virtually no living at all. The elite
of the profession, however, could earn very high incomes. Richard
Findlater estimated that in 1959 stars like Olivier and Gielgud would
earn about £400 a week (or about £20,000 a year), irrespective of film
work.[51] This was the lure that sustained the hopes of the floods of
new entrants and the impoverished lower reaches of the profession.

By 1971 Derek Layder discerns a three-level stratification in the
range of earnings in the profession.[52] An elite of 5 per cent earning
£4000 to £10,000+ in 1971 were the stars. Closely associated with
them were the outer circle of actors earning £1500 to £4000 and
comprising another 18 per cent. Casting directors tend to ask for
such actors rather than actors having to seek work. The elite and
outer circle are handled by the top 60 agents, through whom most of
the work is channelled. This leaves the vast mass of the rest, 76.6 per
cent of the profession, earning less than £1500 in 1971. The median
income for actors in 1971 was actually about half of that, at £785. In

personal terms it contains, for example, a RADA medallist in fairly regular television employment who was earning only £616 by 1966 after five years' experience.[53] At the top end of the mass would be a leading actress at Salisbury Playhouse, who earned from £1000 to £1500 in the early 1970s.[54] The mass endured their low pay, buoyed by the actor's constant belief in the 'break' or success that may come late, the rational calculation that very rapid social and financial advancement is more likely to be encountered in acting than in any other career they might follow, and the sheer love and gratification of the art itself.

Since the 1971 Survey actors' earnings have risen. There is, of course, no scale of salaries for actors, but the basic indicator is the West End Straight Play minimum. This has risen:

1972	1977	1983
£25	£42	£120

Prices have risen fourfold between 1971 and 1983. This nearly five-fold increase in the basic indicator of actors' wages suggests that Equity, for all its troubles, has been able to keep remuneration in line with and even slightly ahead of inflation. This is, however, of little comfort for those receiving these low minima and the many more whose unemployment deprives them of even these. It is worth noting that even a whole year's work on the West End minimum would yield an income of £6240, considerably less than the 1983 national average income of £8700. In 1983 Equity raised the provincial minimum to £90.50 a week after the threat of a strike.

Given these high and permanent levels of unemployment and low levels of income, the modern actor has to resort to a great deal of part-time, non-theatrical work to supplement his income. The almost full employment of the post-war years, until recent times, has accordingly eased the actor's position. Equity noted that 'the profession is therefore dependent to a peculiar degree upon the maintenance of full employment in industry as a whole in order to cushion the effect of casual labour within entertainment.'[55] Cleaning work is a popular standby; indeed Domestics Unlimited, which specializes in employing unemployed actors, is run by a former actor, Malcolm Taylor. Minicab driving is also increasingly resorted

306

to, with building site labouring for men and market research for women.[56] A group of young players trying to get established in their careers had variously taken to secretarial work, waiting, advertising modelling and working in a meat factory.[57] Failing that, the actor had to resort to the Employment Office. For example, of 1243 unemployed people registered at the Camden Employment Office in September 1973, 104 were 'resting' actors and actresses, reflecting a concentration of theatrical people in north-west London.[58]

The high unemployment, intermittent work and low pay took their toll in the large numbers who abandoned their careers. Since 1950 there has regularly been an annual wastage of from 1000 to 2000 actors leaving the profession; this was usually somewhat less than the advent of new applicants. In some years, 1949–50 and 1953–4, there was a massive annual shedding of 2600 and 2700, resulting in an actual fall in membership overall.[59] It suggests that many who had taken up acting during the War, when the theatre boom and call-up of actors had made it easy for the unfit to get on the stage, were cutting their losses and quitting unsuccessful careers in the early 1950s. Several must have been people who inflated the student numbers at RADA in the 1940s and 1950s. While most drama students could get a start in the profession, little more than a half actually stayed in it as a career.[60] Most married or gave up after the second or third job. A group of 1950s RADA graduates interviewed twenty years on in 1979 revealed this interestingly.[61] Of the five interviewed, one woman had given up to marry and now worked in a bookshop, one man had become a restaurateur, another a writer. Only one, Susannah York, had been really successful in her theatrical career. The fifth member of the party had been a moderately successful actor, Alan Thompson, whose persistence revealed another important truth about an actor's career. An actor in his twenties competes with others in the ratio of 100–1. Such is the fall-out that an actor surviving to his forties competes in a ratio of 4–1. Mr Thompson was finding that in middle age he was reaching a point where he was spending more of the year in, rather than out of, work. Most were not prepared to risk waiting so long and left the stage for marriage or other careers. At the present time about 2700 members (nearly 10 per cent) leave Equity annually, most driven out by the failure to find the employment to sustain a career.

307

The only way to tackle the problems of chronic unemployment and the consequent bad pay at the lower levels of the profession was some form of restricted entry. This was an old debate between advocates of free or restricted entry which dated back to before 1914. There was some concern to regulate entry immediately after the Second World War because there had been an influx of untrained and unsuitable actors during the War due to the boom in the theatre coinciding with the call-up of fit actors. A subcommittee of Equity considered this problem but decided against any regulation of the free flow of talent.[62] During the 1960s, however, membership rose very considerably, from 10,000 to 17,000, and this inevitably brought the issue to the fore once again. By the late 1960s Equity was tackling it with strict casting agreements allowing only a small proportion of newcomers in any cast. This has had the effect of sharply reducing the numbers of new members admitted into certain areas.

	Admissions in year before Agreement	Date of Casting Agreement	Admissions 1981
West End	50	(1968)	20
Provincial Theatre	1324	(1971)	607
Television	641	(1969)	99

The union also proposed a new structure of membership, with probationers who have to complete a Work Record Card as an apprenticeship. Full membership was to be difficult to obtain and easier to lose for those in arrears.[63] It considered that new members should not exceed 400 a year rather than the over 1000 a year they were accepting. Most important, it determined to co-operate with the drama schools as potentially the key regulative mechanism controlling the flow into the profession. A Drama School Committee was established which met with the DES, Arts Council and principals.[64] The matter is now much better controlled and the National Council for Drama Training (Equity, Theatre Managers, Drama Schools) is now very keen that half of new Equity cards should be reserved for graduates of their validated drama schools who obtained employment. This has divided the Equity Council into the old

308

schisms of free versus restricted entry. In 1982 the Equity Council decided to allow privileged entry to graduates from NCDT drama schools, reversing an earlier opposite decision in 1981. This has aroused a furore, not least from the NYT.[65] However, with Equity membership continuing to grow from 17,005 in 1970 to 29,151 in 1981, about half of whom are legitimate stage actors, continued severe measures of control remain necessary.

Another important element in this whole process of entry into the profession is the agent, and here too there have been significant changes in recent years. Few agents now sign up young performers. In the 1950s agents used to go to drama school performances to spot talent, making contracts with graduating students for whom they might speculatively expect a lucrative future. Nowadays agents still take a close interest in the drama schools, but rarely to make contracts. Most young actors get their first jobs on their own initiative and without the benefit of an agent until they become sufficiently well-known to start winning television and film work.[66] The changed position of the agent *vis-à-vis* the novice actor and the drama schools has further increased the difficulties of starting a career.

V

The low pay of the rank and file and the high levels of unemployment have underlain increasing political tensions within the profession. A violent ripple of politicization and anti-politicization disturbed Equity in 1949. In the context of severe Cold War, Russian control in Eastern Europe and the UnAmerican Activities Committee in the USA, three Equity organizers resigned because of their fear of Communist influence in the union. One of them had actually been a Communist himself. Lewis Casson dismissed this as nonsense, but an unofficial committee was formed as a pressure group to campaign to restore Equity as a non-political organization.[67] This affected the elections to Council of 1949, and many very valuable members were not re-elected because of their left-wing sympathies. They included former presidents Beatrix Lehmann and Sir Lewis Casson, who had both been active in Socialist theatre activities in the 1930s, and Peggy Ashcroft. They

309

had been victims, in the Secretary's words, of 'rip-roaring Red scare', and Casson said that it would take him a long time to get over it.[68] Thirty-five out of the forty of the newly-elected Council were 'approved' by the anti-political campaign. It is a curious, long-forgotten episode, but presaged the more rifting clashes of the 1970s. In particular it raised sharply the issue of whether Equity should be a non-political organization and whether it needed defending to keep it so.

It was in the early 1960s that a number of actors manifested public political attitudes usually in favour of nuclear disarmament. John Neville, noted for his Socialism and practical anti-racialism, was arrested and fined after a ban-the-bomb demonstration in 1961.[69] A number of Central School pupils, including Judi Dench and Fiona Walker, were supporters of the Committee of 100, while Julie Christie appeared handcuffed in the Church of St Martin-in-the-Fields to commemorate Human Rights Day, 1962.[70] Most important was another Central alumna, Vanessa Redgrave. It was the Hungarian Revolution in 1956 that first sparked off her political interests, and the conviction that good things did not come about 'unless you take your share of fighting the evil things'.[71] In the early 1960s her activity took the form of participation in CND. There was a supposed Leftwards movement of influence in the two major companies, with Olivier veering to Socialism and Joan Plowright, Tynan and Gaskill committed to the Left.[72] Both the National and the RSC, especially the latter, espoused the work of committed Left-wing playwrights – Gorki, David Edgar, Trevor Griffith and Howard Baker.[73] As the theatre acquired a rather Leftish tinge in the 1960s, so actors were received freely at receptions given by Prime Minister Harold Wilson at 10 Downing Street. Conversely, the *Daily Telegraph's* lampooning of its fictitious actor 'Sir Osric Fenton', in the satirical Peter Simple column, was calculated to deflate whatever sense of importance they may have acquired therefrom.

Political divisions rifted Equity in the 1970s. To preserve its closed-shop status the union registered under the controversial Conservative Industrial Relations Act of 1971. This evoked the strong opposition of members on the Left, who advocated a policy of non-co-operation with the Act, and Equity was accordingly expelled from the TUC in September 1973. As it happened, a Labour

310

government was elected in the following March and repealed the Act. Equity subsequently rejoined the TUC after a referendum in December 1974, the issue of registration under the now defunct Act having been removed. Matters were further smoothed as Hugh Jenkins, a former Equity general secretary, became Minister for the Arts.

The Left also wanted Equity to give financial support to the miners during their strike in the early months of 1972. Equity traditionalists or moderates emphasized that solidarity depended on their trade union remaining non-political and 'not entangled with industrial or political disputes of other unions outside our own sphere'.[74] Although the Left was unsuccessful in the elections in 1973, by 1974 three groups had become differentiated.[75] The traditionalists, or moderates, or 'right-wing Establishment', such as Marius Goring, Olivier, Nigel Davenport, wished to keep things as they were – politically unaligned and, very importantly, with all members voting for all members of the council. In the middle was an important new group, CRAPE (the Campaign for Reaffiliation and Progress of Equity), formed by Miriam Karlin and Hugh Manning and with the prestigious membership of Dame Peggy Ashcroft. CRAPE's policies were immediate reaffiliation to the TUC, a union structure based on local branches and delegates (rather than the individual votes of all members), inter-union co-operation and a tougher trade-union stance *vis-à-vis* employers. On the Left was a group associated with the Workers' Revolutionary Party and led by Vanessa and Corin Redgrave. They wanted not only a delegate structure but more far-reaching demands, such as the nationalization of the entertainment industry and the extension of Equity member-ship even to marginal entertainers such as striptease artists, with national actors' strikes to raise wages.

Conflicts were further exacerbated by the internal institutional arrangements of the union. Decisions of the Council could be reversed by a referendum of all members, but a referendum decision in turn could be reversed by a Special General Meeting called by forty members, and an SGM decision could be reversed by the Council. As the secretary, Peter Plouviez, noted, 'our union is caught in a vicious circle'.[76] The Council was fearful of being taken over by tiny minority political groups – which the replacing of a total

311

vote by a delegate system could make possible. The Rule Revision Committee established in 1973 had recommended a branch and delegate system but this had been rejected by the Council and a referendum equally fearful of the influence it would give to minorities. On the other hand the Council was not favourable to Davenport–Goring moves to have it formally stated that the union was 'non-political' since, as Plouviez pointed out, 'non-political' does not make sense when it comes to much of the work the union must do.[77] 'Act for Equity', the moderates' organization led by Davenport and Goring, was accordingly set up to defend the union against the Left politicization of the Redgrave group on the one hand and the 'branch and delegate' abolition of the total vote approach of CRAPE.[78] These troubles were the waves above deeper swells of change. The sheer increase in the size of Equity, from around 4000 before the War to 20–22,000 in the 1970s and to nearly 30,000 by 1983, had created organizational problems of representation less felt among the smaller more homogeneous profession of the 1930s. Probably more important, the social class change in the origins of the actor and its admixture of working-class entrants aided the Left politicization. A substantial body of actors now had no doubt and no shame that they were 'workers' rather than professionals, and had to fight their corner with employers in a competitive capitalist entertainment industry. It is notable that the leaders of the moderates, Davenport and Goring, are both products of major public schools and universities, and that several of the actors standing for Council on the Act for Equity platform in 1978 are noted for their 'upper-class' personas – John Barron, Derek Bond, Hugh Burden, Isabel Dean, Anthony Quayle, Margaret Rawlings, for example. The post-war influx of actors from working-class and even quite poor backgrounds has broken up the social homogeneity of the profession and makes the pointing-up of these contrasts inevitable.

These rifts and conflicts have shown little sign of diminishing in the last few years, while Equity's general position has been weakened by financial troubles. The union's financial position changed from one of surplus in 1979 to deficits of £4000 by 1980 and £100,000 in 1981 and 1982, with fears of this rising to £250,000 by 1983. The root of the problem was twofold. Firstly, the revenue from members' subscriptions was too low, an average of £25 per member in 1981–2. Too few members admitted to higher earnings over £3000 which would entail paying higher subscriptions. Also the majority voted against raising subscriptions, which they suspect as a device to drive the poorer actor out of the profession altogether. Secondly, the union has found its restricted resources bled by the costs of successive referenda. These have arisen from the institutional difficulties referred to earlier. In 1980 a new Council was elected dominated by the Conservative Act for Equity group, led by John Barron. This found itself at loggerheads with groups of activists in specially called SGMs and accordingly appealed to the mass of membership over the heads of such General Meetings by means of referenda. This triangular blocking, with Council decisions being opposed by General Meetings whose views in turn tend to be opposed by referendum decisions, has caused great frustration in the running of the union. It is also very expensive, contributes to the financial problems and in turn has faced Equity with another political crisis.

In 1982 the Council decided to accept government money to assist with the cost of secret ballot referenda. This brought them into risk of a second expulsion from the TUC in circumstances reminiscent of 1973. Equity's position was dire, with fears that the union would barely survive 1982 and talk of selling its Harley Street offices for £1 million. It was also deeply feared that by accepting government money and being expelled from the TUC, Equity would be left powerless to resist the attack on the closed shop embodied in Norman Tebbit's Employment Bill of 1982. The closed shop had been the very basis of Equity's existence since the 1930s, and its abolition would return the actor to the vulnerability of the 1920s.

In these anxious circumstances the Conservative Act for Equity group were ousted from their control of the Council in the elections of 1982. The Council from 1982 to 1984 consisted of thirty-two Centre Forward members (largely the former CRAPE), twenty-eight Act for Equity, four Independents and one All Trades Union Alliance. It is evident that the extreme Left which attracted so much attention in the 1970s is not now significant. The 1984 elections represented a swing to the Right with the Act for Equity group winning 46 of the 66 seats, the Centre Forward 19 and with no Far Left candidates elected.

313

The 1982 Council determined not to accept government money, still less to risk expulsion from the TUC. On the contrary, it sought to help the TUC's fight against the Employment Bill by making a 10p per head levy on Equity members to contribute to the TUC's fighting fund. This in turn has led to further conflicts as trustees Marius Goring, Wendy Hiller and John Clements sought to prevent the payment to the TUC being made and a further trustee, Derek Bond, withheld 10p from his subscription as an unwarranted political levy. What will be the implications of the government's trade-union policies for Equity's closed shop, and the position of Conservative members of the union when they do become apparent, remain to be seen. An important difference of principle has recently emerged with clarity between Left and Right. Hugh Manning and the Left are firmly of the opinion that Equity can no longer regard itself as non-political. However much it eschews a party-political stance, much of its activity, especially in relation to the Employment Acts, must be political in form. The Right deplores this as a betrayal of the non-political professionalism out of which the union grew in the 1930s. Whatever these differences of Left and Right among the actor members of Equity, the strength of the union is underpinned by its permanent officials, led by Peter Plouviez. Their success in extending the areas of Equity contracts in the media and in improving financial terms are the more remarkable in the light of the histrionics of some of the members they serve and the frustrations of the system within which they have to operate.

VI

Off-stage, the actor in recent years has shown less interest in the kind of glamorous social life that characterized the 1890–1939 generation, but the more altruistic charitable and religious social organizations continue to flourish. In the 1940s and 1950s there were some echoes of the social life of the interwar years. In 1947 Mario Gallati moved from the Ivy to start the Caprice Restaurant, with some financial backing from Ivor Novello. Gallati claimed that 'my clientele is predominantly drawn from the theatre';[79] indeed, rather bizarrely, part of the cast of the 1953 film of *Romeo and Juliet* was chosen from habitués of the restaurant. The country house tradition

314

of theatrical entertaining found its last fling in the Oliviers' residence at Notley Abbey in Buckinghamshire in the 1950s, where the artistic and fashionable were regular weekend guests. Noel Coward similarly was at Goldenhurst, though his guests tended to be literary rather than Thespian.[80] Coward left Goldenhurst in 1956, Olivier left Notley in the late 1950s, and there are no real successors. The older generation of interwar actors is now too elderly to enjoy a hectic social life. The modern actor is too burdened with income tax to run country houses, and often too hardworking or serious or family-minded to spend long evenings in nightclubs. Nor is the old style of social life a significant aid to a career, as it was in the days when a fashionable appearance and contacts were important to the drawing-room actor.

On the other hand the less stylish, more private, benevolent forms of social life continued to be important. Various changes took place in the profession's pastoral care of its members through its own religious and charitable organizations. The Actors' Orphanage, which had been founded in 1896, continued to flourish under Noel Coward's presidency. Its house, Silverlands in Chertsey, had been requisitioned during the War and many of the children had been evacuated to America. A new house in Lennox Gardens, Chelsea received the returning children.[81] The Theatrical Garden Party, whose proceeds had supported the Orphanage since 1903 and which had ceased during the War, was revived in 1947 but abandoned in 1952 due to the now prohibitive costs of setting it up.[82] So vanished one of the oldest and most popular features of the theatrical scene, which had brought actors and audiences together in a charitable purpose. In 1962 the Orphanage was taken over by the Actors' Charitable Trust.

The Actors' Charitable Trust also absorbed the profession's other residential provision, Denville Hall for elderly and infirm retired actors. It was begun in 1926 by Alfred Denville, actor, theatre proprietor and Newcastle MP. The Hall was opened formally as a Home in 1926, with Gerald du Maurier as chairman of the trustees. The Variety Artistes followed suit with a home of their own in 1933. By the end of the War Denville Hall had cared for some 200 actors and actresses, of whom forty-eight had died there.[83] The Hall was taken over by the Actors' Charitable Trust in the late 1960s, and it

315

flourishes today with about forty residents in the house at Nor-
thwood, which has been expanded by the ACT under a very active
and concerned committee of theatricals under the presidency of
Lord Olivier and the chairmanship of Sir Richard Attenborough.[84]
Olivier is also the president of the Actors' Benevolent Fund, which
continues its work in support of elderly, ailing or financially hard-
pressed actors and actresses who could remain in their homes
without needing the special care of Denville Hall. The annual outlay
on regular weekly allowances to clients has risen sharply from £4000
a year in 1949 to £63,602 by 1982.[85] In 1977 Equity decided to take
responsibility for running the Evelyn Norris Home in Worthing,
which had been operating for the previous seven years as a retirement home for Equity members.

Pastoral care in the profession was also exercised by the two
religious organizations, the Actors' Church Union and the Catholic
Stage Guild. To a marginal degree they were contiguous in function
with the secular charitable agencies, and post-war changes had more
dramatic effects on them than on the charities. The Actors' Church
Union had enjoyed a fairly stable existence in the interwar years,
with about 1000 members and 600–700 chaplains. Some change was
already becoming evident in the 1930s as the advent of the cinema,
displacing live theatre, obviated the need for chaplains to minister to
actors in the provinces.

Yet it was during the 1950s that very drastic change was experienced by the Union in response to wider changes in the theatre
nationally. The *raison d'être* of the ACU had been its service to the
touring actor in the provinces. As late as 1954 it noted that 'the
strength of the Union is in the Provinces rather than in London'.[86]
The impact of television, in closing down many provincial theatres
and leading to a decline of touring, had a profound effect on it.
Firstly, there was a sharp drop in provincial activity, with a decline
from the 700 chaplains of the 1930s down to 200 by 1959 and a
slimming of membership down to a now stable 400–500. Secondly,
while activity diminished in the provinces, actors became more
focused on London.

Actors though better off financially now spend increasing amounts
of time resting and it has become more economical to remain for

long periods unemployed and waiting for television contracts than to work full time on the road or in repertory. Not only is the demand for provincial live theatre diminishing daily, but the economics of employment encourage this situation.[87]

Accordingly the ACU refocused its activities on London, with a detailed chaplaincy network providing each West End theatre with an Anglican chaplain. Thirdly, this in turn had an effect. It might be thought that the lower level of post-war activity of the ACU merely reflects the decline of religious faith and observance in society at large. To some extent this is so, but in the early 1960s there was an influx of actors into the ACU. Very many of the best-known names in the West End and television became members,[88] a trend running counter to the secularism and permissiveness of the 'swinging sixties'. Finally, in recognition of this new *rapprochement* with the London theatre, the headquarters of the ACU was moved in 1970 to St Paul's Church, Covent Garden, 'the Actors' Church', a step away from the theatres and show-business premises of the Strand, the Aldwych and the environs of Leicester Square.[89]

Round the corner from the ACU its counterpart, the Catholic Stage Guild, is housed in Corpus Christi Church in Maiden Lane. Since its founding just before the First World War, the Guild too had enjoyed a stable existence in the interwar years. In 1927 it opened the Interval Club in Old Compton Street run by Mary and Molly Hewitt and greatly appreciated by young and struggling actors. As well as these secular services the Guild continued its spiritual work for actors, holding Masses and retreats and encouraging actors on tour to attend local churches. It occasionally put on Catholic plays and called for a better moral tone in the commercial theatre at large.[90] In 1937 there were 466 members, of whom I would reckon twenty-five as well-known names on the legitimate stage.[91] Faced with the impossibility of keeping running during the War, the Guild temporarily ceased in 1942.

The modern Guild was revived in the 1950s. The immediate circumstance was the centenary celebration of the restoration of the Catholic hierarchy in England in 1850. A vast pageant was held at Wembley in 1950, narrated by Robert Speaight and produced by Alan Rye. Cardinal Griffin, on learning that there was no longer an actors' Guild to take part in the theatrical representations of the pageant, asked Rye to revive it.[92] This he did, and at a meeting in the Charing Cross Hotel on 10 June 1951 the Guild was reconstituted with Ted Kavanagh (the writer of ITMA) as chairman, Rye as secretary, and the distinguished actors Marie Ney and Robert Speaight on the committee.[93] The new Guild started with 300 members and by 1953 had over 500, and 110 chaplains.[94] It was able to establish a theatrical presence, with some notable productions of a play of *The Dream of Gerontius* at the Scala for the Festival of Britain in 1951 and *Fotheringay* at the Embassy in 1953. Otherwise it continued its normal activities of visiting theatres, holding Masses, publishing a lodgings list and organizing social events. By 1958 it had 464 members, of whom 182 were dramatic stage actors (as opposed to being in variety, ballet and other forms of entertainment), and of these, twenty-six may be regarded as well-known.[95]

The 1960s were a lively period for the Guild, and several factors lay behind this.[96] For most of the decade up to 1969 the Guild was under the dynamic chairmanship of Eamonn Andrews, whose energy and wide range of contacts benefited the organization. An ambitious programme of social events, charitable balls and supper dances brought the Guild to an unusual prominence in the theatrical scene. Secondly, there was an expansion of the chaplains' activities. The Manchester branch began in 1957 and has run since under Joe Gladwin.[97] By the mid-1960s there were twelve chaplains in major provincial towns and six who divided the London theatre between them. Their work was greatly helped in 1967 by Cardinal Heenan's removal of the ban on priests visiting the theatre. It had hitherto been a curious disadvantage, not shared by Anglican clergymen, that Catholic priests had to contact actors in bars and backstage but could not actually see the plays. The provincial chaplains, however, met certain difficulties in the modern context of theatrical work compared with conditions in the 1930s. One of them, who had experience of both periods, perceptively compared the two:

> In the 1930s there were still several theatres in every large city, at least one in each town. The Guild had to provide cards, get in touch with priests who were willing to call at the theatre or at least be available to touring actors who could not easily get to the

church. The majority of professional actors for the greater part of the year were a race apart, they belonged to no settled community. But now my friends in Sheffield go to the most convenient church if they go at all. They don't lead a separate life. They move on as individuals, look also for jobs in radio and television from their own homes.

Also, as regards television, 'I just don't see how we can walk round studios meeting people any more than we can call into factories.'[98] The decline of touring, the actor living as a relatively fixed resident in the town of his playhouse, and the rise of the television studio made the role of the chaplain, whether of the ACU or CSG, both more difficult and less relevant.

In recent years the Guild has moved in certain directions in response to changes in the wider religious and theatrical worlds. Eamonn Andrews had suggested a link-up with the Actors' Church Union in 1971,[99] and in practice there has been increasing co-operation, with joint retreats and services. It is fitting that the present chairman of the Guild, Mr Michael Williams, is supported by his wife Miss Judi Dench, who is a committee member of the Actors' Church Union. Secondly the Guild, like the Union, has been increasingly concerned about the pornographic element in the theatre in the 1970s.[100] The fact that actors are no longer a race apart needing special separate religious ministrations, the changed relation of the provinces and the general decline of formal religious observance has changed the position of both ACU and CSG compared with the period of their Victorian and Edwardian origins. But they both thrive as witnesses to a Christian belief that is more widespread among the 'vagabond' profession than the public may suppose.

V

Public recognition of actors since the War has taken various forms. In 1964, to mark the 400th anniversary of Shakespeare's birthday, a garden party was held by the Queen at Buckingham Palace for 400 actors and others from all walks of the theatre. The universities have been generous in the award of honorary degrees to actors, notably Oxford, which has awarded the D. Litt to Olivier, Gielgud,

319

Richardson, Guinness, Edith Evans, Flora Robson, Peggy Ashcroft, and Lewis Casson and Sybil Thorndike. In addition Paul Scofield, Richard Attenborough, Michael Redgrave and Albert Finney hold honorary degrees from other universities.

But the most important symbol of the public status of the actor has been the award of knighthoods and various degrees of the Order of the British Empire.[101]

	Knights	Dames	CBE		OBE		MBE	
			Actors	Actresses	Actors	Actresses	Actors	Actresses
1945–1949	3	1	1	0	1	0	0	1
1950–1959	5	1	12	8	2	0	0	0
1960–1969	5	4	5	2	1	3	0	1
1970–1979	3	2	9	8	6	5	0	1
1980–1983	1	1	2	2	4	1	2	1

This does not include honours to significant figures like Dame Judith Anderson, Donovan Maule and others whose theatrical work has been chiefly in the Commonwealth rather than in England. Perhaps the most significant of all has been the award of a life peerage to Laurence Olivier in 1970, the first to an actor and as significant a landmark as Irving's knighthood. Olivier is thought to have felt some of Irving's reservations about the assumption of an unprecedented honour – that it would distance him from the audience, or that some untitled distinction might be more appropriate.[102] On the other hand it has been said that 'he is very aware of his place in English hierarchy . . . He likes being a member of the English Establishment and he thinks he should be.'[103] Sir Harold Hobson deplored in the early 1970s that 'yet there is a general . . . reluctance to admit that he is actually a peer of the realm',[104] perhaps partly fostered by Olivier's reported preference for 'Sir Laurence'. This 'reluctance' must largely have dissipated over the decade as lord musicians, journalists and historians have taken their

320

seats in the House. Perhaps the rarest honour accorded Olivier was the naming of a major British Railways locomotive after him in 1980, a distinction he shares with Harold Macmillan. In 1981 he was awarded the Order of Merit.

Other high honours have followed to other actors. Sir Bernard Miles was also made a life peer in 1979. Sybil Thorndike was the first actress to be made a Companion of Honour in 1970, to be joined by John Gielgud in 1977. In the 1970s, in fact, there seems to have been a tendency to use the scale of honours more widely for actors, with the introduction of peerages and the CH at the top end, but also far more OBEs than used formerly to be the case. In these ways the profession is firmly fixed as a part of the national life, to be valued and honoured. After Olivier's peerage nothing symbolized this more in the post-war years than the opening of the National Theatre building at the Old Vic in 1963 and on the South Bank in 1976 with its main auditorium named after Lord Olivier – all this after some three-quarters of a century of advocacy and planning.

The actor has become an important figure in the life of the country. At the economic level this is obviously so. In 1980, for example, over twelve million people came into Britain as tourists and spent £315 million on entertainment.[105] Britain gains four times as much from taxes on the theatre as the government provides in subsidies.[106] In 1968 58 per cent of all organized parties of tourists from America went to the theatre.[107] The actor draws income into the country not only through tourism but also through exports, some £40 million worth of television shows being exported from Britain in 1979.

Important as this is, the claims of the actor rest on loftier ground. Drama has been the special genius of the English, as has music of the Germans and painting of the Italians. We have the finest theatre in the world and, in this century, the best actors. Drama and theatre are a sphere of human endeavour in which Britain performs especially well. The leading British actors of our own time have accordingly placed a high value on their art, as did Irving. For Olivier, 'an actor must be a great understander . . . that puts him on the level with a doctor, priest or a philosopher.'[108] The actor is 'the illuminator of the human heart'[109] and the theatre 'the first glamor-izer of thought'. Similarly, Sybil Thorndike has reflected that the

321

chief satisfaction of her career had been to help people 'feel that they are working towards some better existence . . . [and to] understand more about human beings.'[110] Amid the tawdry tat, trivial sensationalism and strident commercialism that has always trailed around show business from the fairground booth to the television advertisement, this solid purpose and ideal remains. It is as ineradicable as the story-telling and make-believe urge itself, and the actors who embody it are an esteemed part of the nation's cultural life and heritage.

NOTES

1 See Appendix 1.
2 *Going on the Stage, a Report to the Calouste Gulbenkian Foundation on Professional Training for Drama*, 1975, p.14.
3 *Ibid*.
4 Equity Annual Report, 1977–8.
5 Sir Tyrone Guthrie, Llewellyn Rees, Hugh Hunt, Michael Benthall, Glen Byam Shaw, George Devine.
6 G. P. Bancroft, Sir Kenneth Barnes, John Fernald, Hugh Cruttwell.
7 Sir Peter Hall, John Barton, Trevor Nunn, David Brierley (the General Administrator), Ian McKellen.
8 *RADA Prospectuses*, 1945–7.
9 Ronald Harwood, *Sir Donald Wolfit* (London, 1971), p.xii.
10 Denys Blakelock, *Round the Next Corner* (London, 1967), p.124.
11 *Ibid*.
12 Hugh Whitemore in *My Drama School*, ed. M. McCall (London, 1978), p.181.
13 *Theatre World*, March 1964 and *RADA Prospectus*, 1966.
14 *RADA Prospectus*, 1963.
15 *Equity Report*, 1945–6.
16 *RADA Prospectus*, 1950, 1956.
17 'Class of '66', *Sunday Times*, 4 September 1966.
18 Blakelock, *op.cit.*, pp.137, 140.
19 *RADA Prospectus*, 1960.
20 Gwynneth Thurburn, 'My Life with Many Voices', *Woman and Home*, April 1959.
21 Irving Wardle, *The Theatres of George Devine* (London, 1978),

pp.105–18, 131–8. Lee Montague, 'The Old Vic Theatre School', in *My Drama School*, ed. M. McCall.

22 *The Stage Year Book*, 1950.

23 Irving Wardle, *op.cit.*, p.200.

24 *Going on the Stage, A Report to the Calouste Gulbenkian Foundation* 1975, pp.26–7.

25 *Gulbenkian Report*. Appendices D2, D3.

26 Simon Masters, *The National Youth Theatre* (London, 1969).

27 Papers of Gwynneth Thurburn, Letters and memorandum from Michael Croft to Miss Thurburn, 1964–5.

28 Ralph Loveless, 'Drama and the Schools', *The Stage*, 23 April 1953.

29 The number of 18-year-olds in the population rose from 533,000 in 1959 to 812,000 in 1965.

30 Bristol Old Vic Archives. Letters from applicants, 1951.

31 Calculated from playbills for 1961 in *Who's Who in the Theatre*, 1967. Shakespearian productions are excluded from my calculation, since these would artificially tilt the ratio even further to the advantage of male actors.

32 Minutes of University of London Diploma in Dramatic Art, 23 May 1939.

33 Minute, 10 March 1948.

34 Report on RADA, 12 May 1953, by Lewis Casson.

35 Memorandum by John Fernald, 22 September 1959.

36 Sir Lewis Casson, 'A Note on the Diploma in Dramatic Art', 5 May 1960.

37 Report on the Central School, 21 February 1969, and Minutes, 23 October 1969.

38 W. P. Eaton, 'The Yale School of Drama', *RADA Magazine*, March 1947. Sawyer Falk, 'Drama Departments in American Universities', in *The Universities and the Theatre*, ed. D. G. James (London, 1951).

39 Glynne Wickham, *The Relation between Universities and Films, Radio and Television* (London, 1956), p.44.

40 Reports of Bristol University Drama Department 1946/7–1975/6. Glynne Wickham, 'The Study of Drama in the British Universities 1945–1966', *Theatre Notebook*, Autumn 1966.

41 Michael Richards, 'UK University Drama', *Theatre Quarterly*, No. 15, August–October 1974. Glynne Wickham, 'A Revolution in Attitudes to the Dramatic Arts in British Universities 1880–1980', *Oxford Review of Education* Vol. 3, No. 2, 1977.
42 'An Actor's Career', *The Observer*, 9 January 1966.
43 *Going on the Stage, op.cit.*, pp.14, 21. The Gulbenkian Report found from four university drama departments that only 10, 15, 20, 30 per cent of their graduates went into the theatre.
44 Equity Annual Report, 1952–3. *The Stage*, 17 July 1952. Equity Annual Report, 1953–4. Employment Survey April–Sept. 1953. Equity Annual Report, 1954–5. Employment Survey Oct. 1953–April 1954.
45 *The Observer*, 9 Jan. 1966, 'The Actor's Career'.
46 'There's No Business', 'Aquarius', LWTV, 9 Dec. 1973.
47 'In Britain Now' BBC Radio 4 22 March 1978 and Peter Barkworth, BBC Radio 4, 12 Aug. 1980, both cite this.
48 Equity Survey of Employment and Earnings for 1971.
49 Laurence Olivier, *Confessions of an Actor* (London, 1982), p.40.
50 Employment Survey in Equity Annual Report, 1953–4.
51 Richard Findlater, *The Future of the Theatre* (Fabian Tract 317, London, 1959), p.11.
52 Derek R. Layder, *Occupational Careers in Britain with Special Reference to the Acting Profession* (University of London PhD, 1976) p.208 based on the Equity 1971 Survey of Employment and Earnings.
53 'Class of '66', *Sunday Times*, 4 Sept. 1966.
54 'Panorama', BBC 1, 2 Dec. 1974.
55 Equity Annual Report, 1953–4.
56 *Sunday Telegraph*, 7 Jan. 1972 and TV *Times*, 4 March 1978, are illuminating on this.
57 'There's No Business', *op.cit.*, 'Who Zat Kid?', *Thames TV*, 26 Sept. 1978.
58 *Evening Standard*, 22 Nov. 1973.
59 Calculated from Equity's Annual Reports.
60 Ronald Hasting, 'A Career on the Stage', *English Digest*, October 1960. This was the view of Hugh Jenkins, then Asst. Gen. Sec. of Equity.
61 'Twenty Years On', BBC 2, 4 Feb. 1979.

62 Equity Annual Report, 1945–5.
63 Equity Annual Report, 1968–9.
64 *Ibid.*
65 Michael Croft in *The Stage*, 12 Nov. 1982.
66 *The Stage*, 5 June 1980. Peter Dunlop. Mr Dunlop has been a leading agent for 30 years, founder of Fraser and Dunlop and chairman of the Personal Managers Association, which comprises 50–60 of the chief theatrical agents.
67 *The Stage* 7 April 1949. The Committee included Clifford Mollison, Henry Oscar and Richard Attenborough.
68 *The Stage*, 2 April 1949.
69 J. C. Trewin, *John Neville* (London, 1961), p.109.
70 The Newscuttings Books at the Central School, 1961–2, record such events.
71 *Woman*, 6 October 1962.
72 Nicholas Tomalin and John Elsom, *The History of the National Theatre* (London, 1978), pp.149–50, 152.
73 Bernard Crick, 'The Political in Britain's two national theatres', in *Drama and Society*, ed. James Redmond (Cambridge, 1979).
74 For example, Margaret Webster, *Daily Telegraph*, 17 March 1972. Miss Webster was of course Dame May Whitty's daughter and active in the union from its origins.
75 Ian Jack, 'Loud Alarums', *Sunday Times*, 9 June 1974.
76 Robert Chesshyre in *The Observer*, 9 Nov. 1975.
77 *Ibid.*
78 Bernard Levin in *The Times*, 24 May 1978.
79 Mario Gallati, *Mario of the Caprice* (London, 1960), pp.119, 132–3.
80 Cole Lesley, *The Life of Noel Coward* (London, 1976), p.351.
81 *The Stage*, 30 May 1946.
82 *The Stage*, 4 Sept. 1952.
83 *The Stage*, 22 May 1947.
84 I am grateful to Mrs K. Kirby, the Matron, for being able to visit the Hall and talk to her in September 1978.
85 *The Stage Year Book*, 1949–69, contains ABF accounts. I am also grateful to Miss A. G. Marks and Mrs Rosemary Stevens of the ABF for data on their finances.
86 ACU Annual Report, 1954.

87 ACU Annual Report, 1959.

88 It would be invidious to disclose names in this private matter, but of 94 new members in 1960, 15 are very well-known, 10 of the 49 new members of 1961, 6 of 48 of 1962 and 4 of the 39 of 1963. Of the 35 'very well-known' new members 1960–4, 7 hold decorations at various levels of the Order of the British Empire.

89 I am grateful to Miss Phyllis Brown and Rev. Michael Hurst-Bannister of the Actors' Church Union for discussion of its activities.

90 Eric Bridson, MS Reminiscences of the Catholic Stage Guild. Also *The Stage* for the period.

91 Catholic Stage Guild Yearbook, 1937.

92 Alan Rye, MS Reminiscences of the Catholic Stage Guild. Also letter from Mrs Gwendoline Rye to the author, 3 September 1979.

93 *The Stage*, 14 June 1951.

94 *The Stage*, 21 May 1953.

95 List in *The Catholic Stage Guild*, 1958.

96 Catholic Stage Guild MS Minutes, 1963–78. The Minutes prior to 1963 are unfortunately lost.

97 Mr Gladwin is a Northern actor well-known for many character parts on television. He was made a Papal Knight of St Gregory for his CSG activities. Mr Andrews had received the same honour in 1964.

98 CSG File on Provincial Chaplains. Letters from Fr E. Quinn of Sheffield, n.d. and 15 May 1975.

99 CSG Minutes, 2, 15 February 1971.

100 Minutes, 26 May, 15 Sept., 23 Nov., 1976.

101 Calculated from *Who's Who in the Theatre, Stage Year Book, Who's Who in Television, The Times*.

102 Laurence Olivier interviewed by Dick Cavett, BBC 1, 17 February 1974 (a recording made in 1973).

103 John Osborne in Logan Gourlay (ed.), *Olivier* (London, 1973).

104 Harold Hobson reviewing *Long Day's Journey into Night*, *Sunday Times*, 2 January 1972.

105 *British Tourist Authority Annual Report*, 1981.

106 Feargus Montgomery MP speaking in the Commons; *The*

Stage, 4 March 1982. Mr Montgomery is Parliamentary Consultant to the Society of West End Theatres.

107 *The Theatre Today*, Report by the Arts Council Theatre Enquiry 1970, p.21.

108 Irving Wardle, *The Theatres of George Devine* (London, 1978), p.105. citing Olivier's address at the Old Vic School, 24 January 1947.

109 Olivier in *Great Acting*, ed. Hal Burton (London, 1967), p.23.

110 Sybil Thorndike in *Great Acting*, *op.cit.*, p.61.

Appendices

Appendix 1 – The Social Origins of the Acting Profession in England 1880–1980

	Landed or Titled Status		Professions		Commercial/ Industrial		Artistic and Literary Occupations		Theatrical Occupations		Clerical/ Lower Sales men		Artisan/ Manual		Working-Class Shops	
	M	W	M	W	M	W	M	W	M	W	M	W	M	W	M	W
Starting pre-1880, acting post-1890 M 64 W 34	1 (1.5%)	1 (2.9%)	21 (32.3%)	2 (5.8%)	12 (18.5%)	2 (5.8%)	5 (7.7%)	4 (11.8%)	24 (36.9%)	24 (70.6%)	1 (1.5%)	0	1 (1.5%)	1 (2.9%)		
Starting 1880–9, acting post 1890 M 155 W 94	5 (32.%)	1 (1.1%)	69 (44.5%)	32 (34%)	22 (14.2%)	10 (10.6%)	9 (5.8%)	15 (16%)	45 (29%)	35 (37.2%)	3 (1.9%)	0	2 (1.3%)	1 (1.1%)		
Starting 1890–1913 M 189 W113	10 (5.3%)	0	111 (58.7%)	52 (46.0%)	21 (11.1%)	8 (7.1%)	8 (4.2%)	10 (8.8%)	35 (18.3%)	40 (35.4%)	1 (0.5%)	2 (1.8%)	3 (1.6%)	1 (0.9%)		
Starting 1914–45 M 148 W 97	5 (3.4%)	7 (7.2%)	70 (47.2%)	50 (51.5%)	28 (18.9%)	11 (11.3%)	4 (2.7%)	6 (6.2%)	31 (20.9%)	23 (23.7%)	7 (4.7%)	0	3 (2.0%)	0		
Starting post-1945 M 114 W 105	3 (2.6%)	3 (2.8%)	31 (27.2%)	33 (31.4%)	14 (12.3%)	22 (20.9%)	5 (4.4%)	10 (9.5%)	25 (21.9%)	24 (22.8%)	2 (1.7%)	2 (1.9%)	28 (24.6%)	9 (8.6%)	6 (5.3%)	2 (1.9%)

Appendix 2 – Actors' Wages in the Productions of Sir Herbert Tree, 1903–1914

Production	Date	(a) Pennies per actor per performance	(b) Annual average	(c) 5-point moving average	(d) Converted to index 1905=100	(e) National occupational Wages Index	(f) National Price Index
Richard II	Oct 1903	431	431				
Oliver Twist	Sept 1905	448	448	552*	100	100	100
Nero	Feb 1906	735	735	536	101.8	101.9	107.9
Antony and Cleopatra	March 1907	561	561	604	114.8	107.5	112.5
Edwin Drood	Jan 1908	554	500	615	116.9	105.3	100.9
Faust	Sept 1908	447					
School for Scandal	April 1909	887	777	628	119.3	105.3	105.6
False Gods	Sept 1909	668					
Beethoven	Jan 1910	378					
The O'Flynn	Feb 1910	440	505	639	121.4	105.3	112.5
Henry VIII	Sept 1910	699					
Macbeth	Nov 1911	799	799	644	122.4	106.4	118.32
Trilby	Feb 1912	566					
Othello	April 1912	751	616	635	120.7	109.8	120.64
Oliver Twist	June 1912	523					
Drake	Sept 1912	627					
School for Scandal	May 1913	644	526				
Joseph and his Brethren	Dec 1913	409					
Darling of the Gods	Jan 1914	584	732				
Pygmalion	April 1914	881					

* 1904 calculated as an average of 1903 and 1905

Notes on Appendix 1
The data on the Social Origins of actors 1880–1980 is based on a sample of 1133 players (670 actors and 443 actresses). There is no one source where this information may be found. Accordingly I have called evidence of the occupations of fathers of sample from obituaries, interviews, the theatrical press, memoirs etc. over several years research.

Notes on Appendix 2
From the Account Books of Sir Herbert Tree it is possible to calculate the payments made in actors' wages. These can be expressed in terms of old pennies (240 pence per £) per actor per performance for each of 20 productions between 1903 and 1914 (a). An annual average can then be calculated for each year (b). To even out the incidence of expensive and less expensive productions these annual averages are converted to a 5-point moving average (c). For example, the moving average for 1910 is the average of the five years 1908–12 inclusive. These can then be converted to an index of wages costs with a base of 1905=100 (d). This index can then be compared with the national wages index of A. L. Bowley (e), similarly adjusted to a base of 1905=100. The wages of Tree's actors considerably outstripped those of other occupations in the country at large. Both (d) and (e) can then be compared with the National Price Index by P. Rousseaux (f). National wages did not keep pace with price inflation. Those of Tree's actors did.

The Bowley and Rousseaux indices may be found in B. R. Mitchell, British Historical Statistics (Cambridge, 1962), pp.60, 344. For the purposes of this Appendix both have been converted to a base of 1905=100.

Appendix 3 – Actors' Earnings in Stage and Film Work 1916–1939

SILENT ERA

	Date	Stage Earning per week	Film Earning per week	Earning per picture
Noel Coward[1]	1916	£4	£5	
Owen Nares[2]	c. 1918	£10	£250*	
Ivor Novello[3]	1921	£60	£100–200	
	1923		£350	
	1927		£500–600	
	1928			£3000
Matheson Lang[4]	1920s			£4–5000*

SOUND ERA

	Date	Stage Earning per week	Film Earning per week	Earning per picture
Gracie Fields[5]	1930s			£40,000
Jack Hawkins[6]	c. 1932	£30	£40	
Anna Neagle[7]	1932		£50	£200
	1933			£300
	1933			£300
Emlyn Williams[8]	1933	£20 (1930)	£100–200	
Laurence Olivier[9]	1934–5	£100 (1934)	£600 (1935)	
Margaret Lockwood[10]	1930s	£12	£50	
			£75	
	1937		£77	
	1938		£115	
Rex Harrison[11]	1936		£48	
Bruce Belfrage[12]	1930s	£10–12	£75	
Michael Redgrave[13]	1939		£150	
Robert Donat[14]	1938			£25,000
Vivien Leigh[15]	1935		£26 small-part	
Deborah Kerr[16]	1939		£26 players	

* offered, not accepted

334

1 Noel Coward, *Present Indicative* (London, 1937), pp. 60, 71.
2 Owen Nares, *Myself and Some Others* (London, 1925), pp. 195–7.
3 W. MacQueen Pope, *Ivor* (London, 1951), pp. 165, 179, 217.
4 Matheson Lang, *Mr Wu Looks Back* (London, 1941), pp. 147, 154–7.
5 Basil Dean, *Mind's Eye* (London 1973), p. 209.
6 Jack Hawkins, *Anything for a Quiet Life* (London, 1973), pp. 30, 49.
7 Anna Neagle, *There's Always Tomorrow* (London, 1974), p. 76.
8 Emlyn Williams, *Emlyn* (London, 1973), p. 292.
9 Felix Barker, *The Oliviers* (London, 1953), pp. 63, 71.
10 Margaret Lockwood, *Lucky Star* (London, 1955), pp. 41, 54.
11 Rex Harrison, *Rex* (London, 1974) p. 48.
12 Bruce Belfrage, *One Man in His Time* (London, 1951), p. 76.
13 Richard Findlater, *Michael Redgrave* (London, 1956), p. 43.
14 J. C. Trewin, *Robert Donat* (London, 1968), p. 98.
15 Anne Edwards, *Vivien Leigh* (London, 1977), p. 42.
16 Eric Braun, *Deborah Kerr* (London, 1977), p. 43.

Select Bibliography

UNPUBLISHED PAPERS

Bristol University
a) Papers of Sir Herbert Beerbohm Tree
   Ledger HMT 1903–4; Treasury Payments by cheque 1905–11, 1912–14; Treasury Book No. 2 1909–1914; Analysis of Treasury Payments 1904–15.
b) Bristol Old Vic archives. Letters from applicants.

British Theatre Museum
Papers of Sir George Alexander, Robert Lawson, Olga Lindo, Cecil Madden. Pigott Collection.

Catholic Stage Guild
MS Reminiscences of the CSG by Molly Veness, Joyce Carpenter, Alan Rye, Eric Bridson.
Minutes of the CSG 1963–70.
Files of provincial chaplains.

Central School of Speech and Drama
Papers of Principal Gwynneth Thurburn, OBE.

Equity
Minute Books of Annual General Meetings 1930–39.
Minutes of the Executive Council 1931–39.
Correspondence and negotiations between managers and Equity 1935–43.
Proceedings of the Equity Arbitration Committee 1933–9.

Organization Committee's figures on weekly employment in London theatres 1935–8.
Minutes of the London Theatre Council 1935–9.

Garrick Club
Minutes 1890–1940.
Applications for admission 1890–1940.
Percy Fitzgerald Collection.

London University
Minutes, memoranda, etc. of the University of London Diploma in Dramatic Art 1922–70.

Public Record Office
Ministry of Labour Files.
Lab 6/170 Lord Lytton's Committee.
Lab 6/175 Determent of Actors.
Lab 10/19 and 20 London Theatre Council.

Royal Academy of Dramatic Art
Letterbooks of the Administrator (G. P. Bancroft, Sir Kenneth Barnes) 3 volumes, 1908–14.
Administrator's Diaries 1915–1939.

Typescripts
Brian Crozier, 'The Theatre Audience 1880–1900'.
Derek R. Layder, 'Occupational Careers in Britain with reference to the Acting Profession' (University of London, PhD, 1976).

ORAL EVIDENCE

I *Personal interviews*
   Miss Phyllis Brown (the Actors' Church Union), 13 September 1977.
   Miss Fabia Drake, 20 August 1976.
   Miss Edna Farrand (Actors' Association and ACU), 1 November 1977.

Miss Kathleen Harrison, 7 August 1978.

Mrs Kay Kirby (Matron of Denville Hall), 6 September 1978.

Mr Esmond Knight, 23 August 1978.

Mr and Mrs John Laurie, 1 August 1977.

Miss Marie Ney, 2 and 6 June 1978.

Miss Athene Seyler CBE, 23 August 1976.

Miss Nora Swinburne, 23 August 1978.

Miss Gwynneth Thurburn OBE (Principal of the Central School), 3 September 1976.

Mr Austin Trevor, 13 September 1976.

Mr Timothy West CBE, 6 November 1975.

II *Radio and television interviews, memoirs, etc.*

'There's No Business', LWTV, 9 December 1973.

'An Actor's Life for Me', BBC 2, 16 December 1973.

Laurence Olivier interviewed by Dick Cavett, BBC 2, 17 February 1974.

'Curtains for the Arts?', *Panorama*, BBC 1, 2 December 1974.

Richard Bebb, 'The Voice of Henry Irving', BBC Radio 3, 23 October 1975.

Bryan Forbes, 'That Most Despicable Race,' BBC Radio 4, 13 November–9 December 1977.

'Bioscope Days', BBC 2, 10, 18, 25 May 1978.

'Who Zat Kid?', Thames TV, 26 September 1978.

Sir John Gielgud, 'An Actor in his Time', BBC Radio 4, 18 October – 22 November 1978.

'Twenty Years On', BBC 2, 4 February 1979.

Keith Darvill, 'Unity Theatre 1937–1975', BBC Radio 3, 28 May 1979.

'Ma, a Celebration of the Theatrical Landlady', BBC Radio 4, 16 September 1979.

Roy Plomley, theatrical interviews in 'Desert Island Discs', *passim*.

III *Historical tapes*

Sir Johnston Forbes Robertson, Matheson Lang, Cyril Maude, in Cecil Madden Collection, British Theatre Museum 1964/A/74.

REPORTS, HANDBOOKS, ETC., OF ORGANIZATIONS

I *Parliamentary*
1892 XVIII Report of the Select Committee on Theatres and Places of Entertainment.
1909 VIII Report of the Joint Select Committee on Stage Plays (Censorship).
1919 XXX Cmd 484. Report of the Committee . . . Licences to Children to take part in Entertainments.
The Teaching of English in England, Report of the Departmental Committee appointed by the Board of Education, 1921.

II *Private bodies*
Reports of the Proceedings of the Dinners of the Actors' Benevolent Fund, 1891–1902, 1906, 1909.
Actors' Church Union Annual Reports, 1899–1970.
Actors' Church Union Report on the Education Problem, July 1913.
Actresses' Franchise League Report, 1912–13.
Arts Council, The Theatre Today, 1970.
British Actors' Equity Association Annual Reports, 1931–80.
Catholic Stage Guild Yearbooks, 1937, 1938.
CEMA Bulletins, 1940–5.
Garrick Club, Lists of Members 1880, 1890, 1900, 1910, 1920, 1930, 1940, 1950.
Going on the Stage, a Report to the Calouste Gulbenkian Foundation on Professional Training for Drama, London, 1975.
Left Theatre handbook, 1936.
London Theatre Council Annual Reports, 1936–39.
Royal Academy of Dramatic Art Prospectuses and Reports, 1905–70.
Proceedings of the International Conference on Speech Training, 1927.
Unity Theatre handbook, 1939.

339

SELECT BIBLIOGRAPHY

NEWSPAPERS, PERIODICALS AND DIRECTORIES

British Equity (a monthly periodical published by Equity), 1934–6.
The Call Board (an Actors' Church Union publication), 1930–58.
Era.
The Genesian (a Catholic Stage Guild publication).
The Ministry of Labour Gazette.
Plays and Players.
Royal Academy of Dramatic Art Magazine, 1946–7.
The Stage.
The Stage Year Book.
Theatreland.
Theatre World.
The Thespian.
Viva Voce (a Central School of Speech and Drama publication).
The Green Room Book, 1907.
Who's Who in the Theatre 1912–77.
Who's Who on Television 1980.

Newscuttings Books (by subject)
Sydney Carroll (in British Theatre Museum).
Central School of Speech and Drama (at the CSSD).
Equity (at the Equity Offices, Harley Street).
Miss Marie Ney (in the British Theatre Museum).

BIOGRAPHY, AUTOBIOGRAPHY, MEMOIR

(Place of publication London unless otherwise stated)
Adam, Ronald, *Overture and Beginners* (1938).
Albanesi, E. M., *Meggie Albanesi* (1928).
Allen, D. R., *Sir Aubrey* (1982).
Aria, Mrs., *My Sentimental Self* (1922).
Arliss, George, *On the Stage, an Autobiography* (1928).
Asche, Oscar, *His Life* (1929).
Ashwell, Lena, *Myself a Player* (1936).
Aspel, Michael, *Polly Wants a Zebra* (1974).
Bancroft, G. P., *Stage and Bar* (1939).
Bancroft, Sir Squire and Marie, *The Bancrofts, Recollections of Sixty Years* (1909).

340

Bancroft, Sir Squire, *Empty Chairs* (1925).

Barker, Eric, *Steady Barker* (1956).

Barker, Felix, *The Oliviers* (1953).

Barnes, J. H., *Forty Years on the Stage* (1914).

Barnes, Sir Kenneth, *Welcome Good Friends* (1958).

Batters, Jean, *Edith Evans, a Personal Memoir* (1977).

Belfrage, Bruce, *One Man in His Time* (1951).

Benson, Constance, *Mainly Players* (1926).

Benson, Sir Frank, *My Memoirs* (1930).

Bettany, F.G., *Stewart Headlam* (1926).

Bingham, Madeleine, *Henry Irving and the Victorian Theatre* (1978).
   The Great Lover, the Life and Art of Herbert Beerbohm Tree (1978).

Blakelock, Denys, *Finding my Way* (1958).
   Round the Next Corner (1967).

Blow, Sydney, *The Ghost Walks on Fridays* (1935).

Bogarde, Dirk, *A Postillion Struck by Lightning* (1977).

Bolitho, Hector, *Marie Tempest* (1936).

Brambell, Wilfred, *All Above Board* (1976).

Braun, Eric, *Deborah Kerr* (1977).

Brent, J. F., *Memories of a Mistaken Life* (1897).

Brereton, Austin, *H. B. and Laurence Irving* (1922).

Brookfield, Charles, *Random Reminiscences* (1902).

Brough, James, *The Prince and the Lily* (1975).

Brough, Jean Webster, *Prompt Copy* (1952).

Bull, Peter, *I Know the Face But . . .* (1959).

Calvert, Mrs Charles, *Sixty Eight Years on the Stage* (1911).

Campbell, Mrs Patrick, *My Life and Some Letters* (1922).

Carmichael, Ian, *Will the Real Ian Carmichael . . .* (1979).

Casson, John, *Lewis and Sybil* (1972).

Chapman-Houston, Desmond, *The Lamp of Memory* (1949).

Child, Harold, *A Poor Player, the Story of a Failure* (Cambridge, 1939).

Clarence, O. B., *No Complaints* (1943).

Coffin, Hayden, *Hayden Coffin's Book* (1930).

Cole, Marion, *Fogie, the Life of Elsie Fogerty CBE* (1967).

Collier, Constance, *Harlequinade, the Story of My Life* (1929).

Colman, J. B., *Ronald Colman* (1975).

Compton, Fay, *Rosemary* (1926).

341

Cooper, Lady Diana, *The Light of Common Day* (1959).

Cooper, Dame Gladys, *Gladys Cooper* (1931).

Cotes, Peter, *George Robey* (1972).

Cottrell, John and Cashin, Feargus, *Richard Burton* (1971).

Cottrell, John, *Laurence Olivier* (1975).

Counsell, John, *Counsell's Opinion* (1963).

Courtneidge, Robert, *I Was an Actor Once* (1930).

Coward, Sir Noel, *Present Indicative* (1937).
   Future Indefinite (1954).

Craufurd, Russell, *The Ramblings of an Old Mummer* (1909).

Croxton, Arthur, *Crowded Days and Nights* (1934).

Dean, Basil, *Seven Ages, an Autobiography 1888–1927* (1970).
   Mind's Eye (1973).

Denham, Reginald, *Stars in My Hair* (1958).

Denison, Michael, *Overture and Beginners* (1973).

Derwent, Clarence, *The Derwent Story* (New York, 1953).

Devlin, Diana, *A Speaking Part, Lewis Casson in the Theatre of his Time* (1982).

Drake, Fabia, *Blind Fortune* (1978).

Drinkwater, John, *Inheritance* (1931).
   Discovery (1932).

Druxman, M. B., *Basil Rathbone, his Life and his Films* (1975).

du Maurier, Dame Daphne, *Gerald, a Portrait* (1934).

Dunbar, Janet, *Flora Robson* (1960).

Edwards, Anne, *Vivien Leigh* (1977).

d'Egville, Alan, *Adventures in Safety* (1937).

Fagan, Elizabeth ('A Stage Cat'), *From the Wings* (1922).

Fairbrother, Sydney, *Through an Old Stage Door* (1939).

Findlater, Richard, *Michael Redgrave, Actor* (1956).
   Lilian Baylis (1975).

Fleetwood, Frances, *Conquest* (1953).

Flynn, Errol, *My Wicked, Wicked Ways* (1960).

Forbes, Bryan, *Notes for a Life* (1974).
   Ned's Girl (1977).

Forbes Robertson, Sir Johnston, *A Player under Three Reigns* (1925).

Forsyth, James, *Tyrone Guthrie* (1976).

Fortescue, Winifred, *There's Rosemary . . . there's Rue* (1939).

French, Harold, *I Swore I Never Would* (1970).
  I Thought I Never Could (1973).
Fyfe, Hamilton, *Sir Arthur Pinero's Plays and Players* (1930).
Gallati, Mario, *Mario of the Caprice* (1960).
Gielgud, Sir John, *Early Stages* (1939).
  Stage Directions (1963).
  Distinguished Company (1972).
Gielgud, Kate Terry, *An Autobiography* (1953).
Gill, Maud, *See the Players* (1938).
Gourlay, Logan (ed.), *Olivier* (1973).
Graham, Joe, *An Old Stock Actor's Memories* (1930).
Green, R. L., *A. E. W. Mason* (1952).
Greenwall, Harry J., *The Strange Life of Willy Clarkson* (1936).
Hamilton, Cicely, *Life Errant* (1935).
Harcourt, F. C. Vernon, *From Stage to Cross* (1901).
Hardwicke, Sir Cedric, *Let's Pretend* (1932).
  A Victorian in Orbit (1961).
Hare, Robertson, *Indubitably Yours* (1956).
Harrison, Rex, *Rex* (1974).
Harwood, Ronald, *Sir Donald Wolfit* (1971).
Hawkins, Jack, *Anything for a Quiet Life* (1973).
Hawtrey, Sir Charles, *The Truth at Last* (1924).
Hayman, Ronald, *John Gielgud* (1971).
Henderson-Bland, R., *Actor, Soldier, Poet* (1939).
Henson, Leslie, *My Laugh Story* (1926).
Hepworth, Cecil, *Came the Dawn* (1951).
Hicks, Seymour, *Twenty-Four Years of an Actor's Life* (1910).
Higham, Charles, *Charles Laughton* (1976).
Hird, Thora, *Scene and Hird* (1976).
Hobson, Sir Harold, *Ralph Richardson* (1958).
  Indirect Journey (1978).
Howard, Leslie Ruth, *A Quite Remarkable Father* (1960).
Hutchison, Percy, *Masquerade* (1936).
Irving, Laurence, *Henry Irving* (1951).
  The Precarious Crust (1971).
Isaac, Winifred, *Alfred Wareing* (1951).
  Sir Philip Ben Greet and the Old Vic (1964).
Jacob, Naomi, *Me* (1933).

Jacobs, David, *Jacob's Ladder* (1963).

Kane, Whitford, *Are We All Met?* (1931).

Kendal, Dame Madge, *Dame Madge Kendal* (1933).

Kendall, Henry, *I Remember Romano's* (1960).

Keown, Eric, *Peggy Ashcroft* (1955).

Kerr, Fred, *Recollections of a Defective Memory* (1930).

Kingston, Gertrude, *Curtsey While You're Thinking* (1937).

Knight, Esmond, *Seeking the Bubble* (1943).

Kulik, Karol, *Alexander Korda* (1975).

Laceby, Arthur, *Stage Struggles of a Bad Actor* (Edinburgh, 1904).

Lanchester, Elsa, *Charles Laughton and I* (1938).

Lang, Matheson, *Mr Wu Looks Back* (1941).

le Gallienne, Eva, *At 33* (1934).

Lesley, Cole, *Life of Noel Coward* (1976).

Leverton, W. H., *Through the Box Office Window* (1932).

Lion, Leon M., *The Surprise of My Life* (1948).

Lockwood, Margaret, *Lucky Star* (1955).

Loraine, Winifred, *Robert Loraine, Soldier, Actor, Airman* (1938).

McCarthy, Lillah, *Myself and My Friends* (1933).

Mackenzie, Sir Compton, *My Life and Times, Octave 3, 1900–7* (1964).

Mackenzie, Faith Compton, *As Much as I Dare* (1938).

McCowen, Alec, *Young Gemini* (1979).

Malleson, Constance, *After Ten Years* (1931).

Maltby, H. F., *Ring up the Curtain* (1950).

Manvell, Roger, *Ellen Terry* (1968).

Martin Harvey, Sir John, *Autobiography* (1933).

Mason, A. E. W., *Sir George Alexander and the St James Theatre* (1935).

Massey, Raymond, *When I Was Young* (1977).
A Hundred Different Lives (1979).

Matthews, A. E., *Matty, an Autobiography* (1952).

Maude, Cyril, *Behind the Scenes* (1927).

Melford, Mark, *Life in a Booth* (1913).

Millward, Jessie, *Myself and Others* (1923).

Mitchell, Yvonne, *Actress* (1957).

Moore, Eva, *Exits and Entrances* (1923).

More, Kenneth, *Happy Go Lucky* (1959).

344

Morley, Robert and Stokes, Sewell, *Robert Morley, Responsible Gentleman* (1966).

Morley, Sheridan, *Gladys Cooper* (1979).

Murray, Pete, *One Day I'll Forget My Trousers* (1975).

Nares, Owen, *Myself and Some Others* (1925).

Neagle, Dame Anna, *There's Always Tomorrow* (1974).

Neilson, Julia, *This for Remembrance* (1940).

Nesbitt, Cathleen, *A Little Love and Good Company* (1975).

Newton, H. Chance, *Cues and Curtain Calls* (1927).

Nicholson, Norah, *Chameleon's Dish* (1973).

O'Connor, Garry, *Ralph Richardson* (1982).

Olivier, Laurence, *Confessions of an Actor* (1982).

Osborne, John, *A Better Class of Person* (1981).

Paxton, Sydney, *Stage See Saws* (1917).

Payne, Ben Iden, *Life in a Wooden O, Memoirs of the Theatre* (Yale, 1977).

Pearson, Hesketh, *Thinking It Over* (1938).
   Beerbohm Tree (1956).

Peile, F. K., *Candied Peel* (1931).

Pemberton, T. Edgar, *John Hare, Comedian* (1895).
   Sir Charles Wyndham (1904).

Pertwee, Michael, *Name Dropping* (1974).

Pertwee, Roland, *Master of None* (1940).

Philips, F. C., *My Varied Life* (1914).

Phoenix, Pat, *All My Burning Bridges* (1974).

Playfair, Sir Nigel, *Hammersmith Hoy* (1930).

Pope, W. MacQueen, *Ivor* (1951).

Purdom, C. B., *Harley Granville Barker* (1955).

Rix, Brian, *My Farce from my Elbow, an Autobiography* (1975).

Robins, Elizabeth, *Both Sides of the Curtain* (1940).

Robyns, Gwen, *Margaret Rutherford* (1972).

Rosslyn, Harry, *My Gamble with Life* (1928).

Rozant, Ina, *An Actress's Pilgrimage* (1906).

Salter, Elizabeth, *Helpmann* (1978).

Selby-Lowndes, Joan, *The Conti Story* (1954).

Semon, Sir Felix, *Autobiography* (1926).

Sherek, Henry, *Not in Front of the Children* (1959).

Smith, Dodie, *Look Back with Mixed Feelings* (1978).

345

Smythe, Arthur J., *The Life of William Terriss* (1898).

Speaight, Robert, *William Poel and the Elizabethan Revival* (1954). *The Property Basket* (1970).

Sprigge, Elizabeth, *Sybil Thorndike Casson* (1971).

Steen, Marguerite, *A Pride of Terrys* (1962).

Stokes, Sewell, *Without Veils* (1953).

Storey, Anthony, *Stanley Baker, Portrait of an Actor* (1977).

Sutro, Alfred, *Celebrities and Simple Souls* (1933).

Thesiger, Ernest, *Practically True* (1927).

Thorndike, Russell, *Sybil Thorndike* (1929).

Thorndike, Dame Sybil and Russell, *Lilian Baylis* (1938).

Trewin, J. C., *Edith Evans* (1954).
Sybil Thorndike (1955).
Paul Scofield (1956).
Alec Clunes (1958).
Benson and the Bensonians (1960).
John Neville (1961).
Robert Donat (1968).

Trewin, Wendy, *All on Stage, Charles Wyndham and the Albery's* (1980).

Tynan, Kenneth, *Alec Guinness* (1961).

Ustinov, Peter, *Dear Me* (1977).

Vanbrugh, Dame Irene, *To Tell My Story* (1948).

Vanbrugh, Violet, *Dare to be Wise* (1925).

Ward, Dame Genevieve and Whiting, Richard, *Both Sides of the Curtain* (1918).

Wardle, Irving, *The Theatres of George Devine* (1978).

Warner, Jack, *Jack of all Trades* (1977).

Warwick, Lou, *The Mackenzies called Compton* (Northampton, 1977).

Watson, Thomas A, *Exploring Life* (New York, 1926).

Webster, Margaret, *The Same Only Different* (1969).

Wilcox, Herbert, *Twenty Five Thousand Sunsets* (1967).

Williams, Bransby, *Bransby Williams* (1954).

Williams, Emlyn, *George, an early Autobiography* (1961). *Emlyn* (1973).

Wilson, E. A. Rathmell, *Pre-War* (Epsom, 1937).

Winn, Godfrey, *The Infirm Glory* (1967).

Wood, Alan, *Mr. Rank, a Study of J. Arthur Rank and British Films* (1952).
Young, Patricia Don, *Dramatic School* (1954).

OTHER BOOKS

Armstrong, C. F., *The Actor's Companion* (1912).
Arthur, Sir George, *From Phelps to Gielgud* (1936).
Ashwell, Lena, *Modern Troubadours* (1922).
    The Stage (1929).
Baker, Michael, *The Rise of the Victorian Actor* (1978).
Balcon, Michael, *Twenty Five Years of British Film 1925–1945* (1947).
Ball, R. H., *Shakespeare on Silent Film* (1968).
Barbor, H. R., *The Theatre an Art and an Industry* (1924).
Barker, Kathleen, *The Theatre Royal Bristol 1766–1966* (1974).
Barnes, John, *The Beginnings of the Cinema in England* (1976).
Beerbohm, Sir Max, *Around Theatres* (2 vols, 1924).
Benson, Sir Frank, *I Want to Go on the Stage* (1931).
Betts, Ernest, *The Film Business, a History of the British Cinema 1896–1972* (1973).
Billington, Michael, *The Modern Actor* (1973).
Bishop, G. W., *Barry Jackson and the London Theatre* (1933).
Boas, Guy, *The Garrick Club 1831–1947* (1948).
Borsa, Mario, *The English Stage of Today* (1906).
Bourne, John, *Actors by the Thousand* (1944).
Briggs, Asa, *The History of Broadcasting in the United Kingdom* (4 vols, Oxford, 1961, 1965, 1970, 1979).
Burnand, F. C., *Personal Reminiscences of the ADC Cambridge* (1880).
Burnham, Barbara, *Actors – Let's Talk Shop* (1945).
Burton, Hal (ed.), *Great Acting* (1967).
    Acting in the Sixties (1970).
Calvert, Louis, *Problems of the Actor* (1919).
Charques, R. D. (ed.), *Footnotes to the Theatre* (1938).
Dark, Sydney, *Stage Silhouettes* (1902).
Davy, Charles (ed.), *Footnotes to the Film* (1937).
Day, M. C. and Trewin, J. C., *The Shakespeare Memorial Theatre* (1932).

347

Dean, Basil, *The Theatre at War* (1956).

Donaldson, Frances, *The Actor Managers* (1970).

Dunbar, Malcolm, *Theatre Ownership in Britain* (1953).

Elder, Eleanor, *Travelling Players, the Story of the Arts League of Service* (1939).

Elliott, W. G. (ed.), *Amateur Clubs and Actors* (1898).

Elliott, William J., *How to become a Film Actor* (1917).

Elsom, John, *Theatre outside London* (1971).

Post-War British Theatre (1976).

Ervine, St John, *The Theatre* (1933).

Evans, A. J., *The Stage Golfing Society 1903–1953* (n.p., n.d.).

Findlater, Richard, *The Unholy Trade* (1952).

The Future of the Theatre (Fabian Tract 317, 1959).

At the Royal Court, 25 Years of the English Stage Company (1981).

Fitzgerald, Percy, *The Garrick Club* (1904).

Gielgud, Val, *British Radio Drama 1922–1956* (1957).

Glasstone, Victor, *Victorian and Edwardian Theatres* (Harvard, 1975).

Goddard, Arthur, *Players of the Period* (1891).

Godfrey, Philip, *Backstage* (1933).

Goldie, Grace Wyndham, *The Liverpool Repertory Theatre 1911–1934* (Liverpool, 1935).

Hammerton, J. A., *The Actor's Art* (1897).

Hardwicke, Sir Cedric, *The Drama Tomorrow*, The Rede Lecture (Cambridge, 1936).

Hayman, Ronald, *The Set-Up, an Anatomy of the English Theatre Today* (1973).

Hole, Donald, *The Church and the Stage, the Early History of the Actors' Church Union* (1934).

Holledge, Julie, *Innocent Flowers, Women in the Edwardian Theatre* (1982).

Hornblow, Arthur, *Training for the Stage* (Philadelphia, 1916).

Howard, Diana, *London Theatres and Music Halls 1850–1950* (1970).

Howe, P. P., *The Repertory Theatre, a Record and a Criticism* (1910).

Hunt, Hugh *et al*, *The Revels History of Drama in English, vol VII 1880 to the Present* (1978).

Irving, Sir Henry, *The Stage as it is* (1881).

The Art of Acting (1891).

Irving, H. B., 'The Calling of the Actor', 'The Art and Status of the Actor', in *Occasional Papers* (1906).

James, D. G. (ed.), *The Universities and the Theatre* (1952).

Keeling, Frederic, *Child Labour in the United Kingdom* (1914).

Kemp, T. C. and Trewin, J. C., *The Stratford Festival, a History of the Shakespeare Memorial Theatre* (Birmingham, 1953).

Leacroft, Richard, *The Development of the English Playhouse* (Cornell, 1973).

Low, Rachel, *The History of the British Film 1918–1929* (1952).

Luttrell, Grace, *Letters of an Actress* (novel; 1902).

McCall, Margaret (ed.), *My Drama School* (1978).

MacDermott, Norman, *Everymania, the History of the Everyman Theatre Hampstead 1920–6* (1975).

Mackinnon, Alan, *The Oxford Amateurs* (1910).

Macleod, Joseph, *The Actor's Right to Act* (1981).

Masters, Simon, *The National Youth Theatre* (1969).

Maule, Donovan, *The Stage as a Career* (1932).

Morley, Malcolm, *The Theatre* (1935).
    Margate and its Theatres (1966).

Morton, Cavendish, *The Art of Theatrical Make Up* (1909).

Motter, T. H. Vail, *School Drama in England* (1929).

Nathan, Archie, *Costumes by Nathan* (1960).

Nicoll, Allardyce, *A History of English Drama, vol.5 1850–1900* (Cambridge, 1959).
    English Drama 1900–1930 (Cambridge, 1973).

Parts I have Played (Westminster, 1909).

P.E.P., *The British Film Industry* (1952).

Perry, George, *The Great British Picture Show* (1975).

Pertwee, Roland, *An Actor's Life for Me* (novel; Oxford, 1953).

Playfair, Sir Nigel, *The Story of the Lyric Theatre Hammersmith* (1925).

Pogson, Rex, *Miss Horniman and the Gaiety Theatre Manchester* (1952).

Reid, Erskine and Compton, Herbert, *The Dramatic Peerage* (1891, 1892).

R.M.S. (ed.), *Letters of an Unsuccessful Actor* (1923).

Roberts, Peter, *The Old Vic Story* (1976).

Rowell, George, *The Victorian Theatre 1792–1914* (Cambridge, 1978).
    Queen Victoria goes to the Theatre (1978).

349

SELECT BIBLIOGRAPHY

The RADA Graduate Keepsake and Counsellor (privately printed, RADA, 1941).

Rozant, Ina, *Life's Understudies* (novel; 1907).

E.F.S., *Our Stage and its Critics* (1910).

Shubik, Irene, *Play for Today* (1975).

Sieveking, Lance, *The Stuff of Radio* (1934).

Speaight, Robert, *Acting, its Idea and Tradition* (1939).

Swaffer, Hannen, *Really behind the Scenes* (1929).

Swift, Clive, *The Job of Acting* (1976).

Taylor, George, *History of the Amateur Theatre* (Melksham, 1976).

Taylor, John Russell, *Anger and After* (1969).

Tomalin, Nicholas and Elsom, John, *The History of the National Theatre* (1978).

Trewin, J. C., *The Birmingham Repertory Theatre 1913–1963* (1963).

Wagner, Leopold, *Roughing it on the Stage* (1895).
How to Get on the Stage (1899).

Wickham, Glynne (ed.), *The Relation between Universities and Films, Radio and Television* (1956).

Williams, Harcourt, *Vic Wells, the work of Lilian Baylis* (1938).

Wyndham, Horace, *Audrey the Actress* (novel; 1906).

Wyndham, Horace, *The Magnificent Mummer, Some Reflections on the Twentieth Century Stage* (1909).
Limelight (novel; 1914).

ARTICLES

Armstrong, William A. 'The Nineteenth Century Matinée', *Theatre Notebook*, Winter 1959–60.

Ashwell, Lena, 'Acting as a Profession for Women', in Edith J. Morley (ed.), *Women Workers in Seven Professions* (1914).

Barnes, Sir Kenneth, 'G.B.S. and the R.A.D.A.', in S. Winsten (ed.), *G.B.S. at 90* (1946).

Crick, Bernard, 'The Political in Britain's two national theatres', in James Redmond (ed.), *Drama and Society* (Cambridge, 1979).

Eigner, Edwin, 'British television drama and society in the 1970s' in Redmond, *op.cit.*

Ervine, St John, 'Protecting the Actor', *The Nation and Athenaeum*, 21 July 1928.
350

Felice, James de, 'The London Theatrical Agent', *Theatre Notebook*, Spring 1969.

'The Finding of Employment for Artists', *International Labour Review*, Vol. 18, Oct–Nov 1928.

Hughes, Alan, 'Henry Irving's Finances, the Lyceum Accounts 1878–1899', *Nineteenth Century Theatre Research*, Vol. 1, No. 2, Autumn 1973.

Kent, Christopher, 'Image and Reality, the Actress and Society' in Martha Vicinus (ed.), *A Widening Sphere* (Indiana, 1977).

Macht, Stephen R., 'The Origin of the London Academy of Music and Dramatic Art', *Theatre Notebook*, Vol. XXVI, No. 1, Autumn 1971.

'The Modern Theatre', Special Supplement, *New Statesman*, 27 June 1914.

'Organisation among Intellectual Workers', *International Labour Review*, Oct–Nov 1928.

Poel, William, 'The Economic Position of English Actors', *Nineteenth Century*, Vol. LXXVI, September 1914.

Richards, Michael, 'UK University Drama', *Theatre Quarterly*, No. 15, Aug–Oct 1974.

Tree, Herbert Beerbohm, 'The Academy of Dramatic Art', *Review of Reviews*, Vol. XXIX, Jan–June 1904.

Whiteing, Richard, 'How they train actors in Paris', *The Nineteenth Century*, Vol. LV, June 1904.

Wickham, Glynne, 'The Study of Drama in the British Universities 1945–1966', *Theatre Notebook*, Vol. XXI, No. 1, Autumn 1966.

'A Revolution in Attitudes to the Dramatic Arts in British Universities 1880–1980', *Oxford Review of Education*, Vol. 3, No. 2, 1977.

Index

Cassell, Sir Ernest, 90
Casson, Sir Lewis, 25, 37, 157, 159, 174, 215, 221, 222, 239, 240, 248, 250, 257, 263, 264, 271, 301, 302, 309, 320
Caste, 211
Casting Agreements, 4, 308
Catalani, Madame, 73
'Cathedral Steps' pageant, 271
Catholic Actors' Guild, 150
Catholic Stage Guild, 150–2, 174, 201, 317–19
Catholic Suffrage Society, 110
Catterick, 169
Cavalcade, 201
censorship, 104–5, 210
Central Pool of Artists, 262
Central School of Speech and Drama, 2, 32, 38, 47–50, 191–2, 193, 194, 196, 222, 281, 294, 298, 301, 302, 310
Centre Forward, 313
Ceylon, 261
Chamberlain, Neville, 255
Chandos Hall, 36
Channel 4, 284, 286
Chant, Mrs Ormiston, 119
Chaplin, Charlie, 118
Charing Cross Road, 185
Chariots of Fire, 286
charities, theatrical, 86–92, 315–16
Charles and Mary Lamb, 224
Charlot, André, 182, 240
Chatterton, Balsir, 56
Cheer Oh Cambridge!, 49
Chekhov, Anton, 191, 192, 223
Chekhov, Michael, 192
Chelsea, 90
Chelsea Royal Hospital, 91
Cheltenham, 287
Cheltenham Ladies' College, 16
The Cherry Orchard, 191, 256, 264
Chester, Elsie, 43
Chevalier, Albert, 129
Chichester, 287
Child, Harold, 58, 59

child actors, 69–74
Child Performances Regulations (1968), 74
Childrens Act (1889), 70
Childrens' Act (1908), 71
Children and Young Persons' Act (1963), 74
Christie, Julie, 310
Chu Chin Chow, 163
Church, Esmé, 193
Church Pastoral Aid Society, 146
Church and Stage Guild, 146–7
Churchill, Sir Winston, 119, 136, 267, 271
The Cigarette Maker's Romance, 211
cinemas 123, 128, 218, 247, 268, 285
Cinematographic Films Act (1927), 213
Ciro's night club, 168, 199, 201
The Citadel, 216
City of London College, 37
civic playhouses, 287
Clarence, O.B., 58, 238
Claretie, Jules, 39
Claridges, 231
Clark, Kenneth (Lord), 258
Clarke, Sir Edward, 89
Clarkson, Willy, 60, 139, 173, 199
Clements, Sir John, 216, 219, 276, 314
Clifton College, 220
closed shop, 4, 101–2, 112, 236–9, 242, 250, 283, 284
clothing coupons, 277
clubs, actors', 136–9, 199–201
Clunes, Alec, 263
coach parties, 279
Coburg, 8, 26
Cochran, C.B., 237, 240
Cockburn, Lord Chief Justice, 135
Colefax, Sybil, 198
Coliseum, 117, 122, 123, 124, 126, 127, 128, 172
collars, 145

366

374